DOING ANTHROPOLOGY
IN CONSUMER RESEARCH

DOING ANTHROPOLOGY IN CONSUMER RESEARCH

Patricia L. Sunderland and Rita M. Denny

Walnut Creek, CA

LEFT COAST PRESS, INC.
1630 North Main Street, #400
Walnut Creek, California 94596
http://www.LCoastPress.com

Library of Congress Cataloging-in-Publication Data

Sunderland, P. L. (Patricia L.)
    Doing anthropology in consumer research / Patricia L. Sunderland and
Rita M. Denny.
        p. cm.
    ISBN 978-1-59874-090-5 (hardback : alk. paper) --
    ISBN 978-1-59874-091-2 (pbk. : alk. paper)
    1. Business anthropology--Research. 2. Consumers--Research. I.
    Denny, Rita Mary Taylor, 1956- II. Title.
    GN450.8.S86 2007   658.8'34--dc22   2007034206

Printed in the United States of America

⊖™The paper used in this publication meets
the minimum requirements of American
National Standard for Information
Sciences—Permanence of Paper for Printed
Library Materials, ANSI/NISO Z39.48–1992.

All photos, unless otherwise noted, were taken by
and (c) Patricia Sunderland and Rita Denny.
Figure 5.1 reprinted with permission of Photosport Ltd,
P.O. Box 99804, Newmarket, Auckland, New Zealand.

Cover design by Lisa Devenish

Dedication

To Mekonnen and Steve
Two of the most patient and supportive souls this world has ever produced.

To Sarah
A master of the nuanced cadences in her mother's replies (grunts) to her home-from-school greeting, "How's the book?"

With love and thanks.

To our research participants and to our teachers, our muses throughout.

Contents

List of Illustrations

Preface: Ethnographic Consumer Research and Anthropological Analysis

We have been conducting ethnographic consumer research for corporate and institutional clients since the 1980s. We have worked with the producers, suppliers, and advertisers of consumer goods ranging from drain cleaners and power drills to 24-carat-gold ingots and fine art. We have worked with financial, healthcare, and educational institutions, retail conglomerates, energy and emerging technology industries, and governmental nonprofits. Our cultural analyses have helped clients to brand and market their goods and services in relevant and resonant ways as well as to think about entirely new products and services.

Over these twenty years, we have witnessed what one could call a seismic shift in the location and integration of ethnography within the consumer research world. The arena shifted from one in which "ethnography" was an esoteric term and as a mode of research was only rarely commissioned, to one where ethnography has become so commonplace that virtually every company offering qualitative consumer research has had to incorporate ethnographic work into the toolkit in one fashion or another. Advertising agencies and other business corporations have hired ethnographic specialists, and many have created entire departments dedicated to ethnographic inquiry.

As anthropologists, it is difficult not to applaud these developments. Ethnography has been the hallmark methodology of cultural anthropology for almost a century, and to see the methodology move beyond the bounds of our arguably niche academic field is to envision the influence of anthropology in a wider sphere. However, there is also no question that it is one-handed applause. Traditionally, for anthropologists, the applause might have been one-handed because anthropologically based insight was being incorporated into corporate pursuits. But the troubling reality of the situation is that this is precisely what has not always happened. The misuse and misappropriation of ethnography in consumer research has been part and parcel of its use. A myriad of research

13

techniques within consumer research (from the few-minute in-store intercept interview, to the one-hour "depth interview," to the online focus group) have become redefined as "ethnographic" with barely any change in the underlying assumptions regarding method or analysis. Researchers have transformed themselves into "ethnographers" with few changes in practice beyond the name. In moments of need or desperation, clients have embraced ethnography as a crystal ball or magical resolution of their business problems, rather than as a mode of understanding and analytic catalyst for business-relevant ideas.

The truly troubling side of the proliferation of ethnography in consumer research, then, has been the relative absence of an accompanying proliferation of anthropological cultural analysis. Within anthropology, ethnography as a methodology has been honed in the service of understanding sociocultural phenomena and practices. "Culture" and "society" are at heart concepts with long histories, and long histories of disagreement among specialists. In the last decades, anthropologists have been active in combating notions of culture as static phenomena or as geographically located entities. There have also been strong efforts against cultural essentialism, or the "the X do this because of their culture" school of thought. In current anthropological conceptualizations, individuals are not pawns of the social or the cultural; rather, they are simultaneously its agents and its pawns, its creators and its destroyers, its advocates and its adversaries. Despite theoretical differences and disagreements, what anthropologists have generally maintained is an interest not only in the individual but in the extra-individual. The social milieu or metaphoric space that supports, catalyzes, organizes, and transduces, as well as confounds and constrains, individual thoughts and practices is seen as crucial. But in the use of ethnography within consumer research, the problem one frequently witnesses is that the goals of the research do not include any understanding or interest in analyzing the lived context of people and brands, that is, in the shared or contested cultural meanings and values imputed to brands or products and the common (and contested) cultural practices that surround categories or brands of products. Rather, ethnographic inquiry is too often embraced as simply a means to obtain a deeper psychological understanding of a target audience. In essence, even when the "new" methods of ethnography have replaced the traditional focus groups and other qualitative techniques within consumer research, ethnography has simply been subsumed as another technique of psychological research. An implicit paradigm and theoretical framework that assumes individual motivation and make-up are the key to consumption practices has been left intact.

Among anthropologists in consumer research, one can see the implicit expectation and interest in cultural issues in the names given to firms and departments—for instance, "Cultural Connections," "Cultural Discoveries," "Cultural Research and Analysis," and the like. Our goal in writing this book is to help make these implicit anthropological expectations and interests explicit. In so doing, our desire is two-fold. On the one hand, we want to provide a means for the increased appreciation and use of anthropological analysis in corporate consumer research circles. On the other, we want to bridge the gap between the corporate and academic consumer research realm and academic anthropology. Within academic anthropology, there appears to be a renewed and increasing interest in applied anthropology generally and applied consumer research in particular. In recent years, both the National Association for the Practice of Anthropology (NAPA), the American Anthropological Association's designated subdivision for practicing anthropology, and the Society for Applied Anthropology have considerably increased their general visibility as well as their specific attention to and embrace of corporate and consumer research. Within academic circles, consumption has also been incorporated as a topic of interest and theoretical import. Still, as a rule, practicing and academic anthropologists and academic consumer researchers are talking within their own separate circles.

With this book, we would like to bring the various divided conversations of the consumer research realm and academic anthropology together. To do so, we use a series of case studies. We see these case studies as a means for the increased appreciation and use of anthropological analysis in corporate consumer research circles as well as an introduction to the intricacies of doing anthropology in the corporate arena for those within academic anthropology. We have specifically chosen *not* to write this book as a how-to primer on methods. There are already many good texts of ethnographic research methods. Recent works of note include Karen O'Reilly's *Ethnographic Methods* and Hy Mariampolski's *Ethnography for Marketers*, which, as its title suggests, is specifically geared to the corporate consumer research realm. It would be difficult to significantly surpass the contributions these authors have already made. Rather, our aim with the present book is to show what it means to re-attach cultural analysis in ethnographic consumer research using first-person case examples. In so doing, this book tells "how to" but, more specifically, "how to apply and appreciate cultural analysis in the practice of consumer research." We want to show that the real magic and difference of ethnography lies in the cultural approach and analysis, not in a different kind of data gathering. We will show, in fact, that one can do anthropology even in context of the focus group room.

Organization of the Book

To provide readers with a better sense of the background and context surrounding current practices, we begin with a brief chapter on anthropologists and anthropological outlooks in consumer research. This introductory chapter is in some ways itself an experiential case study, as, in addition to written sources, we have drawn on discussions with business colleagues and our own personal experiences. We focus largely on developments in the United States, where our own consumer research practice has been based, but also footnote some developments in the United Kingdom and France, again drawing on discussions with others and personal experiences as well as written sources. Chapter 2 then introduces readers to the specifics of what we mean by a cultural approach and analysis. Chapter 3 builds on this foundation by focusing on some of the methodological considerations that motivate the research process. We do so through the presentation of a "what is coffee?" exercise we have used to train corporate clients as well as other consumer research professionals. We show how coffee, its consumption, and its meanings are cultural matters that can only be understood with attention to cultural context, whether in Benton Harbor, Michigan, or Bangkok, Thailand. We also demonstrate how a cultural analysis can be generative for clients while simultaneously illustrating that ethnography as a method is inherently multimodal and analytic (e.g., about listening as well as observing, about actions as well as artifacts, and about analyzing as well as asking).

The book includes a number of forewords by other authors. Our purpose in including these forewords is to help bridge gaps and tie strands of the varied fields together. In the section "Engaging Approaches," the major case study section of the book, we begin with forewords by anthropologists Donald Stull and John Sherry. Their unique vantage points and bases of experience in applied anthropology and academic marketing, respectively, help bridge the divided conversations of anthropology and marketing. Chapters 4 through 7 thereafter provide readers with in-depth examples drawn from our own consumer research practice. The first of these, "The Social Life of Metaphors: Have We Become Our Computers?" calls attention to the ways metaphoric understandings are frames with which consumption and other life endeavors are imagined and enacted. It builds on multiple research projects and analyses and examines how metaphors of computing have entered into American cultural definitions of self, other, work, and play. This chapter also demonstrates the way attention to small details in how people organize the everyday spaces of their lives gives clues to highly salient cultural matters.

Chapters 5 and 6 illustrate the integration of ethnography with text-based analyses or semiotics. These chapters, a cultural reading of trans-Tasman identities and an examination of the cultural constitution of emotion among young people in the United States, United Kingdom, and New Zealand, draw on work carried out over a number of years with partners and colleagues in those countries. In discussing these projects, which included examinations of the semiotics of moving and print ads, we also want to show how semiotic analysis is inherently a cultural analysis, ideally paired with ethnographic inquiry. Chapter 7, "Diagnosing Conversational Details," draws from an even more traditional consumer research technique—the focus group—and demonstrates how this research context is also a site for cultural analysis. Viewing the focus group setting as a conversational event, we look at how people talked about and framed their expectations of utility companies as the clue to their implicit expectations of relationships with these services. Using insights from linguistic anthropology, we show how the ways individuals choose to talk reflects—and creates—those implicit relationships.

The next chapters, 8, 9, and 10, form the "Engaging Entanglements" section of the book. These take a different tack as case studies in that, rather than focusing on a particular research method, question, or project, these chapters focus on recurrent issues we encounter in the course of our work as anthropologists in business. Our goal in this section is to make the entanglements of differing epistemologies, politics of power, institutionalized exigencies, and practicalities ethnographically explicit. The issues we have chosen to focus on—matters of ethnoracial consumer segmentation in Chapter 8 and visual representation in Chapters 9 and 10—are further contextualized through a foreword by Vilma Santiago-Irizarry and Frederic Gleach, anthropologists at Cornell University, and the foreword by Russell Belk, professor at York University's Schulich School of Business, who, along with Robert Kozinets, has been a primary ambassador and advocate of visual representation in consumer research.

In Chapter 11, the concluding chapter, we provide a few final words regarding what we see as the possibilities and promise of a re-attachment of cultural analysis in the practice of consumer research. We suggest that playing in the interstitial spaces between anthropology, academic marketing, and practice not only has great merit, but also has benefits. Convergence between the work—academic and applied—of consumer research/researchers and anthropology/anthropologists has the power to enrich both academic and applied thinking and practice.

Acknowledgments

Our understanding and perspective has been mediated by a polyphony of voices and thus we, and the existence of this book, owe much to many people.

For the questions, conundrums, projects, and perspectives that have inspired us over the years, we particularly thank Michael Angelovich, Ellen Arnold, Bruno Asselin, Steve Barnett, Mike Bean, Marlene Bellis, Karen Blu, Liz Boyd, Don Cass, Cathy Dowdell, Craig Dunaway, Starkey Duncan, Patrick Duquesne, Kathryn Fields, Frank Gaynor, Erving Goffman, Cari Groppel, Anne Gudwin, George Hay, Jen Josephson, Herb Leff, Rachael Lovelace, Tom Luke, Owen Lynch, Tamara Maier-Jones, Maryann McCabe, Dick Nelson, Bill O'Connor, Lee Pavach, Ernie Perich, Ellen Plusker, John Prevost, Michael Silverstein, Jacqueline Smart, Roz Rago, Lisa Robinson, Donna Romeo, Patrick Roney, Bambi Schieffelin, Dan Sygar, Roger Thompson, Tom Townsend, Russell Tuttle, Brian Van den Hurk, Lisa Wilcox, Connie Williams, Julie Wittke-Smits, and Judith Wright, as well as Bud Causey, long an ardent supporter of our ethnographic approach, who once, in inimical style, labeled us "ethnogeeks."

As our cultural understanding is often constituted through visual media, we also wish to thank Matthew Belanger, Mark Cassar, Sarah Teitler, and Nelly Trillon, who, as editors, have brought there own sensibilities to bear in illuminating ethnographic sojourns. Kaleb and Belain Eyob, Dennis Frank, Byron Kelly, JoanE O'Brien, Robert Moïse, Bruno Moynié, Mark Pirro, Maria Rosenblum, and Sarah Teitler, as videographers in the field, have energized, supported, and sometimes saved the ethnographic endeavor—whether as anthropologists, professional videographers, filmmakers, or simply astute observers. To our clients who have held cameras for many an hour, you, too, have been muses.

For those who read proposals or chapters, or agreed to be grilled for their perspectives, we want to thank Elise Andaya, Malcolm Baker, Steve Barnett, Ulla Berg, Elizabeth Boulter, Luc Chelly, Malcolm Clark, Elizabeth Denny,

Dominique Desjeux, Michael Donovan, Adam Drazin, Daniel Eyob, Ayala Fader, Vanessa Hayward, Doug Holt, Cate Hunt, Angela Jenks, Mekonnen Ketsela, Hy Mariampolski, Grant McCracken, Saúl Mercado, Hartmut Mokros, Ian Phillips, Annie Rorem, Paitra Russell, Charlotte Sector, Hannah Shakespeare, Irina Carlota Silber, Jaqueline Smart, Robert Spector, Gigi Taylor, Sarah Teitler, Susan Terrio, Christina Wasson, and Bob Yovovich.

Our goal to bring in multiple trajectories of scholarly writing would not have been achieved without the help of Luther Elliot who took the spirit of our task to heart. Annie Rorem did yeoman's duty in mastering Endnote for us. Meredithe Applebury, who otherwise lives a life of a molecular biologist, stood in at all hours as technical support to neutralize our deficiencies in electronic referencing.

The foreword authors, Russell Belk, Fred Gleach, Vilma Santiago-Irizarry, John F. Sherry Jr., and Donald Stull, we cannot thank enough. We are deeply grateful, not only for their very careful readings, written contributions, perspectives, and powers to orient, but for the generosity of spirit with which they donated both their time and attention to gently correct our oversights, answer our questions, and simply to help us out. We thank Jennifer Collier, our editor at Left Coast Press, who has shepherded us through this process without ever losing her sense of humor or balance. Jennifer's insight and advice has made this a better book, as did the thoughtful, careful comments of our reviewers, and the copyediting of Ginny Hoffman. Of course, all errors, oversights, and lapses of judgment in this book—no matter how large or small—are our own.

We also owe much to the Practica Group enterprise without which we would not have had the latitude to write. Thanks to Ed Bovich and George Hunt for unfailing graciousness and humor; to Michael Donovan, fellow anthropologist, whose voice is found in many of the case studies we discuss; and a special thanks to Sue Silaj, whose friendship and faith in us as colleagues has kept the book (and us) going. Sue's unequivocal belief that there is a solution, if there is heart, has long bolstered us in our work and in the writing of this book. Without the assistance, often late at night, of Elke McAteer and Dawn Hackett, we could not have made it work, either.

Writing amid densely packed work schedules is an exercise in the creation of time. It has been situated in interstitial weeks, days, hours, and moments. To our families, and to our friends, who have nurtured our illusion that time can in fact be created, we thank you for your unequivocal support in the endeavor, recalibration of time on our behalf, and patience with our whining. We owe you many days, not to mention dinners. And we owe you laughter. For those of you still wondering why we haven't written the blockbuster bestseller (after all this effort), we duly sympathize. Perhaps next time.

To Thelma and Louise, many, many thanks. We had no idea what it would take in time, effort, tenaciousness, efficiency, and heart to write this book. It has been a collaborative effort from the start, made possible only because of friendship, shared vision, great trust, and huge respect. We have traded off taking the lead in getting ourselves into messes (okay, new territories) over the past ten years, and this book, the topics written about, and the writing of its chapters are no exception to that tradition. It was shocking to discover that it has become impossible to know who wrote what. This somehow is fitting, as even clients of longstanding mix us up.

Many of these chapters have drawn on prior published work in thought or deed. We are grateful to the following publishers for permission to excise liberally:

Patricia L. Sunderland (2006), "Entering entertainment: Creating consumer documentaries for corporate clients," in Russell W. Belk (ed), *Handbook of Qualitative Research Methods in Marketing*, Cheltenham, UK: Edward Elgar, pp. 371–383.

Rita M. Denny (2006), "Pushing the boundaries of ethnography in the practice of market research," in Belk (ed), *Handbook of Qualitative Research Methods in Marketing*, pp. 430–439.

Rita M. Denny, Patricia L. Sunderland, Jaqueline Smart, and Chris Christofi (2005), "Finding Ourselves in Images: A Cultural Reading of Trans-Tasman Identity," *Journal of Research for Consumers*, www.jrconsumers.com, Issue 8.

Patricia L. Sunderland and Rita M. Denny (2005), "Connections among people, things, images, and ideas: La Habana to Pina and back," *Consumption, Markets and Culture* 8(3):291–312 (http://www.tandf.co.uk).

Patricia L. Sunderland, Elizabeth Gigi Taylor, and Rita M. Denny (2004), "Being Mexican *and* American: Negotiating ethnicity in the practice of market research," *Human Organization* 63(3):373–380.

Rita M. Denny and Patricia L. Sunderland (2005), "Researching cultural metaphors in action: Metaphors of computing technology in contemporary U.S. life," *Journal of Business Research* 58:1456–1463.

Rita M. Denny and Patricia L. Sunderland (2002), "Strange brew: How semiotics became au fait with au lait," *Research*, Issue 438:21–24.

Patricia L. Sunderland and Rita M. Denny (2002), "Performers and partners: Consumer video documentaries in ethnographic research," in *Qualitative Ascending: Harnessing Its True Value*, Amsterdam: ESOMAR, pp. 285–303.

Rita M. Denny (1995), "Speaking to customers: The anthropology of communications," in John F. Sherry Jr. (ed), *Contemporary Marketing and Consumer Behavior*, Thousand Oaks, CA: Sage, pp. 330–346.

Patricia L. Sunderland and Rita M. Denny (2003), "Psychology vs anthropology: Where is culture in marketplace ethnography?" in Timothy Malefyt and Brian Moeran (eds), *Advertising Cultures*, Oxford, UK: Berg, pp. 187–202.

For permission to use the "office" illustration that starts Chapter 2, we thank Robin Jareaux; we are indebted to her for her willingness to redraw the original illustration and to Matthew Belanger for recreating the original caption.

Part I
Introduction

Figure 1.1 *USA Today*, February 18, 1999

1

Anthropologists and Anthropology in Consumer Research

The headline pictured at left, "Hot asset in corporate: Anthropology degrees," appeared in the business (i.e., "Money") section of a February 1999 issue of *USA Today*.[1] Popular press articles detailing the virtues of anthropology, and more specifically those praising the value of ethnography as a tool for consumer research, flourished around that time. Articles featuring ethnography as the "new" means for companies to "really understand" consumers appeared with an almost predictable regularity in the decade from 1995 to 2005. A wide variety of publications, not only *USA Today*, provided this attention—*The New York Times, American Demographics, Fast Company, U.S. News & World Report, Harvard Management Update, The Wall Street Journal, Fortune Small Business, Newsweek, The Smithsonian, The Financial Times*, and many others took part in spreading the news.[2]

Radio, television news and documentary, and video snippets on the Web also played a role.[3] Highly visible among these was "The Persuaders," a 90-minute documentary that initially aired on public television's *Frontline* in November 2004.[4] This portrayal of the market research industry was clearly fascinating for many. And it also appears to have made Clotaire Rapaille—well known in corporate arenas for his research work associated with Chrysler's PT Cruiser, and variously cited in the media as "medical anthropologist," "psychiatrist," and "car shrink"—a bit of a celebrity.[5]

Within business circles, the interest in anthropological viewpoints and ethnographic research is real. Many Fortune 100 firms do hire anthropologists, whether celebrities or not, and as we write this in 2007, ethnography is a standard offering of qualitative consumer research firms in the United States.

Theorists and practitioners alike have located much of the business interest in ethnographic methods to a shift in marketing's focus—from the production of things to a production of experiences in the marketing of brands.[6] While it can be argued, and we would, that consumers have always encountered experience with products and brands, i.e., creatively produced meanings and experience in the act of consumption, there is no doubt that focus on "experiential marketplaces" (Disney to Nike Town to ESPN Zone to Starbucks) spurred marketing managers and advertising researchers to consider new models and alternative methods of research.[7] There is also no doubt that crowded shelves, the unending array of products for sale, the widespread availability of credit, and the loss of "loyalty" to brands (a standard metric in the industry) also produced a sense of urgency for marketing managers to find a way to make their products stand out. The use of ethnography has often become a kind of Holy Grail quest in the effort to sell one's brand.

Without question, many of the ways ethnography has been understood, as well as implemented, in consumer research have not been in line with the ways in which most anthropologically oriented researchers would frame their work. As we discuss further in Chapter 2, quite often ethnography has been embraced as simply "observation" and combined with an individual-oriented frame of analysis both in the United States and in the United Kingdom.[8] In the hands of unskilled and/or creative market researchers, ethnographic efforts have also, at times, careened toward the absurd, be it maddening or comical. Some of these developments have undoubtedly been driven by the passion of the quest, and as Intel anthropologists Nafus and Anderson have trenchantly noted, "There are quacks in every profession."[9] Nonetheless, a crucial result of this heyday of ethnography in applied consumer research has been the flourishing of high-quality, theoretically informed ethnographic work carried out by serious practitioner-scholars—many of them working, quite explicitly, as practicing anthropologists.

Our goal in this chapter is to provide a bit of context surrounding this movement of anthropologists and anthropological outlooks into consumer research. In doing so, we want to illuminate relevant strands in academic consumer research (generally carried out by researchers in business schools), as well as among anthropologists engaged in the practice of applied consumer research. We do so, necessarily, from our vantage point as anthropologists engaged full-time in the practice of applied consumer research, and in the spirit of ethnographic inquiry, we want to show some of the lived realities that comprise this movement. There seem to be a number of activities currently aimed at melding academic anthropology, academic consumer research, and applied consumer research together in the United States. A question for a later history is whether these activities will actually forge a meaningful and durable bond. Our contextual review has the vantage point of U.S. developments, but the world of consumer research is carried out on a global stage and cannot by any means be seen as limited to the United States, nor necessarily from this point of view.

Popular Attention: Incipient Norm or Irregularity?

The attention in the popular media to the commissioning of ethnographic research and the hiring of anthropologists in business during the 1990s may seem a clear indication of the impending normalization of ethnography and anthropologists within the business world. On the other hand, the flourishing of attention in the popular press might simply be an indication of the fact that ethnography and anthropology remain non-normative cultural and research practices. As Sidney Levy, a professor of marketing recognized in academic marketing for his enduring contributions to symbolic analysis, maintained in a masterful essay on the history of marketing and consumer research, "Regardless of the long history I am describing here, it is a sign of the irregular situation of qualitative research that examples of its application still turn up in the press as if it were some remarkable newcomer."[10] As he reminded readers, "reinventing the wheel is a common occurrence."[11]

Notably, in September 2006, the *Journal of Advertising Research* published a special issue devoted to ethnographic research. This issue was co-edited by Joseph Plummer, the chief research officer of the Advertising Research Foundation. In an editorial that introduced the issue, Plummer wrote of his embrace of ethnographic work, maintaining that he felt "pleased to see an approach that was so valuable to advertising early in my career enjoying such a resurgence" and hoped the interest would not be "a passing fad."[12] Plummer's early advertising career was spent at the Leo Burnett advertising agency in the 1960s. Plummer recounted that he had taken several courses in anthropology in graduate school, was "smitten" by ethnographic methodology, and then had been inspired to incorporate "ethnographic thinking" into his research work for Leo Burnett when he attended a talk given by Burleigh Gardner "on the value of personal observations of rituals and symbols apparent in consumption or purchase of consumer goods."[13] After an initial ethnographic study in the late 1960s successfully led to Kellogg's trademark "A Kellogg Kind of Morning" campaign, Burnett often used ethnographic research. Ethnographic research was applied, per Plummer's list, to develop advertising for detergents, beer, washing machines, homeowners insurance, and air travel, before it was "abandoned by agencies and marketers" and replaced by focus groups.[14]

Crucially, part of the long history that Levy described in his essay were his activities in the late 1940s and 1950s at Social Research, Inc. (SRI), a Chicago company founded in part by anthropologist Lloyd Warner, along with Bill Henry and Burleigh Gardner, whose talk had inspired Plummer to apply ethnographic methodologies. SRI, which provided organizational consulting as well as consumer research for advertising agencies and companies, was, as Levy pointed out, dynamically infused by the charged intellectual climate of the University of Chicago at the time. The interdisciplinary Committee on Human Development, in which Levy was a graduate student, and the departments of sociology, anthropology, and psychology provided both people and ideas to SRI. The climate at the time included the teaching and ideas of not only Lloyd Warner, but also, among others, Carl Rogers, Robert Redfield, Everett Hughes, Herbert Blumer, David Reisman, and Donald Campbell. Among Levy's fellow graduate students and friends, peer interlocutors in philosophical, topical, and methodological debates, were Erving Goffman, Herbert Gans, Anselm Strauss, Lee Rainwater, and Gerald Handel; the latter two also became core members of SRI. Brand image was one of the concepts that emerged from SRI's work, along with groundbreaking studies on the social symbolism surrounding consumer behavior and products ranging from cigarettes (at the time symbolic of virility and potency) and television (then relatively new) to Coca-Cola, soap, the telephone, baseball, flowers, and cars. Levy described his ten years of work at SRI, which entailed living "SRI from breakfast until bedtime, brooding over methods of data-gathering and seeking penetrating insights" as "among the most exciting and intensely absorbing" in his life.[15] These years also led to Levy's influential articles "The Product and the Brand" (coauthored with Burleigh Gardner) published in 1955 and "Symbols for Sale" in 1959, both in *The Harvard Business Review*.[16]

Disdain-Induced Separation (Exceptionally Transgressed)

If the decade of the 1950s was a time of acknowledged links between applied consumer research and the academy, as well as between anthropology and consumer research applied to business, these links were subsequently both obscured and severed. As Levy, again trenchantly, put it, "The receptivity to qualitative research by business offends people who despise business and those who study consumers on its behalf."[17] Levy hinted, citing Veblen, that this disdain-induced distancing from the "base" world of actual marketing and selling is not, culturally, a novel idea either, and it exists *within* as well as outside of marketing departments and business schools. One need only attend a few sessions of an Association for Consumer Research (ACR) meeting to realize that this is true. ACR meetings are comprised of academics who work (for the most part) in business schools. As someone looking into the field with the eyes of an anthropologist, the naïve expectation might be that there would be a celebration of consumption in the context of business practices. An embrace of consumption practices does reign, but the affection frequently resides squarely in the "pure" pleasure of the analysis.

Certainly, within U.S. anthropology, the cultural and professional climate of the 1960s and 1970s produced great efforts among anthropologists to symbolically distance themselves and the field not only from business, but also from business schools. This sentiment was perhaps heightened for anthropologists because of the covert research scandals of the 1960s, resulting in the 1971 American Anthropological Association (AAA) Principles of Professional Responsibility that prohibited anthropologists from undertaking research that could not be openly published (business research is often proprietary, at least in part).[18] But distancing practices were very strong and have had enduring impact. For instance, despite studying anthropology at the University of Chicago and New York University, universities with prominent business schools, as students we had no contact with the business schools, and (implicitly) learned to think of business dismissively.[19] At the University of Chicago in the early 1980s, anthropology graduate students could look out their office windows on Friday afternoons and down on the business students having their usual Friday barbeque in the quad. We often did; it was a matter of smug pride to be working while others played.

This culturally produced sentiment has carried through years and generations. In the mid-1990s, while teaching an undergraduate course in linguistic anthropology at New York University, one of Patti's students who was such a pleasure to have in class and so clearly delighted in and enjoyed the material, was also studying business. As he discussed one day after class how he felt about the fields, he maintained that while anthropology was interesting to him, business was not; his study of business was based solely in matters of practicality. Moreover, not only did anthropology have the courses he liked, they were more intellectually challenging and required more work. He may not have liked his business courses, but he did not have to work at them either; they were easy. In other words, again, a form of double disparagement—business (in the abstract, at least), though practical, was not only boring, it was stupid. Anthropology was for the more intellectually inclined. About ten years later, at the meetings of the Society for the Anthropology of North America, after Patti had given a paper discussing consumer research in anthropology, a graduate student in anthropology approached her. This student had an MBA, had worked for many years in business, and had quit her job to go to graduate school in anthropology. What perplexed (and annoyed) her was the way business was so frequently characterized in such simplistic terms among anthropologists, and meanwhile anthropology was conceived in different, but equally simplistic, terms by her business friends. Straddling and aware of both worlds, she could not help but be troubled because she knew that neither caricature fit.

This does not mean, however, that a few pioneering anthropologists did not navigate the terrain of business schools and/or business. In the late 1970s anthropologist Steve Barnett was a vocal proponent of anthropology's methods and theory in applied consumer research. Arguably, it was Barnett who made anthropology visible to Madison Avenue during these years through both his consulting practice and his column in the trade periodical *Advertising Age* in the 1980s. His column enlightened on issues such as why cultural beliefs sunk issue ads, why lifestyle was a myth that deserved debunking, how consumers had become performers, and the ways "I seem, therefore I am" had become culturally true. By charismatic force, a discourse of "symbols and meanings" in proposals as well as reporting, a savvy awareness that to be heard cultural analysis needed at the time to coexist with survey results, Barnett demanded that clients consider an alternate way of knowing.[20] Trained at the University of Chicago, Barnett introduced others into commercial practice during the 1980s, including us.[21]

In 1984, anthropologist John F. Sherry Jr. was hired by Northwestern's Kellogg School of Business, not coincidentally into a department chaired at the time by Sid Levy. Since that time Sherry has worked—tirelessly it would seem—to incorporate (or perhaps more accurately, to help reinstate) a cultural, anthropological frame into consumer and marketing research. And the epistemological grounding of marketing's consumer culture theory has clearly felt the impact of work by Sherry as well as colleagues Belk, Hirschman, Holbrook, Wallendorf, O'Guinn, Schouten, Venkatesh, and others—a collaboration forged by the Consumer Behavior Odyssey project in the mid-1980s.[22] The Behavior Odyssey project was a collaborative venture undertaken with the conscious intention to break away from the hardening mold of quantitative research at some remove from "the real world with real people."[23] Nonetheless, academic marketing as a field still takes significant cues from statistics, economics, information processing in particular, and experimental, quantitative paradigms in general—the frameworks that have maintained, in Sid Levy's words, "the irregular situation of qualitative research."[24]

Since the mid-1980s, Grant McCracken has also successfully and consistently inhabited a liminal space between anthropological theory, academic marketing, and marketing practice. He has held positions at Royal Ontario Museum in Toronto, McGill University, Harvard Business School, Convergence

Culture Consortium Laboratory at MIT, has an ongoing consultancy that includes Fortune 100 companies, and, throughout, continues writing about consumption and brands, both theoretically and practically.[25] At the time of this writing, though, anthropologists engaged with academic marketing remain in short supply. Even though anthropologists Eric Arnould, Annamma Joy, Janine Costa, and Barbara Olsen also all found independent paths to positions in business schools in the 1980s and early 1990s, anthropologists and the anthropologically oriented on the whole do not necessarily have an easy time within business schools due to their "irregular situation." Anthropology and marketing continue to be oppositional fields, and anthropologists, as a group, continue to keep their distance.

Stigmatized and Shameful

In the crucible of anthropological time and place in which our professional identities were formed, the label "applied" was stigmatic. No doubt resonant with an entrenched dichotomy of theory versus method and practice, and broad cultural distinctions and preoccupations about thinking versus doing, applied work was deemed as less theoretical, less sophisticated, and ultimately less valuable. Once again, the same dichotomous reasoning that allowed anthropology in general to be deemed valuable because of theoretical sophistication and business as less so and simplistic was in action. The ingoing assumption about applied work was also that it was less "pure" and always a little compromised. Moreover, if "applied" in general was "dirty,"[26] consumer research or "marketing" was filthy—wickedly so, in fact. And, discursively, at least in terms of certain industries, it clearly still is.

For instance, when we recently conducted a study for a fast food company, we wanted advanced anthropology graduate students to be part of the research team. In our effort to find qualified students, we sent out the word through our academic contacts. Later, on an e-mail trail which we were probably not intended to see, we noted that the subject heading, penned by a student to a fellow student, read, "Selling yourself to the devil for a few days." For the same project, someone who helps us in video editing, someone with an M.A. in anthropology and ethnographic film, refused to work with us on that job. It was not to be believed that the corporate goal was *truly* to create healthier options. Even accepting that the corporate interest was grounded in a larger financial interest in surviving changes in the cultural climate, the desire was not considered real. Clearly, once framed as the devil, it is difficult to consider any corporate actions as "good."[27] Thus when we tell people that the clients with whom we worked on these fast food projects have been among the nicest, most thoughtful, most cuisine-interested we have come across, they find it difficult to believe. (Okay, originally it was a bit shocking to us, too.) But the first time we met in Los Angeles, they suggested we do so at a trendy Asian-French restaurant that had been recommended by their corporate head chef. The people we met there cared about food, cared about theory (yes, one had a Ph.D., we learned over dinner), and cared about their kids as well as the well-being of others' kids. The world—and people—are complex and multifaceted. This complexity may not fit our analytic (folk) models, and perhaps we cannot help but revert to oversimplification, but we also recreate the divide when we do so.

In 2002 we carried out a study for faculty and administration of the School of Foreign Service at Georgetown University. They were in the process of restructuring the Culture and Politics curriculum and hired us to conduct focus groups with Culture and Politics majors as a means to incorporate the student viewpoint into the process. Studies like these do sometimes feel—in the abstract, at least—somehow better, loftier, and more worthy than those on drain cleaners. As Lila Abu-Lughod has pondered in reference to the study of television, "Does the taint of lowbrow status and the apparent banality of television rub off on those who study it?"[28] Yes, it can sometimes seem, and feel, that it would be worthier or more important to study the intricacies of an elite university's curriculum than to study drain cleaning.

But in the doing, there is no question that studying drain cleaning captures and holds the analytic imagination. One need only think back to the emotion and social drama that surrounded the last time a toilet overflowed in your home, or when you stopped up one in the home of someone you barely knew, or when your shower drained slowly enough to feel the water creeping up on your ankles. Moreover, just as a study of garbage hauling leads one to issues of dynastic families and to study television viewing is to look into the very fabric of sociocultural life, stopped-up drains are not trivial issues. An overflowing toilet means one stops everything else and attends to it, and it leads not only to trauma but also to domains of established sociocultural importance.

Based on our experience, we must agree with Sid Levy that applied consumer research work is "exciting and intensely absorbing," an experiential state shared by the graduate students and anthropologists in academic positions who occasionally freelance for us. There is on-the-ground reality of engagement, curiosity, fascination, and commitment to the research goals. In the end, for us, as it is for many other practicing consumer researchers, the work is a long-intertwined explorative ethnography of contemporary life, of people's lives in and around the world of consumption and corporations. We have also found Levy's statement about living the work from "breakfast until bedtime, brooding over methods of data-gathering and seeking penetrating insights" to be very true.[29] The current compression of corporate time schedules combined with cultural expectations of speed and productivity also assure the "until bedtime" part.[30]

Methodological, Substantive Connections

Within academic anthropology, the traditional notion of research based on in situ, face-to-face, participant observation carried out in one geographic location for a year or more, has been both challenged and upended in the face of contemporary sociocultural realities. Remaining still and focused on one place is not sufficient for understanding a world characterized by the rapid flow of people, objects, and ideas across geographic boundaries. A confluence of available digital technologies, media resources, transportation possibilities, and the like, alongside shifts in geopolitical power and concomitant assumptions, has changed the world, anthropological research, and representational strategies. Multi-sited, multi-modal, multiple vantage point research, that considers and accounts for both changes and endurances across time and space, has been called for. Anthropologists practicing in the applied world of consumer research have noted these same sociocultural realities and frequently commented on how the particular habitus of the business milieu stretches and compels one to come to grips with new forms of research, new technologies, and new representational strategies.[31]

Within business environments the social facts of flatter organizations, portable communications devices, broadband, e-mail, and other technologies have effectively put managers into the perpetual present. While a standard research cycle for product innovation, concept testing, positioning, and branding might remain the same as before, it certainly seems as if now a particular project lies dormant in the pile on the desk (as piles often do on academic desks) until it reaches the surface, at which point it must be put into action. Compression then occurs in every aspect of our work: recruiting, fieldwork, analysis, and reporting. The result is aggressive scheduling and intense, compressed time.

In response to time (and space) compression, ethnography in practice has routinely become one of multiple places, multiple vantage points, and multiple methods. In terms of multiple places, for marketers, that a "moderator," as leaders of focus groups have traditionally been called, would travel to conduct groups with "respondents" in a variety of different geographic locations for a given research project has been standard for decades. This practice, often driven not by the anthropological desire to specify the local, but rather by an inverse desire to assure that data were not "skewed" by geographic specificity when a product or brand was a national or international one, has been carried forward in ethnographic studies.[32] In our experience, only rarely are studies undertaken to understand the particularities of one context—we instead are often looking for the aspects and insights of what is shared across a larger sociocultural and geographic terrain. In a sense we are hired to consider shared consumerscapes, brandscapes, and globalscapes.[33] Current realities of global brands as well as global product distribution also mean that the ethnographic work of corporate consumer research is often carried out "elsewhere," a traditional, if now deeply contested, standard of honor among academic anthropologists. Much of the ethnographic work currently discussed by consumer researchers—in the academic as well as the popular press—includes an international aspect.[34] Some of our favorite projects, perhaps speaking to our own anthropological predilections, have been ones that have taken us beyond the bounds of the United States. We have investigated the meanings of home in Moscow (in the early 1990s, a time of great change); the meanings of gardens and lawns in the United Kingdom, France, and Germany; refractions of the Chrysler brand in Germany, France, and Japan; the social constitution of emotions among young people in New Zealand, the United Kingdom, and the United States; and trans-Tasman identities.

Multiple eyes and minds focused on a project are likewise a routine part of consumer research practice. In applied consumer research this, too, has roots in the history of focus group rooms in which groups of commenting clients would sit behind one-way mirrors. In the practice of in situ ethnographic work, client presence has generally been incorporated into encounters either by becoming explicitly part of the encounter, or in mediated ways. For instance, in our in situ encounters, we typically have clients join as videographers, note takers, and observers. In the process, considerable emergent tensions must often be managed, as our anthropological outlook to let meanings emerge and to embrace "mistakes" and gaffes as moments of enlightenment tends to conflict with implicit (and explicit) models of expertise and efficiency (see Chapter 8). However, clients' alternate points of view often serve to enrich the impact on what we know and on how we answer the culturally framed questions with which we started. In the topics their priorities bring to the fore (and even in what they implicitly prioritize on tape in their role as videographers), we gain. Engineers specializing in research and development key into details we might not otherwise notice. Numerous ethnographic consumer researchers have noted this positive value of multiple vantage points. For instance, pointing to practices at E-Lab, an ethnographic research firm where many other currently practicing consumer research anthropologists once worked, Christina Wasson noted that the process of data analysis—which included researchers, designers, and clients—created results that "were certainly far more robust than they would have been if only one or two of the three groups had been involved."[35] Lovejoy and Steele have discussed how the use of Microsoft's Photo Story application, in which product development team members can see photos, hear accompanying narration, and participate in an accompanying blog is helpful in bringing alive the day-to-day of nonlocal research and allows (remote) team members to pose questions during the course of the research project.[36] Erickson and Høyem have also discussed the ways that blogs have been an extremely helpful way to include clients in the research process on work undertaken with young people and technology in China.[37] Ever more frequently, research respondents are also becoming active participants in such blogs.

Routinely, the metaphorical frame of these multiple perspectives is the collaborative team.[38] In fact, from the earliest days of our practice we have undertaken ethnographic and other research projects as a collaborative team effort. This has often been a pragmatic decision undertaken out of the need to complete a large, multi-sited project quickly, but also is not without theoretical grounding.[39] The incorporation of multiple vantage points meshes with epistemological orientations current within academic anthropology, even if these are not always easily realized. As Wasson noted in her discussion of the analyses conducted at E-Lab, one of the reviewers of her article pointed to the positive contribution of multiple vantage points, noting that "such a three-way collaboration, 'even in today's age, is quite unusual' in bridging both disciplinary and organizational boundaries."[40] Notably, in academic consumer research, a team approach (even if only within the discipline) has been more often the rule, not the exception. The Consumer Behavior Odyssey project mentioned earlier is, again, a case in point. Other classic, culturally oriented studies have also been undertaken with teams: Arnould and Price's on white-river rafting, Schouten and McAlexander's ethnographic work on bikers, Sherry, Kozinets, and others on the ESPN Zone and now American Girl.[41]

Augmenting the traditional in situ, face-to-face encounter is also often a pragmatic necessity in commercial consumer research. This augmentation likewise has benefits in terms of the process and outcome of the research, and is an epistemological fit with the realities of studying contemporary sociocultural life. While we incorporate in situ, in-person encounters, we routinely go beyond them by asking participants to reflect for us through diaries, essays, or poems, whether they be verbal or photographic, still or video, before and after our encounters. More and more, methods in applied ethnographic work are also iterative—both in analytic time and in real time. For instance, in a project focused on out-of-home food consumption among twenty-somethings, we first started with annotated photo diaries and focus groups. Half of the participants were then selected for ethnographic interviews in which our tours of Los Angeles were calibrated by food establishments (including mothers' homes). Realizing in the process that the wee hours were crucial food consumption moments, we then decided to ask our respondents to create video diaries for us of their eating events in the following week. We thereafter gathered them all for a debriefing—a bit of a party as it turned out. Life events had unfolded in the hours bracketed by the focus groups; the boy and girl friends lost and gained turned the final encounter into a palpable singles scene. Moreover, in this project, the clients were a catalyst for geographically dispersed teams, which then came together for the final analysis. The clients commissioned one consulting group to carry out ethnographic work in France, another to carry out work in China, and us to carry it out in the United States. The three consulting groups were then gathered together for a multi-day, mutual debriefing and analysis session in which multiple parties from the corporation were also present. It worked.

Finally, in terms of representational strategies, videographic and other visual representations have been exceedingly important to applied consumer research.[42] As we discuss in more detail in Chapters 9 and 10, visual media have been central to both the process and the representation of our own ethnographic work for many years. In fact, photographs and video have become central in the work of virtually all ethnographic consumer researchers. Visual representation is a *must*—in some ways this is problematic in that ethnography reduced to observation is then simply transduced to photographs and videographic representation. But, as with developments in the terrain as a whole, this emphasis has also created opportunities, and linked us with both longstanding concerns and new developments within academic anthropology and marketing.

In the End

We are, perhaps, inhabiting (yet again) a unique moment of convergence in market research, consumption theory, and anthropology. The voice of anthropologists has been felt in consumer culture theory in business schools. In anthropology, there has been an increase in the numbers of practicing anthropologists working in the fields of technology and design,[43] enhancing the status and recognition of practicing anthropologists and leading to the advent of forums like EPIC (Ethnographic Praxis in Industry Conference), whose mission is to explicitly bring anthropology's theoretical voice into business practices.[44] Clearly, given events and activities during the last decade, there is an underlying momentum that perhaps also propels a sense of optimism.

The challenge, as we see it, is how to ensure the endurance of this movement. Optimism must be balanced by the realities of entrenched practices and attitudes—in business schools, anthropology departments, and commercial consumer research. The impact of such entrenchment is evidenced when popular media and the trade press not only continually rediscover ethnography and anthropology, but also frequently get it wrong. We hope this book will help lead to a better understanding of anthropological ethnography, or even—and perhaps more importantly—that its practice will no longer be deemed noteworthy because it will simply have become "too normal."

Notes

1. Jones (1999).
2. See Gomes (2006), Green (1999), Gross (2004), Koerner (1998), Larson (1993), McFarland (2001), Murphy (2005), Tett (2005), Tischler (2004), Wellner (2002). Without question, some of this flourishing had to do with the active marketing efforts of practitioners themselves, but other times the interest in ethnography was clearly part of the popular Zeitgeist, and the press undertook active efforts. We were cited in the *Harvard Management Update* because they contacted us. *The Wall Street Journal* also contacted us, suggesting that they accompany us on a study and then create a story—in essence conduct their own ethnographic investigation. The story never happened, as we did not find a client willing to take part.
3. See, for example, video of Intel anthropologist Genevieve Bell, http://www. podtech.net/home/technology/1267/pcs-in-bed-beyond-genevieve-bell-intels-top-anthropologist, accessed January 28, 2007. See also Goto and Subramanian (2004).
4. This documentary currently remains available online, http://www.pbs.org/wgbh/pages/frontline/shows/persuaders/.
5. Rapaille is quite charismatic for U.S. audiences, aided by a French accent, neo-royal bearing, and his discussion of the importance of things like the "reptilian brain" (see Gross 2004). While the reptilian brain is clearly not part of typical explanatory frameworks of cultural theorists in the United States today, without question Rapaille's name has become, if not a household one, then at least a cocktail party one. On numerous social occasions we have had to explain to those outside the field how what we do is similar and different from what Rapaille does. Most recently, one of us was pulled into a lengthy discussion of the consumer research field at a 2007 New Year's Day party, spurred by the genuine curiosity of an actor/waiter who had seen "The Persuaders." As Russell Belk (2006:193) has written, in a cultural climate in which documentary filmmakers make films about business and consumer behavior that enjoy wide viewership and popularity (e.g., Morgan Spurlock's "Supersize Me"), it is time to take pause and note that "consumers have become a hot topic."
6. See Suchman (2000). There is no question that interest in what consumers were doing with "stuff" became a focus of attention in both popular and trade presses during this time. As Barnett observed in the mid-1980s, serial reinvention of one's

sense of self was pervasive (Barnett and Magdoff 1986). Propelled in part by rapid changes in technology that elided time and space dimensions, values of stability were backgrounded to ideas of transformation. In the mid-1990s, we observed that Las Vegas tourists saw themselves as both participants and spectators. Participation at face value, in which tourists felt part of a larger experiential moment (e.g., being a high roller or feeling glamorous), coexisted *interchangeably* with spectatorship—finding enjoyment in the recognition of the ersatz and absurdity. Continued technological developments in the 1990s provided further momentum for creating new experiences. Brands (even a "brand" such as Las Vegas), become fodder for performative acts within this backdrop.

7. See, for instance, Arnould and Price (1993), Carù and Cova (2007), Kozinets (2002), Sherry et al. (2001).

8. As Abrams (2000:211) wrote, "In strict academic terminology, *observational research* is actually a branch of ethnography. However, for the last few years the marketing community has used the two terms almost interchangeably" (italics in original). See also Sue Squires' (2006) comments on how ethnography has sometimes been implemented. The dislocation between ethnography and cultural analysis is also evident in U.K. marketing research practices, where ethnography is often defined as observation (see, for example, Smith 2007, www.turnstone-research.co.uk, www.lawes-consulting.co.uk), a practice no doubt influenced by the practices of Mass-Observation in the 1940s (see Stanley 2001 for an intellectual history of Mass-Observation). An explicit concern for cultural analysis, an emergent paradigm in market research in Britain (see Imms 1999) has been propelled by the visible, if not large, practice of semiotic analysis (a deconstruction of texts such as advertising, packaging, Web sites) in both the United Kingdom and France (see Valentine and Evans 1993; Valentine 1995). Virginia Valentine was among the earliest proponent for semiotic analysis in Britain's market research world. Other prominent voices today, such as Malcolm Evans and Greg Rowland, spent time at Semiotic Solutions, a firm Valentine founded in 1987. Note also the comments on observation in U.K. market research by academic marketers Lee and Broderick (2007).

9. Nafus and Anderson (2006:230n1).

10. Levy (2003:104). This essay focuses on activities centered around the University of Chicago. See also Levy's (2006a) similar, but more broadly focused, analysis and history of qualitative research methods in marketing.

11. Levy (2003:104).

12. Plummer (2006:245).

13. Ibid.

14. Ibid.

15. Levy (2003:101).

16. See Levy and Rook (1999) for reprints of these articles.

17. Levy (2003:104).

18. See also Baba (2005a, 2005b) and Baba and Hill (2006).

19. To be fair, this sentiment also clearly extended beyond anthropology. Patti attended graduate school in psychology at the University of Vermont in the early 1980s. It was a matter for considerable discussion and joking when a best friend and fellow graduate student fell in love with a man in an MBA program. Patricia Sachs, an anthropologist who has had a successful business and workplace consulting practice

for many years, also comically wrote about how these sentiments operated within her medicine- and arts-oriented family, "The rules were as follows. First: Be a neurosurgeon. Second: At least be a professor. Third: Thank God you got your doctorate. Fourth: Never, ever go into business." The rules in her anthropology graduate program at the City University of New York were, "First: Be a professor. Second: Refer to the first" (Sachs 2006:153).

20. Column examples are from Barnett's "Observing" column in *Advertising Age* during the years 1986–1988. Barnett continued to influence via positions with Nissan North America, CitiCorp, Ogilvy & Mather Worldwide, GBN (a strategic business consultancy now owned by Monitor), the Wharton School, and his own consultancy. At the time of this writing, he hosted an Internet environmental program, The Paradise Parking Lot.

21. It is notable how many of the anthropologists who work today in consumer research, especially in small consumer research practices on the East Coast, have first- or second-generation connections to the companies Barnett headed—not only ourselves, but Maryann McCabe, John Lowe, Ilsa Schumacher, Tim Malefyt, Robert Moïse, Michael Donovan, and Tom Maschio.

22. See Belk (1991) for the collection of work coming from the Odyssey project. See also Sherry (1983, 1991, 1998), Belk, Wallendorf, and Sherry (1989) and Belk, Sherry and Wallendorf (1988). The last two papers were nominated for best article in *Journal of Consumer Research* and the 1989 paper winner of Best Article Award, JCR 1989–1991. As a whole, they illustrate the development of the interpretative frame (and Sherry's anthropological one) on academic marketing. See Arnould and Thompson (2005) for a synthetic overview of analyses over the last two decades within academic consumer research which fall into this research tradition, which they term "consumer culture theory." See also Arnould and Thompson's chapter in Belk and Sherry (2007) regarding their purposes for creating this label and the pros and cons of its reception within the field, as well as other papers in the volume of proceedings of the inaugural consumer culture theory conference held in 2006. Note, as well, Moisander and Valtonen (2006).

23. Belk (1991:iii).

24. See the discussion regarding this situation in the chapter by Arnould and Thompson in Belk and Sherry (2007). This situation within business schools, and the quantitative versus qualitative, anthropology-versus-other-frameworks divide applies quite clearly in France as well. Olivier Badot, anthropologist and marketing professor with posts in both France and Canada, admirer and creator of anthropologically informed analyses of consumer behavior and environments, has told us that the situation in France is just as it is in the United States—in which a cultural theory perspective is niched and, as such, not the recommended means by which to advance one's early academic career if one wants to be at a top business school (Badot, personal communication, January 2007). See also Desjeux (2007) for his perspective on the situation in France.

25. McCracken (1988a, 1996, 2005, 2006a). See also his ongoing blog at www.cultureby. com.

26. Hill and Baba (1997:16) noted that, among Western countries, "Practice is viewed as a far removed, downstream and 'dirty' activity which may serve utilitarian

purposes, but is not relevant or useful to theory-building." Note Rylko-Bauer, Singer, and van Willigen's (2006) comments on the academic-applied divide in U.S. anthropology and their call for reclaiming applied anthropology within the discipline. See also the important discussions of the "pure" and the "impure" and the academic versus applied distinctions of anthropology in Britain in Pink (2006c), especially the three chapters by Simon Roberts, David Mills, and Adam Drazin. Mars (2004) also discusses the consequences of the separation between academics and applied anthropology for British anthropology departments.

27. Note also the resilient negative framings of utility company actions discussed in Chapter 7.

28. Abu-Lughod (1999:111).

29. Levy (2003:101).

30. Note McCracken's (2006a) *Flock and Flow*.

31. Discussions regarding the importance of multi-sited, multi-perspective ethnographic work have been carried out among academic as well as practicing researchers; see Appadurai (1996), Gupta and Ferguson (1997a, 1997b), Marcus (1998), Olwig and Hastrup (1997), Ong and Collier (2005), Pink (2006b), Roberts (2006), Sherry (2006), Tsing (2005), and Wasson (2002). See also Jones and Ortlieb (2006) for an example of a multi-sited, multi-perspective commercial consumer research project on social software (blogs, wikis, etc.) and their comments on space and place as metaphoric and theoretical concepts.

32. Note, this means that it is often counter to the reason that anthropologists have gone to specific places—where they go to find specificity. See, for example, Tsing (2005).

33. See Appadurai (1996), Ger and Belk (1996). Note also Ong and Collier's introductory framing of "global assemblages" as "anthropological problems" as well as the ethnographic examples and analytic comments regarding globalization by a range of anthropological scholars in their edited volume, *Global Assemblages* (2005). See also Hackenberg and Hackenberg (2004).

34. See, for instance, Ger and Belk (1996), Lovejoy and Steele (2004), Nelson (2001), Pink (2004b), Thomas and Salvador (2006), Wilk (2006).

35. Wasson (2000:385).

36. Lovejoy and Steele (2004).

37. Erickson and Høyem (2006, 2007).

38. See Erickson and Stull (1998), Lassiter (2005), Sherry (2006). Hy Mariampolski has been a strong and active catalyst in the creation of worldwide teams of ethnographic consumer researchers through trainings he has provided at ESOMAR (Europe's premier association of market research professionals) throughout the past decade. In recent years he has extended those trainings to China and Latin America. See also Sando and Sweeney's (2005) discussion of clients as team members.

39. See Arnould and Wallendorf (1994) and note 38 above.

40. Wasson (2000:385). See also Lamphere's comments on collaboration and the convergence of practicing and academic anthropology in her 2004 article, "The Convergence of Applied, Practicing, and Public Anthropology in the 21st century."

41. Arnould and Price (1993), Diamond et al. (n.d.), Schouten and McAlexander (1995), Sherry et al. (2001). See also Sherry (2006).

42. Sarah Pink, based in Britain, has been an extremely strong voice for the use of visual methodologies and has been an advocate for an applied visual anthropology (Pink 2001, 2004b, 2006a).

43. While anthropologists have been in the design field for some time, it is arguable that the collaborative efforts of Lucy Suchman, then at Xerox/PARC, with Rick Robinson at the Doblin group catalyzed the growth and visibility of anthropology and design on the U.S. map. Later a founder of E-Lab along with other Doblin employees, Robinson, though not an anthropologist himself, hired many anthropologists and has continued to be an important figure in the applied practice of ethnographic research (see Wasson 2000 and Robinson 2005). E-Lab was sold to Sapient in 1999 but by early 2002 many of its anthropologists had fled or been shed, which meant more anthropologists for hire, and now competent in the discourse of business. The AnthroDesign list serve, catalyzed by the efforts of Natalie Hanson, has been a visible and community-creating presence for practicing anthropologists in design as well as consumer research. See also the collection of articles focused on anthropologists in the field of design edited by Squires and Byrne (2002) as well as van Veggel (2005, 2006). For a history of ethnographic efforts at Microsoft, see Sanders (2004).

44. The organization of EPIC (Ethnographic Praxis in Industry Conference) in 2005, with the stated aim of providing "a forum for ethnographic practitioners in business to exchange research, insights, methods and other information," has been a significant development. The EPIC mission statement asserts that "the conference aspires to promote the integration of anthropological perspectives, methods, and theory into business practices," as well as "to promote public recognition of practicing ethnographers as a profession; and to support the continuing professionalization of the field." Based on the highly positive comments from those who attended as well as the subsequently published proceedings, the two annual conferences that have taken place up to this point have been extremely successful in creating an intellectual exchange among highly trained, highly experienced, anthropologically oriented researchers outside the traditional halls of academia. EPIC has been organized as a joint effort between Ken Anderson from Intel and Tracey Lovejoy from Microsoft, with an advisory board and sponsors and some links to academic partners and organizations. The 2006 Web site had a corporate support heading that featured the logo of the American Anthropological Association alongside that of Intel, Microsoft, PitneyBowes, and the National Agency for Enterprise and Construction (see http://www.epic2006.com). See also Baba (2005a, 2005b), Baba and Hill (2006), Jordan (2003), Meerwarth, Briody, and Kulkarni (2005). There have also been important developments in the United Kingdom and France, among anthropologists and the anthropologically oriented, which converge in bringing together applied and academic anthropology and consumer research. See, for instance, Desjeux (2006), Pink (2006c), Pulman-Jones (2005), and Thorpe (2003). Note also the Web site (www.edlglobal.net) of the U.K.-based consumer research firm Everyday Lives, with links that lead directly to academic anthropology resources and institutions. Developments in the United Kingdom and France also converge with developments in the United States through joint conversations and interactions among researchers (see note 38).

2

What Does Cultural Analysis Mean?

For 21st-century anthropologists, the office cubicle will be as exotic as Samoa.

Figure 2.1   Image accompanying the article "Into the Wild Unknown of Workplace Culture: Anthropologists Revitalize Their Discipline" in *U.S. News & World Report,* August 10, 1998

The image of anthropologists at work in the illustration above involves a great deal of misunderstanding relative to the way that most contemporary anthropologists frame or practice their research. The problem is not simply the unflattering iconography of people who seem part Puritan, part Sherlock

43

Holmes, and part Girl Scout, but rather the assumptions regarding what this and surrounding iconography imply about the anthropological process. In this chapter, we want to detail what we mean by cultural analysis and make explicit some of the implicit assumptions involved in anthropological ways of thinking and conducting research. To do so, we believe it is necessary to first deconstruct some of the widely held—and largely misleading—ideas about anthropological work, as evidenced in this chapter's opening image.

On the level of misunderstanding easiest to resolve, the depiction of researchers as pith-helmeted, bent over, and peering through a magnifying glass harbors within it a notion of archaeology that, as a rule, is fairly distant for most anthropologically minded researchers currently working in business or consumer research. Yet the creator of the image cannot be faulted for incorporating this understanding.[1] For one, many of us studied in programs using the traditional "four field" approach which included at least some archaeology as part of our training. Moreover, the perception of anthropology *as* archaeology is a surprisingly common one, at least in the United States. When we meet people who are taking part in a research project with us, we often tell them that we are anthropologists, and many times we hear this archaeology association in response—replete with joking references to digging things up and/or confusion over how archaeology fits with the questions at hand. However troubling, one of the easiest ways to clear matters up remains a quick reference to Margaret Mead. That Margaret Mead had other concerns as an anthropologist, concerns that befit a cultural anthropologist rather than an anthropologist-as-archaeologist, is generally appreciated, if not fully understood. Notably, the use of Samoa in the caption that accompanied that image is undoubtedly a reference to Mead, as her trip to Samoa is mentioned in the article's second paragraph. But that cultural anthropology is only, or primarily, perceived in terms of Margaret Mead's study in Samoa is a problem.[2] Her primary influence in cultural anthropology is now roughly three generations thence, and while she undoubtedly deserves considerable acknowledgment and respect within the field, including for her efforts to bring anthropology to a wider public, truly a lot has happened in cultural anthropology since then.

Moreover, this outside-observer-of-everyday-action imagery of anthropological work recurs again and again. For instance, in a 2005 *Fortune Small Business* article about Microsoft's "dispatching" anthropologists to study small businesses, anthropologist Nelle Steele was also featured in photographs as studiously observing from outside, and above, an office cubicle.[3] This type of imagery involves a profound misinterpretation of what Margaret Mead was doing in Samoa, as well as how most anthropologists have carried out their work ever since Bronislaw Malinowski's 1922 exhortation to imagine ourselves set down and in the middle of the village.[4] For nearly a century the goal of cultural analysis has involved not only observation, but also modes of participation (at least in the form of conversation) that aimed at acquiring, among other things, an insider's view of things. This was part of Mead's purpose in Samoa as it was Malinowski's in the Trobriand Islands.

This emphasis on understanding—and taking seriously—participants' points of view in contexts different from one's own also firmly established not only a tradition of the appreciation of relativity or perspectival knowledge, but also an awareness of the crucial role of symbolic matters in human affairs. Otherwise, how could one adequately account for the fact that in the Trobriand Islands the houses used to store yams were more elaborately decorated than the ones in which people lived? Or how else could anyone, including Trobrianders, appreciate that ownership and gifting of large yams were demonstrations and creations of status for men, just as skirts, painstakingly created from banana leaves, were a means for women to demonstrate and create status, realized, for instance, when offering these skirts to others during mortuary rituals.[5]

However outdated or exotic these Trobriand examples may seem, these are the types of realities—the very real, human practices—that formed the basis of anthropological inquiry as well as our academic training. The process of exoticization is widely perceived as implicit in the anthropological project, as the opening illustration's caption, ". . . the office cubicle will be as exotic as Samoa," also suggests. Yet, imprecision again resides in this framing. As students, examples such as elaborately decorated yam houses or the exchange of banana-leaf skirts were taught *not* to encourage us to view the world as a cornucopia of exoticism, but rather to develop an appreciation for the symbolism that was embedded and constituted in the matrix of ongoing social life. We learned to consider whether a large home, car, clothes, an elaborate yam house, or a banana-leaf skirt signified wealth and well-being. We also learned to consider what "wealth" and "well-being" meant in this context. How were they demonstrated and achieved? And, importantly, did they even matter? Thus, the fundamental assumption that informs cultural analysis as we practice it is not that cultural worlds are necessarily the stuff of special difference and exoticism, a topic we will return to later in this chapter, but that symbolic, socially created meanings are inherent in human life.[6] Anthropology taught us to recognize the human capacity to spin, twist, turn, invent, tangle, tear, and live by, through, and between symbolic meanings in the way we look at the world and to incorporate that appreciation into our research projects.[7]

The concept of socially constituted meanings and its corollary, the partiality of knowing, are ideas that have been embraced by many in the last few decades via the direct and indirect avenues of postmodern philosophy.[8] An appreciation of the crucial role of symbolism in the workings of everyday life and the symbolic saturation of objects, no matter how seemingly mundane, is also part of the currency of advertising, design, and the attention to media—by specialists and others. But drawing from anthropology's intellectual history and traditions, cultural analysis also carries the premise that the realm of the social context—embedded in and emergent from human interactions—is important, not only the realm of the individual. Much of the marketing world, at least in the United States, is permeated with implicit notions of psychological motivation. There is a strongly held (but often unnoticed) belief that psychological issues are what matter. Psychology as an intellectual tradition provides the fodder and framework through which consumption is thought to be generated as well as best explained. The importance here is that in psychological analyses, the individual and individual psyche are as a rule the unit of concern.[9] What psychological features or personal tastes make these individuals different from those individuals? What is *this* person's "relationship" to the brand? What is his or her emotional attachment to the brand? Even when more than one person is involved, the analytic focus on the individual is often retained. It is thus not surprising that within the anthropologist-at-the-cubicle imagery of the opening illustration, there is only one person being examined—one person with things, not one person interacting with others, not even multiple one-person cubicles being observed. In the depiction of the man observed by pseudo-Pilgrims, it is one person, in one cubicle, being examined.

But, in general, this is not the reality of anthropological practice. Individuals are rarely observed—or considered—in isolation from other people and social context.[10] As Dominique Desjeux, a professor of anthropology at the Sorbonne with an active consumer research consultancy, has formulated it, in anthropological practice, the research focus, "the zoom," is set to a different scale of observation, the scale of the social. More specifically, as Desjeux notes, the heuristic scale for "ethnomarketing" (a term he coined with Sophie Taponier to refer to the application of anthropology to marketing) is often the micro-social (the realm of personal interactions and small groups) with consideration of the meso-social (organizations, institutions, systems of actions) and the macro-social (national, international, global) scales as context.[11] The focus of cultural analysis on the social scale means that the kinds of questions one asks of data in culturally analytic consumer research are often different than those asked in other consumer research analyses—the issues are examined through a different lens of refraction—and thus the answers one derives are different as well, even if at first glance the questions can seem the same.

For instance, in guest lectures to business students and marketing professionals, we often include a video excerpt from an interview with a New York woman, a respondent in a study for which the marketing question was whether gold could be sold on the Internet to the general public. The ultimate client was Anglogold, a large South African mining company looking for new markets. (It was also the late 1990s, in the heyday of Internet commerce possibilities.) In this bit of video, about three minutes long, one sees the woman showing a jewelry box in which she stores pictures of jewelry torn from catalogs and newspapers. She discloses that the jewelry box was originally a present from her to her husband, but that since he did not use it, she had decided to—putting in it things that she would like her husband to buy for her. We also hear in the background a child noisily banging toys. When we show this video, we ask the audience to answer the question, What is gold for this woman? The answers we get are usually along the lines of gold is "fulfilling a need that her marriage cannot provide," or "her motivation is status." We also get reactions of laughter and antipathy—she is often not liked: "She's manipulative," "she's depressed," "I'd hate to be her husband." The language is psychological: Its terms are needs, motivations, and emotional underpinnings. Students and professionals alike are generally quick to offer the psychographic profile.

A cultural inquiry, on the other hand, focuses primarily on the sociocultural, symbolic meanings, practices, and situations surrounding gold (treasure, gifting, investment) versus the interpersonal emotions, on the relevance of these meanings and practices in ongoing life (versus the personal motivations), and on marketing opportunities (versus individuals' needs) that arise therefrom. We are interested in the symbolic meanings and practices that are shared (or contested) among respondents, and while we might garner the existence of these through ethnographic interviews with individuals, we are not interested in the individual's singular personal dynamics per se. While motivations and needs are ubiquitous marketing terms, the *sine qua non* legitimizing market research projects, they are also, per anthropological analysis, *analytic* constructs tied to psychological models of behavior.

This gold example also demonstrates how the researcher and the observer are implicated agents in the creation of meaning, even when just watching a video excerpt of an interview. The cultural analytic research paradigm is, importantly, not one of objective distance—as per the scientific Scouts with magnifying glass and notepads standing above and outside "the data"—but rather one of inextricable involvement in the process of discovery, knowing, and understanding. Thus, the process of cultural analysis must be one of constantly questioning presuppositions—examining the role of our own assumptions and points of view and interrogating what we think we know and why we think we know it. For the Anglogold project, the analytic, cultural questions were: What is gold? What is investment? What is the Internet? And these were not only the questions we asked of our research participants, but the questions we asked ourselves. We answered these questions iteratively through what we asked, saw, heard, observed, wrote down, videotaped, photographed, and reacted to, and by what bored, embarrassed, or inspired us. The jewelry box as treasure chest, gold as jewelry and something to be gifted, the relevance of "treasure" in harried daily life, were significant "observations" that were also by no means mere observation—they were based in talk, reflections, stories, observed objects and events (including a distracting child). From our vantage point, markets are not constituted by segments of people with specific and profiled "needs," rather they are constituted by systems of interwoven meanings and practices that may or may not have resonance for a product, brand, or experience. Gold seen through a cultural lens transcends individual life stories of marriage tensions, career angst, or the status of being a wife. It involves cultural notions and practices surrounding gifting, investment, the marking and making of relationships, trickery, treasure, magically endowed materials, and the like.

As another example, consider not gold, but the study of household floor cleaners. When we conduct studies on household cleaners, we also look for the symbolic cultural meanings, categories, creations, and practices that organize people's perceptions and actions. Thus, while watching someone cleaning a floor we might be contemplating: What is a floor? What is clean? What is a cleaner? What is cleaning? In asking ourselves (or others) these questions, we do so to discern the assumptions about floors, cleaning, or cleaners that contributes to a person's cleaning the floor in a particular manner. As a mode of illumination and amplification, we would also contemplate comparatively. What is different about a clean floor versus a clean chair or table? So what is the cultural difference and importance of a table, floor, and chair? A sense of "making visible the invisible" is often associated with cultural analysis because cultural matters can be so familiar or so tacit that neither the research participants nor the researchers can immediately discern their existence.[12] As we are researching, we are trying to make the very familiar, the very tacit, and the very new (for instance, new ideas of what constitutes a clean floor) obvious to ourselves and to our clients. This tradition in cultural analysis was developed because anthropologists traditionally studied in situations where they were unfamiliar with the social or cultural worlds of the participants. So one needed to ask such things as, "What are chairs and their social uses?" because, like yams in the Trobriands, chairs and what was accomplished with them were often not only unexpected, but inexplicable. In our work, we build on this tradition and continue to believe that defamiliarization is an important component of the analytic process, even as we strive to de-exoticize and familiarize what we see. The point is not to "other" the person, situation, or process, but to interpret.

If the caption, "For 21st-century anthropologists, the office cubicle will be as exotic as Samoa," misleadingly evokes anthropologists and anthropological inquiry as necessarily exoticizing (precisely what we attempt not to do),[13] the formulation also rests on problematic ideas of separately located, different cultural systems. For anthropologists, culture is not an idea that is used to refer to a place or a thing, but an idea that refers loosely to the symbolic and practical phenomena that become apparent at a social level of observation, a conceptualization often sorely abused. Within anthropology, culture is not understood as something that resides in a geographic location or something that makes one group of people inherently different from another group, nor as something that can be in operation in one situation and not in another. Thus, culture is not a variable that can be asserted and examined at certain times and not at others. It is not something unchangeable, unmodifiable, or some *thing* really at all. Heuristically, culture is better thought of not as a noun, but rather as an adjective, a modifier of nouns such as meaning, understanding, explanation, and processes, or, alternatively, as an index that points to symbolic meanings and practices constituted by humans which, in turn, are the organizing matrices of ongoing human activity and meaning making.[14]

The misapprehensions of the culture concept are widespread and something we find we must continually re-confront in our work. Culture as a notion is too often reified and essentialized not only in the popular imagination, but also in business and the academy. In business research practices, culture has often simply become a variable akin to others, e.g., psychographic or demographic, inserted in an overall equation of consumer decision making. As Mazzarella as well as Shore and Wright have noted, problems in fact often ensue when "culture" is brought into the discourse. Anthropologists can then find themselves called on to research the "culture" of a group, e.g., elderly, teens, drug users, suburbanites, Mexican-Americans, which puts them in the uncomfortable position of reinforcing the essentialization of culture while at the same time trying to illuminate and nuance clients' understandings.[15] We elaborate our own experiences with such endeavors in Chapter 8.

In essence, then, cultural analysis is a way of looking at and analyzing the world, and for us, ethnography as methodology is intertwined and personally inextricable from that analytic mode. While it would be easy to argue such a case, in actuality there is no necessary and necessarily best fit reason for this cultural analysis–ethnography match, except that ethnographic methods are the ones that have been developed over the years as the companion to this anthropological mode of analysis. And, as has often been, but must still be, pointed out, ethnography is not a method per se, but rather a collection of methods.[16] Over the years of anthropology, ethnography has included long-term participant observation; village censuses, surveys, and maps; life histories; in-depth interviews; projective techniques; audiotaping; videotaping; telephone interactions; attending public events; examining documents online or off; group interviews, and without question much more. These methodological differences have been tied to differences in theoretical orientations, divergent questions, and technological developments. In commercial consumer research circles, one sometimes hears various rules, on the order "it is only ethnography if there is observation," or "video," or "multiple meetings," or "sufficient time," or "face-to-face contact," or "naturally occurring behavior," or ... (filled in with any number of favorite and idiosyncratic rules). But what seems most accurate about ethnography as a companion mode of discovery in cultural analysis is that as a methodology it must be viewed through, and seen as permeated with, the sociocultural. Ethnographers are no different from anyone else in that their perspectives are also culturally constituted by symbolic meanings, the context, and the situation of occurrence. The socially constituted nature of truth is operative in the research context as well. The theories and ideas we have in our heads, as well as what we do, matters.[17]

In the almost ninety years since Malinowski's exhortation to stay in the village, and the forty years since the publication of his personal diary, anthropological theory and ethnographic representation in particular have incorporated self-reflexivity.[18] That there is an unmitigated interaction between observer and what is observed, between subject and object, that researcher and research participant are complicit in the research endeavor, has been accepted and examined for its implications for research and representation.[19] In other words, research never lacks a point of view. Thus, even when ethnography is at its most observational, as in usability applications, it is still crucial to remember that actions do not occur in a vacuum, but are framed by the cultural notions of both the actors and the interpreters. For example, it is important to keep in mind that notions about a computer or microwave are, in turn, predicated on cultural beliefs about offices or kitchens, which in turn are informed by beliefs and practices surrounding work, play, place, and so on. Theoretical presuppositions are made in the interpretive frame, whether explicitly acknowledged or not. The point is that ethnography, like cultural analysis more generally, is inductive, iterative, and in a constant search for meanings.

From an epistemological perspective, data are not understood as "gathered" as much as they are produced; which is to say, our questions, our presence, our assumptions, our views of the situation provide never-ending filters for the questions we ask, what we observe, and what we conclude. In a constant effort to rid ourselves of ingoing assumptions, we ground ourselves in the details of what we see, what we ask, what we hear, and what we experience. Everything counts as data. Anything can be a prop for understanding. We must interrogate our assumptions and our observational filters whatever, whomever, and wherever we are researching. Theory and point of view are central at every stage of the research process. Researcher stance, theoretical perspectives, technologies, and techniques of recording all affect what is found. We find the answers to the questions that we ask, and it matters how we ask them, explicitly and implicitly. Data and analyses are real, and based on real phenomena, but they are produced, not gathered.[20]

Yet in marketing practice, ethnography has, paradoxically, often been embraced because of its apparent transparency of method, not because it problematizes what one thinks one sees. Ethnography is framed as "a method of observation" in which there is an implicit reliance on the ideas that truth is found in observing versus asking, in behavior versus words, and that the surface is suspect versus the truth lurking below. It is a digging metaphor once again, at once archeological and psychological, i.e., digging into those unconscious personal meanings and motivations, getting down to the "real" reasons underneath the surface, those deep inside (not those social ones simultaneously inside *and beyond*) the person.[21] In *Blink*, Malcolm Gladwell's 2005 best-selling book, he notes the importance of gut feeling—an immediate attribution of judgment that occurs without conscious thought—in decision making. He attributes this ability to think quickly to a psychological construct, the "adaptive unconscious," rendered experientially as a feeling. We would suggest that "gut reaction" is most productively understood as "implicit" rather than "unconscious" because the fodder on which such judgments are made is socially and culturally learned.[22] Cultural analysis unpacks and illuminates the implicit.

Thus, we would argue that focus groups, usually the perennial whipping post, are no more superficial (as in false) than an ethnography grounded by a belief that observation (behavior) is truer than talk. We must look at this chapter's opening illustration and not think of it as three objective Puritans, Scouts, or investigators gathering data from the scene, site, or field but of ones whose research practices are producing the data (here, seemingly, a collection of observations of the kind that can be entered into a notebook once refracted through rather Puritanical outlooks and a magnifying lens). In our practice, we engage in a number of methodologies—the one we choose depends on the question and situation at hand. We conduct participant observation and engage in ethnographic encounters, but we also carry out focus groups, engage in interviews, assign diaries, ask consumers to create video documentaries, and undertake semiotic analyses of "texts," which include images and retail environments as well as written words. These methodologies are not "ethnographic" or "culturally analytic" per se, but to paraphrase Geertz, are made so by the intellectual framing of the task.[23] Each vantage point is also a source of illumination. If we put the camera into someone else's hand, we have gained a different voice. If we observe store displays and consumers shopping these displays, we garner a view of another site where meaning is produced through actions, artifacts, interactions, and talk.

At its heart, then, cultural analysis references an anthropological way of looking at the world and it *is* a different way of thinking about and through things than is frequently the default tendency in everyday American life, marketing research practice, and other academic fields. This difference is in many ways its value and power. That is the point. Cultural analysis refers to a mode of inquiry that encompasses a philosophical and epistemological heritage. It refers to the notion that the meanings, artifacts, and environments in which we live are socially created and symbolically saturated, and that these merit elucidation; that understanding, appreciating, and analyzing the social realm is of value; that doing so illuminates our understanding of humans and human life. As cultural analysts we are always trying to elucidate and illuminate sociocultural meanings and practices. We are trying to discern the cultural symbolism, to clarify the associated practices, to understand the cultural or social context, to understand how people operate, use, behave, and think in these contexts.[24] We are trying to make the cultural symbols, meanings, and practices something we can consciously think through, rather than missing them and/or simply thinking and acting through them without reflection.

In the end, for cultural analysts, there is nothing and no one that is not also culturally saturated. The way of thinking, the philosophical and epistemological assumptions, the way of doing research—in the end, it is all cultural.[25] Admittedly, thinking deeply along these lines may produce vertigo. But the point is that thinking along these cultural lines and moving out of a psychological motivation, rational action, or normative frequency box, provides a heuristic framework that is helpful. It is a framework that helps make sense of what people do and it can help foster the development of dynamic new products or services. Most importantly, cultural analysis intrudes into everyday thinking and allows one to think about things differently—and not just about elaborately decorated yam houses, but also about one's own house.

In the chapters that follow, we provide case studies of cultural analysis. In the first of these, we will continue to explicitly illustrate key heuristics of cultural analysis by describing some of our experiences in training clients and fellow researchers in the practice of cultural analysis. That chapter and the chapters that follow are in many ways an ethnographic account of doing cultural analysis in marketing practice.

Notes

1. Notably, contrary to this imagery, the written article also foregrounded practices in academic and practicing anthropology that were contemporary at the time (see Koerner 1998).
2. This problem, of course, is also due to cultural anthropologists' traditional lack of engagement in public discourse in the United States. See Eriksen (2006) and MacClancy and McDonaugh (1996), including the chapter by Mitchell which examines some of the characteristics of Mead's approach and activities that made her so widely known.
3. See Murphy (2005) for the imagery of Nelle Steele as outside-of-cubicle observer.
4. See Malinowski's 1922 introduction in *Argonauts of the Western Pacific*.
5. See Weiner (1976) and Malinowski (1984).
6. In fact, while anthropologists at present sometimes still rely on the value of de-familiarizing or surrealizing the familiar (see Clifford 1988, or Miner 1956 for a classic example) as a mode to communicate their findings, a major concern for contemporary anthropologists has been to not "other" or exoticize the researched—whether studying in one's own typical or atypical social milieu. See Abu-Lughod (1991), Jackson (2005), and our depiction of both efforts and struggles in this quest in Chapter 10.
7. This outlook, and particularly this articulation of spinning, twisting, turning, and tearing symbolic meanings, is indebted to the work of Clifford Geertz (1973, 1983). We thank Karen Blu (1980) for the notion of tangling.
8. See, for instance, Gergen (1991), Harvey (1990), Lyotard (1984), and Marcus (1998). For business and consumer research discussions, see Brown (1995), Cova (1996), Firat and Venkatesh (1995), Sherry (1991), and Thompson, Arnould, and Stern (1997).
9. We have written about this penchant for psychological analysis before, providing other examples and slightly different angles of refraction. See Sunderland and Denny (2003) and Denny (2006). Note also Arnould and Price (2006), and importantly, Valentine and Evans (1993).
10. See also the comments and case study from Thomas and Salvador (2006) on "the fixation on the individual in corporate research" and the need for a reframing in terms of people's relationship with others and institutions.
11. See Desjeux (2001, 2004, 2006). Presentations of his work in English are also to

be found on his Web site, www.argonautes.fr. See also Arnould and Price's (2006) framing of levels, although they label and define these levels somewhat differently, e.g., "The macro-level ethnography perspective focuses on the identification of cultural templates for action and interpretation that consumers draw upon to give structure to their consumption choices and life goals" (p. 252). However, the underlying logic and raison d'être of understanding consumers and consumption within a sociocultural context is the same. As Arnould and Price (2006:254) write, "Distinguishing our meso-level approach is an interest in consumers as intentional actors with personal projects that are embedded in their sociocultural life worlds." And, "Our argument is that customer-centricity is not about 'how does my customer really feel about and use my brand,' but instead is customers using firm-provided resources in the culturally, socially situated practices of everyday life" (p. 261). See also the use of "zooming out for context" by Jane Fulton Suri and Suzanne Gibbs Howard in the same special issue of the *Journal of Advertising Research* (2006:247).

12. See, for example, Suchman (1995). In the realm of contextual design, the formulation of "making culture tangible" and creating "tangible representations for these intangible forces" has also been used (see Beyer and Holtzblatt 1998:112).

13. We recognize both the ink that has been spilled over this issue and the multiple sides to the argument. The anthropological gaze has often functioned to exoticize. The point is that anthropology, as a field, has recognized this distancing, othering function and many anthropologists, including ourselves, make conscious efforts to combat exoticizing in our research interactions and representations (see note 6).

14. See Fischer's (2007) important review of anthropological concepts of culture and the sociohistorical contexts of shifts in its meanings and application. As Fischer also sums up a current conception of culture (p. 39), "Culture is not a variable; culture is relational, it is elsewhere or in passage, it is where meaning is woven and renewed, often through gaps and silences, and forces beyond the conscious control of individuals, and yet serves as the space where individual and institutional social responsibility and ethical struggle take place." Fischer also points to the "jeweler's eye view" of ethnographic inquiry, which involves "not only the ability to bring out the different facets of cultural variability, but also a constant back and forth movement between (loup assisted) close-up viewings and sitting back for a more global view of the settings" (p. 3).

15. See Mazzarella (2003a and 2003b) and Shore and Wright (1997). As Mazzarella has noted, in a globalized advertising world, culture has become an entrenched variable that allows industry (ironically) to become its advocate and make culture into a paying business proposition. Also, despite huge inroads in the last twenty years foregrounding the complex, mutually implicated relationships between culture and consumption, as reviewed by Arnould and Thompson (2005), cultural analysis in the corporate world remains stymied by the lack of privilege of analysis in qualitative applied worlds in the United States in general, and by the privileged position of folk models of behavior in particular that, as noted, are often psychologically based. But see also Marvin's (2006) ethnographic study of foxhunting in Britain, for a wonderful example of how an anthropologist negotiates his/her many responsibilities—to those studied, to commissioning clients, to an

academic department, to government agencies. See also Abu-Lughod's now classic chapter, "Writing Against Culture" in Fox (1991) in which she argued for the need of anthropologists to work against—in theory, ethnographic practice, and writing—an outdated culture concept that functioned to create "others" and "cultures." Note also Santiago-Irizarry's (2001) analysis of the deployment of ethnicity and culture as variables in a medical setting.

16. Mariampolski (2006), O'Reilly (2005), Marcus (1998), Arnould and Thompson (2005), and many others.

17. As Geertz (2002:2) also points out, in describing the proliferation of analytic paradigms in anthropology in the last fifty years and grounding anthropology's theoretical development and interests to larger, contemporaneous historical events: "There is very little in anthropology that is genuinely autonomous; pretensions to the contrary . . . are self-serving. We are, like everybody else, creators of our time, relics of our engagements." See also Fischer (2007) and Sherry (2000).

18. See Geertz (1988) and Malinowski (1989 [1967]).

19. See Behar (1996), Behar and Gordon (1995), Clifford (1997), Clifford and Marcus (1986), Fox (1991), Jackson (2005), Marcus (1998), Ruby (1980), Van Maanen (1995). Academic consumer culture research has problematized representation as well and has, more generally, taken on the notion of produced data and its epistemological underpinnings; see Sherry (2000), Sherry and Schouten (2002), Stern (1998). Note also comments on the representation of qualitative research by Thorpe (2003), a commercial consumer researcher in the United Kingdom.

20. From an anthropological perspective, it is a given that data are "produced" not "gathered" across disciplines, fields, and methods (including the experimental sciences). In the field of anthropology, there is a long history of discussion on how anthropological knowledge is created by theories, methods, and perspectives. These ideas are evident in the early 1900s methodological statements of Malinowski (see Malinowski 1984). They can also be found in the more recent discussions of reflexivity, the writing of ethnography, and the problematics of Malinowski's in situ ideal in a contemporary world of both considerable human movement and nonlocal, remote communication and interaction; see Clifford (1997), Clifford and Marcus (1986), Fox (1991), Gupta and Ferguson (1997a, 1997b), Marcus (1998), and Olwig and Hastrup (1997). As Desjeux (2004) has noted, this perspective does not imply that what one concludes from any given vantage point is untrue, but rather that there are many truths. One must simply be highly aware of the vantage point and the productive matrix of any given truth.

21. From the *Harvard Business Review* (Leonard and Rayport 1997) to *U.S. News & World Report* (Koerner 1998) or *Marketing Week* (2004), whether U.S.-based (Wellner 2002; Yin 2001), British (Barrand 2004) or Canadian (Smallbridge 2003), the fundamental articulation of ethnography has been grounded in metaphors of depth and digging. Truth is somehow fathomable if we just keep on burrowing. Thus, ethnography is still couched as looking beneath, plumbing psyches, getting to underlying motivations, as it was almost a decade ago (Denny 1999). See also Valentine and Evans (1993).

22. Gladwell (2005) in fact acknowledges the learned-ness of what then becomes the source for "gut" thinking, but nonetheless emphasizes a psychological con-

struct in describing the phenomenon. We would only note that this is another instance in which cultural meanings in the analytic understanding of behavior are backgrounded, and in the process tend to remain unrealized or invisible. Crucially, see McCracken (1988a, 2005) for an eloquent argument to the contrary—in a series of essays in both books, he demonstrates and illuminates the importance of a cultural lens in understanding consumption and consumer behavior.

23. Geertz (1973:6).
24. For an excellent illustration of cultural analysis, see McCracken's (2005) chapter on museums and museum-going.
25. Again, see McCracken (1988a).

3

Framing Cultural Questions: What is Coffee in Benton Harbor and Bangkok?

In this chapter, our aim is to further elucidate the meaning and implications of cultural analysis by focusing on methodological considerations that animate the research process. We do so through the presentation and framework of a "what is coffee?" exercise that we have used in training corporate clients as well as other research professionals in ethnographic research techniques. The exercise shows participants how coffee, its consumption, and its meanings are cultural matters. It demonstrates how a cultural analysis can be generative of new product ideas, brand positioning, retail design, and the like. Our goal in these trainings, as it is in this chapter, is to show how ethnographic cultural analysis is inherently multimodal (e.g., about listening as well as observing, about actions as well as artifacts) and analytic (about analytic thinking as well as questioning). In its rendering, this final introductory chapter is also an ethnographic account of explaining cultural analysis.

Coffee in Benton Harbor, Michigan

The first time we posed the question of "what is coffee?" as part of a teaching exercise was in Benton Harbor, Michigan, at the headquarters of the Whirlpool Corporation. Donna Romeo, a cultural anthropologist employed there at the time, had asked us to provide a seminar and training in ethnographic methods for interested staff. The point of the training was not necessarily for everyone to become an ethnographic researcher, but for those attending to be able to appreciate the parameters, use, and value of ethnographic cultural analysis. During the first part of the seminar we covered practical matters ranging from the need to design ethnographic research projects to fit the questions at hand, to some of the nuts and bolts practicalities of recruiting research participants, to strategies for the successful communication of the results within the organization. Amid these issues, we also discussed specific research techniques. The point of the "what is coffee?" exercise was to give everyone a chance to experience ethnographic interviewing in order to garner a feel for the approach.

We divided the group into pairs to conduct ethnographic interviews with one another. Each was to take a turn at both being the respondent and being the interviewer. The interviewing task was to find out what people thought about coffee and about the circumstances of coffee consumption in their daily lives. Consistent with the analytic assumption of the ongoing filtering of what we hear and see, an important instruction for those asking the questions was to remember that their own minds and actions were refracting agents, and thus they needed to be consciously open to matters other than those they already thought or assumed were important. We were trying to instill the appreciation that the focus, resolution, and fidelity (to borrow Fischer's list and metaphoric phrasing) of what is perceived were dependent on their own filtering processes.[1] Participants were urged to really try to understand, in detail, the point of view of the person being interviewed and to remember that something quite other than what they were expecting might be the truly important thing to realize about coffee.

To achieve this openness, we suggested they needed to try to imagine they had absolutely no preconceived notions about coffee. We advised that they could try to consciously garner the perspective of someone from another planet (using the 1984 John Sayles cult classic movie, *The Brother from Another Planet,* as a muse), or, if that perspective seemed too difficult to imagine, to try to take on the perspective of a child's first learning. Their goal here, we maintained, was to attempt to comprehend and appreciate everything that needed to be taken into account, learned, and practiced to become culturally competent in this realm. This stance comes about rather naturally when investigating in an unknown social milieu where the varied mistakes, social faux pas, and "stupid" questions one cannot help but ask actually help to illuminate the symbolic meanings and practices in play. We conceded that it is more difficult to have a naïve stance investigating coffee amid one's own social group, but emphasized that this stance is crucial for cultural analysis, otherwise too much can be left implicit, unanalyzed, unquestioned, unconsidered, or underutilized. The initial challenge was really to listen to others without preconceived notions or constraints about what kinds of information can or should come out of it.

Practically, we suggested they start their interviews simply with the very open-ended question of what coffee meant to the person. For instance, "Tell me about coffee in your life." We suggested they encourage their respondents to tell them about actual instances and specific examples and to elicit stories about coffee events in their lives. We stressed that in the responses, the person's categories of meaning, the conversational direction, the stories that were chosen, the tones of voice that indicated what they thought was important (or not), were *all* telling. We comforted them with the idea that *everything* counted as data—what was talked about or what was not, the way something was talked about (e.g., with pride, embarrassment, a sense of wonder). It did not matter if people could not think of something to say, since this, too, was considered data. We reminded them that in the real world of ethnographic inquiry, it is also important to consider what people do and thus that one should have an eye to the interaction with artifacts, the organization of the environment, the activities, and the match as well as the mismatch of thought, talk, and behavior.[2] So, they should also keep those kinds of observations in mind if their conversational partners were drinking coffee or, in fact, drinking or eating something else during the interview. Finally, we entreated them to pay careful attention to the details. We stressed that stories are often good vehicles for understanding meanings because they are full of telling details (and emotion), often without people even realizing it.[3] We noted that props and behaviors contain details and if one is not in the environment (by necessity, as for this practice) then one needed to ask about those details as well. And as we reiterated before everyone started, all of these details would be the fodder for developing a powerful analysis, thus it was crucial to also record them. So, please take detailed notes.

"But I Don't Drink Coffee"

Asking "what is coffee?" as a training exercise has many virtues. At the outset the question can strike people as mundane; in fact, for many it borders on boring.[4] The meanings and practices that surround coffee, even when fairly elaborate as they now are in the United States, tend to be taken for granted, or at least taken as just the "natural" and "true" circumstances and meanings that coffee should have, even while some people profess that other people do not necessarily know how to appreciate coffee "correctly" and others may contend that those who say such things exaggerate.

In this seminar as in others, when given this co-interviewing assignment, there were the usual types of pleas from some of the participants: "But I don't drink (or don't like) coffee, what can I say?" For us, these utterances are cases in point. As we tend to say, "You can still talk about it; not drinking it does not mean that it does not carry meaning for you. Coffee still exists for you." Moreover, talking to people who do not drink coffee can, in fact, provide considerable, often extremely enlightening information about relevant cultural matters. Among clients commissioning research, we often find much unneeded worrying about having to talk strictly to those defined as fitting the target audience profile. Talking to people with other profiles is frequently conceived of as a waste of time, and when it happens it is often framed as a mistake in respondent recruiting. Yes, it is true that one generally needs to speak to the members of the key audience for a product or service. But as we are not trying to plumb an individual psyche for psychological motivation, but rather trying to elucidate the relevant symbolic cultural meanings and practices, information garnered from those who do not like something is also relevant to understanding the cultural picture. In fact, contestation between points of view and meanings is a crucial aspect of the social dynamic. These nodal points of disagreement and different points of view can be precisely the most intriguing domains of cultural movement and thus new opportunities.[5]

"Is Cappuccino Named after Monks?"

And so we talked to one another about coffee. There were an odd number of participants, so Patti was part of a group of three, including one person who was a proud nondrinker of coffee. She drank tea, she said. There was ensuing talk about caffeine, heart palpitations, and liking Sprite because it lacked caffeine. There was mention of how "weird" it was that people would have coffee when first waking up, that it was a stimulant, like a drug or a "fix." While not liking coffee, she noted with new realization that she liked things that tended to go with coffee, for instance Kahlúa. And, in fact, she liked coffee ice cream. She also thought that the foam on cappuccino made coffee look "cooler" than coffee without foam. She talked of having heard that cappuccino was named after monks, though she did not feel certain that this was true.

From the person who did like coffee, there was talk about relaxing, about coffee being associated with sitting around with friends and taking one's time, not rushing. There was imagery of the special coffee cups at home which were used only on Sundays, of lazy mornings spent drinking coffee made in the French press and reading the *Chicago Tribune* with her husband. There was also talk about specific cups; for instance, for cappuccino she liked a larger cup. The larger cup felt better in the hand; it was more comforting. Coffee was also associated with being out with friends; for instance, during college, coffee shops were places to go hang out, and notably, coffee shops have great desserts.

There were also stories of having studied in Brazil and experiencing the coffee there, which seemed to be remembered primarily in terms of the senses: by the amount of sugar, the little cup, the smell, and of not liking it but in fact of drinking it "out of necessity." There was talk of office coffee, which included issues of paying for it, and powdered creamer, styrofoam cups, and sipping at one's desk. There was the particular story of a new puppy's barking at a time when her husband was traveling, which meant trouble with the neighbors and no sleep, which meant knowing that in the morning, "it was going to be a coffee day." She told of coming into work and "chugging it" which gave the feeling of "finally, something that will help me through the morning." But, like the non-coffee drinker, there was also talk about wanting to stay away from coffee, about not wanting to have too much caffeine, about wanting to try to be healthier and so maybe when feeling desperate at work in the afternoon, going to get a Pepsi instead.

From both of them there was also mention about *adults* drinking coffee, about adult family and friends drinking coffee at the conclusion of a meal, about temperature, about drinking hot things when not feeling well and as a way to stay warm, as well as about iced coffee. There was discussion about coffee makers (having them or not having them at home) and, again, talk of sensations. There was talk of smells, that sometimes ground coffee smells good. And there was more, even though each had talked for such a short period of time. Given the lunch break and that they had interviewed Patti as well, perhaps each person had spoken for approximately ten or fifteen minutes.

"I Never Thought of it that Way"

After these conversations, the next and, as we stressed, crucial step in cultural analysis was to go back and think about it. Part of the reason for writing down, for putting down details, for recording as much as possible was to be able to go back and consider the details. The reason we can now provide the description of bits of the coffee drinker and non-coffee drinker's conversation is because we had taken notes during these practice interviews. Putting things down on paper or in electronic files (or audio- or videotaping) also allows one to think about and (sometimes literally) see and hear things and connections not noticed before.

Epistemologically, cultural analysis is true to its name: It assumes that analysis is part of the process. Even though one must truly try to consciously open the mind and erase preconceived notions that could inhibit discovery for as long as possible while "in the field," there is always a filter. Even in the midst of a conversation, there is the filter of conversational and situational context. There is also always ongoing analysis. Once one has begun an ethnographic inquiry and started sorting out the symbolic terrain and practices, it is a constant, iterative, ongoing case of analytic learning, even as one continues to try to be open to surprises and other unexpected avenues along every step of the way. An analysis at the end is also crucial: If the ethnographic process is to remain open-ended, there will be some potentially irrelevant things included in the record; although, what is irrelevant? One must really think about it. Data are not transparent; meanings are not transparent. Different people and different researchers often come away from encounters with different insights because it is about making connections. In our research practice, we encourage clients to accompany us during fieldwork or to look at videotaped recordings of these encounters. We want clients to engage in the lived worlds of their customers. But we do not believe that we are necessarily all thinking about, or attending to, the same things in that environment. Meaning is not transparent, but we sometimes experience that assumption when clients who join us in the field are surprised by what we "took away."

The process of final analysis can be slightly idiosyncratic. (Patti's favorite mode is to first make an exhaustive, uncensored brainstorming-fashion list; Rita's favorite is first to write down the overarching categories that seem to have emerged and then to see how other bits of data and ideas mesh, or not, with those initial categories.) There are many other good suggestions to be found in the literature, but whatever one does should ideally fit with one's most productive or at least most pleasurable mode for thinking.[6] Because in the end, at its core, cultural analysis is about going back through one's materials and thinking as hard and as long as possible about what has been said or done and what it all implies. This thinking and rethinking can sometimes happen long after the exploration began (see, for instance, Chapters 8 and 10). Cultural analysis is about looking for connections and disconnections, similarities as well as contradictions, among what has been said and done. And at this stage it is about utilizing every single synapse and every single particle of any ideas, however recessed in the mind, to find every metaphor, meaning, and connection. The goal is to try to discern what it all means and implies and to use every other bit of cultural knowledge to help interpret the matter at hand, thus also connecting everything that is in the nonempty mind with what has been taken in with as open a mind as possible.[7]

And so, in the margins of the interview's notes from that day, one can now find "Tea is the comparison beverage" scribbled next to the strong statement of "I drink tea." Alongside this is also scribbled, "iced tea, iced coffee," a scribble that would indicate that the later mentions of both iced tea and iced coffee seemed further indication of the parallel nature of coffee and tea. "Addictive things" is written next to "stimulant," "drug," and "fix" and about it being "weird" that people drink coffee when first waking up. Near the notes about cappuccino and monks and the foam looking "cool," there are notations of "cooler" and "folklore." In other margins, one finds "energy," "relaxed," "the temperature of coffee really important," "smell," "ways of preparing," "ways it didn't work" and "coffee as friend/enemy." This list is also telling. There were perhaps fifteen minutes of analysis time that day. Besides trying to be relatively uncensored (and thus noting things that just jumped out such as "temperature is important" and "energy"), one can see the attempt to make connections, thus the notation of tea as the comparative beverage, as well as the attempt to understand some of the metaphoric and more complex symbolic meanings, thus the notations of drug like addiction and coffee as friend/enemy. That coffee's connection with adulthood, a culturally constituted life stage and category of personhood, was deemed an important detail was marked in the notes by an arrow and the slightly larger way in which it was written at the time of the interview.

Coffee also engenders strong emotions; it can be loved. We have no notes for the interview Patti provided as a respondent. But we do still have in the folder that corresponds to this training an image she drew, perhaps to both depict the way she felt about coffee and to make the point that one can ask respondents to select and create imagery which then can be both simultaneously telling and a potent illustration for a report, as in Figure 3.1.

"You Could Get Ideas from This"

After each person had spent some time looking for connections and doing the analysis of their notes, the next step in the training was to gather together the analyzed content. This was done as a group. We collectively voiced the findings, while one person wrote them on a large board, the length of one of the room's walls, meanwhile grouping findings in provisional categories. This concurrent attempt to group the insights into overarching categories and related issues was another analytic step in the process to see connections and garner new insights. Altogether, as a group, perhaps ten to fifteen interviews had been conducted (not unlike what we might do in our actual ethnographic practice, except then the interviews would tend to be three to four hours long and videotaped). Based on this small amount of interviewing time, the board ended up completely covered with tidbits of cultural insight.

What amazed this group were the potential new product innovations and product positionings that jumped out from the insights garnered, even from

Figure 3.1 A cultural expression of an author's musings about coffee

this short, practice exercise. Given this particular group's business focus, products imagined were those that might enhance the smell or foam in coffee, varied automatic ice coffee makers and coffee ice cream makers, as well as, attesting to the value of including those who did not drink coffee, great comparative products for tea drinkers and the like. In terms of positioning products, there was the coolness factor, the relaxation factor, the strength factor—a whole host of potential angles to be considered. It was clear there was merit in cultural analysis. It was generative. You could get ideas from cultural analysis. Good ones, in fact.

Coffee in Bangkok, Thailand

In Bangkok we elaborated this "what is coffee?" training in both methodological scope and time. Here we were training a group of senior qualitative researchers from Japan, India, New Zealand, Indonesia, Singapore, Thailand, Malaysia, the Philippines, China, Holland, and the U.K. They were all senior members of Research International (RI), most of them the lead qualitative researchers of their respective offices. Thus, all were experienced leaders of focus groups and standard qualitative interviews; all were experts in the kinds of things that brand managers, advertisers, and corporate research departments needed to derive from qualitative consumer research. This week-long seminar, a combined training in semiotic analysis and ethnographic methodology, was commissioned by Malcolm Baker, then Global Managing Director of Research International (RI) Qualitatif. It was in the early 2000s, a period in which ethnography and semiotics had become increasingly important in applied consumer research; Baker wanted to be sure that RI played a part.

This time we also gave seminar participants "homework." We often give our ethnographic research respondents a pre-meeting assignment. The reason for homework is twofold. On the one hand, it helps to make research participants partners in the endeavor: As it prepares respondents for the upcoming ethnographic encounter, it invests them in the process and the question. Just as any traditional fieldwork carried out by anthropologists depends explicitly or implicitly on the willingness of those who are the focus to go along with the endeavor—on their partnership—so does ethnographic consumer research. The second reason is that homework, especially in the form of diaries—video, photo, or audio—helps extend the ethnographic inquiry across time and space. Diaries allow the research to continue beyond the face-to-face encounter and for the researcher to be there without being there. In corporate consumer research, this is often needed given the limited time frame of the research. In anthropological research more generally, there has also been the realization of the need and value of extending ethnographic interactions beyond the face-to-face given the spatially dispersed, telephonically, electronically mediated nature of much contemporary interaction.

In this instance, prior to meeting, we assigned participants articles to read (not something we generally do in our research, although it would perhaps be a novel method worth trying), and we asked them to take photographs. These photos were to include the places in their countries where coffee would typically be consumed or purchased. We asked them to take photographs of the interiors, the exteriors, the details they found interesting, as well as to take photographs of whatever in their minds captured a given place. We also asked them to take photographs that would bring to life what coffee meant in their own homes. Here we used the comparative example of Rita's home where the photos included the coffee grinder and coffee maker in their prominent place on the kitchen counter, the beans in the freezer, the cups, and the favorite places for reading while drinking coffee. Given the aspect of the training that involved the semiotic decoding of advertisements, we also asked participants to bring along examples of coffee advertising, which here we suggested meant not only advertisements from magazines and newspapers, but also from billboards.

Advertisements Are Data Too

The advertising examples gained everyone's attention. Large billboard ads from India featured women alone with hands tenderly embracing a cup, or head back, eyes closed, and imagery of wafting aroma, depicting coffee as a private moment of experiential sensations. Among the ads from Japan was one featuring two cups and hands, with the hands referencing the close relationship of a couple. Beyond intimacy, coffee in Japan was also associated with modernity, urbanity, sophistication, self-expression, and style as indexed by the clothes worn by those featured in other ads. Nescafé ads in Malaysia, China, and the Philippines invoked moments of mystery and romance as well as indulgence and getting in touch with the self through imagery of closed eyes, gold cups, and so on. (The billboard ads of coffee in India were also for Nescafé.) Yet in their power to entertain and amaze (at least us), no advertisements quite topped those from New Zealand. These ads took on the addiction metaphor that had been touched upon in Benton Harbor. This brand, *roasted addiqtion*, was uncompromising in its iconography of coffee as a drug with its drug paraphernalia imagery and copy such as "by the hit, by the gram, by the kilo."[8] But it did let you know that it was not really about straight-on addiction via the playful misspelling of addiction in the brand's name (see Figure 3.2). A *roasted addiqtion* card that the participant brought was also printed with the ironic, implicitly playful instruction to "call from a public phone, don't use your real name and ask for 'bob.'"

Emergence of Cultural Categories

When the participants interviewed one another about coffee, we asked that they use the photographs they had taken prior to the training, as well as their collected advertising texts, as stand-ins for being in situ and immersed in the context and artifacts of each other's everyday lives. After interviewing one another, participants then jointly analyzed the results by country and presented these to the whole group. The presenters analyzed coffee in Malaysia as a fashion product, that is, an expensive product consumed outside the home within an upscale, fashion ambience because of its "cool" factor. In other situations, they suggested, coffee was just another drink and even associated in Malaysia with a lower class milieu. For Indonesia, we also heard that coffee could be understood as just another beverage, as well as the articulation that "coffee is not coffee per se" because coffee only existed as a beverage once other ingredients such as milk, chocolate powder, and creamer were added

Figure 3.2 An example of *roasted addiqtion*'s messaging brought by a New Zealand participant to the seminar

to it. From the U.K. we heard about coffee as a ritual of work, as a social drink, just part of the expected daily diet. For China, we observed a recurrence of coffee as a metaphor for work, with the addition that coffee was a symbol of modernity and western urban values. For Holland, coffee consumption was analyzed as a rite of passage, based on the data that the teenage years were a time to take on coffee drinking and that, in fact, in Holland coffee consumption demarcates generations. The myriad rituals and social rules that surrounded coffee consumption in the Netherlands were also noted—the assumptions of fixed times for drinking coffee and fixed times for not, the role of coffee in social obligations and its contribution as social lubricant. For New Zealand, we were told, coffee was an all-occasion drink, as well as tied to social moments. For India, coffee was social and trendy, whereas tea was intrinsic to life, and instant coffee was coffee's traditional form. Two narratives were articulated for Japan. One strand emphasized special occasions, in which time was needed to enjoy the coffee and emphasis was put on issues of purity, genuineness, authenticity, and flavor. The other strand focused on how coffee was about stimulation or getting a kick start, in which the modal form for consumption was out of a can. A dichotomy between the version that stressed masculinity and potency and framed coffee as old-fashioned, versus a new and trendy, younger consumption arena for coffee, was the case presented for Singapore. But there also existed, we were told, a more mundane take on coffee in Singapore as "just a beverage" that could be consumed either cold or hot, along with mentions of unhealthiness and substitutes such as Red Bull, the energy drink.

The fact that these analyses stressed multiple categories of meaning was testament to the additional time given to the task, the sophistication of those analyzing, and the encouragement in the assignment to come up with multiple, even potentially contradictory strands of cultural meanings. For this training we had created an interview guide that extended beyond the general "tell me about yourself and coffee" and had explicitly included probes about different times, places, and people. There were questions about different instances of one's own coffee consumption and its change over time, as well as about oneself versus others in the family, friends, and colleagues. There were also subcategory notations about coffee versus other types of beverages and different brands of coffee. Again, one does get the answers to the questions one asks, and that is precisely why it is also so important to be open to the unexpected.

When is Observation Cultural Analysis?

As enlightening as participants' interview analyses were, these exercises were still only part of practice and subassignments to the major assignment of examining, "What is coffee in Bangkok?" We were all assembled in Thailand for this training and we were asking participants (and ourselves) to conduct an analysis of coffee in Bangkok functionally, symbolically, and aesthetically. What we wanted participants to do was to conduct a semiotic analysis of coffee based on the analysis of retail environments. In this case, the primary goal was to look at retail environments as types of semiotic texts, that is, to look at the codes, the cues, the references, the symbols, the icons, the indexes, in essence the myriad messages locatable in the environments, rather than necessarily to talk to people. There was the practical problem, shared among virtually all of us, of a lack of fluency in Thai. But we also wanted to stress the aspects of

trying to look at environments (architectural layout, artifacts, as well as behaviors within an environment, which would as a rule include the what and
how of speech) as conveyors of potential informational fodder for a cultural
analysis. We supplied participants with an observational protocol (or guide)
that included two major categories: "layout of environment" and "browsing
and consumption patterns." Sub-categories included props, signage, milieu
(table, chairs, floors, lighting, litter), and questions such as, "What do aesthetics
of the setting tell you about coffee?" "Who are the customers?" "Who aren't
they?" "Coffee making and serving rituals?" and "What is a person looking at,
drawn to, touching, talking to, reading?" We then set off in two teams, each
with one of us acting as participant mentor.

We had, in fact, conducted our own exploratory mission for this exercise
before the training. We had arrived in Bangkok a day or so early because we
thought that we should have some coffee places in mind for the teams to visit.
We set our agenda with the help of guidebooks for finding coffee places in
Bangkok. But before taking on our list of possible locations, we first indulged
our own predilections for local markets by going to an open-air market. While
there, our attention was drawn to a vendor mixing coffee with condensed and
evaporated milk and pouring it into a plastic ice-filled bag, then tying it for
easy carrying and puncturing it with a straw (see Figures 3.3 and 3.4). At the
open-air market, we also found a stand of what seemed like a more elaborate
set-up of various coffees for sale, but we did not linger too long as we were in
our search of coffee shops and coffee stores for the upcoming assignment.

Negotiating both guidebooks and public transport, we did find Starbucks,
rather brimming with young, cell-phone-carrying professionals, and UCC, an
expensive place that seemed to give at least as much priority to food as to coffee,
but which prominently featured individual-serving drip pots (see Figure 3.5)
which, we were later told, were very *au courant* at that time in Japan. Many of
these coffee drip pots, in varying states of warming, dripping, and waiting, lined
a highly visible, rather centrally located work counter in the restaurant.

We also found the casually chic Coffee Corner, located in an air-conditioned,
upscale shopping center, replete with menu of individual, specially prepared
coffees and canisters of beans lining the counter. Yet, it was not until after the
training that we located the much-harder-to-find old storefronts in Chinatown
(with their tiled floors, marble-topped tables, and local denizens, largely older
men). These shops, more than any other, gave a feeling of a "really Thai"
place for coffee, even though they also seemed to do a significant business
in food, from sandwiches to the more substantial, in addition to coffee (see
Figure 3.6).

Figures 3.3 Coffee vendor at the open air market in Bangkok

However, what we did begin to realize in our search for varied coffee environments was that the assumption of places centered on coffee consumption was an inappropriate assumption in Thailand. In fact, it was an assumption that unless discarded endangered a full understanding of what coffee was in Bangkok. What became apparent was that while "coffee places" were relatively few and far between and took some searching to find, coffee was, in actual fact, everywhere.

Figures 3.4   Pouring coffee into a plastic ice-filled bag

Figure 3.5   UCC coffee pots

Figure 3.6 Coffee in Bangkok's Chinese storefront restaurants

Coffee was routinely sold in Bangkok at the ubiquitous carts and stands of street vendors, which sometimes also had a few tables for eating nearby. It was just another beverage choice among many (see Figures 3.7 and 3.8). Once one knew to look, the warm pots of waiting coffee could often be readily spotted alongside these stands. It also became clear that coffee's presence was indexically marked by canned milk, often Carnation. That is to say, just as smoke is a semiotic index of fire, if one saw Carnation, coffee was likely nearby (see Figures 3.9–3.11).

Before we accompanied seminar participants on their ethnographic excursion, we did not mention this street vendor coffee. Perhaps we wanted to allow them to experience the process of discovery, and especially the experiential pleasure at the moment of an unexpected realization, or maybe we were just hoping to make a didactic point. In any case, notebooks in hand, Rita's team set out to Starbucks, UCC, and another mall-based location on Rita's mental must-see list. Patti's team set off to explore a small restaurant beautifully and intricately composed of numerous small rooms, trinkets, and flowers; the casually chic Coffee Corner; and the unstated discovery of street vendor coffee. For Patti the process felt a bit like a game in which she had hidden something and had

Figures 3.7 Coffee on the street in Bangkok, one beverage among many

Figures 3.8 Vendors and sidewalk tables

Figures 3.9   Warm pots of waiting coffee

Figures 3.10   Cans of milk, indexicals of coffee on the street

Figure 3.11   Canned milk poured into a plastic bag as an ingredient of street coffee

to watch as participants fumbled around to find it. There were the moments of help—akin to when in such a game the hider says "cold," "warm," or "hot" to let participants know their relative chance of finding the hidden goods in that location. The hints started with the suggestion of getting something to drink from one of the vendors, "because it was so hot," to finally something fairly obvious on the order of raised eyebrows and a moving finger pointed at a sitting coffee pot. Like us, participants had a difficult time finding the coffee at a street vendor's cart because they also were not expecting it; they undoubtedly also were carrying the notion of (closed in, coffee-focused) place in their minds, even if for no other reason than that we had told them to look for "coffee places."

"But Real Coffee is . . ."

At the end of the day when we all reconvened and set about going through notes as a first step in analysis, we reminded participants once again that one of the hardest things to overcome in any cultural or semiotic analysis is the impact of one's own ingoing assumptions. Thus participants were encouraged to use their own feelings and reactions regarding what they had seen and thought of as not "real" or "good" coffee as clues and catalysts for looking more carefully at what coffee *is* in Bangkok. Focusing the initial analysis on what coffee *is not* also served as a useful way to acknowledge and make explicit the group's own ingoing assumptions. As seminar participants noted, in Bangkok:

- Coffee was not black and not hot. What Americans and Europeans consider "coffee" (hot black essence sometimes "diluted" by other elements) was rarely seen. Coffee during the day was routinely poured into plastic bags of ice. Participants concluded that "coffee is an ingredient."
- Coffee, when served, was not "refined" through a mechanical process. Unlike the exceptional and clearly imported (the Starbucks machine or the Japanese drip pot), there was no homage to bean-grinding machinery or dripping process; there was an absence of mechanical spectacle. Vendor coffee sat waiting in pitchers of warm/hot water, in its filter sock, poured out when someone ordered it. While instant coffee was found on the shelves in local groceries, coffee was not often found in freshly ground or bean form. A seemingly ubiquitous use of old instant coffee jars as containers for other things also suggested that instant coffee had an appeal.
- Coffee did not have its own places. As a group, we set out looking for coffee places: cafés, special stores, boutique environments. Instead, we did not find any stores specifically dedicated to coffee and we found that coffee typically had no special place dedicated to its drinking; along with other drinks and food, it was routinely found with the street vendors. The assumption of a place focused around coffee was simply another assumption we had carried with us.[9] A Western import like Starbucks, truly a *place* for coffee, was inhabited by young, cell-phone-carrying professionals. Starbucks is about fashion and social currency. Coffee more generally, was not.

Thus, traditionally at least, coffee was neither a visual nor a conceptual focal point in places where it could be purchased, and the "freshness" of coffee was not fetishized, as coffee, in general, was not fetishized. The lack of differentiated status among beverages (at least as it was sold), its lack of focal point for social activity, its lack of physical place for consumption all seemed to indicate "unelaborated commodity." But this would be viewing coffee in Bangkok solely through a Western lens—as black, hot, espresso machines, aromas, beans, and places for coffee (coffee shops or cafés) are signs (symbols and indexes) conventionalized in our own terms for carrying meaning about coffee (potency, performance, intensity, productivity, depth).

So, we then asked participants to try to think about coffee in Thai cultural terms. Though truly an impossible task given that most of us had spent a total of two days in Thailand and no one spoke fluent Thai, it was important to try to examine coffee from a Thai point of view, to try to see it in those terms. The provisional analysis was provocative. As we reasoned, perhaps:

- Coffee was a deftly constructed concoction (akin to a good bartender's movements) that is like Thai dishes in its medley of ingredients, its place on the streets, and its to-go form. Just as Thais seemed to evaluate food as better when there were more individually, thoughtfully added ingredients, a really good coffee we were told was achieved by first adding the condensed milk, then the coffee, then the evaporated milk, and so on.
- Coffee was refreshment, more ubiquitous than soda, an antidote to city heat while making one's way from point A to point B. Sold in the same beverage stands as fruit drinks (also served on ice in bags with straws), street coffee, at least, suggested interlude.
- Coffee forms were symbolic of larger cultural discourses and flows between East and West, tradition and modernity. Participants from Malaysia, Indonesia, China, Singapore, and India extrapolated from similar cultural and coffee phenomena in their own countries to reason that Starbucks and similarly processed and packaged coffees operated as icons of Western modernity. Consumption of the "traditional" Thai street vendor coffee as opposed to Starbucks or UCC could thus make a statement about people's values in addition to their taste preference. A participant who had spent time in Thailand further observed that instant coffee had once been the symbol of westernized modernity. The seemingly ubiquitous old Nescafé containers, now filled with other things, were thus reminders of an earlier time.

The results we outlined above are based solely on a few hours of seminar participants' Bangkok observation coupled with the few extra hours of preparation on our part. Given this time frame, we believe the results to be truly a testimonial to the power of cultural analysis. At the same time, we would argue that they are woefully incomplete. We encouraged participants to try to think in Thai "insider" categories as we maintain that without the insider's point of view, cultural life is ultimately always misunderstood, filtered to obscurity given its view only through the eyes of the observer. To do the study as a research project, not just a training exercise, one would need to talk with Bangkok coffee drinkers, to understand what they think about coffee, to hear how they talk about coffee, to know what goes on in their heads and what things they do as they take their first, middle, and last sips, to know what they think and do when drinking different types of coffee, to know what they are thinking about while waiting at the street vendor or in the Starbucks. If the study had been a full one, we would have perhaps heard that, in fact, morning coffee is often drunk hot, and that we were just not touching that part of the elephant, focused as we were on the afternoon. In fact, a man with a small storefront, who sold us some more sock-steeped coffee poured over ice, told us that he sold more coffee in the morning and that, at that time, he sold it hot.

Figure 3.12 A Bangkok vendor, with the coffee "sock," who told us he sells more coffee in the morning than in the afternoon . . . and sells it hot.

Notes

1. Fischer's (2007:3) more complete formulation was, "Objects, theories, and techniques change in focus, resolution, or fidelity (to draw on visual and sonic descriptive modalities) as we vary our cultural concepts."

2. Discussion of the match, and particularly the mismatch, of what people say they will do and what they do has been considerable within the academic literature of consumer research as well as psychology. We actually originally heard the tripartite construction—thought, talk, and behavior—used by Dominique Desjeux during a seminar he organized in January 2007. The tripartite model including thoughts as well as voiced opinions and action seems a more precise model for this phenomenon than simply talk vs. behavior, which, in the actual training described, is what we most likely said.

3. Note also Levy (2006b), who discusses the role (and consumption) of stories in negotiating identity.

4. See Sherry (1995b), who, in an analysis of coffee, using American TV programming as data, comments on coffee's ubiquitous presence in living, its consumption akin to breathing.

5. See Thompson and Arsel's (2004) discussion of anti-Starbucks discourse and places as a case in point in the domain of coffee.

6. For background and discipline, see Glaser and Strauss's 1967 classic, *The Discovery of Grounded Theory*. See also Strauss (1987), McCracken (1988b), and Chapter 8 of Barrett (1996) including what he has to say about the modes of analysis suggested in these other works. Note also Arnould and Wallendorf (1994), Thompson (1997), and Valentine (1995). Developed out of the growth of ethnographic research in realms of product design, the use of affinity diagramming and other means of visualizing connections and analysis have also gained currency; see Beyer and Holtzblatt (1998).

7. As Malinowski wrote in 1922 in *Argonauts of the Western Pacific* (1984:8–9) "Good training in theory, and acquaintance with its latest results, is not identical with being burdened with 'preconceived ideas.' If a man sets out on an expedition, determined to prove certain hypotheses, if he is incapable of changing his views constantly and casting them off ungrudgingly under the pressure of evidence, needless to say his work will be worthless. But the more problems he brings with him, the more he is in the habit of moulding his theories according to facts, and of seeing facts in their bearing upon theory, the better he is equipped for the work."

8. See their Web site, www.roastedaddiqtion.co.nz, for other examples of the metaphor. Coffee has long been viewed as a drug; see, for example, Dufrenoy and Dufrenoy (1950). See also Gladwell (2001) and compare Roseberry (1996).

9. The assumption of place, given coffee's social history (see Clayton 2003; Hattox 1985) and contemporary Western practice, is understandable if not forgivable. As Sherry observed in his analysis of coffee in American TV programming, coffee emplaces—its presence is a magnet, "people are drawn to the site of its production" and "the coffee machine and the beverage it produces help emplace and embed consumers in existentially profound quality space" (1995:359). This also provides a case in point of how meaning is constituted through social practice, and how difficult it can be to relinquish assumptions of what is "real." Note also Thompson and Arsel's (2004) analysis of the influence (and flourishing) of local coffee places in light of (opposition to) Starbucks' globally branded places.

Part II
Engaging Approaches

The Ordinary Matters: Making Anthropology Audible

Donald D. Stull

University of Kansas

Anthropology, or any other subject, cannot avoid the context in which it is done. And we cannot afford to be out of touch with our times.

Paul Bohannan (1980:512)

Whether it survives, flourishes, or becomes extinct depends on anthropology's ability to contribute: to become integral and significant to our culture and society without becoming subservient.

James L. Peacock (1997:9)

[P]ractice is not an option for anthropology if it is to survive. Practice is part of the discipline's destiny and needs to be at the center of discussion about anthropology's future.

Barbara Rylko-Bauer, Merrill Singer, and John van Willigen (2006:179)

These epigraphs, all from the *American Anthropologist*, suggest a convergence of anthropological opinion: our discipline must not only be involved with the world in which it finds itself; it must also demonstrate that it can be of use to that world. Given that the first two quotes came from presidential addresses to the American Anthropological Association, it would seem that such an idea has considerable currency within the field. Would that it were so.

Sadly, the steady escalation and amplification of calls for a more relevant and engaged anthropology, ushered in by Bohannan, have not bridged the chasm between academic anthropology on the one hand and applied and practicing anthropology on the other. In fact, those who cry the loudest for a new and more relevant anthropology pointedly ignore the long-standing tradition of application within the discipline. And it was from this convenient amnesia that Rylko-Bauer, Singer, and van Willigen sought to reclaim the rightful place of application and practice in anthropology's past, present, and, most importantly, future.

Misconceptions about applied and practicing anthropology abound, but the most persistent—and the most pernicious—is that it is lacking in theory (Rylko-Bauer, Singer, and van Willigen 2006:184). Applied anthropologists have repeatedly debunked this disciplinary fantasy (see, for example, Hill and Baba 2000; Schensul and Stern 1985), but, like so many urban legends, it simply won't go away. Perhaps this is due, as Partridge (1985:141) suggests, to the failure on the part of applied and practicing anthropologists to make the role of theory in their work explicit. This is certainly not the case here. Never have I seen a more eloquent or forceful argument for how theory informs and is informed by practice.

Patti Sunderland and Rita Denny are practicing anthropologists, who by dint of their positions as marketing researchers, are especially well situated as ethnographers—and chroniclers—of our postmodern age. This book is a gem, and one long awaited by academic applied anthropologists like me. I have taught courses in applied anthropology and ethnographic research methods for many years, and several of my former students have gone on to careers in market research. Had I had access to such a text earlier, my students would have been far more aware of, and far better prepared for, the careers that awaited them.

Doing Anthropology in Consumer Research consists of a series of what are essentially "letters from the field," eloquently written with wit and candor, and filled with intriguing vignettes illustrating just how important the work of practitioners can be in advancing anthropological theory and method. Their use of multiple methods within the overall ethnographic framework, including rapid appraisal and semiotic analysis, is a model for contemporary fieldworkers, regardless of the location or domain of their work. That their findings and analyses of necessity are partial, provisional, and positional is instructive for researchers of every stripe. After all, our understandings of the social world are always tenuous and malleable. It cannot be otherwise.

The chapters in the following section, "Engaging Approaches," are superlative examples of the interplay between theory and practice, forged in the topsy-turvy world of applied research. They also reveal, in the authors' deceptively casual manner, theoretical and methodological sophistication that brings new, and at times quite surprising, insights into the nature of work, national identity, gender, companionship, emotion—the very stuff of life itself.

Like a lot of my friends and colleagues, I spend more time at the office than at home, and while in the office I can usually be found staring at or banging on my laptop. Personal computers are ubiquitous, and they have become absolutely essential, even for stubborn Luddites like me. In Chapter 4, "The Social Life of Metaphors: Have We Become Our Computers?" Sunderland

and Denny artfully combine visual and conversational data to demonstrate how the computer serves as a powerful metaphor for postmodern society—in "the office" and far beyond. But the computer is more than metaphor; it shapes our lives in significant and often insidious ways. Computers have transformed our vocabulary and even our grammar; molded our interpersonal relations; influenced how and where we work and play; collapsed space and time. Perhaps most revealing of just how potent computers have become is the young man who described to Sunderland and Denny his annoyance with traffic lights because they are not "smart" enough to "read" the traffic and turn from red to green to suit (his) traffic needs.

Super Bowl Sunday is an American institution. And in a land where "party" has become a verb, only New Year's Eve out-parties the Super Bowl. Counterintuitively, perhaps, Super Bowl commercials have become as much a part of the event as the action on the field. Advertisers pay millions for a 30-second spot, and viewers reportedly record the game so they can view the commercials over again.

What can commercials and advertisements tell us about culture? Quite a lot, actually. Advertising is a form of discourse between advertisers and consumers. And like any other discourse, to be successful, both parties must share systems of meaning. In Chapter 5, Sunderland and Denny employ semiotic analysis to penetrate the meanings behind ads for automobiles, convenience food, and beer in Australia and New Zealand. Drawing on collaborative research with advertising professionals from Sydney and Auckland, they take readers on a captivating tour of Australian and New Zealand cultural identity (with an occasional side trip to the United States). At its end we come away with crucial insights into national identity, as well as cultural constructs surrounding gender, friendship and kinship, sport, notions of the place of humans in nature—and the parameters of trans-Tasman identity.

The comparative method was a cornerstone upon which anthropology was built, but early on it came under attack (Boas 1896) and the ethnographic case study became the method of choice of cultural anthropology. Nevertheless, comparison, if carried out systematically, is the basis for ethnological generalizations that reveal cultural processes, which, after all, are the primary goal of applied social science. In Chapter 6—"Contextualizing Emotion: When Do Boredom, Paranoia, and "Being Strong" Become Emotions?"—Sunderland and Denny put the comparative method to excellent use in an exploration of the social construction of emotional states among young adults in the United Kingdom, the United States, and New Zealand.

I must confess that at first I found their decision to restrict their sample to six middle-class youths each in New York, London, and Auckland to be off-putting and suspect. After all, New York City is hardly a "typical" American community. But in reading their analysis of "stress" as the "key example . . . in elucidating the U.S. sociocultural terrain of emotion" (p. 152), I was struck with how much the young people they interviewed in New York sounded like my students and colleagues at the University of Kansas. And their comparative research showed just how important culture really is—in emotions, no less than in the languages we speak, the gods we worship, the clothes we wear, or whether we drink our coffee black, "regular," or *con leche*.

In reading "Contextualizing Emotion" I was struck, as I have been throughout this book, with how methodologically rigorous—and imaginative—Rita Denny and Patti Sunderland are. Asking research participants to keep a diary is a well-established technique, but how many researchers would think to ask teens to record their location, activities, and moods on the inside of the candy wrappers they consumed during the study period? I can only shake my head in admiration, and mutter: Well, what better way to uncover boredom as a teenage emotion?

Ethnography is all about getting to know a group of people, and ethnographers will tell you that it takes time. After all, my candidate for the inventor of ethnography, Frank Hamilton Cushing, spent four-and-a-half years at Zuni (Erickson and Stull 1998:2). Following in Cushing's footsteps, and those of Bronislaw Malinowski, who has been lionized as the first ethnographer, anthropological fieldworkers have sallied forth to faraway places, lived among the natives, partook of their wisdom, and returned in a year or so to "write up their notes" on "their people." This archetype was passed down over the years in the "1:1:1 ratio—one man, one village, one year" (Hackenberg 1993:13).

That was then. . . .

In today's world of social research, funded increasingly by research contracts, time is in short supply. Anthropologists have had to diversify their traditional ethnographic toolkit beyond participant observation and in-depth interviews to include an array of other research methods often subsumed under the umbrella of rapid research methods, or rapid appraisal (see van Willigen and Finan 1991). Chief among these rapid research methods is the focus group. Most ethnographers, I suspect, certainly this one, are skeptical, if not downright disdainful, of focus groups. But in Chapter 7, "Diagnosing Conversational Details," Sunderland and Denny demonstrate that focus groups are performative events, potentially rich in information and insight. They masterfully dissect the focus group as a method, showing how industry concern with this research technique has led to a growing interest in ethnography.

Denny and Sunderland ground their research in the ethnography of speaking, which recognizes the "messiness, variability, systematicity, and creativity" of verbal communication, and employ "language-in-use as a means for understanding broader social codes and the dynamics of change and meaning" (p. 192). In so doing, they interpret public concerns over possible health risks associated with electrical power lines to utility corporations. More broadly, their work reveals "the implicit relationship between speaker and subject," as well as the mutual unintelligibility that so often characterizes public "communication."

Anthropologists are fond of quoting Laura Nader's (1972) dictum to "study up," but few have tried it, and none with greater success than Patricia Sunderland and Rita Denny. How better to understand our society than by working with those who shape it. They lure their readers out of the cloistered halls of academia and lead them on a journey to the shores of corporate board rooms, through the cubicles and offices of ad agencies and public utilities, and into the homes and shops of everyday people on several continents. We drink coffee with them and ponder its meanings in Michigan and Thailand, explore race and ethnicity in the United States, delve into sports and advertising in Australia and New Zealand, experience the innermost emotions of young people of three continents, view the people and landscapes of Cuba through their eyes. In so doing, we are given an advanced seminar in modern ethnographic research methods and anthropological ethics. And perhaps most important of all, our eyes are opened to the cultural freightings of the prosaic, the ordinary artifacts of our everyday lives—coffee, chocolate, household cleaners, the Internet, TV, the brands that frame who we are and dictate what we buy.

In "The Anthropology of Trouble," Roy Rappaport (1993:295) advocated "the relocation of both engaged and domestic research from anthropology's periphery toward its center." He also reminded us that "[i]t is one thing to make discourse intelligible and quite another to make it *audible*" (1993:301, emphasis in original). For Rappaport—and for anthropology—this is both a "deep theoretical as well as practical problem" (ibid.). Patricia Sunderland and Rita Denny have devoted their careers to making anthropology both intelligible and useful to nonanthropologists. In *Doing Anthropology in Consumer Research* they have shown the rest of us the way. It now falls to us to see more clearly the anthropological lessons in the world around us and to speak more intelligibly and audibly to those who shape our world.

Apposite Anthropology and the Elasticity of Ethnography

John F. Sherry Jr.

University of Notre Dame

Rita Denny and Patti Sunderland have written an intensely personal account of their practice of consumer ethnography. This section in particular—"Engaging Approaches"—calls forth a personal response. My dissertation advisor inducted me into the discipline by intoning this mantra:

> There are as many anthropologies
> as there are anthropologists.

I've always repeated this gift in iambic pentameter, and sometimes shift the words to make it scan more pleasingly, but its instress has been unerring. We bring our own madness to our method, and that bringing—the intraceptive intuition that emerges from our immersion in theory tempered by fieldwork—dimensionalizes us as instruments and distinguishes the discipline.

As an anthropologist, a professor of marketing, and an active industry consultant, I am intrigued both by the ways the authors have involved us with their ideas, and by the substantive findings they turn to their disciplinary and managerial purposes. Like good seminar leaders or skilled facilitators of unfocus groups, they introduce most of their findings with questions, inviting us implicitly to tack from text to margin, documenting our conversation in penciled notes of assent or elaboration, or even still, of disagreement, because the stuff of their discourse is just so compelling. We are led through their musings, and encouraged to meander on our own, by the simple conceit employed by every successful nondirective interviewer. "Tell me about ____," they beseech their informants, and so also are we imbricated in that telling.

Throughout this section, we are challenged to connect methodology with the theoretical orientations that determine its deployment in the field. We see that elegant design and technical sophistication, detached from a theoretical

89

lens, yield idiosyncratic insight of potential projective value, but systematic intuition about neither the lived experience of consumption nor the cultural templates framing it. The marriage of cultural theory with rigorous yet flexible methodology is what separates more reputable market-oriented ethnographers from Sahlins' hucksters of the symbol.

Notwithstanding the semiotic orientation Rita and Patti adopt—it is, after all, the preferred perspective of ethnographic consumer research—we are treated to an old-school four-fields analysis of the commercial enterprise. They are relentlessly holistic in their attention to language, behavior, artifacts, and the nature-nurture interface. They adeptly depict the tension inherent in developing (versus merely applying) theory in an applied realm. I hope readers are motivated to explore the exhaustive source material that informs the authors' consideration of their consulting practice, for, just as anthropology has been periodically "discovered" by industry, so also have traditional anthropologists been frequently surprised to learn of the existence of marketing and consumer research disciplines informed by ethnography.

The presence of our discipline's elders invests the early pages of this section of the book. The authors' description of the emergence of a cybernetic sense of self, manifested in this case through technology and possessions, resonates with Gregory Bateson's life work. Their discussion of the dynamics of root metaphors in the material and metaphysical construction project that results in identity would please Victor Turner, had he trained his sights more specifically on the role of commodities in postmodern life. Much of my own recent work on brand meaning has drawn from these wellsprings, which offer valuable insight into the ways that projection and introjection cause marketing to become a principal engine of both individual apperception and of cultural stability and change. Here again, elders like Mary Douglas have leveraged such insight to help make both an academic and applied anthropology of marketing and consumer behavior possible. The authors' fascination with dialectical processes (if not semiotic squares) is a timeless one as well. Convergence/collapse, implosion/fusion, and space/place are primed here, and will hopefully dispose readers to consider the many other cogent couplings that a global marketplace has fostered. I'd call with my own two favorite pair: production/consumption and resistance/accommodation.

The authors are most compelling where they are most particular. Their focus on language is exquisite. The metaphors of fictive kinship, sport, gender, epidemiology, and electricity are probed to produce insight not only into commercial category, but also into cultural mediation. The plasticity of emotion is revealed in their detailed unpacking—and their creative use of crucial emotions as cultural keys—to be both a structured and structuring lived experience negotiated in real time. Their indictment of the focus group (and what anthropological treatise on marketing would be complete without such gleeful skewering?) is turned toward the illumination of the polylogue of stakeholders, to demonstrate the holistic demand ethnography makes of its practitioners. I trust Rita's and Patti's plumbing of consumer behavior in exotic settings will inspire readers to train the ethnographic imagination on the invisible medium of the familiar in their own lives.

That ethnography can be an elastic enterprise without being atheoretical the authors make abundantly clear. Inquiry might begin with introspection, recollection, the examination of an artifact, or passive observation; it may begin as well outside of the inquirer's conscious awareness. Inquiry might proceed casually via conversation or formally via systematic interview; it may proceed as well in nondirective fashion, as the inquirer cedes control to informant by using projective tasks to elicit understanding or insight. Inquiry might conclude with emic commentary on etic interpretation incorporated into a white paper, or an evocative multimedia presentation with intellectual and visceral bite; it may conclude as well in open-ended fashion, with the inquirer applying substantive findings and newly developed portable skills to the client's (or another client's) next challenge. Emergent design, a generalized toolkit, and a playfully paramilitary predisposition to improvise, adapt, and overcome, all harnessed in the service of consumer insight, suit the market-oriented ethnographer to the task.

Fifth-column critics in either camp are alive to the limitations of consumer ethnography as a managerial practice that Rita and Patti allude to in their case studies. Length of field immersion in any one project is governed by the client's ambition, which ranges from modest to vaulting. While degree of access and prospects for comparison may be vastly improved by corporate funding, the conventional ethnographic year (our analog to the psychoanalytic hour) is typically realized, if at all, in installments over many years. Multisite ethnography within and across categories—coupled with the consultant's concurrent nonproprietary or "academic" research—is the order of the day. Most often, the consultant practices a form of diagnostic research of the rapid ethnographic appraisal type common in development work that stems from methodological and topical expertise honed in similar circumstances over many outings.

Anthropologists studying consumer behavior as an academic specialization have the luxury of time, if not always of access or funding, to pursue inquiry to the limits of its hedonic appeal. Being housed in a college of business may or may not facilitate an ethnographer's inquiry more handily than a liberal arts and sciences demesne, and may or may not catalyze the transition to consultancy more urgently, but it certainly has long driven demand for an anthropology of marketing and consumption we see emerging in the home discipline. Further, the diffusion of ethnography within academic marketing is fueling ever greater attention to the societal impact of marketing practice; ethical and policy implications that preoccupy our home discipline ramify to the stakeholders dwelling in the host. These issues of duration and consequence in the building of a research arena are latent in the authors' discussion of advertising, for instance, as both a commercial and cultural discourse: Marketing shapes and reflects the cultural worlds we inhabit.

For better and for worse, meaning and milieu are mediated by the market. Anthropologists need to study this mediation in order to influence its evolution in prosocial directions. They also need to influence it in order to understand it. Just as physicians incorporate treatment into diagnosis in developmental fashion, so also do practicing ethnographers conduct directed interventions into consumer behavior, to see what might serve the interests of market and polity, economy and ecology. Consumer ethnographers in the academy, ever mindful of the unintended and unanticipated consequences of responding to unarticulated wants and needs that ramify throughout experience, must direct their work to ever more diverse audiences, so that the cultural ecology of marketing is more fully limned and more thoroughly debated.

Spurred on by a cultural habit of mind and a curiosity for techniques admitting us to increasingly intimate domains of experience, anthropologists are in the vanguard of frontier consumer research. Rita and Patti have shown us how we might use our own idiosyncratic fascination with the circumstances of everyday life to set the wheel of inquiry-insight-intervention-inquest-inquiry spinning in interesting new directions. Whatever type of anthropology you might pursue, you'll find an entree to the field in the following pages.

4

The Social Life of Metaphors:
Have We Become Our Computers?

What we would like to do is basically wipe the board clean, like, you know, pressing the reformat button on the computer and say to skin cells, "Forget you're a skin cell . . . become a heart muscle cell."

(U.K. physician Alison Murdoch, describing the purpose of stem cell cloning research, February 3, 2006, National Public Radio)

In this chapter we want to demonstrate the value of using everyday metaphors as a prism through which to conduct cultural analysis in consumer research. We call attention to the ways, such as the "reformat button" in the quotation above, that metaphoric understandings—in this case one built on familiarity and use of computers—are frames with which consumption and other life endeavors are imagined and enacted.

In our ethnographic work, we frequently draw on the concept of metaphor as a key analytic and strategic tool. For instance, in 1999 we conducted ethnographic research on the meanings of drugs and drug practices among U.S. "tweens," young people ages ten to thirteen. We found that while they articulated marijuana in terms of plant and organic substance metaphors, other drugs were surrounded and permeated with chemical metaphors, framed as much more direct and harmful to bodily function. Inhalants, for example, as prototypical chemicals, "cut off oxygen to the brain." But, marijuana, as a plant, became dangerous only when "laced" or combined with other drugs. In the case of cigarettes or alcohol (also considered drugs by the tweens), chemical damage was not the worry per se, but the effects of pollution on physical appearance were, e.g., yellow teeth and bad breath from cigarette smoke. Among our recommendations to the client, responsible for creating anti-drug use advertising, we pointed to the need to play on the cultural metaphors of *pollution* and *chemicals* that resonated so powerfully for tweens. We also pointed out that a cultural reading of plants as safe, organic, healthy, and benign posed a challenge in dissuading tweens from marijuana's use.[1]

In recent years metaphor has gained attention in academic as well as applied marketing and consumer research circles. A prime catalyst for this attention can be located in the work of Zaltman and Coulter. Their ZMET technique, a multi-step analytic procedure, has been framed as a means of uncovering consumers' metaphors through guided conversation, storytelling, collage building, and explorations of visual and other sensory imagery.[2] Additionally, consumption practices have been a locus for applying a metaphorical perspective. Specific topics that have been brought into focus with a metaphorical analysis include the meanings of various dog breeds and relationships with pets in general, spectatorship at the baseball park, relationships with cars, models of entrepreneurship in the United States, the ways information technology is integrated in corporate life, and readings of the body with implications for organ donation practices.[3]

The use of metaphor as a theoretical construct in consumer research has often relied on cognitive linguistic, psycholinguistic, and literary views which position metaphor as an organizing principle used by individuals to construct conceptual understandings of the world.[4] While there has been much debate on the privileged position of metaphor in the construction of thought, in which cognitive linguists and more culturally grounded theorists have been in opposition,[5] cultural mediation of metaphoric constructions has been increasingly recognized.[6] Though debate continues as to whether metaphors organize or reflect cultural models, there is little question that uses of metaphor in everyday talk are contextualized by cultural realities—by the circumstances of their instantiation, salient symbols or ideologies, or simply social conventions.[7]

In this chapter we want to show how metaphors are a prism for socially embedded and contextualized consumer action, discernable through ethnographic study. Our approach is to decipher metaphors as they are instantiated in social action, including behavior, speech, organization and artifacts, and thoughts.[8] This emphasis on metaphors as they are articulated in conversation and social action assumes language is a social resource that is itself a culturally defined practice.[9] We take as a premise that language not only reflects and inflects cognitive processes but, in its use, is a creative cultural practice, in which artifacts, environment, and social action are all catalysts of new forms of expression.

To illustrate the heuristic value of this approach for consumer research, we use the example of metaphors of computing technology (as in the chapter's opening quotation) and describe some of the ways these have been integrated into everyday practices and discourse in the United States. We want to call attention to the ways computing metaphors have become a frame for which other life processes are imagined and enacted. The examples, drawn from multiple research projects, show how these metaphors frame life events, and also demonstrate the way attention to small details in how people organize the everyday spaces of their lives provides clues to these metaphoric frameworks.[10]

As a narrative framework, we begin with the catalyst for our pondering of the migration of computing metaphors into other arenas: a client's request in 1999 for us to address the topic of how people organized information in offices, a question we embedded in the larger question of what constitutes an office. Given the rapid and continuing changes in computing technology over the last two decades, this and many of the subsequent examples necessarily read as dated, if not archaic. But we believe that the datedness is also what makes the example an illuminating one. The reality of its datedness fosters insight into the changing, socially constituted nature of metaphoric frameworks and makes clear the need for researchers to constantly be aware of emerging, newly operative metaphors as they change over time and circumstances.

What is an Office?

In late 1999 we were asked to speak to a Fortune 100 company about the impact of technology on the ways people organized information in offices, either at work or at home. As the anthropological voice among the handful of assembled business experts, our assignment was to address "the human need to organize." This company, in the business of paper, labels, file folders, and dividers, but not computers, was seeing the effects of electronic communication and storage. If the office were to become more digital and electronic—in the word of that time, "paperless"—what were the implications for their business?

Drawing on our experiences in consumer environments, our talk covered the multidimensional aspects of organization—the aesthetic, the functional, and the symbolic. Illustrated by in-home photos (see Figure 4.1), we emphasized the fact that organization occurs in a living space—whether office or home. And as a living space, it would be landscaped by symbols of what was valued and, invariably, of the self.[11]

The underlying question we raised was, What constitutes an office? Across much of the last century, the answer would have foregrounded a space that

Figure 4.1 Offices: infused with aesthetic, functional, and symbolic elements

included a desk with drawers, a chair, paper, pens and pencils, a phone, filing cabinets or other form of paper storage, and a wastebasket, with the addition, just in the last few decades, of a desktop computer and then a laptop. But, in 1999, we argued, the office *was* the computer—wherever it sat (on the kitchen counter, park bench, in a backpack, hotel room, airplane, Starbucks counter—wherever). We suggested to the company that it was no longer in the file folder and divider business, but rather it was in the "computer" business because people looked to the computer not only for functionality but as a model for organization. In short, the computer had become the generative or source metaphor, and to develop organizer ideas that would resonate with consumers, one would have to start with the computer as the metaphoric model.

It was not clear that the company found our suggestion to mine the implications of the computing metaphor as promising as we did. But shortly thereafter, we observed the generative power of computer and Internet metaphors in other quarters. BellSouth, for example, recast its Yellow Pages as a virtual store, consciously referring to itself as a database and search engine.[12] A December 1999 *New York Times* article included a photo of a Toronto broadcast news station whose format clearly modeled itself on a Web page (see Figure 4.2).

MEDIA

A 24-hour all-news cable station in Toronto, CP24, offers an extreme example of a trend to put more information on television screens.

BROADCAST SIGNAL
The traditional video part of the screen.

HEADLINES
About 180 national and international news headlines that rotate throughout the day.

STOCK INDEXES, EXCHANGE RATES AND SPORTS SCORES
The indexes and exchange rates change to sport scores when markets are closed.

STOCK PRICES AND LISTINGS
Sixty largest stocks on the Toronto Stock Exchange; gives entertainment events and venues when markets are closed.

DATE, TIME AND CHANNEL NAME
Appears even during commercials.

TEMPERATURE
Rotating list of current conditions.

Rotates between a three-day and a 24-hour forecast.

ADS (LOGOS)
Sponsor for local forecast or traffic conditions.

TRAFFIC CAMERAS
Images from 139 video cameras on major roadways around Toronto change every few seconds. Sometimes switches to video feed from local transit authority headquarters.

Figure 4.2 Toronto station news format mimicking a Web page in 1999

(Though now virtually all U.S. news programs have an "Internet" look, in 1999 it was a new phenomenon.) Jaron Lanier, a chief architect of Internet Two, also noted in 2000 that reality TV was more like a Web page than a television show.[13] This recasting of traditional book or broadcast media in computer terms was just the sort of metaphor mining we had suggested that our client should be thinking about for the paper-and-desk office.[14]

Taking a Step Back

Reversal of Source Metaphors

If by 1999 the computer had become the resonant model organizing other domains, the early design of desktop computers actually pointed to the prior potency of paper, filing cabinet, and desk metaphors. Desks and what surrounded them had been the source metaphor for the target of computing. Starting with Xerox PARC and mainstreamed by Apple and Microsoft, was the "desktop," a two-dimensional screen on which file folders neatly sat. The "trash" icon sat in the corner of the screen, invoking the office of yore (now "recycle bins") and Mac trash even included visual and sound effects when used. Word-processing software was designed with paper as its iconic frame, so that when one used a word-processing application it was as if writing a letter. Keyboards were like typewriters.

But with computers came other organizational opportunities. For instance, files, coded with the visual icon of "folders," could be named and put wherever one wanted, and importantly, endless embedding of file folders within file folders could occur. Embedding could be done with impunity because there were search functions for finding things quickly. And there were multiple sorting possibilities. Files could be viewed and sorted by name listing, icon, type, or date. The instant sorting capability that computers offered to mix and match in any number of ways meant that eventually, linked to the Internet, doing things like spinning incoming e-mail by date, author, recipient, or other self-defined subject became common.

With the proliferation of personal computers on desks, the source and target of the desk-computer metaphor could also become reversed: It became possible to mimic our computers mimicking our desks. In this scenario, real desktops could be piled high with folders because of an increasing dependence on a visual cue (fostered by the visual icons on computer desktops) for locating what one needed.[15] In 2001, we observed a tech-savvy individual doing just this. On coming into the office he set up a model of his computer "desktop" on the floor by his desk: File folders were laid out from his backpack, opened up when in use, then closed when tasks were completed or the day was done. His actual desktop was piled with folders of less temporal immediacy (see Figures 4.3–4.5).

In essence, the way of doing things in noncomputer realms had begun to metaphorically mimic what was done with computers. Hence, the perceived value of retrieval systems in the noncomputer world could also suffer in comparison to what had become possible via the computer's desktop. As one of our early-thirties research respondents, Travis, commented in 2000, "Technology makes information management easier. You can save virtually forever. You have multiple search tools and can search through the hard drive real quick, unlike file cabinets where everything is just kind of stacked there." For a client in the file folder and divider business, it clearly was time to consider these other, metaphorically inspired ways of doing things. What could be invented for floor-based filing systems that mimicked the computer desktop filing systems? What could be invented as computer-inspired ways of embedding, embedding, and embedding within folders? What could be invented for the retrieval properties of paper products, akin to what had become normative with computer retrieval (e.g., visible arrays as well as electronic tags)? These were the kinds of questions we believed the company's strategists needed to consider as they rethought their business in 1999.

Figure 4.3 An array of files on the floor mimicking the computer's desktop. Files on the floor were opened and closed (picked up, used, put down) throughout the day, as needed, then put into the backpack at the end of the day.

Figure 4.4 The actual desktop, i.e., the desk's, arrayed with files whose information was less immediately needed. These files might not be touched day to day.

Figure 4.5 The computer's desktop was visually parsed by file folders and photos of his son, which once might have been framed and displayed (arrayed) on the desk.

From Humanly Negative to Personally Positive

In the United States, another metaphoric migration occurred with the proliferation of personal computing technology—from conceptualizing computing technology as humanly destructive to seeing it as personally empowering. In the United States there has traditionally been an articulated ambivalence toward technology. Technology has frequently been seen as a force that drives society forward, but also as an equally powerful anti-human force—one that makes technology "cold" and something that can deprive the world of humanity, emotions, and feeling. Earlier on in the advent of personal computers and particularly the Internet in the United States, research respondents would recite urban legends (as did the mass media) of people who would stay at their computers and online, no longer caring about their family or friends—for instance, mothers who spent so much time online that the children went neglected and unfed.

But, by the beginning of 2000, when we interviewed consumers we heard computers and technology referred to as "good," "friends," and "helpers." Metaphors of friendship and assistance had become the order of the day. This is not to say that the paradoxical nature of technology or the ambivalence surrounding its presence had lessened, but clearly the terms had changed. At the base of the newer, positive articulation of computing technology lay a change in the conceptualization of its power.[16] People moved from understanding the technology of computers as a social force (outside of an individual's power) to understanding it, and experiencing it, primarily in embodied (part of a person's power) terms. It was seen as virtually inside of a person, as part of a person.[17] The world had changed since the early 1970s when mainframe computers were specters of alienation.[18]

In the early 2000 conception, computing technology was articulated not as something that masters humans, but rather as something that makes humans masters—people help themselves, and help others, with personal computing technology. These positive aspects were foregrounded in conversations about computers which we conducted among the less knowledgeable as well as the "tech-savvy" of the time, a level of savvy that is now mundane for many in the United States. As they told us in 2000:

- Customizing a homepage, showing specific stock quotes and news, means, "I manage the flow of information. I get what I need," and having a PDA makes me feel that "I'm supremely in control of my destiny" (Wall Street investment advisor, early thirties, who bemoaned, though with some pride, that with his Palm Pilot he had become "directory assistance" for his less-connected peers).

- "With the Internet I can find the information myself. I can communicate directly with people all over the world. I can find the medical information I need to get—or stay—well. I can help others with their problems" and "I have improved my husband's health condition" (Mother of two elementary school children and for whom Internet access at home was a recent acquisition).

- "Using the searchable OED means I manipulate the information. I get what I want. With information that is sortable, I can do things with it I really could not do before" (Contracts lawyer, fifty-eight, self-described as a technology early-adopter).

- The quadruple boot: "My system I'm really proud about because I can boast that I can quadruple boot operating systems. I've got DOS on there, Windows 98, Windows NT, and Linux all on one system. I can boot into any of those four operating systems, and that just shows, I don't know, the computer geek in me, but just the bright, creative energy that I put in my system" (Web site designer, in his early twenties, excited by the possibilities technology afforded).

What was particularly striking at that time about the homes of the tech-savvy was not the elimination of the desk from the office, but the elimination of books. For these individuals, by 2000, computers and related peripherals had replaced books as the icons and symbols of knowledge as well as organization. If books had once surrounded, embellished, decorated, and defined the intellect of the office (at least the intellectual office), digital technology appeared to have taken on that role. The smart office of the day demonstrated access and management of up-to-date, changing information, with the computer in the central position. The symbols that mattered, and the ones proudly displayed, were those that assured a person access to the outside world, and that organized and synchronized information. Internet-ready computer screens, telephones, PDAs with their synchronizing cradles, and sometimes back-up disks or drives were what sat on desks. Reference CDs and software manuals and boxes had replaced the books on office shelves. (Of course, by 2007 displayed CDs and software boxes would no longer telegraph "smart" or "with it," in fact, likely the opposite.)

This more celebratory sense of computers and the Internet, a positive evaluation fostered by personal use of these personal machines, was built on—and built—the metaphor of the computer as personal power. In practice, computational technology did often provide people with a sense of expanded memory and communication. Respondents told and showed us how their mobile devices took "the fear of forgetting out of life" and that through the use of e-mail, increased contact with others across space and time were maintained.

By the early 2000s, one could also observe the routine re-articulation of computing metaphors in the everyday framing of how minds worked. In the course of an ethnographic encounter, for instance, one respondent told us about how his wife accused him of being a "binary thinker," thus using a computer-inspired metaphor to express her exasperation over what, in another time, she might have described as his "black and white" thinking, his inability to think in shades of gray. Brains became easily imagined as "hard drives" and memory lapses as "deletions." And as the Internet became increasingly synonymous with the computer, the Internet was also rendered an important source for mental processing metaphors. "Bandwidth" was now part of the figurative vocabulary, as in "do you have the bandwidth for that?" roughly glossed as available time and ability. And if heads were once "wrapped around an idea," the phrase could now be to "download" or "link" to ideas, as one downloads and links to sites on the Internet.[19]

Metaphoric Reconfiguring of the Self and Social Life

Along with forging their way into notions of personal power and the ways in which minds worked, computing metaphors affected cultural definitions of the self. This argument is well known from the work of Sherry Turkle, who has argued, for instance, that people have developed a Windows-influenced sense of themselves as both multiply refracted and flexible in light of computer familiarity and use. Turkle has also argued that cyberspace as a metaphor has become a catalyst for a conscious reconsideration of assumptions about identity in the popular imagination (from a unitary, indivisible entity to one of multiplicity and divisibility).[20]

Other authors have argued that in light of computing technologies, performance antes were upped not only for selves, but also in the expectations for products and the functioning of life processes in general. As Gleick argued in his 1999 book, *Faster*, with computers, speed became *the* assumed standard for calibrating anything from intelligence to productivity, and faster was always better. This standardization of speed paralleled the development of microprocessors—computers offered an ever finer ability to parse time. And so developed the rather oxymoronic, perhaps absurd, situation of finding relevance in chunks of time both imperceptible and measurable, e.g., the milliseconds by which races are won, or the seconds by which appliances save time.

Yet, it is not just the computer's speed that infiltrated notions of work, productivity, and intelligence and fostered a perpetual state of immediacy. The surfing, the e-mailing, the embedding, the instant messaging and chatting, the finding, the inserting, the linking also provided new cues for comprehending and interpreting the larger world, and for enacting and re-enacting that reality. Consider that nonpublic communication can now be referred to as an "offline" conversation. Consider also whether interpersonal encounters have become more like e-mail—brief, casual, unpunctuated, and immediate? Are physical places "surfed" as are Web sites? In any case, without question, it is not only the idea of speed, but the model of what the computer does and the conventions derived from use that have made the computer a potent metaphor and model for productivity more generally. A tech-savvy respondent in his twenties told us in 2000 that he got impatient and irritated at red lights not because the lights were slow, but because the lights were not "smart"—they should be able to "read" traffic needs—and therefore be green when there is no traffic. While a "fast" processing computer was seen as a "good" computer, a "fast" computer was also one that allowed one to carry out multiple processes, to simultaneously open up multiple windows, to do things like quadruple boot.

We would also add that the current portability of the computer and related technological devices must also be considered. The portability of these contemporary devices has allowed for a reconfiguration of the sense of social space and place. Geographer David Harvey has discussed the concept of "time-space compression" that has arisen in light of interconnected capital, transportation, and communication technologies of the modern and postmodern worlds.[21] As Harvey has pointed out, many have noted—with varying degrees of alarm—the seeming collapse of social space and time in light of these developments. In 2000 we did observe that portable devices and wireless communications gave people the ability to collapse temporal and physical space between home and office, private and public, work and play. The kitchen counter, park bench, hotel room, airplane, and the spot at Starbucks did become workspaces when one pulled out the laptop. Laptops, Internet access, cell phones, and PDAs allowed for the dislocation of white-collar work from set workplaces.

Because the spatial divide could be collapsed, and one could work where once one only played (or play where once one worked), it has sometimes been argued that traditional boundaries between cultural domains such as work and home have collapsed. Technology has provided the potential for increasing the integration between these domains functionally and, subsequently, conceptually.[22] But, as Harvey noted, spatial barriers are only collapsible through the production of other spaces (e.g., air travel's reduction of spatial distance is achieved via airport "spaces"),[23] and even as spatial distance has become less relevant for capital, the search for the most advantageous geographic location remains highly relevant. Similarly, we would argue that the seeming elision of boundaries between cultural categories has also been structured. With Windows as the culturally articulated metaphor, the cultural categories of work and play that were once defined by particular senses of place can be maintained in computer windows. Truly interesting are the ways the very same technologies that have afforded the space-time collapse between cultural spheres can simultaneously be the means by which their functional and symbolic separation is assured.

In 2000 our respondents' actions maintained the separation of cultural categories. Cell phones were taken to work for making and receiving personal calls. People had created separate e-mail accounts—one for personal, one for business—or several—the junk mail account, the friends and family account, the chat account, plus the business accounts. People played games, perused banking or investment sites, downloaded music, and watched sports events during work hours, but these were in different windows—a click away from the windows of work. In essence what we witnessed people doing was not merging, but rather holding up the longstanding cultural boundaries between work and play, private and public, home and office, but doing so with the aid of their technological devices. Taking us full circle, the computer and related technological devices really had become our office dividers.

Moving Forward?

Cultural categories and metaphors are rooted in history and sociocultural life. The physical separations necessitated by early industrial processes had a huge hand in creating the contemporary symbolic divisions between public and private, work and play. At the same time, metaphors, as we have noted, are lenses which refract cultural assumptions and values. Moreover, metaphors not only provide a prism through which to understand the world, but, in their use by individuals, create ways of seeing and interacting with the world. And metaphors change—as new technologies are "consumed" or integrated into daily life, we must expect new refractions.[24]

There is also no question that metaphors are used for rhetorical purposes whose intent is motivated by agendas—political, personal, commercial, or social. Consciousness surrounding metaphorical uses implicitly or explicitly guide commercial, legal, social, or political practices.[25] Office or library metaphors, widely pervasive in professional classes, for example, are not equally accessible by all social groups. The institutionalized implementation of these metaphors in the practices of schools, government, or professional archiving thus can serve to reinforce existing asymmetries in cultural capital and render relationships more problematic.[26] Similarly, evolutionary metaphors in relation to technology (i.e., the implicit or explicit articulation of technological change as inevitable progress with overtones of Social Darwinism) obfuscate a more nuanced history as well as commercial or governmental interests in the outcome.[27] The transparency of connectivity, as though "place" is erased, that has characterized popular articulations of the Web hides the very real importance of place as a geographic and imagined (cultural) entity in the (commercial) construction of virtuality.[28] And turning things full circle, computer scientists are not only conducting research on metaphors implicit in users' actions and their articulations of action, but are using metaphor as a means to direct research and development applications and to construct how cyberspace is thought about by a wide variety of users.[29]

Yet, too often, metaphoric discourses forget themselves. That is, it is forgotten that they are metaphoric. For instance, the notion that the "virtual" world is distinct from the "real" world has itself been grounded not in a reality-that-must-be but by convention deriving from normative constructions of time-space relationship deriving from cultural traditions and ideas. (How is it that playing a board game could be considered "real" while playing an online video game is to traffic in the virtual realm?) "Virtual" in operation is a cultural symbol, yet has often been evoked as a separate space and place, as though these virtual spaces were not embodied and defined by the practices of users, themselves social and cultural beings.[30] That cyberspace is a metaphor, not a place that exists independently of meanings grounded in cultural practices (even as behavior is constrained and regulated by computer code[31]), is sometimes forgotten. If metaphors of architecture have resonance for western societies generally, metaphors of the frontier and cyberspace are particularly grounded by American ideological discourses.[32] But if, as many have noted, metaphors can be invoked and evoked by a particular discussant, they can also be revoked. Meanings of metaphors are never singular; they are open and therefore contestable.

But to contest, we need to remember that metaphors they are, not reality-as-is. The shift toward visual arrays in technological formats (is there anything without a screen?), visualization of communication (Web cams, telephone screens), and even the apparently greater nuances that biomedical picturing technologies afford, makes this last point particularly important.[33] Visualizing, in our cultural norms, brings with it a sense of what really exists, a taken-for-granted belief of substance that can then obscure the conventions, assumptions, and social definitions of images and imaging, rendering their metaphorical contribution less visible, and therefore less contestable.

In the early 2000s, Windows provided the model for a kaleidoscopic lens, in which multitasking and a recalibration of linear time were framed. One must expect, moving forward, that what it means to work or to play or what counts as private and public, will fundamentally change as post-Windows technology and metaphors offer new frameworks for interpreting the world. One cannot know what will happen as wireless Internet access becomes completely normative in public spaces or as we become an increasingly seamless part of the show (as is occurring with blogs, and the uploading of personal video and photos onto commercial Web sites). But, we do know that metaphorical trajectories have their foundation in cultural practices permeated with ideas and beliefs—how else could metaphors of both the virtual and the real find themselves to be in circulation and yet not contested enough?

Notes

1. This research was conducted with fellow partner and anthropologist Michael Donovan, and was one among several research initiatives conducted for ONDCP that, in the end, fed into Ogilvy & Mather Worldwide's "Truth—the anti-drug" campaign, an advertising campaign targeting tweens. While we might have wished that our analysis was more widely embraced, and we did present in person to ONDCP, acquiring an effective voice in policy decisions is always a challenge.

2. See Zaltman and Coulter (1995) for a more detailed description of the technique. See also Zaltman (1997) as well as Coulter and Zaltman (2000). As it is generally framed, the ZMET technique leads to the extraction of consumers' conscious and unconscious ("hidden or deep") mental models and reasoning processes, a cognitively oriented frame that differs from a culturally oriented one we would apply.

3. See Hirschman (2002) for a cultural reading of dog breeds, Dodd (2002) for a textual analysis of entrepreneurship, Belk (1990) for a treatment of organ donation practices, Belk (1996) for relationship to pets, and Kaarst-Brown and Robey (1999) who use metaphor as a way to analyze different experiential relationships with information technology (IT) in the workplace. Holt (1995), in an analysis of baseball spectators at Wrigley Field in Chicago, offers a typology of consumption behavior

that is metaphorical, e.g., consumption-as-play vs. consumption-as-experience. Piller (1999) provides an analysis of metaphors in automobile fan discourses. In reference to brands, Hanby (1999) discusses the need to shift marketers' conceptualization of brands from brand-as-product-extension to brand-as-idea.

4. See Coulter and Zaltman (2000), Dodd (2002), Hanby (1999), McQuarrie and Mick (1996), Piller (1999), Stern (1989), and Zaltman and Coulter (1995) as examples in academic marketing. The theoretical basis on which marketers are often relying include Gibbs (1994), Kövecses (2002), Lakoff (1987), Lakoff and Johnson (1980), Low and Cameron (1999), and Ortony (1993).

5. See Alverson (1991), Fernandez (1991), and Quinn (1991).

6. See Gibbs and Steen (1999) and Kövecses (1999).

7. See Eubanks (1999) for contextualization of conceptual metaphors in social practices, Ohnuki-Tierney (1991) for metaphor as a cultural symbol, Gibbs (1999) and Emanatian (1999) for the impact of sociocultural experience on defining embodied (conceptual) metaphors.

8. See Cohn (1987), Fernandez (1991), and Martin (1987, 1994).

9. See, for example, Hanks (1996), Schieffelin (1990), Schieffelin, Woolard, and Kroskrity (1998), and Silverstein (1976). See also Chapter 7.

10. The observations reported here were based on projects undertaken from 1995–2001. They span more than sixty ethnographic interviews whose focus, one way or another, was on the integration of technology in everyday life. The research participants ranged in age from eighteen through fifty-five and included singles, families, and empty-nesters. While by no means a representative sample in the United States today—household income was 40K+ and respondents lived in urban metro environments (e.g., Los Angeles, San Francisco, Seattle, Chicago, Atlanta, Boston, and New York)—they do represent a spectrum of involvement with technology—from self-described technophobes to users to tech-savvy.

11. See Belk and Watson (1998) for an analysis of academics' offices.

12. See Linnett (2000) for description of Bell South's advertising campaign and strategy.

13. See McClain (1999) who describes the Toronto TV station's new Web-like format and Schrage (2000) who interviewed Jaron Lanier.

14. In essence, television was remediated by computer conventions; see Bolter and Grusin 1999. Note also comments on remediation in Chapter 9.

15. In a 2003 research project on how people manage all the stuff in their lives, we noticed the importance of and dependence on visual arrays in their organizational retrieval systems. If things were not visible, they were often "lost."

16. See Mick and Fournier (1998), who delve into the types of paradoxes articulated by consumers around technology. Particularly salient articulations of paradoxes revolved around control vs. chaos and freedom vs. enslavement. Their observations are consistent with the notion of transitional movement from computers-outside-of-us to computers-within-us. That is, the articulation of the paradoxes presupposes a personal relationship—one that did not exist in the 1970s.

17. Note also Downey's 1998 ethnographic account, "The Machine in Me," focused on computer-aided design and computer-aided manufacturing (CAD/CAM) training and industry.

18. See Snyder (1972).
19. The use of these tropes illustrates, again, the generative or source status of the computer metaphor—which foregrounded organization, powers of retrieval, and productivity of the mind versus more creative, figurative dimensions (even if in programming and artificial intelligence circles, articulations of computer processes have gone far beyond mere retrieval and calculation); see Turkle (1995).
20. See Gleick (1999), Harvey (1990), and Turkle (1984, 1995, 1997, 1999). Note: We cite their work in this section given their influence on these discussions and the relatively wide readership of their work. There are many other highly significant analyses of the impact of computing and other technologies on contemporary configurations of self and social life as well as the impact of new technologies on ways of conducting research. The literature is increasingly vast, and would include currently prominent voices in anthropology and consumer research (e.g., Michael M. J. Fischer, Alladi Venkatesh, Daniel Miller). Given that our goal is to provide an example of the heuristic application of metaphor in research practice, rather than to provide a review or contribution to these discussions per se (we have chosen to keep it "dated"), we have also been highly selective in citation and discussion. We recognize that it is highly truncated.
21. See Harvey (1990).
22. See Venkatesh et al. (2001) for a case study in integration of technology into everyday life. See Nippert-Eng (1996) for a case study illustrating a shift in conceptual articulation.
23. Harvey (1990:232).
24. See Venkatesh (1998) and Venkatesh et al. (2001).
25. See, for example, Lessig (2001) who discusses the relationship between Internet architecture and innovation. He argues that the Internet is being re-architected for control through changes in law and changes in architecture. Though he is not concerned with metaphoric uses per se, he speaks to the larger domain over which metaphoric battles are waged. See Venkatesh (1998) for examples of how language of the Internet has been appropriated by industry, e.g., use of "communities" rather than "markets."
26. See Duncker (2002).
27. See Berland (2000).
28. See Mosca (2000) who argues that geographical place and cyberspace are mutually constituted, conceptually and commercially, but whose constitution is often overlooked by the metaphor of (transparent) connectivity.
29. See Butz and Krüger (2006), Ishida (1998), Johnson (1994), Maglio and Matlock (1998), Palmquist (1996), and Pantzar (2000) as examples.
30. See Doostdar (2004), Dumit (2004), Elliot (2004), Hakken (1999), Miller and Slater (2000), and Wilson and Peterson (2002).
31. We do not wish to minimize the impact of computer code on what is experienced in cyberspace (see Lessig 1999), nor of the interests of commerce and government in creating specific code. Our point is that cyber behavior is framed by offsite symbols, meanings, and practices and that, like code, its impact can often be overlooked.

32. See Adams (1997) for a careful analysis of metaphoric domains currently in play. He also discusses issues of power, privacy, and property.

33. See Dumit (2004), who studied the impact of PET scans on understandings of identity. With the advent and now proliferation of visual formats in computer technology, we wonder whether visual formats will obscure the ability to fathom the metaphorical nature of these discourses.

5

Finding Ourselves in Images: A Semiotic Excursion

What does it mean when an Australian announces, with a note of obvious pride in the voice, "New Zealand has always been a country that punches more than its weight"? Beyond the situational perspective of the speaker, what does it say about cultural ideas that are salient or assumed? Or, if rugby, barbeques, and backyards are considered by New Zealanders and Australians as iconic images of the trans-Tasman region[1] (see Figures 5.1–5.6), what are the embedded corollary meanings and implications? And what if one delves deeply into contemporary advertisements, the symbolically saturated combinations of images and words that so permeate our contemporary world? What, for instance, does a Tooheys beer ad in which New Zealand and Australian teams spar in a bottle-cap competition say about the relationship between Australia and New Zealand and about culturally shared values as well as territories in which meanings and values diverge? What are New Zealand and Australian advertisements communicating about the region—and each other?

In taking mediated texts (advertisements and photographs) as the starting point, our goal in this chapter is to illuminate the use of semiotic analysis in consumer research practice. Our point is to show how advertising, beyond its product or brand discourse, is a cultural discourse, one that can then be mined for cultural insight. But we demonstrate the inherently ethnographic analytic project that semiotic analysis must become because advertising is a discursive event—meaning is produced in the interaction between text and readers. While this chapter focuses on New Zealand, Australian, and trans-Tasman cultural identities and is based on research conducted in Auckland in 2004, our goal is to show the heuristic value of an ethnographic semiotic approach more generally.

The research was conducted as part of an immersion in semiotic and ethnographic practices for the New Zealand and Australian offices of FCB Worldwide. It began with the agency's selection of automobile, convenience food, and beer advertising as relevant categories to explore for cultural understanding. In preparation for the session, FCB gathered contemporary examples of billboard, print, and television advertising from each country (with an eye on inclusion and exhausting the universe, not preselecting a sample) and sent them to us. Australian and New Zealand FCB team members also created diaries of images which were then collectively discussed and analyzed during

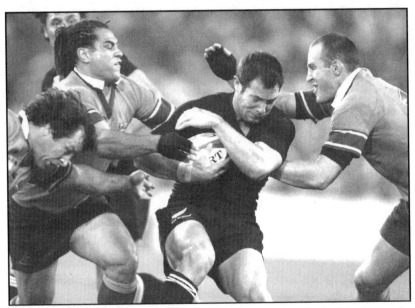

Figure 5.1   Icon of the trans-Tasman region, Australia–New Zealand rugby match

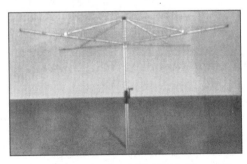

Figure 5.2   Icon of Australia, the Hill's Hoist, Photo Diary, Australia

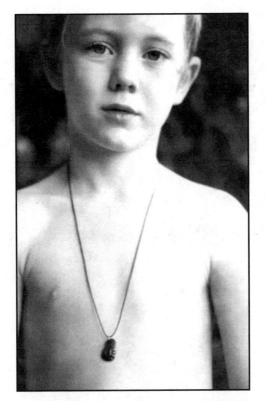

Figure 5.3 Icon of New Zealand, "Boy with Tiki," Photo Diary, New Zealand

Figure 5.4 Icon of the trans-Tasman region, surfing, Photo Diary, Australia

the seminar.[2] In addition to the decoding and discussion sessions among the team (comprised of two Australians and four New Zealanders), five ethnographic interviews were carried out in Auckland-area households with

Figure 5.5 Icon of the trans-Tasman region, the barbeque, Photo Diary, New Zealand

Figure 5.6 Icon of Australia, "Aussie boy," Photo Diary, Australia

recruited consumer respondents. Members of these households were asked to complete the same photo diary assignment, as were two agency student interns, with whom we carried out a joint discussion on the final day.

While we began a semiotic decoding of the Australian and New Zealand advertising before we crossed hemispheres, it quickly became apparent that despite our formal analysis of the ads sent to us, we did not have a clue as to their meaning. We could and did map out hypotheses concerning key symbolic terrains, metaphors, presuppositions, and assumptions made by the ads about cars or beer; yet we could do no more than make hypotheses. It was only in contextualizing our formal analysis with informants' help that we made headway. Team members from Australia and New Zealand needed to explain the cultural background—in detail, iteratively. In this, the team members became ethnographic informants, not dissimilar from the recruited respondents.

In what follows, we present highlights of the analysis. Clearly, given that this session took place in Auckland and all recruited ethnography respondents were New Zealand residents, the analysis favors New Zealand issues.[3] This fact, as well as the scope of the data more generally (produced in the context of a week-long training session), make the analysis illustrative, not definitive. Nonetheless, the analysis offers a unique vantage point on the question of what is trans-Tasman. It further speaks to, and bears witness to, not only the cultural constructions that give advertising meaning, but the significant role of "readers" in the creation of meaning of advertising texts.

Advertising as a Text

The analysis of advertising is not a new endeavor practically or theoretically. Among advertisers it is a common, in fact necessary, practice to conduct brand and benefit audits of existing advertising and to keep tabs on the terrain. The language of these analyses is grounded in industry models of how advertising works—brand essence, consumer benefit, reason to believe, brand relationship. Tonality, especially as it relates to imputed brand personality, is also an object of attention. Competitive brands can thus be arrayed in a matrix to discern trends, opportunity areas, or overlapping domains. Analyses such as these, animated by industry concerns for their brands, are generally also bounded by brand, as an analytic (marketing-based) category.

Among scholars there is a long tradition of analyzing advertising as social commentary and lens onto consumption practices.[4] Advertisements are, without question, cultural texts that incorporate (or co-opt) cultural conventions, metaphors, values, and ideologies into the space of the ad to give a brand meaning. Williamson's (1978) classic text speaks to how advertisements align cultural meanings with products to imbue the latter with emotional, functional, and symbolic salience. From a variety of disciplines, a number of authors have looked at how ads do this—that is, focused on the codes and conventions that organize and convey meaning.[5] If semiotic analysis has illuminated how meaning is constructed in ads, it can sometimes seem as though advertising texts live as singular entities, as though each could exist independently of past ads, of the entire discourse of advertising, or of its actual readers.[6] Our view is essentially an anthropological one—that there is no text that does not have both sender and intended receiver implicated in the text itself, a view that has a long history in linguistic anthropology and a more recent one in advertising research.[7]

We would also argue that precisely because of the process of semiosis, the juxtaposition of signs, ads become a rich source for understanding not only the advertised brands, but also ourselves and our sociocultural worlds. Viewed in a semiotic frame, advertisements are performative events and, as such, offer an inherently ethnographic (con)text for analysis.[8] Thus, advertising matters not simply in its narrow sense, that is, in its intent to persuade target audiences to purchase a brand or product. Advertising matters in its larger sense, as a discourse that infuses daily life.[9] In its inherently semiotic process, advertising brings into focus symbolic spaces in which products and categories are given meaning. This symbolic space is not only the fodder with which brand and category meanings are created but, as such, becomes a lens for understanding cultural issues (cultural assumptions, symbols, values, metaphors) quite independent of the product being advertised. These cultural spaces can be illuminated through analysis.

By way of example, consider two U.S. Nike ads appearing in 2002. These double-page print ads contested definitions of femininity in the United States.[10] In one ad, a young girl, a tween or younger, has just raised her hockey mask and is looking off center. She has, one surmises, just finished a hockey game or practice and has a look of quiet confidence. There are two sentences in the ad, "I like pink. I like sports." The second ad captures an older girl, a teenager, in the midst of boxing practice; the camera has seemingly caught her in the act of throwing a punch. Her face is a study of concentrated determination. The two sentences are, "I wear muscles. I wear dresses." These ads, by juxtaposing two stereotypic symbols of masculinity (ice hockey and boxing) with young women, are telling us that girls can be tough, powerful, determined—traits traditionally ascribed to masculinity in the United States. Young girls and boys (third and fourth graders, in our experience) can tell you the message: "It's saying you can be a boy or a girl," (though they also voice skepticism: "It *is* an ad"). The power of the ads, their effect, is only possible because of huge differences in cultural notions of what it means to be male or female—notions that are carefully continued through the symbolic invocation of pink and dresses. The cultural values, symbols, or metaphors on which a brand relies to create meaning are also those which people use to frame their ways of seeing the world. To illuminate the implications of this perspective, our task in this chapter is to delve into ads and diary images for what is culturally presupposed about trans-Tasman identity and to demonstrate the benefit of this kind of analysis and understanding. Notably, if ads are relying on meanings people use to make sense of their worlds more generally, they hold the potential to reframe these understandings as well.

Symbols of Trans-Tasman Identity

Mates

The overwhelming majority of images and pictures chosen by team members as representative of Australia, New Zealand, and the trans-Tasman region carried an assumption of maleness.[11] Men and women were equally represented among team participants and consumer respondents, yet masculine images were chosen by both. The array of images that opens this chapter was among them. Few would contest the selection of the All Blacks team as iconic New Zealand or an Australian–New Zealand rugby match as a good representation of trans-Tasman-ness; that image is only the most obvious, not the most telling. If team wins and losses could affect stock prices, as team members informed us, surely such an image can—and should—be included as a marker in the cultural stakes. More striking was the cumulative effect of other images, for instance, the (male) surfers serving as a marker of the trans-Tasman region or, for Australia, the image of a turned-around baseball-capped man as "Aussie Boy," and "Boy with Tiki" (as he was labeled in the digital image) to represent contemporary New Zealand. The barbeque, an icon that surfaced again and again in both New Zealand and Australian diaries, was explained as the site of men's cooking. The barbeque is implicated in family rituals and thus is obviously important in multigendered events, yet the barbeque as icon nonetheless foregrounds men in the cultural story. Was not the Hill's Hoist clothesline clearly female oriented, however? No. The image was explained as the invention that gets women's work out of the way, so male sports could be played in the backyard.

Where were the girls? Where are women in the symbolic construction of national identity? In an Australian Tooheys television advertisement, she is the hero who triumphs in a bar bottle-cap contest among rival Australian and New Zealand teams by shooting the winning bottle-cap from her navel. In one sense she wins by cleverness—both the rival team and her own are astonished by her behavior. At the same time, she wins by being one of the guys and playing the mates' game, beating them in a male sport. In essence, she has become the honorary male. In New Zealand, an Export beer television spot was a riff on the mainstream, ubiquitous wheelbarrow. A female is the expert commentator on the ingenuity of young guys as they dissect, reassemble, and reconstitute the barrow as a technological invention. Yet the creativity is all male—the female, as narrator, is the bystander. While the prism of reflection was clearly constrained by the (male) category of beer ads, the underlying motifs on which these beer advertisements played go beyond the brands and the category. Just as in the American Nike ads, Export and Tooheys were calling on cultural symbolism that involves tacitly understood categories of gender relations to create meaning for their respective brands; otherwise, the ads would make no sense.

One could argue that the selection of beer and automotive advertisements as the categories selected for analysis predisposed the focus on male imagery; at least in Australia, beer is gendered male.[12] True. But once aware of the lurking underlying assumption of maleness and the involvement of masculine imagery at the heart of trans-Tasman, New Zealand, and Australian cultural identities, team members also queried themselves. Had that cultural predilection itself influenced the choice of categories on which to focus? The gendered inflection of cultural identity also appeared in the convenience food ads. For instance, an Australian Maggi advertisement ("Emma: Darren's new girlfriend and new SNACK STOP fan"), shows Emma—young, effusive, and a bit clueless—giving a testimonial on the benefits of Snack Stop as her two male flatmates look on, bound together by their shared derision of what she is saying. This ad drew not only on contemporary stock comedic characters for its humor but, at its heart, on the highly culturally salient concept of mates. In this case it was not the obvious way the woman was made a fool in this advertisement that spoke to the gendering of cultural identity, but how a male defined concept of matehood was tacitly accepted and assumed.

The explanatory *mates* emerged repeatedly in discussion of photo diary images, advertisements, or in stories told to us in ethnographic interviews; which we (the culturally naïve) initially glossed as *friends*. Whether the topic centered on adventure, sport, the pub, the flat, the girlfriend, the wife, advice, or, it seemed whatever, mates emerged as an explanatory element. An Australian

Tooheys New advertisement ("Nice Things to Say") simultaneously addresses many of these as it shows four mates in a pub, jointly creating a list of nice things they could say to female partners as strategies that ultimately allow their joint and male-only attendance at a rugby match. One younger man's suggestion of "will you marry me?" momentarily stops and silences not only his mates, but the entire pub. He is willing to go that far for his mates. They click glasses and the seemingly oldest mate writes it on the list.

Mates' age differences and the acknowledgment of a mentorship function are perhaps what made the mate concept so striking from an American perspective. (The United States has no equivalent cultural category; "friends" comes closest, but mentoring, even if it occurs, is not a culturally understood or necessarily expected part of that relationship.) So, from New Zealand, a Speights beer ad in which a younger man uses the two free tickets provided by an attractive young woman to go with his older mate to a dance was, at first, almost inscrutable for us, the Americans. Was the older man the father of the younger? What happened here? The difficulty in cultural reading was not shared by participants from either side of the Tasman. Saturated with the flavor of southern New Zealand and its regional values, the narrative was transparent nonetheless. The two men were mates and the older had (somewhat shamelessly) manipulated the situation to his mateship advantage. Team participants understood how this advertisement drew on notions of being true to your mate, of putting your mate first. For Australia this notion was interlaced with ideas of survival—of the need to look after mates because of the need to depend on them in the face of isolated and harsh conditions. Hence, one heard of sayings such as "rely on your mate, your horse, and your dog." Laudable values of loyalty were brought to the fore in this cultural emphasis on (male) mates, yet where does this framework leave, and put, relationships with women? Women, just as in these beer ads, have not been picked up as part of the main cultural narrative but rather viewed apart.[13]

History plays a role. Mates, as a social and cultural category, can be traced historically to male labor crews in the history of both Australia and New Zealand.[14] But aspects and "facts" of history never assure the whole cultural story. Male crews were part of U.S. history as well, and yet did not survive as a culturally salient category. In the United States male crews were reduced symbolically to the lone individual—the cowboy who does it alone, e.g., the Marlboro Man, as he, through the semiosis of ads, is also now known.

Notably, if the U.S. cultural value of (male) individualism tends to erase emphasis on relationships and dependencies on others, both male and female, notions of mates on both sides of the Tasman provide men the space to openly express emotional facets and bonds of male-male relationships. As one ethnographic respondent said of the periodic departures of mates and colleagues during his multiyear employment in the Antarctic, "it was quite special really, and emotional, to say 'goodbye.'" In the United States, women's friendships are the culturally ascendant model, implicitly and explicitly used as a comparative standard.[15] This model of women's friendships assumes talking and "sharing," which implies foremost the confessional sharing of secrets, not the sharing in activities such as work or sport. Oprah, a long-running cultural phenomenon, is a clear cultural fit.

The use of the female friendship model as a comparative norm (further aided by a psychotherapeutic worldview) has meant that for decades men in the United States have been criticized for not talking often or explicitly enough about feelings, moods, deep-seated dreams. At present, there reigns a sense that men are "coming around," that is, men are talking more and as such are demonstrating a capacity for competent (i.e., culturally ideal) interpersonal relationships. Undoubtedly, this lurking comparative model helped to produce our feelings of surprise when both male and female ethnographic respondents in New Zealand declared men, not women, as undisputedly easier to live with as flatmates. It was not only that men were viewed more even-tempered and accepting, while women were said to bitch and complain, whether chronically or cyclically. It was that respondents attested that male-only flats tended to "always" work interpersonally. Female-only flats were "disasters," an observation later nuanced with the distinction that actually that was not the only case; rather the case was that the outcome tended to be one of two extremes—either disaster or total sisterhood. Again, the point is not what the realities were or were not, but that the male situation was deemed normative, the one with which situations with women were compared—in this case as extremes relative to the norm. If, at present, many flatmate configurations are actually multigendered, and an ideal image consists of a flat with both men and women (abiding by the rule of "don't screw the crew," though in reality many do), there lingers the notion that it would be better in those situations if the women were more like the men, not the inverse.

Of course, in everyday life all of these perspectives are refracted through other, simultaneously operative perspectives, e.g., gendered and sexual identities and interests in partners who are female, male, or both. Notably, our purpose here is not to create or reinforce stereotypes or to overly simplify a messy reality. Life as it is lived, in New Zealand, in Australia, in the United

States, includes both men and women, and innumerable kinds of relationships among men and women. The point is the play of cultural narratives and symbols within that reality, and how we as cultural actors, analysts, advertisers, consumers, residents, and citizens make our way, carve out niches, and create new spaces amid the cultural geographies. Illustrating that note, it would also not be fair to continue without some mention of the place of sports in the construction of trans-Tasman cultural identities.

Sports Is a Currency

In both New Zealand and Australia, sports was an understood, shared form of communication and measurement, or currency. Explicitly, achievement in sports was a symbol of success and standing beyond one's borders in both countries. It has been a historical and cultural marker of national identity and a means to demonstrate difference from Britain and each other for both Australia and New Zealand.[16] There were stories and more stories of wins and losses in rugby and, for New Zealand, of the days of mourning following the loss of the America's Cup in 2003. Loss of the America's Cup was further discussed as an index of national predilections, not only shame. The basic thread of the narrative was "we produce the best sailors in the world, but we won't pay them their worth, so they go elsewhere and win for other countries." New Zealand: Always producing among the best in the world. New Zealand: Always shooting itself in the foot.

The cultural emphasis on sport and the use of sports as valuable currency was discernable in advertising in which play was often articulated as a sport. In both of the aforementioned television beer advertisements, the Export wheelbarrow reinvention (New Zealand) and Tooheys bottle-cap competition (Australia), games devised to entertain and pass time took on the motif of sports (teams, winning/losing, competition). In New Zealand car advertising, a vehicle easily becomes the technical equipment in an extreme sport. For instance, when an Audi Quattro pulls an extremely competent wakeboarder through the water, it does more than take a man and his gear to the beach. Ford cars and trucks not only do work and drive through water, they also drive easily across frozen terrain with snowboarders in tow. Mitsubishi 4x4s, not to be fenced in, go through water, pull snowboarders, and climb rocky barriers in the middle of city streets. While it is important to note the mainstreaming of extreme sport and its co-opting in mainstream branding endeavors,[17] for us, what is crucial is the presence of these symbols at all. These metaphors and iconography would not be symbolically resonant in U.S. culture—they are culturally specified tropes of the trans-Tasman region.

Team sports, in addition to their salience in national identity, were viewed as salient symbols of community and, like the mate concept, a way of celebrating the group over the individual. Photo diaries included many images of group games of cricket and rugby, formal as well as the informal kind played on beaches and in backyards with friends, family, countrymen. Nonetheless, respondents suggested that team sports were losing salience as a currency. In Australia, this was expressed by the increasing adoption of "take away" sports, i.e., signing up for an activity rather than embracing sports as a metaphor for living. In New Zealand the replacement of team sports with music was also noted as significant, as was the shift toward individual sports, as seen in the icons of sports used in advertising, e.g., the snow- and wakeboarding, the luge, cycling, rock climbing, and running. Ethnographic respondents talked of their workouts in the gym, pursuits distinctly focused on the betterment of their individual bodies. Even if carried out in the context of a group class, this was not a team sport, but a matter of individual betterment. National pride can still attach, however. Les Mills, for instance, was described as a first-rate fitness training program that New Zealanders have provided the world.

Given the discussion of male icons above, perhaps it goes without saying that not only in the traditional team sports, but also in the individual and extreme sports currently celebrated, men's activities were foregrounded. Even when women were featured, traits of physical and mental strength typically associated and understood as masculine (strength, courage, daring) were the ones highlighted. Just as the concept of the male boxer frames and informs Nike's U.S. ad of a young female boxer, so the statement, "New Zealand has always been a country that punches more than its weight," is informed by male-inspired metaphors.[18]

Common Ground of Identity-making, but Different Inflections

Older and Younger Brothers

The rhetorical question that started this essay regarding New Zealand's "punching more than its weight" queried not only this phrase, but what it could mean when announced by an Australian, with a note of obvious pride in the voice. The phrase carries the notion of a boxer, but its delivery implied more. Clearly there *is* a relationship between New Zealand and Australia that spans time, trade, and alliances in wars. Just as clearly, this historical relationship has been continually reconstituted through migration, tourism, sports, and business enterprises in more recent times,[19] even if the extent of the relationship has been downplayed by modern historians of each country.[20] *Trans-Tasman* is a resonant category, for residents on both sides of the Tasman. Diary images of trans-Tasman-ness included references to interactions during wartime, trans-Tasman travel, and geographic proximity.

Not surprising given history, the relationship was construed as familial but, more specifically, it was articulated as brothers in which New Zealand is the younger. It was not twins, not siblings, not sisters, not mates, but younger and older brother. The metaphor of *brother* captures the intense national rivalry in sports as well as the ongoing sparring that occurred through words, jokes, smiles, and intercultural insults among the assembled New Zealanders and Australians in the seminar. *Younger brother* not only reflects New Zealand's smaller size in land mass as well as population, but also accounts for the intense mutual interest in how New Zealand fares relative to Australia—in economics, sports, accomplishments on a world stage, interethnic domestic relations, standards of beauty, the role of sheep, wine, virtually everything.

Importantly, *brothers* is itself a cultural category that carries with it a set of implicit meanings. Given the common ground of history in which Britain was the espoused symbolic parental nation for both countries (despite more complicated realities and intricacies of settlement), the category of brothers is nuanced by the British tradition of primogenitor which valorizes the elder brother. If the first son inherited family wealth, carried the family title, held greater status, and was seen as more established vis-à-vis society at large, the younger brother made his own way in the world, perhaps without wealth and certainly without title. Given both the similarities between these two countries in time and patterns of immigration, as well as the huge differences of circumstances of immigration and relations with resident populations, it could be considered remarkable that *older brother* and *younger brother* was the current metaphor for expression of relationship between Australia and New Zealand. At the least, one might ask, why not cousins or, indeed, mates? And why is Australia granted the status of elder brother? In fact, through the lens of American eyes, why are these countries not just *neighbors* as, culturally speaking, Canada is to the United States?

The cultural underpinning of *brothers* is further nuanced through an ontogenetic or developmental metaphor articulated by residents of each country, e.g., as in New Zealand is still "growing up" or adolescent and Australia is an adult. In the conversational spaces of both New Zealanders and Australians, New Zealand was not imagined as the fully grown yet younger brother, but as a still-growing younger brother who had not yet achieved the full adult growth (i.e., maturity) of the older brother. Notions of progress, development, and evolution were prevailing metaphors for social analysis in Anglo American theoretical traditions from the mid-1800s to the early 1900s. In the foundational writings of theorists such as Herbert Spencer, other societies were compared in a developmental framework and classified as "earlier" forms of the researchers' own more "complex" society. Similarly, in biology the theory that ontogeny recapitulates phylogeny spoke to the notion that evolutionary development of a species could be observed in the stages of biological development of the organism.[21] While both these theories are now defunct in academic theorizing, each seemed to live on implicitly in folk theories informing New Zealanders' and Australians' articulations of cultural identity, e.g., "You're more advanced than us."

Without doubt, the intense rivalry in the brother metaphor also speaks to great commitment. Brain versus brawn was a well-worn dispute on both sides of the Tasman. Winning and losing were typical terms of engagement. We would just emphasize once again that these terms and the larger metaphor of *brothers* are cultural constructions, not in any sense the way it must be, merely the way it happens to be.[22]

Ingenuity versus Resourcefulness

Ingenuity born of scarce resources on the part of New Zealand was contrasted to an Australian sense of resourcefulness. A narrative of ingenuity runs through New Zealand advertising, as it did in the photo diaries and ethnographic interviews. Ingenuity in design was articulated by images of fashion and architecture and stories of bikes and boats, for instance, the many-times-told tales of New Zealanders' invention of cars that morph into boats and of engines that, by virtue of operability in very shallow water, allow boats to almost work on land. The sheep and dairy industries were seen as historic testaments to ingenuity, the developing wine industry as a contemporary one. Perhaps not unrelated to traditional social roles of the British younger brother, was the overall mantra and recurrent refrain in New Zealand of "making the best out of what you have." As one respondent said, "In New Zealand the question is how can we do more; do better with what we've got here." It was also the uniqueness of contribution that is a crucial bit of New Zealand cultural identity.

New Zealand, we were told, does not want to play on the world stage as others (or brothers) have defined it, as much as it wants its achievements to make unique contributions to that stage. Narratives of achievement came in the form of "nothing less than first class," carried out with a distinctive New Zealand ingenuity as well as connection to the country. At the time of this research project, this was exemplified by Peter Jackson's *Lord of the Rings* movies.

In New Zealand's Toyota advertising, even the cars were clever. For instance, in a spot for the "smaller, bigger, smarter" Echo, the Echo is, to the tune of "The Pied Piper," *the* pied piper that other brands follow, emptying the town to the consternation and confusion of their owners. At the edge of a cliff overlooking the sea, the Echo swiftly turns and observes as the long line of following cars careens over the cliff. There are no drivers, the cars drive themselves. In an advertisement for a new Corolla model, scored to the tune of "Please Release Me," owners find themselves trapped by their cars, their vision blocked whenever they try to get a glimpse of a passing Corolla. A door slams shut catching a coat; another door locks an owner inside; sun visors and convertible tops clamp down; seats, mirrors, and emergency brakes work on their own accord; an air bag explodes. The car here is not only a technological device to be mastered; it is a clever, sentient, inspired, ingenious being.

New Zealand's past was invoked by New Zealanders as a reason for current ingenuity. The narrative was traced through New Zealand's history and imagined that it has always been such. As one South Islander now living in Auckland reflected, "We are inherently innovative; perhaps we got that from the Māori." In his detailed, two-volume work, historian James Belich provided several examples of Māori inventiveness. These include the pattern of Māori engagement in the first hundred years of contact that dictated the value of what traders had to offer (from trinkets to guns) and ingenious uses of trade goods (from Te Puhi's iron patu in 1815 in which an iron bar became a weapon "beaten with infinite patience," to earrings from bits of glass, to nails made into chisels and fish hooks).[23] Whether or not Māori inventiveness was recognized as such at the time, it does seem that inventiveness has become a salient symbol in contemporary stories about being a New Zealander.

One might assume that given the attention to the vast amount of desert that makes much of Australia barely habitable, ingenuity would also be prominent in the narratives of Australian identity. But this was not what we observed. Rather, Australian narratives emphasized self-sufficiency and resourcefulness in which survival skills, technical knowledge, physical strength, and stamina are foregrounded. In Australia, the Toyota Landcruiser 100 is described thus:

"with earth-moving V-8 power . . . the most powerful Landcruiser ever," and shown as a vehicle that reverses global rotation when it reverses gears.

Culture in Nature

On the surface, both New Zealand and Australian national identities were grounded by a shared symbol of nature. Advertising and photo diaries from both countries were replete with images of gardens, plants, camping, the sea, the beach, the ubiquitous barbeque, and love of outdoor cafés. There the similarities end. Nature as a symbolic category was nuanced differently in each country. In Australia nature was something to be mastered; in New Zealand, it was something with which to partner.[24]

As seen through photo diaries that included images of snakes, brushfires, and remote vistas, nature in Australia was framed as harsh and potentially deadly. It could kill you by virtue of its sheer vastness, the deadliness of flora and fauna, and extreme climactic conditions. Nature was explained as something to be mastered: It is important to be proficient in one's survival skills and resourceful. In a similar vein, nature was something to tame or domesticate. Climactic differences notwithstanding, swimming pools as icons of the outdoors loomed large in Australian diaries. Nature is engaged, but not as a partner; it must be controlled for one's own welfare, for one's own benefit.

In New Zealand it was important to engage and challenge nature—to push the boundaries of one's own limits. The Audi Quattro ad in which the car pulls a competent wakeboarder through the water is a good example of this. Photo diary images of "modern" New Zealand typically included individual sports such as bungee-jumping or winter skiing. There was also a Subaru ad that shows the car going through water and rough terrain, scenes that were interwoven with high-flying, flipping snowboarder Glen Sisarich (two-time New Zealand downhill champion) cycling New Zealand's remote hills, Steve Gurney (Coast-to-Coast winner) running nature's more rocky spots, and, it seems for good measure, Angela Paul (Olympic luge champion) on a luge barreling down a city street. In all, what loomed large was an intense, personal engagement and interaction with nature. Fear and mastery was not the issue, except perhaps of oneself. Nature was a partner, a partner in endeavors, a partner in culture. And technology could be partnered with nature. The combination of nature and technology was not an immediate disconnect (as it would tend to be for Americans).

In ethnographic discussions with New Zealanders, the therapeutic function of nature was articulated. Images of traditional New Zealand, such as a secluded beach cove, a barbeque at the beach, or a picnic in the park all spoke of personalizing experiences in nature. Through the engagement with nature—whether through camping, rowing on the bay, sailing, walking the beach with the dog—one's very being was seen as reconstituted. We observed in Auckland homes the extent to which the outside was brought inside through porches, plants, open and unscreened windows, the barbeque always somewhere, even if squeezed onto a very small balcony. In New Zealanders' partnership with nature, they have, in the language of semiotics, an indexical relationship with nature in which the acts of participation with the outdoors are at the heart of it (see Figures 5.7 and 5.8). In the United States, by contrast, the "doing" is not the issue; nature is more like a museum—something to witness or "see." For New Zealanders it was the doing that mattered; to separate New Zealanders from the land would be akin to severing an artery. The derogatory "JAFA" ("just another f-ing Aucklander") was in part based on the perception that Aucklanders have in fact severed the tie to nature in their pursuit of commercial success. In turn, Aucklanders' wariness of recent immigrants may be in part because these immigrants were not *doing* or *engaging* nature in the way New Zealanders implicitly would, and thus were violating deeply held, implicit, cultural convictions about the way life is lived, in this case, in a "doing" relationship with nature.

Multicultural versus Cosmopolitan

New Zealanders prided themselves on their multicultural history and multicultural attitude. Māori images, symbols, and art were pointed to proudly (Figure 5.3 is one example).[25] In part, multiculturalism was a way to articulate a clear separation from Australia in which national history with Aboriginal populations provided, for New Zealanders, clear evidence of Australia's monocultural leanings. The history of Māori and European engagement and the extant presence of Māori cultural forms were cited by informants not just to separate New Zealanders from Australians, but also to distinguish New Zealand from other countries which share similar settlement history or patterns, e.g., the United States and Canada. Thus New Zealand, because of its Māori history of engagement, could be seen as unique.[26]

The Australian images collected in photo diaries or in advertising made no implicit or explicit claim to multiculturalism. Rather, the Australian value was articulated as contemporary cosmopolitanism with the goal of playing (and being recognized) on the world stage. Diary images selected to express "modern" or contemporary Australia included images of restaurants and chefs,

Figure 5.7 A photo diary image, in which the respondent took a photo of herself standing in a pool of water, connects the person quite literally to nature, as though one's legs were a plant stem, and feet, the roots.

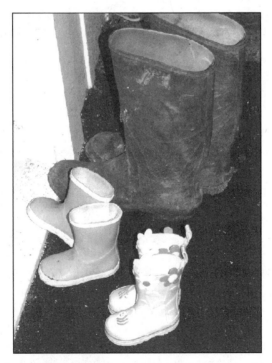

Figure 5.8 One of many observations of Aucklanders' relationship to nature—in this case, muddy boots of family members on the threshold

international foods, the gay and lesbian Mardi Gras parade. These images, as well as advertising that assumed acceptance of cosmopolitanism and male metrosexuality (e.g., imagery of parties, restaurants, music that could easily be located in many of the world's elite cities; a Birds Eye advertisement in which a young man knows better than his date how to cook a stir-fry and use chopsticks), became for respondents evidence of Australia "taking the best from other cultures," that is, a selective integration of symbols from elsewhere inserted into contemporary Australia.

In both Australia and New Zealand, current immigration practices were in tension with the articulated values of cosmopolitanism and multiculturalism, respectively.[27] Australia's policy of turning immigrant boats away from its shores, the Tampa incident of 2001 keenly recalled by team members at the time of this fieldwork in 2004, made visible the heavy-handedness with which "cosmopolitan" could be constructed. Aucklanders' angry reactions to recently immigrated Chinese populations (often glossed as "Asians") contradicted a professed acceptance of ethnic diversity that the term "multicultural" would imply. Notably, although the agency made great effort to assure that Māori and Pacific Islanders were included among ethnographic respondents, recent Asian immigrants were not included. Some respondents railed against Chinese cyber-cafés and shopping centers or areas that have only Chinese signs and included such images in their photo diaries. Others vented disgust at the fact that some young teenagers who come to New Zealand to go to school "stay inside and study all the time," thereby changing the norm for the New Zealand students.[28] Again, for Aucklanders it seemed not that ethnic difference per se was so offensive, but that recent immigrants were not *doing* in the way New Zealanders could understand and accept. That is, by not participating in and engaging with nature, by separating inside and outside so thoroughly, perhaps by not embracing ingenuity New Zealand-style and melding shopping centers or language use more ingeniously in an Anglo-Māori world, immigrants broke tacit rules. Again, we offer the United States as a comparative frame. In New York or Chicago, a taxi driver can be forgiven for not speaking English, for cell phone conversations in another language, for not knowing the landscape of streets and directions, *if* there are concomitant signs of shared values—in this case, that the person is there because of a shared belief in liberty, opportunity, or democracy. These signs might include an American flag on the dashboard, a conversation about higher education or children in school, and even a posted sign of what wearing a turban means to a Sikh. In the United States, what counts is the demonstration of a sharing of ideas and values, a state of psychological, intersubjective sharing; in New Zealand, the crucial signs are those attesting to engagement with nature and doing.

What are Ads Selling?

The foregoing analysis is necessarily incomplete, limited by very real constraints of time and space. We have not mentioned the New Zealand emphasis on step-wise goal setting, health as the road to success, or the iconic Kiwi holidays. Nor have we touched on the trans-Tasman nuances vis-à-vis tall poppies, global youth culture, or new images of crime. Yet we would hope that this essay nonetheless offers a glimpse into the value and potential power of an analysis deconstructing the cultural details and messages that are implicated in the advertising images that both reflect and constitute our cultural worlds.

There is little question that advertisements co-opt symbols and values and by semiotic juxtaposition give brands meaning. There is also little question that advertising can redefine category landscapes. Apple Macintosh, for example, reframed the discourse of "what is a computer" with a series of print advertisements that introduced cultural categories of art and design in 2002. Apple's visual treatment of the Macintosh as an aesthetic form was in direct contrast to the black box and small print functional specification focus characteristic of mainstream personal computer (PC) advertising.[29] In so doing, Apple shifted the category discourse altogether. Our concerns in this chapter go beyond ways that symbols or metaphors give a brand meaning, to what those symbols or values tell us about larger cultural categories such as gender, friendship, childhood, personhood, or national identity. In this endeavor, advertising becomes an additional discourse, along with movies, music, cartoons, editorial content, or political rhetoric, for observing and under-standing the cultural assumptions we live by.

A cultural analysis of advertising can be an insightful source of understanding or self-realization (depending on one's relationship to the advertisements under scrutiny) not necessarily garnered elsewhere. We do not think that New Zealanders' relationship with nature as a source of explanation for criticism toward recent Chinese immigrants would have been readily revealed through simple discussion. New Zealand and Australian car advertising got us there—by provoking the question of "what is nature" and an analysis of one's relationship to it. That diary images were replete with pictures of nature on both sides of the Tasman told us we were onto something which, in turn, provoked a detailed ethnographic questioning. The link to attitudes toward recent immigrants came much later.

Moreover, understanding the nature of one's immediate and "automatic" reactions offers the potential for altering the reactions. Research team participants from New Zealand were visibly embarrassed, horrified even, by some of the images and statements regarding Chinese immigrants. Criticisms of Aboriginal policy produced bruised looks on the faces of Australian team members. No one was particularly proud of the realization that almost everyone had selected distinctly male-centered imagery as representative of their individual countries as well as the trans-Tasman region as a whole. As anthropologists and social analysts we suggest, however, that one can see the careful deconstructive analysis of cultural imagery as a first step in the strategic rethinking and recasting of those images. That is, with self-awareness comes the potential to shift the discourse.

A cultural analysis requires a recognition that the "truths" on which advertisements depend (e.g., what it means to be a girl or boy or mate or Australian or New Zealander) are culturally constituted. These truths are grounded (though in no way determined) by social, historical, economic, and political forces and, as such, are subject to change—if we notice, if we comment, if we contest, if we question, as scholars, market researchers, or consumers. So, for example, one of the New Zealand participants had collected noticeably more images of women as part of her representations of New Zealand—for instance, the breast-feeding image in Figure 5.10. She cited this image as reflective of a long-standing New Zealand tradition of valuing breast over formula feeding (again an issue with links to ideas about active partnering with nature?), but part of her project was clearly to include women in the representations of New Zealand to counteract the underlying gender bias that prioritized men. Similarly, the man as the caregiver of a baby while overseeing young boys' sports could also be put forward as an image indicative of change in gender roles (see Figure 5.9). But in putting forward alternative images, one must still look further into the cultural assumptions implicit in the images. Are there recurrent images that feature women's caregiving in a nourishing, comforting, passive (sitting down) stance versus men's that indicate active challenging? Is the gender of women's children depicted as mixed or ambiguous while for men the tendency is unambiguous depiction of boys? Are women depicted as caregivers, operating within an adult group situation, while men are going it alone with the kids? A cultural reading of advertisements requires us to question, requestion, and then to question again.

Among scholars there has been much debate on whether ads recycle, reproduce, and thereby perpetuate the status quo or, whether by virtue of

Figure 5.9   Diary image signaling "modern" New Zealand: Dad with baby updates traditional masculinity.

polysemy inherent in semiotic processes, advertising is a more dynamic, open-ended system. Did the Wonderbra campaign deserve the feminist critique or did it in fact chart new territory in foregrounding female power?[30] No doubt it did both, depending on the viewer. The distinction, then, is less important than acknowledging the power of advertising to mediate social worlds: seeing advertising as a source for understanding social meanings of things, a source for gaining currency and therefore competence in what is out there, a source of ideas for personal flights of the imagination, a discourse for talking about things, values, and ideas. If advertising's intent is to sell us a product, it is also "selling" us or at least circulating larger cultural ideas beyond the product. In its rationale as a selling or marketing discourse, advertising can disguise and obfuscate its power to mediate social life in a larger sense. It seems worthwhile, then, to

Figure 5.10 Women's breastfeeding offered as a unique, alternative iconic image of New Zealand. Yet what gendered assumptions do these images still telegraph?

fathom advertising as cultural discourse and to make explicit its construction and production processes to illuminate what else is being sold.[31]

As nations, both New Zealand and Australia seemed intensely and self-consciously interested in working out their own identities as well as their relationships with each other and the world.[32] For scholars, the now classic 1983 works of Benedict Anderson and of Hobsbawm and Ranger made clear how nation and national identity are not natural or static identities but human constructions that are achieved, reinforced, and altered through time.[33] What is so striking to American scholarly sensibilities is the degree to which analysts on both the New Zealand and Australian sides of the Tasman incorporated an acknowledgment of the role of advertising in that creation of the nation and national identity. For example, as Richard White wrote in the introductory paragraph in his now also classic *Inventing Australia*, "This book traces some of these efforts to explain what it means to be Australian, from William Dampier's description of 'the poor winking people of New Holland,' to the corporate advertisements of the 1980s."[34] The acknowledgment of the importance of advertising in the reflection as well as framing and constitution of the cultural milieu is evidenced in the matter-of-factness with which varied scholars draw on advertising messages to make their case regarding New Zealand or

Australian cultural issues.[35] It is thus undoubtedly no coincidence that advertising professionals from New Zealand and Australia would be interested in analyzing existing advertising as a window onto their own cultural identities as well as looking to cultural realities (and tensions) as a medium from which to draw for the creation of future advertising.

There is also little question that resonating with implicitly held cultural truths can make for better advertising whether the objective is to sell cars, increase tourism, or decrease alcohol consumption. Strategic alignment with such truths can be extremely compelling, as seen in New Zealand's Toyota ads in which the cultural value of ingenuity was applied to the cars. Perhaps more importantly, strategically questioning such truths also offers the possibility of reframing identity narratives.

At the end of the week-long seminar, we suggested that advertisers needed to look more closely into questions of how women may be redefining the mate concept or the currency of sports and suggested that one could play with and off the ubiquitous use of male symbols and the *big brother–little brother* relationship. In the process of doing so, one might also alter the cultural terms of understanding—of both the relationships and values of the trans-Tasman region. It is not the fact of a *brother* relationship or even *little brother* relationship across the Tasman that was most important, but recognizing that either is a socially constituted truth that, if brought into focus, can be contested. This goes for advertisers and for consumers. Identity stories are narratives—stories we tell ourselves about ourselves—and advertising has the potential to play a significant role, even while selling us something. Consumers are integral in this process. The consumption of messages is always an active, not passive process; and only through the imaginations and activities of many can the idea of a nation and national culture be achieved.

Notes

1. The Tasman Sea lies between Australia and New Zealand. The trans-Tasman region was the term used by participants in this research to refer to the geographic and metaphoric cultural space that includes the two countries.
2. Each country's participants were asked to create a photo diary of images that captured essential qualities of their country—in both a traditional and modern sense. They were also asked to include images of ideas or values that were counter to either traditional or modern values. Finally they were asked to include images/photos capturing what "trans-Tasman" meant to them.
3. This chapter draws primarily on the conversations surrounding the decoding of images from television advertisements for beer and automobiles and from eighteen

photo diaries (six diaries were created by Australians, all of whom were advertising professionals, and twelve diaries were created by New Zealanders, of which five were created by consumers and seven by advertising professionals or student interns at the agency). At a later date, FCB continued the research process, conducting ethnographic interviews in varied locations in Australia as well as New Zealand.

4. Social science treatments include Barthes (1972), Burke (1996), Goffman (1979), Leiss, Kline, and Jhally (1986), McClintock (1995), Vestergaard and Schrøder (1985), Williamson (1978). Caillat and Mueller (1996), Goldman (1992), Mick (1986, 1997), Scott (1994), and Sherry (1987) treat advertising through the lens of consumer research. Abel (2004), Claudia Bell (2004), Jackson and Hokowhitu (2002), Jutel (2004), Palmer (2002), Pettigrew (1999), and Turner (2004) are all recent treatments of advertising and consumption practices in the trans-Tasman region, either Australia or New Zealand. This is by no means a definitive list, merely exemplars of traditions (and some classics, e.g., Barthes).

5. See Mick et al. (2004) for an exhaustive review of semiotic applications in the consumer research arena, inclusive of advertising. Schroeder (2006), Schroeder and Zwick (2004), and Stern (1996), also from consumer research, bring literary and visual arts analytic constructs into play in the semiosis of advertising. See Scott et al. (2005) for a roundtable discussion of advertising's formal properties emergent in the past twenty years. The interplay between advertising and culture is particularly noted by Holt (2004), who argued that brands achieve iconic status through their mediation of societal concerns and tensions. Advertisements become repositories of cultural meaning whose content can shift over time. Streeter (2005) provides a more general semiotic framework into analysis of media, inclusive of advertising. Bignell (1997), Cook (1992), and McCracken (1990) not only consider the codes of advertisements, but treat advertising as a discourse in which consumers are implicated in the construction of meaning.

6. See Bauman and Briggs (1990) in their discussion of entextualization, "the process of rendering discourse extractable, of making a stretch of linguistic production into a unit—a text—that can be lifted out of its interactional setting" (p. 73). While Bauman and Briggs are commenting on performative speech, we would argue that advertising is also a form of performative speech.

7. See Scott (1994) for a well-reasoned plea to academic consumer research to implicate the readers and readings (plural) of advertising into a larger theoretical discourse of advertising, and Jardine (2004) for a discursive reading of a New Zealand advertisement. See Valentine and Gordon (2000) for their plea to marketing research practice to analyze the discourses of consumers and advertising in consumer research.

8. See Bauman and Briggs (1990).

9. Ritson and Elliot (1999) show how teenage school mates reference and incorporate advertising into their general discourse and social interaction, quite apart from the products being advertised. See also Scott (1994) and Mick and Buhl (1992) who in a phenomenological analysis show how ads are "read" through life themes and stories of "readers."

10. See Goldman and Papson's (1998) analysis of Nike advertising as cultural documents which includes a chapter on the representation of women and gender differences in Nike ads.
11. Consistent with Claudia Bell (2004), Kapferer (1996), McGrath (1997), and White (1981). See also McClintock (1995), who argued that articulations of nationalism are always gendered.
12. See Hamilton (1990) and Pettigrew (1999, 2001a, 2001c).
13. See Ernst (1990) and Kapferer (1996).
14. See Belich (1996).
15. See Oliker (1989) and Rosenzweig (1999).
16. See Bergin (2002), Mewett (1999), Perry (2004), and Turner (2004).
17. See Palmer (2002).
18. See also Henley's (2004) discussion of women's netball in New Zealand and Palmer's (2002) discussion of the gendered morality of risk-taking, e.g., male climbing feats stand unencumbered by family relations, while women's feats do not.
19. See Belich (1996, 2001) for a historian's view and Goff (2001) for a political one.
20. Smith and Hempenstall (2003).
21. See Gould (1981).
22. Contextualizing countries in terms of family metaphors is not unique to the trans-Tasman. See Cohn (1987), who described the use of family metaphors in the talk of nuclear defense intellectuals to capture relationships among countries. Cohn's example provides a case in point of the impact folk metaphors can, could, and do have on a geopolitical scale. Her paper illustrates how ways of talking (e.g., "collateral damage" instead of human death) allow defense intellectuals to carry out their work. It deserves rereading.
23. See Belich (1996:149; 2001).
24. See Clark (2004). Also see Gibson (1993) for a discussion of the undomesticated view of Australian nature and the consequences of this notion for imagery in film. See Jutel (2004) for a discussion of ramifications of the construction of New Zealand nature, including its *Lord of the Rings* image as Middle Earth.
25. If Figures 5.1–5.6 were notable for their maleness, one would also have to note them for their whiteness. Our goal in this section is not to untangle the problematics of "multicultural" in New Zealand either historically or ethnographically (see Chapter 8 for a nuanced treatment of race and ethnicity in the practice of consumer research), but only to note the articulation of "multicultural" as a symbol of national identity among New Zealanders.
26. See also though Jackson and Hokowhitu's (2002) analysis of the (mis)appropriation of Māori symbols and heritage in Adidas advertising, which raises the question of whether Māori icons in consumer circulation serve as evidence of multiculturalism or appropriation by a prevailing white New Zealand.
27. See Abel (2004) and Hudson (1997).
28. See Abel (2004).
29. Historically in the U.S. computer market, PCs have referred to machines running the Microsoft operating system, the prevailing system for computers in the marketplace. Though Macintosh is a personal computer, because it runs on a different operating system, it is not a "PC."

30. See Bignell (1997).
31. See Malefyt (2003), Mazzarella (2003b), and Moeran (2003), who all focus on the process of advertising production within agencies and argue that brand positioning and resulting advertising has more to do with the agency-client relationship than it does with consumers per se, despite a marketing discourse which would suggest otherwise. See also Miller (1997) and Moeran (1996).
32. See Bell and Matthewman (2004), Goff (2001), Horrocks and Perry (2004), Kapferer (1996), Mewett (1999), and White (1981).
33. See Anderson (1983) and Hobsbawm and Ranger (1983).
34. See White (1981:viii).
35. See Abel (2004), Goode (2004), Matthewman (2004), and Pettigrew (1999).

6

Contextualizing Emotion: When Do Boredom, Paranoia, and "Being Strong" Become Emotions?

In 2006 we re-partnered with two of the New Zealand advertising planners we had worked with on the trans-Tasman identities project discussed in Chapter 5. Our collective goal in this project, as it is in this chapter, was to explore the social constitution and expression of emotions among young adults in the United States, United Kingdom, and New Zealand. The genesis and intellectual impetus of the project came from our partners as well as ourselves and incorporated anthropological and advertising concerns, both theoretical and practical. On our side of things, we had been toying for a few years with the question of "When did boring become an emotion?" This question had captured our imaginations in the course of a 2003 project on teens and chocolate.[1] As part of this study we had asked varied teens to keep the wrappers of all the candy they ate for a ten-day period preceding the time of our ethnographic visits. We asked them to make notes on each wrapper telling us where they were, the time of day, what they were doing, with whom, and what their mood was at the time. To our surprise, even given an ingoing expectation of teen expression of restlessness or anomie, was the number of times that teens—quite independently of one another—wrote "bored" as their mood. "Bored" was written as the accompanying mood while eating chocolate and reading a book alone, while playing Sims with friends, when in a store with parents or in a car with parents and siblings, as well as when eating alone in the kitchen. What they wrote as their mood was bored, bored, bored. While "happy" was unquestionably another pole of emotion, expressed at other chocolate times by the teens, bored stood out for us. We wanted to think more about it. We could not help but wonder if there were connections with ubiquitous technologically mediated stimulation. Was it the presence of the Internet, e-mail, IM-ing, cell phones, video, digital games, and television in the lives of teens that produced this sentiment? Working on this project promised us the frame and fodder to think further about it.[2]

For our New Zealand partners, Jacqueline Smart and Rachael Lovelace, the impetus for this project was the success of the first cultural study combined with the pressures and tensions they felt in the wake of the publication of Kevin Roberts' book *Lovemarks*.[3] Roberts' book was an attention-grabbing force to be reckoned with at the time, even if the book's admonition for advertisers to pay attention to feeling and disregard thinking was problematic and its basic tenet of love as the key to astounding brand loyalty—more or less full stop— was frustratingly simplistic.[4] Yet, given that Procter & Gamble chairman A. G. Lafley, widely heralded for his consumer-centric approach, wrote its foreword, and author Roberts was Worldwide CEO for Saatchi & Saatchi (an important multicontinent agency which, per their Web site, dropped "advertising" from its name in 1997 to signal a "shift to an Ideas Company"),[5] *Lovemarks* was a phenomenon that needed a response. Saatchi & Saatchi was at the time also on a visible ascent in New Zealand. In 2006 Saatchi & Saatchi was named New Zealand agency of the year, and Andrew Stone, their New Zealand CEO, was honored as agency CEO of the year, as he had been in 2005.[6] Our partners needed and wanted to distinguish their cultural approach.[7]

Reinforcing our varied interests was the relevance of the project's conceptual content to our more theoretical concerns as consumer researchers and anthropologists. Even if the evocation of love as the single most important key in establishing and understanding loyalty to brands veered toward simplistic overstatement, without question the role of emotion is a crucial topic for brand and advertising specialists to consider. Within the academic field of consumer research, important analyses of the 1990s and 2000s focused on matters such as consumers' relationships to brands, as individuals and in terms of brand communities, in which the role of emotion and emotional attachment were both implicitly and explicitly central in the analyses.[8] For advertisers, best use of emotional evocation and expression in ads remains an important puzzle to solve that varies by brand, by campaign, and by ad.

As Doug Holt's book on iconic brands and cultural branding elucidates, the use of emotional messaging by advertisers is often carried out in ways that are less than effective or beside the point. Using examples of Coca-Cola advertising, Holt points to the highly successful "Mean Joe Greene" ad of the late 1970s. In this ad a young boy offers a Coke to the thirsty postgame football player, Joe Greene, who surprises the young boy with the reciprocal present of his game jersey. This exchange is followed by the boy's surprised thank you and the mean football player's warm smile in response, revealing, as Holt put it, "the warrior's humanity and his momentary bond with the boy."[9] However, when Coca-Cola reworked the ad many years later, then using baseball's Cal Ripken Jr. and the Coke offered by his son, it missed the mark. As Holt reasoned, the ad missed the mark because it had only concentrated on the emotional bond depicted between a sports hero and a child, overlooking that the power of the original ad resided in the fact that Joe Greene was black, the young boy was white, and the bond evoked in the ad spoke to the culturally relevant "symbolic resolution of racial strife."[10] This resolution had been a crucial component of the ad's emotional power as well as its maintenance, in Holt's terminology, of Coke as an iconic brand.[11] For our New Zealand partners, exactly such matters were their concern. They were concerned that in much of New Zealand advertising, emotional depictions tended to the stereotypic, the obvious, and the undeconstructed. While they maintained that they were "always" asked to "build on the emotional aspects" of brands and to "create emotional connections," it also seemed to them that only "happy clappy" ads were deemed acceptable and that emotional appeals were not linked to specific New Zealand cultural meanings, concerns, or target audiences.

For us, as anthropologists, our more general interest was in how emotion and its expression were culturally constituted as well as the ways the discourses and practices surrounding emotion were constitutive of the sociocultural milieu. This outlook was based in work by anthropologists, sociologists, and psychologists that had demonstrated and featured the cultural nature of emotion and emotional expression, often in direct contrast with those who argued for a more universalistic, biological stance.[12] Our intellectual interest had been sparked by the issue of boredom, but this interest was built on the scaffold of work that had shown the cultural specificity of emotions and emotional expression, as for instance, Michelle and Renato Rosaldo's explications of *liget* for the Ilongot in the Philippines.[13] A type of "anger" anchored in issues both of shame and demonstrations of inequality, the Rosaldos have described *liget* as an emotion of energy-building force, ideally resolved—even if now largely historically and/or metaphorically—through the restitution of taking someone's head.

We melded our collective interests into the design of a project. Our research focus was to examine the sociocultural expression of emotion in advertising and among young adults in everyday life. The goal among us all was to better appreciate the ways that expressed emotions in advertising were grounded and linked to larger cultural outlooks, values, symbols, metaphors, practices, and processes, cultural phenomena which were also ethnographically evidenced in everyday life.

How We Did It

We jointly decided to carry out the research in New Zealand and the United States and to add the United Kingdom as an illuminating comparative frame. Arguably, adding the United Kingdom still meant we were conducting the research in sociocultural contexts that would be relatively similar vis-à-vis each other versus some other locations we could have picked. We were not apt to uncover nuances of *liget* or even Germanic *Schadenfreude*. No question. However, we also thought the benefits of (relatively) shared Anglophone-influenced traditions might also aid us. It would aid us practically in conducting the research as well as potentially highlight the ways emotions were socially constituted if we found nuanced differences. In the United Kingdom, our efforts were aided by Liz Boulter, a colleague from the global headquarters of M&C Saatchi, the agency with which our New Zealand partners were then affiliated.[14]

We carried out the research in New York, London, and Auckland. In each city we recruited six young adults ages eighteen to twenty-four as our primary ethnographic interlocutors. These young people were asked to complete two assignments prior to meeting with us. We asked them to create a diary of the actual day-to-day realities of some of their emotions or emotional states. To keep it manageable and "do-able" for them, we suggested they create the diary around three emotions or emotional states that were part of their life at the time. We urged them to take photographs, to jot down notes, to do whatever they needed to show us what these emotions looked like, felt like, and were like in their lives. Their other assignment was to create a documentary of sorts. We asked them to gather together examples of these same three emotions from ads, Web sites, or magazines. We told them we were especially interested in examples that they felt *really* captured the sense of those emotions from their perspective. For this documentary we suggested that they could enlist the help of a friend, a friend who they would then also invite to take part in the ethnographic encounter with us.

We benefited perhaps from this age group's close involvement with scholastic assignments. All carried out the assignment admirably, creating notebooks and disks for us and providing us with almost more images than we could fully process. Most also took to heart the advice to enlist a friend's help in the assignment—many pairs presented us with a set of images gathered by each of them. Thus we garnered the perspectives and associated imagery from twelve young people in each country.

To further focus and ground the study in advertising, we also gathered fairly comprehensive collections of public service, telecom, and beer advertising from each of the countries. We then jointly conducted a semiotic analysis of these collected ads among ourselves and later showed some of the most telling or discussion-provoking examples to the young people in the ethnographic encounters.[15] We had chosen these advertising categories as being of potentially high relevance for this young adult audience, and we chose brands and messages that targeted this age group. Public service messaging was also chosen because of its prevalence in targeting this age group and because of this genre's continual preoccupation with ascertaining the most appropriate and effective uses of emotional content in messaging.[16] Insights and implications for this category of messaging represented a way the New Zealand agency could distinguish itself.

We began the research in New York. Our New Zealand partners joined us there. Our first day was spent in a room, looking at and deconstructing ads. While we had spent some time examining the collected material before their arrival, before this day ended we once again all experienced the reality of how cultural constructions infuse advertising as well as the significant role of "readers" in the creation of advertising meanings. Among us, we often did not understand, or understood differently, the ads from varied countries.

A paradigmatic example was offered by a thirty-second public service television spot from New Zealand. It opened onto a living room where only the loud sound of a ticking clock could be heard. Four young adults were in the room, not talking. Two were young men sitting on a sofa; another was a woman sitting on the arm of a chair, her own arms folded and her purse on her shoulder. Across from them was a young man in a wheelchair and neck brace. The viewer's perspective was initially looking over the shoulder of the young man in the wheelchair. When the camera then moved to show his face, one could see what looked like fresh scars and still bloodied wounds. The woman in the room with folded arms was then shown in close-up, looking at him, with what seemed a hint of disgust and expectation, but without saying anything. Silence still reigned. Then, after a pause, the young man in the wheelchair released a long, breathy sound, smiled awkwardly and said, "Bummer, man." In response, one of the men on the couch was shown looking over to the woman, who then let out a sigh of disgust, frowned, rolled her eyes, got up quickly and walked out of the open front door, arms still folded. The man who had looked over pronounced to the man in the wheelchair, "nice one," and walked out the door. We then see clearly for the first time that the man in the wheelchair has an amputated leg and one arm in an elaborate brace. Quickly thereafter, the other young man from the couch announces, "We'd better go, eh?" and leaves. The young man in the wheelchair is left alone and looks downward.

This spot was inscrutable to us. For the New Zealanders it was crystal clear. The man in the wheelchair had been driving while intoxicated and had an accident in the course of which a mate riding with him had died. The others gathered were the mutual friends, who were there to give him a chance for redemption (but only a chance, as evidenced by the purse still being on the woman's arm, even though she was seated). His attitude and his pronouncement of "bummer" were taken as signs of lack of remorse. The others left him because he had blown the one chance they were giving him for redemption.

Even barring that some of the contextual information of intoxication, car accident, and a mate's death could only be known from other ads and other venues, even when we understood this background, we could not fully comprehend or appreciate the depicted emotions and reactions. The New Zealanders told us that the injured young man had violated the culturally valued "mates look after mates" principle. This was understandable. But why, we asked, would the others not also feel sorry for him? He was irreparably physically hurt himself and obviously he would also be suffering from the guilt of causing the death of a friend. Couldn't it be assumed that he did not know what to say? Could it not also be assumed that their motivation to visit him was to show that they forgave him in order to help him feel better, because obviously he would feel the mantle of responsibility? And if so, why were they acting in the way they did? Wouldn't it be appropriate that they pitied him and his position? What we said seemed somewhat unfathomable to them and the notion of pity provoked a strong response. Pity? No, pity would not be a positive emotion to show, we were told, it would mean that they weren't showing trust and respect, but were rather treating him as lesser, for instance as a kid rather than as someone whom they respected and expected to stand up as an adult. As the conversation continued we assured them that in the U.S. context, pity could be expected and esteemed as a positive response among friends, as it would express empathy.

From this and other bits and pieces and remarks from the day, we all finished the day a bit confused but, perhaps happily for the research project, also convinced that our varied cultural assumptions about emotions were indeed filters for the interpretations of the ads and that the sociocultural frame was clearly of importance in defining what emotions were, which mattered, and what was considered appropriate to express.

In what follows, we present some of the results of this study, highlighting the ethnographic component and detailing what we found as some of the most interesting results from each country. For organizational purposes, we present our findings from the United Kingdom, United States, and New Zealand in turn, bringing in explicit comparisons largely where helpful to make a point of another country clearer. To frame these results as well as to help provide a guide to the nuanced differences for the reader, we first provide an overview in Table 6.1. Throughout this analysis, we place stress on the differences. This is not to imply that there were not similarities. But for the purposes of this inquiry, the differences between the United Kingdom, United States, and New Zealand were more telling and interesting than the similarities. One can think of it as differences within similarities, akin perhaps to differences between driving on the right versus the left side of the road, or differences between a typical spring versus summer day. All part of the same larger system or cultural matrix if one viewed it so, nonetheless also clearly different.

Table 6.1   Overview of Emotion Cultural Matrices

	U.K.	*U.S.*	*N.Z.*
Key Example	Paranoia	Stress	Intensity
Valued in the Expression of Emotion	Intelligence Intellect Public façade	Openness Honesty Release	"Straight up" "Being strong"
Location of Emotions	External Context and situation	Internal Self	Internal Self and others
Emotional Heights and Nirvana	Open expression of felt emotions with friends and family	Strong emotions Feelings of ecstasy and euphoria	Being strong and open
Young Adult Life Goal	Moving upward in position	Making the most of oneself	Making the most of life
Enveloping Cultural Matrix	Matters of social status and relative position	Achievement Race and ethnicity	National identity

Young Adults in the United Kingdom

Listing "paranoia" as a key example in Table 6.1 for young people in London may seem a bit surprising or perplexing. In fact, we were a bit surprised ourselves when paranoia was selected by Mark,[17] who was the first young man we interviewed in London, as one of the three emotional states on which to focus his assignment ("lust" and "relaxation" were the other two). It was not the frequency with which paranoia was chosen by the young people that made it a key in this analysis. In fact, Mark was the only one who chose to focus on this emotion, but we have selected it as a key because it opens up a view onto some of the most important issues in the expression of emotion raised across all of the London interviews.

Importantly, Mark told us that part of the reason that he chose the emotions he did for his journal was because he wanted to make it more interesting, he wanted to pick emotions that showed more thought in the choice. In essence, he did not want to just pick emotions that seemed rather mundane or expected, rather he wanted to choose examples that showed more intellect. His verbal descriptions and nuances of paranoia as an emotional state were vivid and gripping. The instances he recounted were varied. There was the early morning evacuation of the London Underground, a frightful experience in light of bombings that had recently occurred. There was also another public transport experience in which his problem was that he was not able to keep himself from looking at a woman who was drunk and "falling out of her dress," then worried about what other people who saw him looking would think of him. There was the "wake and bake" marijuana moment when he went into a store to buy chocolate and dropped his money on the floor, reached down shakily to pick it up, and felt like the owner knew he was stoned. He also talked about eating chocolate and later finding chocolate on his face, and wondering what other people must have thought. He discussed how he thought the manager at his restaurant job was watching him as he operated the till. He had stolen when he was young and he thought perhaps the manager suspected him now. He also spoke of how his status of "being a student" carried with it a whole set of negative behavioral assumptions, such as being lazy, sleeping late, living in a messy flat, and eating only junk food. These were somewhat troubling and he really didn't like the idea that people might see him this way.

His diary included a small image which he had found on the Web of Edvard Munch's *Scream*, the expressionist painting of a person by a fence, open-mouthed and hands over the ears, red sky in the background. He also included a poem he had written, as well as a reprinted verse, both of which he seemed eager to recite during the interview. This choice to use, create, and recite poetry coincided analytically with Mark's explicit reasoning to choose an emotion that was more "interesting," one that evidenced thoughtful choice. What emerged throughout the U.K. interviews, through explicit statements and implicitly through presentation styles and indirect statements, was the degree to which the involvement of intellect and intelligence were valued in the expression of emotion. In the practice of expressing emotions, intellect and emotion were consistently seen as intertwined, whether it was through the use of poetry as in this example or the frequently noted use of humor or sarcasm to express negative emotions.[18] Young people in London told us of the truism of "the truth is said in jest" and of their own experiences in ways that joking about something can be "a polite, informal warning." We learned that at the workplace, in public, and with people one does not know well, attention is expected from both sender and receiver in discerning what is really being said. In essence, they asserted that emotional expression takes knowledge and skill.

One could argue that the expectation of reading between the lines in the face of unsaids—on both sender and receiver sides—is something that can foster paranoia. But what made this valuation on skill and the intertwinement of intelligence and intellect in the expression of emotion so striking to us was the backdrop of the long (even if disputed) tradition of the bifurcation of thought and emotion in the Western canon, as evidenced in the writings of philosophers, academics, and also the argument of *Lovemarks*. Moreover, this valued intertwinement of intelligence and intellect in the expression of emotion was clearly interrelated with a perceived external, context- and situation-based location of emotion and the interrelated emphasis on maintaining situational and context-appropriate façades.

The young respondents in London provided many direct and indirect examples of how emotions were seen as something that was generated in the external or sociocultural arena, rather than internally within the self. They talked of emotional states induced by drugs and alcohol, such as Mark's "wake and bake" moment, and importantly, focused on the drugs or alcohol as the root and cause of the emotional state, not as simply a catalyst for bringing out what was already there.

James and Angela talked to us about "the Friday feeling," that feeling one has at the end of the work week, or the "Christmas feeling" that one gets around the Christmas holidays. James also talked about how if you "spend time with miserable people, you become miserable," using the example of his sister. He said that his sister had been "bubbly and bright." Then she started hanging out with depressed people and became like them. Now she is around a different group of people and she's happy again. Our respondents noted the creation and sharing of positive as well as negative emotions between people and in situations—how, for example, if you did something nice for someone, such as being polite to your mother, it would also lead to the creation of a positive, shared emotional space. As James also summed up the external causation of emotional states, "Money can't buy you happiness, but it can buy you a few drinks at the pub, which will make you happy."[19]

Among our London respondents, there was an understanding of emotion as forming, occurring, and modified in the external interstitial space between people, rather than as located primarily in the internal, bodily space of a person. One was assumed to feel things in interaction with other people, and what is "out there" and what one "puts" out there was conceived to make a difference. Given this focus on the external genesis of emotions and the correlated attention to the effect of one person's emotions on the emotional state of others, it is then not surprising that there was also considerable attention to mastering and maintaining situational-appropriate façades. Respondents generally framed this in terms of being considerate of others. It was about politeness; it was about thinking of others; it was acknowledging that one's emotions, talk, and behavior could have an effect; and it was about taking care to not hurt or offend someone. Crucially, this cultural façade of politeness was not one that should be seen as diametrically opposed to honesty or "being real." For Americans, a polish of politeness is often culturally interpreted as one of falsehood, of covering up, of not being real.[20] The dichotomy is not the same in the United Kingdom. If a façade is a nice dressing on things, it is not fake. One could perhaps think of it as a bit of sugar and milk in coffee or tea, but not the decaffeination. The façade is the nice front of the house, but this does not mean that it is not also easily deemed and expected to be nice inside.

Aspects of this façade were often seen by respondents as related to "upper lip" notions, which in the United States are often referred to as "the stiff upper lip," and we heard in our interviews also referred to as "the British upper lip." As a rule, in the cultural imaginaries of New Zealand and the United States, this notion refers to a lack of showing of emotion and extends to the idea that the British have a tendency to be cold and unemotional in general. The classic stoic, stone-like stance of Buckingham Palace guards is taken as a notably extreme example, but nonetheless a case in point. In fact, while in London our New Zealand partners witnessed a woman crying while riding the Underground. Others sharing the car with her rather studiously did not look at her and did not say anything to her. There was an aura of acting as if her crying was not even noticed. This was jarring from the New Zealanders' perspective. The reaction of fellow riders was shocking to them on the order of "How could no one say anything?" "How could no one ask her if she was okay and needed help?" In fact, one of them could not resist asking her if she was all right. From our U.K. partner's perspective, the behavior of others in this public site was understandable, normal, appropriate, as well as indicative of consideration. To be able to achieve a façade of "not affected by the situation" was a culturally preferred achievement because to ignore the crying woman's state was to be polite in the sense that it telegraphed to her that her emotional state was not creating discomfort for others. To leave her alone was to not escalate her pain by making her feel that she had also bothered or burdened others.[21]

If a crucial rationale for this polite façade on emotions is related to the under-standing of emotional states as generated foremost in the social and interactional space rather than that of the individual, there carries no implication that there was less inherent emotionality or emotional feeling among people in the United Kingdom. This is where an understanding of the "upper lip" in terms of the absence of emotions misses the mark. Rather, for our respondents there was a sense of great potential for emotion as well as the need for release. The point for our London interlocutors was about expressing and releasing emotions in the right place, at the right time, with the right people. Among friends and with family was the place of living and letting out emotions. In fact, letting down the façade, relaxing, and then giving free reign to emotions was part of the definition of friendship—joint emotional expression was con-stitutive of friendship. Moreover, if a kind of nirvana in terms of emotional expression in the United States was formulated as an out-of-the-ordinary level of positive excitation, a kind of over-the-top happiness or euphoria that could be achieved alone as well as with others, the full-on nirvana feeling for the U.K. respondents was the feeling of comfort in the company of friends that afforded and was afforded by the situation in which it was possible to let down the façade. To be able to not worry about one's own vulnerability and to not worry about the vulnerability of others in terms of the repercussions of emotional expression was a peak and ideal kind of emotional state. The cultural ideal, the state of emotion and relaxation which was spoken of as one that was blissful, was the open-hearted, tell and do whatever with good friends. The general distinction is that emotional expression can make you vulnerable because you put it out there in play, but with friends one does not have to worry about what one should do or say and is not worried about their judgment. For our U.K. respondents, "relaxation" was the letting down of the façade on emotions versus the United States in which "relaxation" was the lack of stress or anger.

A British television spot for Carling beer illustrated this cultural notion of emotional expression and release among friends. This spot opened with a man in his twenties, in a suit, in an office of partially glassed walls within a larger office. We have the idea that it is approaching the end of the workday from his desk posture, the light, and a woman in another office shown putting on her coat. He seems to get an idea and turns to do something. The image then cuts to the office of another young man, who picks up the phone. Then we see the image of the first man, the caller, now slumped in his chair, asking the other man what he's doing that evening. The second man's response is that he's just going to go home and watch "some footie on the telly" and asks the other what he's going to do. The suited man then starts to sit up, as if concerned, and slightly stammering, answers that he's snowed under and won't be home until "much, much later." Meanwhile he's also picking up his keys and starting to get up from his desk. When the call ends, he grabs his coat and starts to run out of the office. The man who received the call then spots the caller running out from his own windowed office, the first time we realize they are part of the same larger office. This sight of the caller running then leads the receiver to jump out of his seat and run out of his own office space so quickly that he knocks a nearby water cooler to the floor. He then gets to the elevator just as the door is closing but he sees the caller inside who pronounces a snide "see ya." As the caller is shown running out of the descended elevator, he is momentarily waylaid by an older man, presumably a senior in the office by the younger man's polite demeanor, by the fact that he stopped running, and the older man said he "got the report." They both then pronounce "Monday," as if they'll see each other and talk about it on Monday, and take leave. Meanwhile, the call receiver is shown running through the lobby. What ensues is a quick cutting of scenes throughout the city, showing the two men in an intense race, including a reciprocal instance of "see ya" when the call receiver gets on a bus that the caller just misses. Toward the end, they are running across rainy streets, in front of traffic, up a stairwell and fire escape, knocking into both people and things. All politeness and decorum are gone. The race finally ends when the caller blasts open the front door, wet and tired, to face the back of a large leather chair situated in front of a turned-off television. The chair swivels to reveal the call receiver already in the chair, Carling beer in hand, who pronounces "cheers." Then the caller hangs his head a bit lower, in a small gesture of disgust, as he still is breathing heavy from running. Meanwhile, the man in the chair lets out a number of guffawing ha-has and raises his hand, holding the television remote in the air, then swivels in his chair to the television to watch the game, and there is the announcement of "Carling, Spot on."

Notably, prior to arrival in the United Kingdom, we had watched this spot and reasoned based on ingoing notions and what U.S. respondents said, that the ad was speaking to the idea of creating strong emotions and emotional tension—that it was about the preference for feeling emotion—almost any emotion—rather than feeling none. And so, in the midst of the mundane routine, two young men had created a competition. When our U.K. partner watched this ad with us, she disagreed with this reading of creating emotions out of a preference for feeling stress and tension rather than no emotions, and pointed out what was immediately obvious to her and what we had missed. The crucial aspect of that ad was that it revolved around the idea of gaining access to limited resources—it was a competition between flatmates for the privilege of sitting to watch the game in their home's only chair. The first man had tried to trick his friend and get home first by saying that he was snowed under. Then the "see yas" were sarcastic, snide, show-off remarks accompanying their relative wins that could be expressed among friends, the kinds of open, emotional expression indicative of friendship. The arm-raised guffawing at the end was the man in the chair's expression of his feeling "chuffed" for the final win—basically he was feeling proud of himself and expressing it—at that moment it did not matter if he made his friend feel badly. In fact, he rather was happy to (good-naturedly) annoy his friend.

But, what was important about this ad was that the smugness of one-upmanship was expressed between relative equals and friends, not between nonequals or casual acquaintances. As our respondents talked about this ad, as well as about the use of humor in general in expressing emotion and displeasure, they impressed that there "is a fine line between feeling good about oneself and feeling better than others." The point is not that a person may not feel or believe themselves better, or better at something, than someone else. Indeed, people did make assessments and distinctions, but the idea was that care must be taken in the expression of those sentiments, especially if not among close friends. Thus, we were told that humor was often used as a social leveler to communicate that you were down to earth and not pretentious, that you did not take yourself too seriously, and to help preserve others' face and feelings. We also heard from our U.K. partner that to be seen as too smart, too driven, and too educated could be bad. As she pointed out, in the workplace it was also generally not good to be too obvious about one's ambitions, as in doing so, it risked showing others up and made them distrustful. To show off, to stand out above the group, is not the desire.

These self-equalizing aspects, as well as her point of the limited resources of the chair, are the other aspects which must be taken into consideration to have a greater appreciation of what was being depicted in this ad and what was involved in the cultural configuration of emotions for our young London respondents. The metaphor of the "ladder" was a highly salient concept for all of our respondents. They talked about their interest in moving up the ladder in their chosen fields, about currently being at the bottom rung of the ladder or about not even being on the ladder yet. James recounted the truism that he told us his father had always said, "It's better to start on the bottom rung of a ladder you want to climb than on the middle of a ladder you don't want to climb." This was the other cultural material embedded in the Carling ad of two young juniors in the office working their way up. Moving up in position was the preoccupation and goal of the young respondents in the United Kingdom; successfully getting on and negotiating the landscape of ladders was the issue.

Implicit in this was a notion of a limited number of ladders as well as limited room on the rungs. The notion was not of a limitless pie, but rather of a limited number of spots in which one was actually in competition with competent others.[22] Respondents often explicitly spoke to the limited resources that framed their realities, whether it was the limited amount of money in their pockets, or James sending out hundreds of inquiries for a paying job, and being one of only five students to get a placement. Fashion design students spoke of the competition out there, which included a crowded field replete with celebrities, even if they maintained that their university credentials would give them "a leg up" on the ladder. They talked of themselves as "creative bombs waiting to explode," but they knew that they were going to have to start on the bottom rung of the ladder, "gritting teeth and bearing it."

The notion of a social environment conceived as one with limited resources, in which persons are distinctly located at varied levels, resonates loudly with the social milieu for which the British have been famously parodied by self and others—a class-based social organization in which attention to distinctions and nuances of class are paramount concerns. Here is where one must ask how the matters of the intertwinement of intellect and emotion, the façade, and the paranoia come together. Many of the politeness efforts can be seen as not wanting to lord something over someone. But are these efforts, this politeness of everyday social action, the leveling of oneself, the primary release of emotions among family and friends, precisely the means that have also allowed class distinctions to maintain? Are these cultural preferences which help to maintain the balance of feeling good about the self without expressing feeling better than others also precisely those which help to keep the fine-line distinctions of class and status intact?

Young Adults in the United States

Based on the diaries and our discussions with young adults in New York, we have chosen stress as the key example for the U.S. discussion. Unlike paranoia for the young people in the United Kingdom, stress was actually selected by a number of our respondents as one of the emotions to focus on in their diaries. Discussions of stress were also central in many of our ethnographic encounters. If at the outset, stress seemed to us a slightly strange choice—we wondered even whether stress could be considered an emotion rather than a set of circumstances—the discussions with the young adults convinced us of both its existence as an emotional state and its merits in elucidating the sociocultural terrain of emotion for the U.S. young adults.

Stress was generally described by the U.S. young people as the feeling of being overwhelmed or having a burden. As one of the young woman detailed stress as an emotion in her diary, "Stress feels like nothing can go right. I have no time to do anything that needs to be done. I have so much to do and so little time to do it." As a young man put it at the very beginning of his diary, "Having to deal with a girlfriend, a job and college, stress unfortunately plays a huge role in my life. Whether it's having the occasional argument with my girlfriend, waking up late for work or having a test, stress always seems to occur." As he then continued in his diary, and as he recounted to us, he tended to "get stressed" from the very beginning of the day, which then affected his mood for the rest of the day. The stress was often from waking up late and subsequently rushing to get to his morning class. But, as he noted, "On the rare occasion I wake up on time with no problem, something else usually causes my tardiness." Another respondent created a PowerPoint report, with photographs and headlines. The headlines for stress included: "School stresses me out; Stressful = my messy room; Stressful = work and getting there on time; Stressful = seeing others stressed out." Accompanying this last headline she had a photograph of a young woman eating at what looked like a cafeteria table, with a paper plate and a large disposable cup that suggested coffee, wearing her coat and winter scarf. Another photograph on that page was of a young man sleeping in a chair, head on a wooden armrest, cushioned only by his hand. Managing and coping with stress was a preoccupation among our U.S. respondents.

As these brief examples perhaps also suggest, the cultural discourse of stress in the United States is also "greedy," in that stress as an emotion appears to be taking over terrain that once was defined in other terms and with other emotions. Included in the diary of the young man who described himself as always late was a picture of two basketball players sitting side by side on the bench. As he explained it, "In the picture above, a pair of college basketball teammates are stressed after losing a game in a tournament. Stress is portrayed by the guy on the left putting his hands on his head, along with a towel. The player on the right covers his face with his hands. After practicing all year, and playing to get so far, to lose one game and go home, is very stressful." Another photograph, this time of a basketball player standing and looking down, bringing his jersey up to wipe his face, was captioned, "The pressure of being the favorite and expected to win something had an added stress factor. The subject of this photo also holds his head down and covers his face with his hands." As we asked ourselves, what happened to frustration, disappointment, sadness, the agony of defeat?

If stress was a greedy cultural discourse for our U.S. respondents, the stress which our respondents discussed was also somewhat self-induced, as some of the foregoing examples simultaneously suggested. Perhaps ironically binding these two sides of the stress issue together, one of our respondents also told us that stressing something equals paying too much attention to it. But, more importantly, that at some level stress is a self-induced emotional state (whether due to waking up late, eating on the run, or something else) is precisely the most telling facet of it in terms of the larger sociocultural terrain in which it resides and operates. For the U.S. cultural context, the idea that you make the circumstances of your life, that you create your life and your world, was the point. Stress was about making the most of oneself, not about making the most of the moment, the day, or the event.

If for our U.K. respondents the social milieu was imagined as metaphorically populated with a distinct number of separate ladders (and so you climb the one you want to be on, not another one), the cultural imaginary for U.S. respondents would need to be one of space for a limitless number of ladders, all of which were built by the users themselves, in the shapes and sizes of their own choosing.[23] Personal goals, strivings, accomplishments were recurrent frames for our respondents in their diaries and in our ethnographic discussions. If the United Kingdom has been caricatured by self and other for an emphasis on nuances and distinctions of class and status, the United States has certainly gained a reputation for its emphasis on the individual, including a certain degree of egomania. Celebrities such as Madonna, Angelina Jolie, and Sean "P. Diddy" Combs are current worldwide ambassadors of this message of larger-than-life, self-creating, and recreating individuals.

While accepting the egocentric self-creation as in part caricature, the truth of this discourse for individuals in their daily lives and the difficulties and challenges it implies can also not be overlooked or downplayed. The young U.S. adults we spoke to were constantly working on themselves, working on their lives, working on getting ahead, working to create a ladder. If in the United Kingdom, a culturally available option to explain one's current lot or lack of success can be to assert one's place in an immutable hierarchy or to note the lack of available spots for competent individuals, in the United States a readily available cultural option is that one is stuck or one does not get ahead because of one's own doing. As a consequence or corollary, our young respondents were constantly hard on themselves, berating themselves for unproductive moments, monitoring their behavior for slipups, deeply concerned about the future they were going to create.

Jon, who discussed the stress he felt because he tended to always wake up late and then hurry to the bus to catch the subway to school, wrote about this berating of self in a direct and self-conscious manner, "When I finally get on the train, I begin punishing myself mentally. In my head, I start disciplining and complaining to myself. I say things along the lines of, 'Damn Jon! You have to wake up earlier than this or you're not going to be successful.' To be a successful person is a goal that I strive for. To achieve this goal, I am particularly hard on myself, so I tend to stress over minor things." This working on getting ahead and working on the self made even small pleasures somewhat fraught.

Another respondent depicted her watching and enjoyment of the popular television show *American Idol* as escapism and guilty pleasure (note: not a pleasure, a *guilty* pleasure). An excerpt from Abraham's diary shows his self-flagellation as well as his intertwined views of productivity and the future. As he wrote, "I wake up at 1pm, and I am frustrated that I could not wake up at a decent hour. Instead of doing something productive such as reading the news-paper or even eating, I slouch in front of the TV and watch garbage. I watch silly shows such as VH1's *The Life of the Rich and Famous*. This show creates a deep longing for the lifestyles of celebrities. This longing leads to an inspiration in which I hope to one day become a wealthy person with many financial options. Later in the day I write short news pieces for my hip hop Web site, so I feel somewhat accomplished and therefore inspired."

If stress was described by the young people as the feeling of being over-whelmed or having a burden, one could easily argue that the social metaphor of creating oneself, and of the freedom to create one's own ladder, also created the burden. It is not easy to carry and create a ladder by oneself, whatever the circumstances. As Jon described another basketball image in his journal, when the team came from behind to win the game, getting twenty-one points in the final six minutes, it "inspired me that despite any given situation seeming bleak or hopeless, there is always time to reverse my fortunes."

Given this cultural emphasis and perceived centrality of the self, it is perhaps not surprising that our U.S. respondents generally imagined and envisioned emotion as located within the person (see Table 6.1). In contrast to the U.K. respondents' external location of the origin of emotion in the context or situation, our U.S. respondents located the genesis of emotions internally, as taking place within their own heads and bodies, and as about the self—emotions were seen to exist and ultimately depend on what was going on inside a person. Even if relationships were seen as cauldrons of emotions and there was an acknowledgment that the actions of another person or the situation could be provocations for emotion, these were also framed implicitly and explicitly as "manipulations." The idea was of a pulling of strings to something that was previously inside of the person (the proverbial "pressing of my buttons"), not of something located outside. "All emotions are created by you," we were told.

As young people maintained, "we are a culmination of all of our experiences and feelings" and "it's my perception, the way I've been raised, it's how I feel it." The young adults depicted themselves and their friends as masters of both their worlds and their emotions.

As Amiri wrote in his diary about events on a night out with friends, "These dudes are stupid. How do they get chicks to talk so reckless? You gotta love them, I say that to myself as I laugh myself into stomach pain. I can't be angry too long, it's silly." As Brenda also wrote, "Finally, I'm indifferent to most of my friends' issues. I don't want to hear you complain about something you got yourself into, that you shouldn't have." Brenda's stated dismissal of her friend's issues is without question an extreme, but her point of getting oneself into things is indicative of underlying conceptions, just as is Amiri's admiration of his friends' ways with women and his own "laugh *myself* into stomach pain."

In fact, the U.S. respondents often invoked and discussed the body as the location and genesis of emotions, whether it was the stomach pain of laughter, the gritting of teeth or tensing of neck in anger, or the giddy feelings of euphoria. Hormones were noted as generators of emotion and as coming from the body, from inside the self. Hormones had also been noted in the United Kingdom as a genesis for emotions, but there it was as if the hormones were almost outside invaders rather than emanating from within.

Coincident with this emphasis on the internal, self-generation of emotions, notions of emotions and emotional differences then also mapped on to categories of personhood salient in the United States. Men and women considered and debated whether their inherent emotional makeups were different and which were "better." Latin-specific machismo was discussed. Differences in emotional expression for black versus white men were salient, a point that is returned to below.

Given the notion that to express emotions is to be real and alive, to not have or express emotions was also to be seen as less than human. To express emotions openly and honestly was also often part of the definition of a "good" person. Brenda spent a considerable amount of time in her interview talking about how her boyfriend, sitting next to her at the time, was in her estimation somehow inadequate because he did not visually and verbally express his emotions. He seemed to unaffectedly take this criticism; it was, in fact, difficult to know what he thought about what she was saying. He did seem unfazed.

A genre of ads which had a lot of appeal among U.S. respondents were ones in which a young person was depicted as talking with or viewing a problematic double of themselves. These spots resonated strongly with notions of working on the self and self-achievement and were frequently deemed highly resonant. U.S. ads from the Montana Meth Project, an anti-methamphetamine campaign,[24] used this technique. One of these, "Bathtub," showed a young woman in a bathrobe, looking into a bathroom mirror and talking on a cell phone. She says into the mirror and to the other person on the phone that her parents think she is sleeping at their house and that she is just jumping into the shower. She is then shown in the shower, first looking relatively relaxed as the water runs through her hair. We then see her look down and get an exceedingly frightened look, making repeated open-mouthed sounds of terror as she gazes into the water at the bottom of the tub that is becoming tinged with the red flow of blood. She turns toward the back of the tub where she screams loudly as she sees her other self crouched in the corner, face scabbed, scarred and discolored, and shaking her head while saying, "Don't do it. Don't do it." Interestingly, we had examples of this doubled-self genre from the United Kingdom and New Zealand as well, in these cases addressing alcohol abuse. With the exception of an ad depicting a woman embarrassing herself at a party, this genre of ads did not seem to resonate well in the United Kingdom. Sometimes the genre was not even understood, for instance, the ad of a N.Z. man talking to his double was dismissed as off the mark because it was not the way friends would talk to one another; it was not understood that he was talking to himself, that he was having an internal dialogue. The U.S. ads, and especially the bathtub spot described earlier, were frequently dismissed as exaggerated by our London interlocutors.

The bathtub and other Montana Meth Project ads were, relative to the ads produced in New Zealand and the United Kingdom, notably extreme. Rather than falling down intoxication, what the U.S. ads illustrated was almost a total disintegration of a physically and morally normative personal and social self. This was not a problem for the U.S. respondents. In fact, what we found to be true among the young adults in the United States was a general comfort with what could easily be defined as exaggeration of emotional expression. The cultural comfort with this exaggeration can be seen as simultaneously generated in the value of an openness and honesty in the expression of one's internal feelings as well as a bit contradictory, i.e., how is emotional expression seen as "open" and "honest" if it is exaggerated? However, another interpretation, and one which provides a fuller explanatory fit of the data, would be to see the exaggeration also as an attempt to make the expression of one's point unmistakable—that the intent (or the interest) of the exaggeration is the transmission of a clear and unambiguous message.

Among the ads we showed to young adults in each of the locations was a series of U.K. billboard advertisements for Vodafone, a telecom company, each

Figure 6.1 U.K. billboard ads, Vodafone, circa 2005

depicting the face and shoulders of a person alone (see Figure 6.1). Among these ads, the one of the man with dreadlocks as well as the woman pictured below him were as a rule taken by all respondents as depictions of people in the middle of music-accompanied movement. It was often imagined that they were at a club or party. In the United States, the depictions of eyes closed, head thrown back in movement so that one's hair was flying, and seeming separation from others, were taken as peak moments of euphoric feeling. These were seen as moments of feeling that one would want to be in—these were feeling at the apex of positive possibilities. Another image, the one which showed a woman as if not moving, but with wet hair falling into her eyes, bare shoulders as if also moist, and a very large smile, was taken as perhaps finished dancing. Her closed eyes and wide grin, with open mouth and teeth apart, was also taken as indicative of enjoying a moment of post-euphoric-peak bliss. The depiction of the intensity was in no way problematic, but rather was seen as a good way to illustrate highly valued emotional states.

In the United Kingdom where these ads appeared, they tended to be read by respondents in a different way. The images were frequently seen as veering into the false and unlikely in their exaggeration. They were imagined as drug-induced states. What was missing from these images for U.K. respondents were also other people—these were not readily imagined as states one reached alone. Thus, the wet-haired woman was imagined as an image about sex, and talking to her boyfriend, i.e., she was not really imagined as alone. Moreover, the ads as a whole were read as messaging that Vodafone was for all different kinds of people. The images were read for what they transmitted about the person, e.g., the man with the dreadlocks was imagined to be third-generation Afro-Caribbean, the woman in the upper righthand corner looking down was described as relatively financially well-off and educated (as evidenced by hair and clothes), the other man's jersey suggested Brazilian soccer and his shaved head an indication of less education, the after-shower woman was imagined as slightly ethnic, perhaps Pacific or the Indian subcontinent. What was striking to us was how this page immediately evoked these nuanced distinctions while the depicted emotions were deemed exaggerated and thus rather dismissed.[25] Granted, it is not at every moment that one has eyes closed and hair flying in the hair, but in the United States these exaggerations spoke as clear depictions of peak emotions.

How U.S. respondents phrased matters in their diaries also spoke to ways that exaggeration was used as a vehicle to make one's point dramatically un-ambiguous. An entry by Amiri, headed with the strongly stated "I Hate Waiting," is a good example. In this he expressed his annoyance at friends who were supposed to pick him up, but who were late and not responding to his repeated calls. As he wrote, "Damn, I need to know where they are in order to reserve the table . . . what the hell is going on? 'Yo, where are y'all going,' I say as they drive right past me. 'What the fuck, you knew I was here, why are you driving right past me?' I call and call without any answer: 10 to 15 calls and no answer to explain. . . . Fuck them, I'll eat by myself." Amiri's "I hate waiting," "what the fuck," and "fuck them" are all emphatic statements that express intensity of feelings. Likewise, his next diary entry involved an instance when his girlfriend called him at three in the morning and woke him up. As he wrote then, "The first thing she asks is what I am doing. She must be stupid 'cause its 3 am. 'I'm sleeping retard.' I humor her because she is slow. I say kindly, 'yo, I'm tired I'll call you during the day.' I know she is slow but the next comment put me over the edge. 'Stay on the phone, please. I'm bored.' You don't have anything to say but because you are bored you want to keep me from my precious sleep. 'Yo, I'll call you later, bye.' Slow selfish people. Back to sleep I go." Again, to frame this interaction as one that "put me over the edge" and his girlfriend as "a retard" involves dramatic overstatement. If in the United Kingdom, poetry was used as a vehicle of expression, dramatic overstatement was a U.S. strategy.

The cultural notion of the importance of release of emotions, especially negative ones, can be seen as another contributor in the cultural allowance for dramatic overstatements. Jon included in his diary a photograph of a man with wide open mouth, closed eyes and grimace, as he captioned, "the male is obviously screaming." As he further interpreted, "He is trying to release his anger by screaming and letting it all out. This is probably the healthiest and smartest thing to do." And he continued, "One does not want to take their anger out on another person, this may lead to a hostile event happening." During the interview, Jon talked a lot about his anger and his strategies for its expression as well as management. He spoke of running up and down the steps of his apartment building as a way of release. He described scenarios in which the intense jealously he felt in reference to others' attention to his girlfriend could turn to anger, an anger that led to confrontation. Jon was a large man, perhaps intimidating to many, a fact of which he was clearly aware, but as he was also keenly aware, interactions can escalate and go bad: "Stress kills people, but anger can get you killed."

In the U.S. context, where emotions map onto categories of personhood, and in which categories of race and ethnicity are highly salient, the situational expression of emotion is also refracted through race and ethnicity. Amiri was African American; Jon and Edward were Latino. Amiri and Edward spoke eloquently about situations in which as men of color they felt forced to squelch and hide feelings of anger and annoyance. These emotions that needed squelching were often described as generated within the ongoing context of a racist world. For instance, Edward, who worked as a plumber, spoke of how his blood pressure could rise in his interactions with white professionals who clearly treated him as an inferior. He spoke eloquently of what it felt like to enter professional buildings in New York in his work clothes as a Latin man. Amiri discussed how as a black man in New York he constantly felt the need to manage his public behavior and perception in ways that kept him safe and far from trouble so he would not be perceived as a threat. The implicit and explicit comparison here is the stuff that "white men get away with." The difficulty of the double standard here is that in a cultural situation in which the release and display of emotion is part of the definition of ideal personhood, men of color are frequently denied the benefits of that ideal emotional expression and personhood.[26]

Young Adults in New Zealand

The emotional states journaled in New Zealand diaries and explicated in the interviews ran a similar gamut to those of the young people in the United Kingdom and United States—stress, love, anger, envy, happy, bored, sad were all included. What we would like to call out in this section is the preoccupation we observed among N.Z. young people with the way emotions are expressed, specifically the intensity of their expression (see Table 6.1). In addressing intensity we are tackling the experiential conundrum for our New Zealand respondents between "being strong" and "being open," both of which are valued emotional states, both of which can be construed and experienced in opposition to each other, and, finally, both of which are avenues for staking one's claim in being an authentic New Zealander. In New Zealand's case, then, we would like to suggest that the display of emotions is a means by which young people establish, negotiate, and contest claims to being New Zealanders in the course of everyday living.

Multiculturalism in New Zealand is a source of national pride, but its realization is not without its tensions and contradictions. In a vein similar to what we heard from black and Latino respondents in the United States, New Zealanders of Māori and Pacific Island (e.g., Samoa, Tonga) descent discussed some of the ways they needed to differentially manage displays of self and emotion relative to New Zealanders of European descent (referred to as *Pākehā* and Kiwis).[27] Clayton, an eighteen-year-old high school senior, rugby player, and New Zealander of Samoan origin, told stories of Kiwis crossing the street at night to avoid passing him and his mates, as well as being in the courthouse for a school project and having an official assume he was there for a court case. As he said of the courthouse incident, "I laughed it off, but is that how people see me?" As Clayton noted, the assumptions of delinquency or violence made by others (generally European, or Pākehā, New Zealanders) make it tough: "They see you as something you know you're not." Displays of anger were, he said, assumed by Kiwis to contain a threat of violence, but as he pointed out, even "happy" could be problematic: "If you're overly happy they might think you're on drugs."

However, what was unique and important about these constraints on emotional expression in New Zealand was the way intensity of feeling was seen as associated with Māori and other ethnic traditions, as well as how that intensity of feeling was part of what defined the valued display of "being strong." Therefore, downplaying and constraining that intensity was a contradiction with "being strong" and a valued multicultural heritage. Thus, in Phillip's description of what stress "looks like" at work (a supply house for hoses used in construction), he was screaming at the other guys to hurry up and swearing at his fellow workers who could not keep up. This scene was perhaps louder in his mind's eye than in actuality, as his fellow workers were "white guys" and he a first-generation New Zealand resident of Tongan origin. Notably as well, the willingness to express emotions intensely (which can also mean just talking about them) was articulated by Ron and Henry, self-described typical Kiwi males, age nineteen, in both ethnic and gendered terms. Henry noted that showing intensity of feelings was a Māori tradition, even in (or perhaps especially in) collective situations. Even "happy" would be done differently among the Māori, according to Henry, as "their 'happy' would be louder." But at the same time, to show too much emotion was also in Henry's eyes to be girlish, glossed as weak. For instance, the French and Russians, in Henry's observation, were seen as more feminine because of the emotion expressed in communicating. Observations such as Henry's are neither remarkable nor limited to New Zealand in their (re)constitution of folk assumptions in which cognition is elevated over emotion and subsequently applied to differentiations of gender or ethnicity (women and ethnic minorities being "the irrational, the emotional"). But what did make these examples remarkable was that intensity of feeling in New Zealand was also part of what defined the valued display of "being strong."

"Being strong," we were told, was to be serious, focused, concentrated, and intent, all of which are conveyed by a stillness of the face. We saw the strong, still face in motion—the game face in rugby (Clayton and Phillip's passion), the face that contemplated the next wave while surfing (Henry's passion), the head that directed the left foot to score a goal in a soccer game in which there were no subs and only an out-of-shape striker (as Ron described the game and himself). In a N.Z. Vodafone television ad, the scene opened in sunny, downtown Auckland, as a kayaker is about to take a run down a three-tiered set of stone steps which are conveniently gushing with water (the result of nearby construction work, one surmises). For our N.Z. respondents, the depicted kayaker was "being strong"—totally committed to his task, intense in the concentration brought to bear, impervious to the attention of his audience. His was a metaphorically recognizable face, resonant and respected. The ad was well liked.

The importance and value of "being strong" was a normative expectation for all of the N.Z. young people with whom we spoke. Cathy, of Māori background, spoke of a time on the train coming home when a guy accosted her. "Stay strong," she told herself, "don't let him know he's freaking me out, don't let him know he's upsetting me." This face was important when in town after drinking and also at school, where, as Clayton told us, tough or fierce was the model. To be otherwise was to risk being construed as weak. The difficulty with "being strong" was that a studied absence of apparent affect (despite intensity required by definition) could be interpreted as a statement of withdrawal and thus was in tension with another aspirational expression of emotion which is "being open" or "straight up."

"Being straight-up" as defined by the New Zealand young adults was to share what is being felt or thought with someone else at that moment. As young women we spoke with explained to us, being straight up is "telling it the way it is, at that moment, so you know what I'm feeling." "You need to be honest with yourself about what you feel and show it. My [Māori] nephew shows so much love to me. He's really open. It's the way everyone should be." "I show emotions when I'm feeling emotions. I'm the black sheep in my [Tongan] family because I do what I want, what I think is right." It is perhaps not surprising that these examples were all from women (who were generally characterized by their male counterparts as being "more emotional"). Yet, what is important to note is that "being open" was an aspiration for all of the young people we spoke to—whether Kiwi, Māori, or Pacific Islander in their New Zealand origins, male or female. The U.K. Vodafone billboard ads in Figure 6.1, some of which from the U.S. standpoint were cited as exemplars of feeling great passion, were uniformly resonant with our N.Z. interlocutors. As in the United States, the N.Z. young adults viewed the individuals in these ads as feeling great passion, being open about and unselfconscious in their expression of feelings. Unlike the U.K. young people, the New Zealanders did not see this series of billboard ads as depicting a variety of people for whom Vodafone would be relevant (e.g., the financially comfortable woman, the soccer player, the third-generation Caribbean immigrant, as U.K. respondents saw them), nor did they invoke an off-camera presence of another interlocutor to make sense of them. Rather, for instance, Cathy, a Māori respondent, homed in on the image of the man with dreadlocks as depicting a state of being free to express one's thoughts and feelings in the moment, a state she would wish were part of daily experience. Notably, the N.Z. young men, regardless of ethnic origins, also interpreted this ad as about "being open"—in Clayton's terms, "letting it out, being open" or, in Ron's words, as "authentic, intense" and what he would have liked to express when he made that left-footed goal in a recent game. His friend Henry likened it to what he feels when he masters a wave surfing. Phillip described the person in the ad as "going full out" and though he said it was hard to feel like that in everyday life, he would like to.

As the reactions to the U.K. Vodafone ads illustrate, emotions were socioculturally articulated in New Zealand as existing within the self, even if brought out in interaction and situational context. This stance was also seen in the reactions to the genre of public service messages in which the subjects of the ads are talking to themselves. As observed among the U.S. young people, but not among the U.K. respondents, internal dialogues with the self were not only viewed as credible and resonant with conversations they had in their own heads, but as exemplars of "being open." In talking to yourself, "as I'm going home, I'm saying I should stop drinking" or "I talk to myself all the time about what I should be doing," there also surfaced a sense of the importance of "being open," even if, in the end, the interlocutor is only oneself.

If "being strong" has historical connection to the practices of New Zealanders of European origin in terms of the control of the display of one's feelings,[28] the value placed on "being open" or "straight up" was a grounded tradition of social interaction among both Pacific Islanders and Māori. Diaries and stories from Clayton, Phillip, and Cathy contextualized happiness and sadness in situations of traditional gatherings (a birthday party, Easter celebration, or funeral) either journaled or recently experienced. These were described as occasions for "outpouring" of emotion, in which hugging, banging on others' arms, yelling, and laughing were normative; these were occasions for strong feeling and "leaky eyes." At a Samoan funeral we were told it was never shameful to cry; at a Māori Tangi (a term that means to cry), the three-day funeral was described as a cacophony of emotions in which a premium was placed on intense expression. These Samoan and Māori practices were seen to contrast with those of "Kiwi families" who generally did not show much emotion, "European families are toning it down I think," and whose funerals were characterized as hour-long affairs lacking in both stories and emotion.

The conundrum and tension for the young people we interviewed was in the desire to be both "strong" and "open." The risks associated with "being open" when too much intensity was expressed in the "straight up" talk (e.g., being seen as girlish, regardless of ethnic origin, or being ethnically stereotyped as violent or delinquent) continued to perplex in everyday life. Henry recounted an occasion in which a friend, who so missed his girlfriend, shared these feelings with Henry and in so doing lost Henry's respect: "I definitely judged him, 'dude, shut up.'" But, this is the same Henry who identified with the face of the man with dreadlocks in Figure 6.1 as what he felt like on a wave and would like to celebrate. Phillip struggled with his girlfriend's "straight up" sensibility, though he admired it at the same time and wished it was not such a struggle. Jim, like Henry, feared too much intensity—humor was the way to talk about something without talking about it, including of his failed kidney transplant that kept him on dialysis. Jim's Māori partner disagreed; she viewed his self-deprecating humor as avoidance. For our respondents, these were dilemmas that mattered. And in the end, "being open" and "being strong" were two prominent discourses in the values of the expression and experience of emotion, often at odds.

Yet "being strong" and "being open" were also interdependent for our respondents. Just as intensity of expression was a defining aspect of "being strong," it must be also noted that "being strong" (serious, committed, focused) was a defining aspect of "being open." This interdependency between "open" and "strong" comes particularly to the fore in the Māori haka. In telling of his school's haka performed before each rugby game, Clayton used it as an example of being "serious," one of the emotions he described and journaled as an integral aspect of his life. It was a haka that he and his rugby mates created based on the All Blacks' haka (now branded by Adidas and broadcast worldwide) and performed before each school game. He valued his school haka, one he even performed for us, because it was "letting it all out" ("being open"), which resulted in "feeling really good about yourself," and because it focused attention and concentration on, and a bit of rage for, the business at hand ("being strong"), where smiles or anything that could take away from the task would be taken as a sign of disrespect. Importantly, in the haka's coalescing of "being strong" and "being open," intensity (whether in reference to openness or strength) becomes no longer a gendered or ethnicized quality, but rather a defining characteristic of both "being open" and "being strong."

The delicate balance between "open" and "strong" in the everyday living of our N.Z. respondents carried with it the additional stakes of what makes for an authentic New Zealander. The most important thing about his team's haka, Clayton told us, was that it bridged and transcended the ethnic origins of the players (whether Māori, Pacific Islander, Kiwi, or Asian). By referencing New Zealand's Māori origins, the haka's performance gave respect to and pride for the past and simultaneously brought the past into the present. The haka "is our identity, something unique to this country," he said, "it makes us one group." There was, in the doing of it, continuity, pride, and a bridging of boundaries, as an eighteen-year-old New Zealander of Samoan origin pointed out. There was, also in the doing, a validation for making intensity a valued quality, for "being open" in one's feelings that does not oppose "being strong" in any way. Henry, whose New Zealand roots can be traced to Europe, agreed that the haka is a "strong" display of emotion, a case where intensity of strength and openness is not seen as "airy fairy." It was the instances of open *and* strong that resonated and counted in some sense as ideal. As the kayaker in the Vodafone ad takes his run down the urban waterfall in downtown Auckland, construction workers and young office workers look on with great delight. One of them takes advantage of his phone to send a video of it to his friend back at the office, who reacts with the joy of one who is actually watching in person. We must consider whether this ad was so resonant because it captured both "strong" and "open." We must also contemplate whether the U.K. Vodafone ads in Figure 6.1 were so well liked because they expressed not only "open," but through single-minded intensity, also "strong."

Multiculturalism in New Zealand is a source of national pride in which Māori origins are explicitly embraced as integral to New Zealand's identity.

We have seen this ideal strived for, contested, and also made vulnerable in the actualities of life as it happens (see Chapter 5). For the purposes of this chapter, it is important to note that expression of emotions (being either "open" or "strong") can become fodder for contesting New Zealand's multiculturalism and making it, as a symbol of New Zealand national identity, simultaneously vulnerable. So, for example, an apparent absence of affect in "being strong" (prevalent in the Pākehā sense of strong as controlling one's feelings) can be seen as saying, "to not care, to not have heart, to not say 'I tried.'" Such an interpretation then feeds a popular conception (and concern) that New Zealand "settles for less," as when swimmer Scott Talbot-Cameron showed no emotion in coming in eighth place in a Commonwealth competition. In not showing how he felt, in contesting sharing (or not "being open"), he prevented an ensuing sense of solidarity. According to Clayton as he told this story, "if you show the emotion, then I can relate; I can know the effort involved." In the apparent absence of intensity, a face of "being strong" was viewed by Clayton as not caring, as "I'm happy with eighth place." Clayton was not alone in this reading; we have heard many stories of how New Zealand too often does not strive to be first.

To what extent is this larger sense derived from systematic but differential readings of expression of emotions? Moreover, to what extent is the absence of intensity in "being strong" and the contradictions with "being open" a rebuke of multiculturalism? If the "game face" is a phenomenon that we observed across countries, in New Zealand's case the Māori haka was seen to give permission for intensity of expression in one's "game face." In supporting intensity, one is thus supporting the symbolic place of the Māori in N.Z. identity. In sharing emotional intensity, one is committing oneself across not only an interpersonal boundary but the (multicultural) boundaries of national identity. One is recognizing, valuing, and perpetuating Māori and Pacific Islanders as New Zealanders. Eschewing intensity can be seen as the opposite—contesting or undermining Māori and Pacific Island ways of doing and thus their claims to be authentic New Zealanders.

If in the United Kingdom the preoccupation of the young people interviewed was getting to the next level, and in the United States to make the most of oneself, in New Zealand the goal was to make the most of life, in which life was inextricably linked to interaction with one's surroundings and the land. (Recall in Chapter 5 that nature was not something to be viewed from afar or as an exhibit and that we described New Zealanders' link to the land as indexical.) This sentiment seemed shared by all our respondents, constituting a common framework in their relationship to New Zealand. In this context, a particular fear was that the expression of intensity of feeling could take you out of life, could make you inactive. For Henry, "I'd be wasting myself being angry or sad. It might make you think about stuff but you might dwell on it and not . . . let life move on." Or Jim's sense of squandering a precious resource, "you are wasting energy indulging in it." If intensity can escalate experienced feelings, as in an argument, not only can it become something to regret or something that tears an interpersonal fabric, it can also be distracting. It is distracting in that it takes you out of the moment, it isolates, it breaches an indexical link to one's surroundings. "Dwelling" in Henry's terms, in which feelings led to too much thinking, was seen as "removal" and an absence of doing. A phenomenology of inaction rubbed against what "feels right" not only for Henry but for the others as well.

In the end, in terms of emotional expression in New Zealand, we are left with some of the same perplexities that faced our respondents. Does "being strong" reference Māori or Kiwi (or Pākehā)? Does "being open" reference immigrant Pacific Islander or indigenous Māori? Does "straight up" put you into the moment or take you out of it? New Zealand is a country in which the cultural imaginary of Māori influence inflected everyone's collective understanding of it. Nonetheless, it is an imaginary constantly contested by the everyday practice of prevailing discourses, in this chapter evidenced in the discourses of emotional expression. These discourses kept what it means to be a New Zealander in play for these young people in which the tensions and conflicts experienced kept the question of whether they were (real) New Zealanders (or not) an open one.

Conclusion

We appreciate that without "being there," this ethnographic account of emotions as explicated by these young people in London, New York, and Auckland may seem to cloud and confuse as much as clarify. While we believe that we gained a significantly enhanced appreciation of the social expression and constitution of emotions from our discussions with the young people in each of these locations, even among us, we did not—and could not—answer all of the questions that the research process raised. Nonetheless, both process and analysis do allow us to reconsider the question of boredom in a more nuanced way, the issue that had sparked our interest in this terrain in the first place. In doing so, we hope to provide a heuristic framework for thinking more generally about emotion and its discursive production in everyday life.

As we noted at the beginning of this chapter, we had originally wondered whether "boredom" expressed as an emotional state among teens was related to technologically mediated stimulation. Was it because of lives routinely enmeshed with electronics and digital media that "boredom" as an emotion was becoming foregrounded? Emerging out of this research, we have gained an appreciation that the boredom expressed by young people in the United States is perhaps not nearly as importantly related to a technologically mediated environment as it is to the U.S. emphasis on self-creation, re-creation, and self-improvement.

In the U.S. social milieu in which one is seen as responsible for one's own success and one's own experience, to be bored was to be not working on the self, it was a missed opportunity for self-betterment. It was to have failed to take advantage of a potentially productive moment (for which only oneself was deemed rightly to blame). The power of boredom as an emotion was that it involved a failure to be constantly productive in the ongoing creation and re-creation of self. It was related to television perhaps, but not because of TV's stimulation but rather more so for the ways that our U.S. respondents berated themselves for actually watching *American Idol* or other "stupid" shows. Through this research we also gained an appreciation of the ways a constellation of emphasis in the United States on emotions as at the heart and definition of personhood, dramatic exaggeration in the expression of emotion, and the idealization of euphoric moments, made the experience of boredom akin to an existential death. To be bored was not to be feeling. Boredom was emptiness, an emptiness of personhood.[29]

Notably, the ways in which boredom was thought about, as well as its embedded social corollaries, were different for the young people in New Zealand and the United Kingdom. In New Zealand, boredom was not the "existential mini-crisis" (as one of our U.S. young people put it), rather it was a neutral zone, where one was safe from the impact and risks borne by too much "intensity" of feeling. Boredom did not risk undermining the ideal life of engaged interaction with the situation and to the landscape of New Zealand as (too much) anger, sadness, depression might do. Rather it was a holding station for being ready and able to grab life's next moment. If for our young New Zealanders boredom was seen as both a waste of time and potential productivity, it was not a threat to personhood, as it was in the United States. For the young adults in the United Kingdom, in line with an emphasis on the external generation of emotion and life possibilities, boredom was described as a catalyst to try new things and as occurring when one was stuck without anything fun to do or when involved in mundane tasks; but self-berating was not a central corollary or consequence.

We did speak with our interlocutors about boredom, but crucially, we did not specifically ask them to focus on boredom as one of the emotions in their diaries; in the interviews we generally waited to see if the topic would emerge. While without doubt, to create a topical focus on boredom was a temptation that we needed to resist, in the end the inductive method of letting our interlocutors determine what was significant to consider in the terrain of emotion did help bring to light sociocultural matters that might have otherwise been overlooked. In the writing of this chapter, we have tried to retain some of this inductive essence by not force-fitting (beyond the introductory Table 6.1 framework) the explications for New York, London, and Auckland into one set format. Rather, we have highlighted the sociocultural issues and practices that were most relevant and telling for each location. Admittedly, this might foster some confusion in quick or initial readings, but we believe that in the end this choice allowed us to present and comparatively nuance some of the more important issues that emerged in each setting. For instance, for the United Kingdom we could detail the understanding of an emotional façade as not one of fakeness but rather one of consideration of others given the cultural understanding of emotion as externally generated and shared in the interstitial space between people. For New Zealand we could detail both the intertwinement and contradictions of "being strong" and "being open," the culturally specific categories of emotional expression that are simultaneously implicated in the definition of New Zealand's multicultural national identity, as well as its less than ideal instantiation in actual practice.

Programmatically, the analysis provided a framework for our New Zealand research partners to create more nuanced creative briefs that could take advertising beyond "the happy and clappy" constraints, or for that matter, the shock and fear of public service messaging. Despite theoretical and folk models that suggest emotional appeals in advertising go directly to the limbic system for processing (kind of like a mainlined drug), we also hope this chapter has shown that "emotional appeal" is an analytic construct in sore need of cultural contextualization. Our ability to discern what is going on is framed by (our) understandings of appropriate display of emotion. To be an expert on emotions in advertising and public service messaging is thus to be an expert on cultural practices. Happy, sad, mad, or glad might be *constructs* we all share, but in *practice* can be inscrutable or systematically differentially understood. One needs to know the cultural stakes involved, e.g., ideas of personhood (United States), friendship (United Kingdom), or national identity (New Zealand), for a particular target—in this chapter, young people, in each of these countries.

It might still be tempting to think of emotions as universal feelings, rooted in a shared physiology, for which (culturally specific) rules of use are overlaid. But this would be unfortunate as such a reading denies the power of emotional experiences to shape and be shaped by world views, values (e.g., achievement, independence, vitality, environment), ideas of personhood, and social milieu. Emotions are both experienced and culturally constituted simultaneously—a convergence that starts with one's earliest interactions with the (social) world. Moreover, a universalistic framework can make us miss the continuous process of change in experiential lives. Nothing is static. In New Zealand, being open and being strong are contested as we write this. It is in the situated-ness of emotions in everyday life with others, always in reference to and linked with larger cultural values and symbols, that becomes the on-the-ground context for new experiences and new readings of those same emotions. Thus, the particularities of emotional experience are not only a lens for further cultural understanding but in practice can shift or bring into focus what are also otherwise implicit in folk understandings.

Notes

1. The 2003 study was carried out by Sunderland and Practica Group partner George Hunt.
2. For another contemplation of boredom, see Musharbash's (2007) ethnographic analysis in which the setting was Aboriginal Australia.
3. Roberts (2004).
4. Note McCracken's (2006b) comments on *Lovemarks* on his blog at www.cultureby. com and his citation of Roberts' (p. 190) advice to "Give your brain a rest. Embrace emotion. Kick the information addiction" as among the problematic assertions.
5. See www.saatchikevin.com/Saatchi_Saatchi_Factsheet. Last accessed March 29, 2007.
6. See CAANZ (2006).
7. As McCracken wrote in his February 24, 2006 www.cultureby.com post, "Here's the thing that really rankles. *Lovemarks* is misnamed. It should have been called *Lovemark*. For it is in fact a lavish, four colour, print ad for Saatchi and Saatchi. I can't believe the other agencies are letting him get away with this."
8. See Aaker and Fournier (1995), Fournier (1998), Muniz and O'Guinn (2001), Schouten and McAlexander (1995). For treatments of relationships with possessions (not brands per se), see for example, Ahuvia (2005), Belk (1988), Curasi, Price, and Arnould (2004), Kleine, Kleine, and Allen (1995), and Wallendorf and Arnould (1988). As examples of how emotion is conceptualized as a variable in advertising research, see Aaker and Williams (1998) and Williams and Aaker (2002).
9. Holt (2004:25).
10. Ibid., 27.
11. See also Schroeder and Salzer-Mörling (2006), whose volume also speaks to the cultural matrices that situate brands.
12. For works focused on the cultural nature of emotion and emotional expression, see, for example, Bendelow and Williams (1998), Hinton (1993), Hochschild (1983),

Katz (1999), Leavitt (1996), Lefkowitz (2003), Lupton (1998), Lutz (1986), Lutz and Abu-Lughod (1990), Musharbash (2007), Reddy (2001), Scheper-Hughes (1992), and Shweder and LeVine (1984).

13. Michelle Rosaldo (1980, 1983, 1984) and Renato Rosaldo (1980, 1984). See also Hinton (1993).

14. Although there is a linked history, M&C Saatchi is a wholly separate, competitor agency of Saatchi & Saatchi.

15. In line with the legal drinking age of 21 in the United States, we did not show or discuss any beer advertising with young people under age twenty-one in the United States.

16. See, for example, Biener et al. (2004), Biener and Taylor (2002), Dahl, Frankenberger, and Manchanda (2003), and Hastings and MacFadyen (2002).

17. All names for young people in this chapter are pseudonyms.

18. Notably, one of our U.K. readers maintained that the great value often placed on figurative and metaphorical usage of language in recounting emotional states in the United Kingdom was a tradition that linked back to the works of Shakespeare, Shelly, and Wordsworth.

19. This external, social-situation orientation of emotion, versus the more internal, individual orientation observed among U.S. young people, coincides with the oft-mentioned traditional focus of British social anthropology on social institutions and organization versus American cultural anthropology's traditional leaning toward cognitive meaning and the individual.

20. A paradigmatic example of the U.S. conception of politeness-as-falsehood can be found in the Eddie Haskel character of the old *Leave It to Beaver* television show. Eddie, the teenage troublemaker friend of Beaver's older brother Wally, and clearly the most morally problematic among all of the boys' friends, was also the one who was portrayed as the most obsequiously polite to the boys' parents.

21. Readers of this chapter have further nuanced this explication of silence in light of others' emotional turmoil in a number of ways. Crucially, they have pointed out that even when the reaction is one of silence and studious acts of "not noticing," there is often an accompanying internal turmoil over whether one should step in. This turmoil, built on concern coupled with worry over whether one would be "invading the space" of the other person, then often leads to a feeling of not knowing what would be the best thing to do. They have also noted that when others are witness to the cause for a person's emotional upset or physical distress, e.g., a bike accident, a large bug crawling on someone, others are often very quick to step in and offer understanding and help. Moreover, at these moments, a feeling of a collective, united spirit can ensue among many, a feeling that frequently remains spoken of as akin to a positive collective spirit that existed in London during World War II. Notably, in these examples, the stress on external causation remains, whether an external situation causing one internal turmoil or the importance of knowledge of the original catalyst as a variable in how one reacts.

22. Note the striking similarity of this respondent framing of that which is desired as existing only in finite amounts and for which one is necessarily in competition with Foster's (1965) classic analysis of the "Image of Limited Good."

23. Of course, access to the unlimited ladders is not equally easy for all in practice in the U.S. as it is refracted by realities of ethnicity and class. See also Cohen's (2003) analysis of the role of consumption and the formulation of citizen as consumer in the United States since the 1930s. The framing of the importance of consumption for the good of the economy as well as others is undoubtedly intertwined in the United States with this limitless ladder outlook.

24. See http://www.montanameth.org. Two ads which we used as part of this research, "Bathtub" and "Laundry Mat," can be viewed. Last accessed March 30, 2007.

25. Distinctions in terms of assumed class and ethnic background were readily assessed and finely tuned as "third-generation Afro-Caribbean" even if the clues and cues remained a mystery to us. As a reader of this paper also pointed out, in recent years there have been many discussions and great sensitivities in the U.K. about "political correctness" and representation in advertising, including quotas on posh accents.

26. See comments by hooks (2004) on the suppression of emotional expression and the self in her analysis of patriarchal masculinity and African American men.

27. Following Avril Bell (2004), we are using the term *Pākehā* to refer to New Zealanders of European descent and moreover as a self-conscious reference to a dominant sociopolitical class. The terms of reference used by our ethnographic respondents for fellow New Zealanders are telling: Pākehā (a Māori word) was a self-referential descriptor used only by middle-class white New Zealanders; Kiwi was used by all our young people to refer to (white) New Zealanders of European descent (which may or may not include themselves); Māori, Pacific Islander, and Asian were also descriptive terms used by all our respondents, whether in reference to themselves or others.

28. Notably, "being strong" was also articulated as being in control of the display of one's feelings and this aspect of "being strong" was articulated as a Pākehā tradition, one that, in its grounding with New Zealanders of British origin, is perhaps related to what we observed in London—the polite façade that is articulated as being in consideration of others, of not wanting to implicate others by explicit expression of one's own feelings.

29. Compare Belk, Ger and Askegaard's (2003) study on the experience of desire, the absence of which was conceived by respondents as akin to death.

7

Diagnosing Conversational Details

"But what are they doing with my money?"
(New Orleans resident, October 1983)

This chapter examines the multiple meanings in people's queries or statements that occur in conversation. The question above, "But what are they doing with my money?" was posed by an electric utility customer in the context of a focus group. Taken at face value, the question was a straightforward query for information. Judged by the supporting chorus of "yeahs" voiced by fellow customers when the question was posed, and the frequency with which it was asked (within virtually every focus group conducted among electric utilities customers in numerous cities across the country at the time), it was a question in sore need of an answer.[1] But efforts by companies to supply the answer often failed to silence the crowd—the information was not believed. For example, when residential customers of electric utility companies were shown direct mail pieces outlining company costs in the form of pie charts, graphs, and the like, these explanations were met with skepticism: How do we know these numbers are accurate? How can fuel, labor, operations (or whatever) cost so much? Surrounded by customer voices such as these, one got the distinct impression that no matter how many times these customers' queries were addressed, their questions would keep coming—lots of talk, lots of apparent answers, but no real answer.

Beliefs about electric utility companies are implicit in the question, "But what are they doing with my money?" Specifically, the question suggests that these companies are accountable to customers in ways other companies are not. "But what are you doing with my money?" is a question not asked of the local supermarket, department store or car manufacturer, Internet service provider or a favorite vendor of computers. It is asked of the government in reference to one's tax dollars and of publicly held companies, if one is a shareholder. The point is that the ways individuals choose to talk, or the questions they believe they have a right to ask, tells us something about the implicit relationships between speakers and subject, and these meanings need to be understood by corporations whenever they "speak" to customers—in the form of services and products, advertising, or policies.

In this chapter we tackle the meaning of words when in context of utterances, that is, conversation. The view taken is that words always occur in context, such that the choice of words speaks volumes, in clear cultural fidelity, about implicit suppositions—whether in relation to fellow interlocutors, situation, or topic at hand. Our goal is to demonstrate the richness of speech-as-it-happens and the benefits of its analysis in consumer research practice. We do so by pulling the conversation of focus groups, a ubiquitous form of talk in qualitative market research practice, into the refractory lens of cultural analysis. The first section of this chapter contextualizes the speech of focus groups practically and theoretically. We situate speech in anthropological perspective. The second section provides a case study of focus group conversations about electromagnetic fields to illustrate the implications of analysis for designing communication strategies. By the end, we hope to have reconfigured prevailing understandings of focus groups so that they are seen as a generative source of cultural meaning and, as such, rich material for cultural analysis.

Bearing Witness to Words in Consumer Research

There is, in U.S. cultural ideology, a sense that words carry meaning beyond their dictionary (or denotational) content. Words can be powerful things—cudgels or insults even when the word(s) might not be at face value (think, "Mom" or "Darling" when said with rolling eyes or sarcastic tone of voice). We understand the power of words when we recognize our own faux pas in conversations, when we find comedy in the inscrutable instructions that come with the gadgets we purchase, when we eschew reading manuals, in the mystifying acronyms of government-speak, in the realization that malapropisms of speech often do not hinder understanding (think, for example, of President George W. Bush and Chicago Mayor Richard Daley), or in our sense that British English accents confer intellectual competence on the speaker. Despite having these senses about language and language-in-use, a sense that we accept pragmatically in daily living, the power of words (outside the boundaries of advertising copy), generally goes unexamined by the U.S. marketing research industry. It is for this reason that we take on focus groups as a generative setting for talk and then ground this discussion theoretically, exploring how talk can be productively understood and analyzed for cultural meanings.

The Focus Group

If ethnography is viewed as a method and setting for cultural analysis, focus groups—the setting for the large proportion of consumer talk in the market research industry—are generally not.[2] Rather, the talk of focus groups is too often assumed by industry to be transparently neutral—what you hear is what you get. And it is rarely, if ever, seen as a site for the production of cultural meanings.[3]

Looking in from the outside, the commercial focus group is an odd convening of consumers ("respondents"), prescreened to meet specific client criteria (demographics, product usage behavior, responses to attitudinal questions, etc.). In the United States (and many other countries), the group typically takes place in a market research facility in specially designed rooms that accommodate client needs for talking, conducting business, eating, or even exercising while watching the groups. The room in which the respondent group convenes has a two-way mirror and is wired for audio and video recording. On the other side of the mirror is the "backroom." The backroom is an important element of the focus group event. Beyond a space, the backroom gains its meaning from its inhabitants, which include the various stakeholders of the project, e.g., commissioning client (usually from the research department of the company), the client's internal client (usually from the brand or marketing group), and outside consultancies, e.g., advertising agencies or packaging designers who have vested interests in the outcome of research. What is important to note is that the backroom can become a tense place, with multiple and competing agendas of its inhabitants and that, frequently, there are more people in the backroom than in the respondent room.

Focus groups are performative events in a number of ways: Recruited individuals are representing themselves and are also acting in their capacity of consumers and in their status as market research respondents. Without question, respondents are finding footing interpersonally and in context of being in a market research discussion. The focus group leader, or "moderator," has dual roles, sometimes in conflict, in relation to the respondents in the front room and the clients in the backroom. And the backroom is also a locus for performance by virtue of its status as collective observer giving witness to "what really happened," which is played out in the ongoing commentary or calling out in accordance with agendas—one's own or someone else's (even if at any given time, individuals in the backroom might be answering e-mail or on the phone). It is, in many ways, an out-of-the-ordinary situation in which an air of normalcy prevails on both sides of the glass—as though there were nothing unusual about the room's design or the presence of recording devices. People on both sides of the glass tend to think of themselves not as attending/doing a performance but rather as observing/doing research.

Despite the presence of a two-way mirror as well as the acknowledgment of both recording devices and the presence of colleagues on the other side, respondents often forget that they are on stage with an audience. If awareness of this role never completely goes away, it is attenuated due to the exigencies of discourse, i.e., the pull of conversation and the need be part of it. Nonetheless, the suspension of awareness of the performative aspect for respondents vis-à-vis the backroom unravels dramatically when laughter or some other explosive comment floats into the airspace of the respondent room. (If two-way mirrors are vision-proof, they are often not sound-proof.) At which point, respondents are forced to remember they have an audience and need to acknowledge it as such: "I guess they didn't like that comment" or "What do you think they think is so funny?" or "Did you hear what he said? That I was wrong, wrong, wrong." But it unravels in less dramatic ways as well whenever anyone takes a moment to contemplate any detail of the surroundings or protocol, in which case their presence as respondents or as consumers can be assumed to motivate what is said and how it is said. It is an environment that is carefully wrought by a particular (and particularistic) idea of a research process. Indeed the focus group, attendant with its environmental trappings, is the marketing research industry's version of a laboratory, with all its positivist overtones. We are calling out performative qualities not to obviate the significance of focus group talk but to contextualize it, thereby showing how focus group conversation (like all conversations) is constructed in part by the circumstances. The particular constraints in which focus group talk is produced might be invisible to observers, but patently not to participants.

We, as moderators, forget the backroom at our peril. If respondents can be chastised (audibly or not) for their opinions, means of expression, contributory worth, or lack of understanding, moderators' talk is also judged, and when deemed wanting a note will be sent in. (Again in particularistic fashion, the note will often be passed to an employee of the market research facility who brings it into the room, rather than being brought into the room in a more direct and time-efficient way by a backroom attendee.) If we are taking our respondents (and ourselves) on a bit of a quest framed by a discussion guide, we cannot fail to be cognizant of backroom needs. The sometimes competing agendas, the explicit research goals, the key analytic questions that in our mind need to be answered, must all be addressed through the ongoing talk of the respondents—even when the backroom might not think so. So, we might (and do) anticipate and forestall backroom consternation and agitation by saying, "I know we're going off track here but . . ." or "I realize we just spent too much time on this, but it was important for me to understand . . ." or "I know we're behind on time, so I'm only going to hit a few key points" or "I know I'm beating a dead dog to death, but I'm curious about the way you said that . . ." These statements are spoken to respondents but are meant entirely for the backroom's benefit. In all, these are ways to indicate to those in the back that a particular flow of talk is intentional, that they should be paying attention to our questions and obsessions, and that they need not worry.

Despite the myriad performative requirements of everyone involved, in the ubiquitous practice of focus group research the transparency of what is said in the respondent room is frequently a taken-for-granted aspect of focus group talk. The tense situations, the need to demonstrate competence, the references to either side of the glass are all taken as peripheral to the talk that is important—what this group of respondents says in the end on various topics of explicit interest. Indeed, it is because of this assumption of transparency, in which what is seen and heard is all too often taken at face value, that the crowds in the back exist in the first place. The idea is that one needs to quite literally be there to weigh in on the significance of what has been heard—to come away with the key takeaways.

Words are of great interest to the backroom when respondents use them to describe the client's or competitive brands, but there is danger when their meaning is taken too transparently, if only because corporate and consumer understandings of the same word can be radically different. Efficacy of bug sprays, for example, means one thing for the R&D developers (killing effectiveness) and quite another for consumers (works in the context of my life). In her book *Goodthinking*, British practitioner Wendy Gordon notes that words can be inefficient communicators—words like "convenience," "relaxing," or "reliable" are deceiving in their simplicity, and some words are "fat" with meaning, e.g., British, American, modern. As she maintains, in both instances more precise meanings must be probed by moderators.[4] Such words need to be contextualized, e.g., "relaxing" to one person might be different for another, or we cannot presuppose that "American" means the same thing from one speaker to another. We would agree, and also note the degree to which advertising and marketing research have themselves created a vocabulary, a genre for speaking about products and brands. Use of "sleek" in reference to cars, "efficient" or "convenient" in reference to most products, is to engage in the genre of speech about products (i.e., to be a consumer). If we need to understand "relaxing" or "reliable" or "American" in context of a consumer's specific experience as Gordon suggests, we also need to recognize these words as symbolic *ideas* constituted through cultural practices (historically, through the lens of consumption, and through specific experience).

Words also take on great significance for the backroom, and are a source of consternation, when a respondent talks too much or talks too forcefully and thereby "dominates the group." The concern with the overpowering voice is that in talking too much and/or too forcefully, the person is swaying the opinion of others, and thereby biasing the results. In the event of the big voice, what is heard is deemed skewed (quite literally), and not what would have been heard had the discussion been more balanced and evenly distributed (the normative ideal for conducting a group). When words are seen to matter, they are too often viewed at face value: countable, immutable, and transparent in their meaning. In the end, the way respondents choose to talk in focus groups is seen as unremarkable. It is what they say, rather than how they say it, that is seen to be of greatest importance.

Focus groups are repeatedly taken to task in the trade press because their set-up invites bias, group think, and the potential to obfuscate what consumers really believe or do in their lives. The enormous support for ethnographic methods in the last decade is precisely the supposed superiority of ethnography (often "observation") to subvert the pitfalls of focus groups. Yet, we would argue, as has Virginia Valentine in the United Kingdom, that focus groups can be venues for cultural analysis.[5] If we think of talk as *always* simultaneously reflecting and creating, of presupposing and performing, then the topic—the research thing—becomes an analytic quest for what *is* in play in the talk and what *is* in contention, that is, what is constructed in part through *how* people talk. In this perspective, the "how" of talk also constitutes the "what" that's being said. And if we pay attention, the how becomes a means for understanding the research issues at hand. Examining how "what are they doing with my money?" is asked allows one to begin to understand that the pie charts and graphs were ineffective responses because they bypassed customers' beliefs about electric companies—beliefs framed by assumptions customers made about big business, monopolies, and the government—and crucially, about the assumed relationship between them, and how they thought the companies think about them.[6]

Anthropology's Perspective

By focusing on how people use words to voice meanings about themselves, others, or the topic at hand, our approach is grounded in the tradition of the ethnography of speaking, a movement within linguistic anthropology that in the last forty years has studied how speech is organized in social life. The early coalition of linguists, sociologists, and anthropologists argued against the notion of a linguistic system that is independent of the cultural context within which it lives, the social processes within which it is cast and toward which it contributes.[7] In the last decade, notions of culture and language have focused even more on the inherent interdependencies between language-in-use and the constitution of cultural ideas. As Hanks noted in 1996, "[S]peech is a form of engagement in the world" such that "language and the world of human experience are everywhere interpenetrated. . . . To speak is to *occupy* the world, not only to represent it" [emphasis added].[8]

Early work in the ethnography of speaking focused on documenting the scope and nature of linguistic regularities in social context. This might mean the differential distribution of speech styles, sounds (e.g., use of post-vocalic |r| across social classes), terms of address, pronominal usage (e.g., use of formal and familiar |you| forms in other languages), taking turns in conversation, or the performative social roles that speech enables.[9] The terms of address used, the form of pronoun chosen, or the way speaking turns are transacted say something about the relationships among the speakers. Qualities such as deference, solidarity, or distance are communicated. What anchored this work was a premise about the way language works—a dynamic system that reflects, perpetuates, and creates social, not merely cognitive, action. In more recent years, there has been great attention to theorizing the impact of language ideology in how it situates and shapes speech practices, and how discursive events (i.e., talk) tap prior (discourse) events to create meaning for what is going on in the here and now.[10] The how of talk is a lens for apprehending the means by which speech negotiates cultural understandings (and in that process performatively creates what has been negotiated).

More simple perhaps, for our concerns here, are the implications deriving from the idea that talk does not belong to its speaker. Talk is social and collectively produced—not merely in the sense that conversation is a summation of all speakers' contributions, but in the sense that talk is collectively produced in any given utterance. In her ethnography of social class on Chicago's south side, Julie Lindquist suggested that argument at the Smokehouse bar was a social event that had the dual effect of invoking and evoking individualness and groupness:

> On one level, to take part in argument is to distinguish oneself from the person on the next barstool; on another, to argue is to do one's part to help the group establish its identity as a social organism. Encoded in arguments at the Smokehouse is information about everything from who's who at the bar to rules governing how belief is negotiated publicly.[11]

If particular individuals were known to instigate and become protagonists in arguing, others, including Lindquist herself, necessarily became mutual participants. In this vein, conversation, inclusive of focus group talk, is never about one person, no matter how much one person talks.

If one considers that the outcome of focus group talk is not what happens by the end, but rather the journey along the way, then it matters not how many respondents said what, who said what how many times, or what the group's consensus was in the end. What matters are the kinds of questions asked, the gambits, responses, moments of tension, and the points of talking over, beyond, or past one another. It matters to whom (fellow participants, the moderator, the backroom) the questions or statements are addressed—implicitly or explicitly.

To illuminate the contingency of speakers' talk on one another and its dependence on discourses extending beyond the room, consider a focus group conversation that took place in New Orleans. The group included ten residential customers of the city's electric and gas utility; all were African American and residents of the neighborhood where the discussion was held (a community center).[12] What was noted at the time in interview notes and now in the recall was the tenseness of the situation. Prices for both electricity and gas had been recently increased, New Orleans had experienced a cold winter, and then, as now, the city's African American residents were among the poorest. Inadequate heat, inability to pay higher bills, and anger with their utility company's explanations for cost increases all meant that company-customer relations were rife with discontent.

In the following excerpts, note two things: a shifting choice of pronouns used in referencing the utility, including the use of "he," in combination with a ranging tone of voice (from measured and reasoned to angry). In this example Edward, an older black New Orleans resident of long standing, was the first to introduce "he" into the conversation and in doing so brought the issue of the company relationship with its customers forcefully into the discussion.[13] Edward provoked the group to link NOPSI (as the local utility was called) to The Man or (white) powers-that-be through his use of "he,"[14] while maintaining an air of reason and factual tone in the process (at least initially). Sam, on the other hand, was the liaison between his community and us, the moderator and observers. (The absence of a backroom meant that the two observers, one client representative and one colleague of the moderator, were hard to ignore, even if silent.)[15] Young, college educated, with a white-collar job, active in his neighborhood, Sam managed to both translate and represent the assembled community group through how he talked. Note how he supported Edward and the group by his own use of "he" to reference the utility (with all the attendant associations of the term) even as he disagreed with them.

> **Edward** (a factual tone of voice belied by the content of his words and the use of "he"): Well NOPSI also indicated that *he* did give us precisely one month in advance, if you can recall and turn back the clock a few hours, *he* did say that your next bill you receive will be double.
> **Sam** (emphatically but without annoyance): Exactly, but you can't—you know, *he* did not say, *he* did not say <u>how</u>, NOPSI did not specify <u>how</u> they were coming to that conclusion and uh, I live in a complex where not one pipe burst, okay?
> **Louise** (tone of resignation and disgust): *He* didn't have to say <u>how</u>.
> **Edward** (increasingly emphatic): I know, I understand what you're saying but *he* did not have to say—and *he* could care less, when, where, or <u>how</u> *he* said <u>how</u> [staccato]—*he* did give you a month in advance [softer].
> **Sam** (measured tone): That would be okay if NOPSI were not subject to regulation by city fathers. And *he* cannot just—NOPSI and no other corporation can just . . . (emphasis on "he" added)

Sam also managed to speak to us, the outsiders, at the same time, often by addressing us directly (e.g., "NOPSI's saying, 'I'm not making a profit . . . you people have to pay for these increases'"). Toward the end of the conversation, though, while agreeing with his fellow neighbors that the company's moral character was wanting, he created a link to us not only by addressing us directly but by his shift to the use of "it" (the normative form of usage) rather than "he." This softened the rhetorical tone, lessened the heat in the room, yet nonetheless fairly represented his neighbors' concerns.

> **Sam:** If NOPSI wasn't so impersonal I don't think you'd [to us] have a lot of problems that you have now. NOPSI is impersonal and cold and is indifferent [nodding of heads and "yeahs" from fellow discussion group participants]. This is New Orleans. This is not New York [a reference to where the moderator lived].

We are not cold. . . . NOPSI, yes. NOPSI is indifferent. *It's* cold and *it's* cunning. *It's* calculating. (emphasis added)

Though perhaps more eloquent in its delivery, the example provides a case in point for the significance of the "how" of talk. Without a consideration of pronominal usage, we wouldn't have understood the multiple sources of discord (as customers, as African Americans, as urban poor, as New Orleans residents) felt by participants. Whether the utility was referred to as "he" or "it" might have seemed less important than what was directly said about rate increases (the topic at hand), but choice of pronoun turned out to tell us quite a lot.

It is because we find such importance in the meanings that emerge from how people say things and the interactions that occur in the conversation among participants that the normative practice of summing-up or a restatement of what's been heard by the moderator at the conclusion of a group (or during topic changes) can become problematic for us. As the moderator sums up, the backroom stops talking among themselves and attends, but we are necessarily inserting our own words into the group as well, affecting what is said, thought, and done next. We do so knowing and evaluating the risks: If we say nothing, we risk a backroom not being sure of what was heard and perhaps wondering whether we the moderators know what has been heard in ways that will answer the research or marketing questions. In this sense, concluding or summing up, as a speech event, is an act offering comfort. It is also an opportunity to remark on something we found particularly interesting, no matter how obscure from the backroom's perspective. As such, it is an act that says, "Pay attention." If we do summarize, however, we risk focusing attention just on the summation (for all parties involved), not on the journey. In this, our actions reinforce the prevailing model of understanding for both assembled consumers and clients—that only *what* was said is important, not the *why* or *how* of what was said. This, of course, we would rather not do.

If the ethnography of speaking has been an arena of study for the last forty years or so, its roots extend much further back, to include at least Sapir, Whorf, and Saussure.[16] The Prague School functionalists of the 1940s and 1950s, a group that included Mukaøovský, Havránek, Trubetzkoy, and, in the United States, Roman Jakobson, viewed language as having distinct functional styles that through careful observation of speakers could be identified and meaning derived.[17] Styles were articulated as being bound to contexts of occurrence— what might be appropriate in one context would not be in another. Contexts themselves were defined linguistically and, more applicable for our interests here, by individuals—their social roles, their reason for speaking, and so on. These styles can be thought of as culturally based ways for communicating or conventions.

In anchoring their focus to context of use, these theorists articulated the significance of indexical, in contrast to symbolic, properties of language. Following the distinctions of Peirce, articulated at length by Silverstein, indexical signs are those "where the occurrence of the sign vehicle token bears a connection of understood spatio-temporal contiguity to the occurrence of the entity signaled."[18] Conversationally based indexicals include sound patterns ("wash" vs. "warsh," for example, points to region and social class), the use of pronouns and deictics (e.g., I, you, this, here, there) or gestures to reference people, places, or things, terms of address indicating social roles, patterns of speech that reference speech genres, themselves tied to particularities of social context. Indexicals are neither icons, which bear a physical relationship to the entity signaled (e.g., pictures), nor symbols which bear an arbitrary relationship to what is referenced (e.g., words typically bear no inherent relationship to its referent—the words "tree" and "l'arbre" in no way resemble the thing growing in the backyard). In their use, indexicals reflect, negotiate, and enact anew social knowledge and roles, identity marking, history, ideologies.

Thus in the question, "but what are they doing with *my* money?" not only is "my" an indexical reference to the speaker, but the question itself indexes stockholder or taxpayer speech. It is clear that the customer assumes money paid to the company is still the customer's (indicated by use of the indexical "my") and, from the form of the question (indexically linked to speech genre), that the company is assumed to be accountable to customers for their spending decisions. While Google users or Microsoft customers do not feel the company should consult them on capital investment decisions, electric utility customers were often angry that the company did not consult them before investing in nuclear plants (or other types of generating plants). These assumptions pointed to expectations of a long-lasting, mutually dependent relationship rather than short-lived contractual arrangements characteristic of American purchasing in general. Similarly, the "he" in the NOPSI conversation was an indexical, in this case of white power, thus pointing to a relationship that was problematic. The mutually dependent relationship customers typically assumed between themselves and electric companies was thus, in New Orleans' case, further refracted by the city's racialized inequities that most recently were brought to stark light in the aftermath of Hurricane Katrina.

In consumer research, the analysis of words, ways of talking, or language-in-use have often been confined to advertising texts[19] or other forms of sales pitches.[20] Somewhat ironically, the methods applied to the analysis of advertising are typically not applied to everyday speech—as though the former constitutes a performance and the latter does not. Notable exceptions would be ethnographic work that includes an analysis of discourse, such as that of Ritson and Elliot who analyzed advertising referents in conversations among teenage school mates[21] or interview data subject to semiotic analysis.[22] It should also be noted that analysis of conversation was a standard procedure at Xerox PARC, introduced by Lucy Suchman in the late 1980s, in their ethnographic studies of people and computers.[23] Thus while ethnographic work is occasionally subject to analysis of its discourse (itself viewed as socially and culturally constituted), group discussions (especially something as applied as the focus group) are generally not—in part because they are not seen as a locus for the emergence of cultural ideas.

We think of the relationship between consumer and producer as always a dialogue, if not always a direct one. Producers "speak" through their products, services, retail environments, or forms of communication (Web sites, packaging, advertising, direct mail). Consumers "speak" in the form of protests, purchases, the ways products and services are used in everyday life, or in the ways they talk about the producer or product. Clearly our notion of exchange is broadly construed and includes the social and symbolic dimensions, not merely the economic.[24]

While the Prague School functionalists might still be our muses, the more general heuristic within which the Prague School falls, and on which we rely in conducting analysis, is the heuristic of habitus, that is, in the context of linguistic anthropology, how ways of talking become normatively produced through experience and, in that process, become indexically linked to that situated use.[25] We think it significant when, for example, a twenty-three-year-old focus group respondent refers to a landline telephone as "the house phone." Whether twenty-somethings do or do not have landline phones in their homes, or whether they feel it is a good or bad thing, the idea that a house has been articulated as being in a possessive relationship with a phone is an important observation to note. This articulation marks a new way to describe a landline phone, one that suggests a different relationship of the speaker to the technology, one that foregrounds a possessive relationship of the phone rather than type of technology. It is only because of an awareness of what is an indexically normative way of speaking that significance comes: The traditional way of referring to house phones (in our experience) is "our" or "my" or "the phone," and the landline aspect of the phone was articulated only when contrasting it to other phone technology, as in "I have the landline for the Internet connection." If older respondents foregrounded their "cell phones" in contrast to "the [landline] phone" in linguistic practice, these younger respondents were foregrounding "the house phone" in contrast to "my [cell] phone."

By awareness of the indexical properties of talk (that is, there are normative ways of talking created through daily life), we can understand the subject (be it product, service, company, or issue) better. Whether we analyze them or not, individuals draw on these conventions to express themselves in everyday interaction; such practices are deployed in and constitutive of social life.[26] They might be linguistic markers such as pronouns, but they might be in the form of metaphors, use of speech events like questions, or the display of apparently contradictory opinions. As a heuristic, we think of someone's talk poetically rather than as an immutable display of descriptive fact. The great significance of "what are they doing with my money?" is that it is an unusual query in the context of U.S. business discourse. A more usual or expected occurrence of this question is in context of governmental use of one's taxes or when posed by a company's stockholders. Culturally and linguistically, then, "what are they doing with my money?" in the context of electric utility customers is a marked or performative use of language.[27] Marking has the effect of transferring indexical meanings to new referents; in these cases, utility customers were referencing themselves implicitly as shareholders in the use of "my" or as objects of corporate exploitation in the use of "he."

Analytically, we scrutinize conversations (audiotapes and/or transcripts or notes) and ask the questions: What must be true about the world for this utterance (or set of utterances) to make sense for speaker and fellow discussants? What is implicit in the speech about the subject at hand? What tones of voice are used? What metaphors surface? How are questions phrased? What is assumed by the query or statement vis-à-vis the speaker's worldview? What descriptors are used by respondents? Importantly, where else have we heard these ways of expression? What is a normative usage? Comparison allows us to discern some of the marked and unmarked uses of talk, i.e., their indexical linkages. In all, analysis unearths some of the cultural baggage that infuses talk. In the following example, we illustrate some of the issues that infused consumer understanding of a particular environmental threat, through a consideration of their talk.

"Currents of Death": Talking about Electromagnetic Fields

By the early 1990s public concern about electromagnetic fields (EMF) had risen dramatically. Paul Brodeur's 1989 book, *Currents of Death*, and subsequent articles and talk show appearances in the early 1990s made EMF a household term. Articles about EMF appeared in *Family Circle* ("Danger in the Schoolyard") and *The New Yorker*. The topic was addressed by Ted Koppel on *Nightline* and Larry King on CNN. The concern focused on the link between childhood leukemia and exposure to electromagnetic fields. While the scientific evidence was not definitive, some epidemiological data supported the claim that exposure to EMF increased the probability of childhood leukemia.

Electric utilities had felt the impact of customer concern because "power lines" were often targeted as the source of EMF by media. As a consequence, the issue was a focus of communication for electric utilities. Impetus for resolving the issue had only grown as lawsuits were filed and received attention.[28] A suit brought against San Diego Gas & Electric for allegedly knowing that high-voltage lines can cause cancer, heard in the spring of 1993, was lost by the plaintiffs.[29] While other suits were met with similar results, the unspoken fear for the utilities was that one day a suit would be won, leaving them extremely vulnerable. As task forces were convened within companies to grapple with the limits of their responsibility and the practical implications of policy decisions, consumer concern grew in fits and starts, locally and nationally. Customers' views of company actions and companies' views of customer needs often elicited looks of dismay and skepticism from company executives and customers, respectively. Resolving the discrepant perspectives was a necessary prerequisite for developing a successful EMF policy.

The data drawn on here were collected in two separate studies. In the first (from 1991), the client was a southern electric utility, concerned about potential fallout from customers in response to EMF publicity. At that point, there was no company policy directing communications about EMF, but the history of nuclear plant communications were still capable of making company executives squirm uncomfortably, and the company had plans to extend high-voltage wires in urban and rural areas. Their goal was to gauge customer concerns about EMF and to construct a communications policy that directly responded to these concerns. In the second study (from 1993), the client was also an electric utility, this time in the northeastern United States. This company's EMF policy was quite developed, involving interfaces with state agencies, individualized response to customer queries, and funding of EMF research. They were also facing an EMF-related lawsuit. The director of corporate communications, our client, still felt that company communications lacked credibility.

In both cases, our role as a research supplier was to provide these companies a way to think about their communications needs—in common parlance, a strategy. What were the problems? What were the constraints? What were the corporate options within these constraints? As anthropologists, the goal was to understand EMF in cultural context. From an analytic standpoint, this entailed a focus on customers' definitions of EMF—the meanings implicitly and explicitly attached to the term, the frames of reference invoked by customers to interpret information on EMF. By understanding this cultural etymology, so to speak, there would be a better chance to respond to customer queries. We agreed with clients that the ways customers spoke in focus groups about the issue could be used as a primary means for understanding EMF meanings.

If a single sentence were to summarize customer concern about EMF that emerged from the focus groups, it would have to be, "Does it cause cancer?"[30] The question is a loaded one, and company attempts to answer it were all too often met with a disappointed (sometimes disgusted) shake of the consumer's head. In particular, the question is loaded with expectations of corporate response which, in turn, stemmed from particular beliefs about business and technology. These beliefs tended to frame customer interpretation of EMF information, reactions to EMF stories, or opinions about the EMF issue.

American Industry

In absence of evidence to the contrary, customers generally assumed that the utility industry would follow the historical precedent of industry in general, or at least their idea of industry and its history. So, for example, respondents believed their electric company might sacrifice safety for profit or withhold key information on EMF:

- "They're avoiding prevention to save on costs."
- "Hey, we'd save a lot of government money if we stopped doing this dance . . . and make them come clean . . . and say 'hey, we know you know' and 'you know we know you know' . . . and get on to the solutions and stop the dance."
- "Are they sharing all that matters?"

These statements assumed an adversarial relationship between customer and company in which EMF was viewed as a consumer problem, not one shared by the company. Moreover, the industry most called upon by consumers as an analogy was the tobacco industry: powerful, greedy, self-interested. The unusual relationship between company and customer (based on long-lasting interdependence) did not provide a counterpoint to the negative view of "industry" in general. Instead, it appeared to compound it and catalyze greater intensity of feeling behind the question, "Does EMF cause cancer?" Resolution of the issue, or an adequate response, was all the more important because of the interdependence characteristic of the company-customer relationship.

Even without the imputation of malfeasance, our respondents tended to be blind toward company actions:

- "I haven't heard them address the problem."
- "We're not condemning the fact that [the company is] standing still but . . ."

And, taken to an extreme, consumers' lack of knowledge itself was seen as an intentional act by the company:

- "Why *weren't* we told?"
- "Why are most people ignorant about EMF? Is it a cover-up?"

Taken together, these statements implied that the company ought to be doing something. Indeed the lack of visible action spurred ever greater skepticism about motives.

Electric Technology

Customers exhibited a lack of surprise when faced with EMF headlines. Nods and an air of resignation were more typical responses. This reaction stemmed in part from ambivalent feelings about technology as it was typically observed in the early 1990s. While technology could represent excitement, innovation, and power over surroundings, it was also thought to threaten social relations and be harmful through unintended effects. Technology was definitely a mixed blessing.[31]

At its most positive, technology was seen to confer power and excitement. Examples cited by respondents included microwaves, which allowed individuals greater control over time; computer networks, which easily overrode traditional limits of geography; and medical technologies, which were seen to have extended or improved quality of life. Consumers expected technology to be a source for future stimulation and fun, an attitude of "the best is yet to come." But with the positive was an expected downside. Technology carried an implication of social harm ("we let technology control us"): "Too much" TV, computer games, and so on, was thought to affect the quality of social relationships. Technology could be harnessed for destruction, e.g., smart missiles, and standing too close to a microwave could cause cancer. Breakthroughs at one time yielded disaster at a later time. The initial headlines about EMF were understood within this frame—another technological feat gone awry.

Electric companies in particular were often singled out by customers. High-voltage wires offered a powerful, tangible construct of danger for customers, offering them a means for visualizing EMF and making it concrete. Customers further elaborated their concerns through their own experience with electricity:

- "It's like static electricity when you walk across the carpet."
- "You can feel your hair stand up near an electric pole."
- "It's what happens when you put a fluorescent bulb in a microwave or near a power line and it lights up."
- "Hear 'em [power lines] singing."

The new information for customers in the EMF discourse was that prox-imity, not just touch, was enough to be dangerous.

Some of our respondents also assumed that EMF was a byproduct of electricity. As such, it was seen to be an avoidable phenomenon:

- "Residual electricity"
- "It's too much current on the line" or "Overload"
- "Why does it have to be leaking out?"

Underlying these beliefs were metaphors of both quantity and containment—more is worse, less is okay (as in, "what is the level that can be tolerated?")—and solutions were technical ones that have to do with containment ("shielding," "wrapping," or, for some, "burying").

A key aspect of electrical technology, then, was control: the ability to manage it. Otherwise, chaos threatened. EMF became an example of "unmanaged" technology, raising the question, Why wasn't it managed better? And how can it best be managed now? As the company was culturally implicated, if you will, in the EMF issue, it was looked upon to respond to these implicit questions.

Implications for Communications

Beliefs about American industry and electric technology together with the customer-company relationship put electric companies in a paradoxical space. Customers would continue to ask their local company, "Does EMF cause cancer?" and not hear, accept, or otherwise favorably respond to the company's answer. Similarly, electric utilities tended to respond by taking the question at face value, thereby perpetuating a talking-past-each-other scenario. Similar to presenting pie charts, graphs, and tables of numbers in response to queries on prices, the form of response failed to answer the question.

In responding to customer questions at face value, that is, solely in their propositional value, companies adhered to a myth of objectivism—a belief that the world is composed of objects whose properties are independent of the individuals who experience them, that words have fixed meanings, and individuals just need to be skilled enough to use words precisely and appropriately.[32] Implicit in this view is that linguistic expressions are objects and communication is likened to a conduit metaphor (fixed message from sender to receiver), an ideological view of language that effectively absolves interlocutors of responsibility for the conversational outcome. Thus, if only customers, employees, communicators, and so on were more competent in using words appropriately, everything would be fine. (This view surfaces in a variety of corporate contexts when designers, marketers, CEOs, or whomever take customers to task for just "not getting it" or believe their communication problems would be solved if customers were "just educated" on the topic.)

In the EMF case, utility companies might or might not have made scientific reports available to customers, but in any case they often summarized such studies by stating that "research is inconclusive," that "more studies are being done," and that the company was making every effort by "continuing to fund research." And so the answers seemed, at best, unsatisfying and, at worst, an intentional obfuscation. Company attempts to explain EMF could also have the same effect. Diagrams sometimes looked as though they had been cut from engineering books, and language could unwittingly play on the concerns customers had without addressing them. For example, EMF was described as "an invisible force" that "surrounds" any flow of current in which "the magnitude of the force" depends on electrical current and proximity to the source. From a customer's standpoint, this sounded like radiation. Common measures of EMF (in milligaus) around the home were sometimes given, yet customers had no way to evaluate the significance of these numbers. Indeed, some companies indicated there *was* no way to evaluate significance.

The question "Does EMF cause cancer?" presupposed an expertise on the company's part. In asking it of the company, customers were granting the company authority on the subject in some way. Given the belief customers had about technology (namely that it has unintended consequences), the content of the question might be rephrased as "What are the unintended side effects of electricity production?" or "What's the downside?" Implied also in the question, though, are the other questions deriving from the assumed relationship: "Why do we have this problem?" and "What are you doing about it?" Beliefs about the way big business functions and the unusual nature of the company-customer relationship were additional factors through which corporate responses were filtered and interpreted by customers. There were a number of implications for utility communications:

- Silence can be damning. Apparent silence, in the face of public concern, could take on a specter of active avoidance. Further, the burden appeared to be on the utility company to get the attention of its customers. It was not enough to be able to point to communications efforts; the company had to be able to point to efforts that succeeded. This would be done most convincingly if customers felt they themselves had been reached. Acting out of the ordinary, as an indication that EMF is not business as usual, would have this effect. Candor about the way customers viewed the company's actions around environmental threats would be a first step. Resonating with customers' ideas would indicate the company had spent time trying to understand their realities. Picture an ostrich on a full page ad in the *Wall Street Journal* or local newspaper with a headline something like, "This is us when it comes to EMF" (a statement that acknowledges customer perceptions), followed with an explanation of why the analogy would no longer be appropriate. (Guaranteed to be seen by customers, but oh so unlikely to get past company legal departments.)

- If central to the (perceived) problem, companies were expected to be central to the solution. This means demonstrating leadership and leveraging their expertise. "Funding research" or responding to customer questions, two frequent corporate responses, lacked a proactive stance that typifies leadership. Instead, inertia was signaled, so the clout that customers associated with big business was not being leveraged for the benefit of customers. Thus, a neutral or "supporting" position was interpreted as an act of noncompliance.

- The utility should be an active guide of consumer understanding. Simply providing data, or "the facts," to customers will not help mediate the perceived opposition of company and customer ("they're passing the buck"). Facts about the issue are important to give, but so is a way to interpret the facts. Customers have to come to their own conclusions; the company cannot do this for them, which occurs when companies respond with a "there is no problem" message. But it is critical that the company provide a means for allowing customers to think through the issue; if they do not, another frame of reference will be invoked, one less complimentary of the corporate position.

Mutual Intelligibility

The need to understand company-customer relationships is particularly acute when the marketplace is changing, bringing corporate entities into focus when they might otherwise be invisible. And change is a constant in today's market. New technology catalyzes a repositioning if not elision of what it means to be a communications, computer, or entertainment company. Deregulation and environmental threats cause gas and electric utilities to be more conscious of themselves and their corporate brand. The mainstreaming of environmental or health concerns brings chemical and pharmaceutical companies and the issue of federal regulations into consumer focus. Rapid technological advances keep the computer industry in a state of flux. Globalization of markets raises the question of whether to leverage the corporate brand as a means for introducing particular products.

In all these cases, the role or equity of the corporate brand (such as Verizon, Procter & Gamble, or Bayer) is at issue, in which we differentiate a brand's fundamental equities deriving from its products and pricing from its symbolic equities, which we define as the set of assumptions consumers make about the company's products, services, or their relationship with the company. These assumptions are based on experience, whether or not they have ever used the products or services. In times of change, companies may well rely on these meanings when they speak to customers via advertising, new policies, or products. Equally likely, they will be constrained, if not hampered by these meanings. In leveraging the corporate brand, the logic behind communications runs something like, "If they know us and like (or trust) us, they'll choose (support, believe) us." Yet, knowing what is meant by liking or trust depends on understanding the sources of distrust and being able to mediate them effectively.

We have argued here that literal expressions of like and dislike cannot be taken at face value, that understanding rests on interpreting the ways opinions or statements are made. Communication is not a closed system. It is not an objective enterprise between sender and receiver. It is messy, it is variable, and, most importantly, it is interactional. It is also systematic. Ethnographers of speech recognize this messiness, variability, systematicity, and creativity and employ language-in-use as a means for understanding broader social codes and the dynamics of change and meaning (re)formation. In applying these principles to corporate and consumer environments, by working with marketers, communications executives, or advertising research directors to understand a customer point of view, the enterprise entails by necessity a focus on, and hopefully an awareness of, the constructedness of their own view.

A critical piece of any communications strategy, whether it is developing an EMF policy or antidrug advertising strategy or contributing to a multinational branding initiative for Bayer, is understanding the (implicit) cultural stakes involved. In the EMF case, persuading customers that EMF was not a problem or was not a utility company's problem was unrealistic and a waste of time, given cultural expectations and beliefs about industry, science, and technology. Persuading customers that EMF was not a utility's problem was similarly unrealistic. A strategy attempt to make consumers into engineers was also not viable. Resorting to the "education" of consumers as the means for implementing change in all likelihood would not work. In doing so, one is not so much imparting knowledge as arguing for a particular experiential worldview and, moreover, arguing its superiority. Rather, we suggested that it might be more useful to construct the goal in terms of a desired (and achievable) company-customer relationship—allies, perhaps, in determining the nature of this particular risk. Given the starting point was an adversarial we-they relationship, the strategy had to include a progression of steps, not least of which was being heard in the first place.

Electric utilities may serve as a good example for the need for ethnographic readings of speech because they have historically made mistakes stemming from misreadings of customer talk. But U.S. utility companies are by no means alone in this; it could be any company. Consumer expectations of corporate behavior and the beliefs spurring these expectations will necessarily vary depending on customer or consumer views of industry distinctions, e.g., mass merchants, banking, pharmaceuticals, electronics, or entertainment to name a few, that change over time (e.g., Microsoft in 1990 vs. in 2006). Defining the constraints against which any communication strategy must work is necessary if it is to be heard as intended. Illuminating implicit cultural assumptions by focusing on how consumers choose to talk about the quotidian—whether skin care, phones, coffee, fast food, gardening supplies or cleaners—is crucial. How corporate or brand advertising and other forms of communication, e.g., Web sites, speak to customers will be based on past "conversations" and the ability to interpret their import. Understanding the ensuing talk in context is key, whether in an ethnographic encounter, a focus group, blog, or other form of editorial. Culturally meaningful speech occurs, whatever the context. The point is to appreciate the context and its telling details and to analyze beyond the face, denotational value of words in ways that highlight and untangle the embedded cultural assumptions.

Notes

1. From 1983 to 1993 Denny's practice included a number of electric and gas utility clients. Though largely concentrated in the southern states, it also included utility companies in the Midwest, Northeast and western United States. The time in which this question was so frequently voiced was in the early to mid-1980s—a time when utilities and their customers were feeling the effects of cost overruns in the construction of generating plants.
2. See Catterall and Maclaran (2006) for a contextualization of focus groups in history, theory, and practice. They suggest that a more cultural approach is currently gaining favor in Britain.
3. See Bloor et al. (2001) who suggested that focus groups could and should be used in social science research as a way to explore shared social meaning(s) but who also noted that academic and commercial applications of focus groups diverged significantly. See also Hy Mariampolski's (2006:14–15) brief but poignant comments about the drift of the focus group in consumer research from the qualitative beginnings of Robert Mertons' focused interviewing techniques joined with Carl Rogers' humanism into mechanistic, pre- and neoquantitative techniques. See also note 5.
4. See Gordon (1999).
5. Valentine has long been a proponent in the United Kingdom of including an analysis of language in qualitative market research. See, for example, Valentine and Evans (1993) and Valentine (1995), who argue that language in qualitative interviews should be decoded for its cultural codes, and Valentine (2002), in which she analyzed the discourse of marketing researchers in an effort to illuminate implicit assumptions practitioners made about themselves and to propel a repositioning through discursive choices. The latter analysis clearly illustrates how linguistic practices are constitutive of ongoing meaning.
6. See Denny and Russell (1994). See Blackston (1992) for his stress on the importance of understanding how consumers feel the brand or company thinks about them.
7. Hymes (1962, 1974a, 1974b) and Gumperz and Hymes (1972).
8. Per Hanks, another entailment of speech (or language-in-use) worth noting is that "Speakers and the objects they talk about are part of the same world, a division between subjects and objects is one of the products of linguistic practice, something people create with language, not the irremediable condition against which language must work" (1996:236). See also Silverstein (2004).
9. The early classics include Austin (1962), Bauman and Sherzer (1974), Friedrich (1966), Goffman (1974, 1981), Gumperz and Hymes (1972), Hymes (1962, 1964, 1974a), Joos (1962), Labov (1972), and Sacks, Schegloff, and Jefferson (1974).
10. See Bauman and Briggs (1990, 2003), Blot (2003), Chernela (2003), Chun (2001), Hanks (1996, 2005), Ochs and Capps (2001), Quinn (2005), Schieffelin, Woolard, and Kroskrity (1998), and Silverstein (2004). See also the *Journal of Linguistic Anthropology* 15(1), 2005, an issue that focuses on current work in the arena of language, ideology, and culture.
11. Lindquist (2002:171).
12. The moderator and two observers were European American; the conversation took place in 1984.

13. The use of "he" to reference the utility company was an unusual occurrence. In our experience the pronouns used to reference utilities were either "it" when referring to the company as a business enterprise, as in "it's been poorly run for years," or "they" when referring to a relationship with customers, as in "what are they doing with my money?"

14. The expression "the man" as a referent for white powers-that-be was current in 1984, when this conversation took place.

15. Whether they spoke or not, we would argue that the observers were interlocutors. More generally we consider observers to be interlocutors in focus group conversation even when they are not visible, as the two-way mirror signals their presence.

16. See Mandelbaum (1949) for a collection of Sapir; see also Whorf (1956) and Saussure (1966).

17. See Havránek (1964), Jakobson (1960, 1980), and Mukaøovský (1977).

18. Silverstein (1976:27).

19. See McQuarrie and Mick (1992, 1996, 1999), Mick (1986), Sherry (1987), and Stern (1988, 1989, 1996). While Brown et al. (1999) use Bakhtin as a muse for analysis (one whose work also figures significantly in the concerns of linguistic anthropologists today), Brown and his colleagues apply Bakhtin's theories to advertising, not consumer discourse generally.

20. See Pinch and Clark (1986), Sherry (1988), and Sherry and Camargo (1987).

21. See Ritson and Elliot (1999). See also Wooten (2006), who showed how brands become active ingredients in the social discourse of teenagers, specifically as a resource for ridiculing peers. While his research wasn't ethnographic per se, it illustrates how discourse is creative of cultural practices.

22. See Mick and Fournier (1998).

23. See Suchman and Trigg (1991) and Wasson (2000).

24. See Levy (1978).

25. See Hanks (1996, 2005). Ways of talking are not only normatively produced through experience, but simultaneously frame what is experienced. To reiterate, "[S]peech is a form of engagement in the world" (1996:236), not "with the world." Habitus, then, is "both a product of history and part of what produces history" (1996:239).

26. See, for example, Mendoza-Denton's (1995) analysis of pauses in the Clarence Thomas/Anita Hill Congressional hearings.

27. The notion of markedness stems from the Prague School, a characterization derived from Havránek's distinction between automatized or foregrounded uses of a particular convention within contexts of speech (see Havránek 1964). When an occurrence of a sign (an indexical in Peircean terms) is an expected or usual event, it is automatized; its use would function as a simple affirmation of shared knowledge. When appearing in an unexpected time or place, then the use is marked or foregrounded, bringing shared assumptions into new contexts. In our research we still find the heuristic of markedness useful.

28. See Richards (1993).

29. See Lane (1993).

30. The data consisted of ten group discussions, each group having ten to twelve participants. Four of the groups took place in Louisiana in 1991, the remainder in the

northeastern United States in 1992–1993. In each case, the participants reflected a local demographic profile. In each group, half the respondents were male and half were female, ranged in age from 25 to 60, and tended to have children at home. In the South, income ranged from $20,000 to $50,000 and education ranged from high school to college graduates. In the Northeast, household incomes were higher ($30,000–$70,000) as was educational level (reflecting the client's sense of the key target audience for EMF communications). Participants were only recruited if they felt they were at least "somewhat familiar" with EMF. Concern with the issue varied from none at all to extreme. Each group was audiotaped and the Louisiana groups were also transcribed. Like typical focus groups, our respondents were recruited by local market research facilities, screened for designated criteria, asked to participate, and paid for their time. Each discussion was about two hours long. Unlike traditional focus groups, these conversations were organized with a series of "tasks" that respondents completed as a group, with minimal intervention by us (a format initiated by anthropologist Steve Barnett in 1980 and referenced in Barnett 2003). These tasks were designed to get at potentially significant issues and allow respondents to use their own language to voice their opinions. For example, groups in the Northeast were asked to "write" an editorial for the *New York Times* on EMF. Group participants were asked to debate positions or outline magazine articles on new technology. Participants completed these tasks aloud through a discussion that was managed more or (often) less by an appointed leader. The editorial, for example, would have had a designated editor-in-chief who would direct the group's discussion of what points to include in the editorial, the stand the group wanted to take, and so on. While the scope of topics was determined by us in the "task" format, the ways in which opinions, concerns, or beliefs articulated were relatively unconstrained. Finally, the goal was not the completion of each task, but the examination of the process by which respondents gave voice to their thoughts. Our aim was to discern the meaning embedded in their talk—in this case, about EMF and about electric utilities.

31. See Mick and Fournier (1998), Sherry (1984), and Chapter 4 of this volume for a more recent cultural reading of technology.

32. See Lakoff and Johnson (1980:187) on the myth of objectivism.

Part III
Engaging Entanglements

Entangled

Russell Belk

York University

The chapters in this section are so deeply reflexive and honest, as well as so evocative of the common realities and dilemmas of fieldwork and presentation of findings, that I winced as they led me to think of my own research entanglements. The discussion of issues involving race and ethnicity in Chapter 8 brought to mind an invitation I foolishly accepted a few years ago to give an address at the annual meeting of the International Academy of African Business and Development being held in Atlanta. A little knowledge can be a dangerous thing, and in my case my only Africanist credentials were a year in Zimbabwe teaching MBAs and a few papers and videos I produced on African consumption issues. It was only after accepting the invitation that I learned that the other speakers at the conference were to be the former president of Ghana and Andrew Young—the same person for whom the street outside the hotel was named. Would that this was my only cultural blunder. During a sabbatical year in Romania just after the end of communism, I used to feel sorry for the people who had chickens or rabbits running around in their yards, until I realized that these were the *rich* people of the town who could afford to have a reliable supply of meat and eggs. And one time my wife and I accepted a dinner invitation from a professional couple in the town, only to be told upon our timely arrival that our hosts were sorry that they had already eaten, but wouldn't we please eat and they would sit and talk with us. It was only after this happened a second time with another couple that we realized that our dinner hosts had enough food for two, but not for four; they went without eating in order to be good hosts.

At least in hindsight, getting into predicaments and misunderstandings such as these is easy to criticize. The more difficult issues are more subtle and deserve more delicate consideration. This is exactly the treatment such issues

199

receive in the careful retrospective analysis of the photos from Cuba in Chapter 10. Because this chapter resolves some of the problems highlighted in the two chapters that precede it, I will focus most of my comments on it. It brings to mind Roland Barthes' exposition of his semiotic concept of visual mythology: "I'm at the barber's shop, and a copy of *Paris-Match* is offered to me. On the cover, a young Negro in a French uniform is saluting, with his eyes uplifted, probably fixed on the fold of the tricolour" (Barthes 1972:116). This is only the simple denotative meaning of the photo, however. At the deeper level of the implicit and unspoken myth, a more troublesome reading can be derived: "France is a great Empire, that all her sons, without any color discrimination, faithfully serve under her flag, and that there is no better answer to the detractors of an alleged colonialism than the zeal shown by this Negro in serving his so-called oppressors" (Barthes 1972:116). This deeper mythological reading is more insidious precisely because such meanings go unattended and therefore unquestioned. They are tacitly accepted and wash over the viewer without calling upon us to consider their veracity. Such visual myth-making is also a powerful force in creating brand meanings through advertising. While consumers and the U.S. Federal Trade Commission might well question the truth of denotative and written advertising claims (e.g., new Tide gets clothes cleaner), deeper visual mythological meanings (e.g., Tide is used by successful and beautiful young Caucasians and you will be like them if you use this brand) escape recognition and regulation. We take for granted the myth that is being established or reinforced.

Other subtle biases occur in ethnographic image-making as well. For example, in an analysis of the Web site war photos of American veterans of the "Vietnam War," Doan Nguyen and I find that while American soldiers tend to be ennobled and heroized through upwardly angled camera shots, the Vietnamese depicted tend to be infantilized and lessened through downwardly angled shots (Nguyen and Belk forthcoming). These framing decisions by amateur photographer-soldiers were not likely conscious choices, but they reveal consistent prejudices. In other cases, the biases of photographs that seek to demarcate "them" from "us" are more conscious, as Lutz and Collins (1993) found in their visual analysis of *National Geographic* and as Albers and James (1988) found in their analysis of postcard depictions of Native Americans. On the other hand, Sunderland and Denny show us that the subtleties of visual image making can also be used intentionally for more positive purposes. In describing their Cuba photos they reveal a desire to show a place "where connections between people constituted an infrastructure, were a currency seemingly more salient than money" (p. 285). What they do in photos of Cuba, Rohit Varman does in videos of India (Varman, Belk, and Costa 2006). This short version of a longer video shows merchants in a Calcutta market who freely borrow merchandise from one another when one of them is out of stock, do not demand immediate payment from their customers, trust debts to be paid eventually despite a lack of record keeping, and generally embed their business transactions within the deeper and more significant fabric of human relationships.

Nevertheless, a salient issue that Sunderland and Denny raise is whether such treatments of the humanity of markets in the less affluent world treat these markets as nostalgic projections of our own imagined cultural pasts. We are tempted to portray the Other as unchanging, far away, and frozen in time (Fabien 1983; Helms 1988). Like the Gary Larson cartoon in which the natives scramble to hide their televisions and VCRs from the approaching anthropologists, lest they destroy the anthropologists' illusions of their "primitivity," we have been more likely to hide or ignore reflections of our own consumer culture when we encounter it in the less affluent world (e.g., see Clifford 1997; O'Hanlon 1993). Thus the Cuban photos showing contemporary cars, Coca Cola cans, a Mercedes Benz wheel cover, and a contemporary Chevrolet logo are trenchant reminders that Cuba is not as distant as viewers might otherwise imagine. But there is also an opposite danger here of valorizing our own consumer culture by implying that everyone covets the possessions of those of us in the more affluent world (see Lindstrom 1993). Noting the scarcity of Melanesian "cargo cults" in Aboriginal Australia, Swain (1993) observes that "[s]ome scholars appear almost affronted that it was not more widespread; as though 'primitives' were honour-bound to ritually lust for White goods" (p. 217). One thing that might better balance the depiction of these American, German, and Japanese goods in Cuba would be to show images of the simultaneous presence of Cuban goods such as cigars, music, and rum in the more affluent world as well as images of the tourists flocking from these nations in order to consume Cuba. Although this might better emphasize that the effects of culture contact are always two-way, with the exception of showing the foreign tourists, it would be difficult to achieve this balance in a photo essay about Cuba.

While Cuba's ability to attract such tourists may be good economically and psychically, this need not mean that it is good culturally. We should not imagine that these tourists gain a good cultural understanding of Cuba from their travels. If they are experienced and well-trained ethnographers like the authors, that is one thing. But more casual tourists to Cuba are likely to see a very different country. Whether they are families, couples, snowbirds, or sex tourists, vacationers to this "island paradise" bring a tourist gaze with them that only sees certain things and in certain ways. A video that very effectively emphasizes this point is Stephanie Black's (2001) film, *Life and Debt*. The film begins with calypso music and a planeload of American tourists flying in to Kingston, Jamaica, and being whisked away to an island resort where they are fed, entertained, and allowed to bask in the sun. Intercut with these touristic images are interviews with the eloquent former Jamaican prime minister Michael Manley, Jamaican farmers driven out of work by low-cost imports following the IMF-mandated removal of trade tariffs, and seemingly uncaring comments by the IMF's Stanley Fischer. Gradually the film becomes an indictment of the New World Order, with Jamaica Kincaid narrating the tragedy and a Greek chorus of Rasta men sitting around a fire lamenting it. Although the film has been characterized as being as much polemic as documentary or ethnography, it is highly effective in raising issues of global justice and the power of the more affluent world by contrasting everyday Jamaican economic realities and the blissful naïveté of the tourist.

The visuals discussed and presented in this section are one form of storytelling. The compelling written narratives of these chapters are another. We might well ask what sorts of stories both are telling. Are they polemic tragedies like Black's film on Jamaica? Are they closer to Van Maanen's (1988) confessional tale than his realist tale or impressionist tale? In Clifford's (1986, 1988) terms, are they tales of lost authenticity, ethnographic surrealism, or allegories of some sort? I would suggest that they do not belong neatly to any one of these genres. In effect, the narrative constructed in Chapter 10 merely uses the visual story told in a previously published photo essay (Sunderland and Denny 2005) as a visual elicitation or "autodriving" stimulus in order to reflect on the meanings of the original story, interrogate the authors' own motivations and biases, and raise postmodern issues involved in creating and presenting visual narratives. That is, it is a tale of a tale. It is the director's cut commentary. It makes the original story more polyvocal by discussing alternative scripts and alternative readings. Moreover, it raises questions of ethics, the meaning of informed consent, and the power of representation. And more than anything it is a deeply reflexive account. Jay Ruby (2000) describes the ideal of reflexivity succinctly:

> To be reflexive in terms of a work of anthropology, is to insist that anthropologists systematically and rigorously reveal their methods and themselves as the instrument of data generation and reflect upon how the medium through which they transmit their work predisposes readers/viewers to construct the meaning of the work in certain ways. (2000:152)

There could hardly be a better demonstration of this process than the deconstruction of the original photo essay on Cuba. Coupled with the further consideration of the discrepancies between filmmaking realities and audience assumptions presented in Chapter 9 and the forthright discussion of the entanglements of race and ethnicity in Chapter 8, the authors provide a provocative problematization of ethnography and videography. After raising these issues in the first two chapters, they conclude with a compelling demonstration of an exemplary resolution in the third of these chapters.

If there were any doubts in encountering this book that it would be a self-congratulatory set of triumphant war stories, the three chapters that follow will quickly dispel them, if earlier chapters have not already done so. If there was any suspicion that this would be an applied book without academic relevance (or, for that matter, an academic book without applied relevance), these illusions will be thoroughly shattered as well. "Entanglements" implies that we are all interconnected, across disciplines, businesses, universities, and cultures. What follows is an enveloping organic narrative with wonderful tendrils that will tickle and tease. But as the reader becomes ever more entwined with the narratives nurtured in these chapters, be alert for the occasional well-placed thorn that should prick our complacency and pierce our consciences.

Reflexivity and Visual Media: Entanglements as a Productive Field

Vilma Santiago-Irizarry and Frederic W. Gleach

Cornell University

In the decade or so since "reflexivity" became a central issue in American anthropology, we have become inured to angst-laden or breast-beating presentations in which the reflexive anthropologist and his/her ever-so-enlightened concerns about the relationships between research and those researched, between subject and scholar and audience, occupy a central ground. Even though these concerns go back virtually to the origins of the discipline, many identify a turn toward awareness of the politics of interrelatedness in these domains with works like *The Predicament of Culture* (Clifford 1988) and the contributions in *Writing Culture* (Clifford and Marcus 1986). These works and others of the mid-1980s—part of the trend often labeled as "postmodern"—were undeniably critical in shaping this as a popular positioning in the field, but other, possibly more useful, strands can be found in earlier work that seems less well known (or at least less frequently cited). And the domain of visual representation, reflexively explored in the following chapters with a refreshing absence of angst or arrogance, was a crucial focus for some of those earlier developments.

We take as particularly significant here the efforts of Jay Ruby to bridge the arts and sciences and develop an anthropological mode of visual expression (e.g., Ruby 1971, 1975, 1976, 1980, and many more recent works). This project grew out of the foment of the 1960s and early 1970s, perhaps best expressed in the anthropological literature by the contributions to Dell Hymes's collection *Reinventing Anthropology* (1972)—but with roots going even deeper. Reflexivity, in Ruby's terms,

> is to structure a product in such a way that the audience assumes that the producer, process, and product are a coherent whole. Not only is an audience made aware of these relationships, but they are made to realize the necessity of that knowledge. . . .

205

[T]he producer deliberately, intentionally reveals to his [sic] audience the underlying epistemological assumptions which caused him to formulate a set of questions in a particular way, to seek answers to those questions in a particular way, and finally to present his findings in a particular way. (1980:157)

Reflexivity in this sense does not foreground the anthropologist as an act of self-involvement or promotion, but rather contextualizes the work so that viewers/readers can better evaluate it. And happily, the latter is what we find here. That this should occur in a work that would be classified as practicing or "applied" anthropology may be less surprising when considered in this context, as "relevance" was a key concept in many of the reinventions contemplated in the 1960s and 1970s; this is a type of work that inescapably and openly confronts the power relations that always are at play in ethnographic work and its presentation.

The complicated relationships between academic and "applied" anthropology are interestingly highlighted by these considerations of reflexivity and context. Despite reflexivity having become doxic, in Bourdieu's term, for U.S. anthropology since the 1980s, many anthropologists remain curiously uncritical concerning our institutional locations, epistemological purposes, and overall relevance in a conflicted world. Or perhaps this is not so curious: A parochial and inbred reflexivity conveniently supports the seeming dominance of academic praxis. Sunderland and Denny appropriately invoke Bourdieu's concept of habitus, and given his theoretical treatment of institutional and professional cultures, that theorizing provides a productive analytical frame for our comments (or perhaps our attention to this may be due to the fact that Vilma is currently reading Reed-Danahay's [2005] analytical and intellectual biography of Bourdieu). Turning to Bourdieu also reflects the theoretical place he is currently accorded in academia, as well as his felicitous critique of it as a field. We do not mean to reassert academic primacy into the very challenges and advocacy that Sunderland and Denny are raising as they interrogate the underpinnings of a line of distinction that is more honored in its breach than otherwise. But we find resonance in Bourdieu's work—much as in Foucault's (Vilma's biography is particularly embedded in praxis, after toiling in law and in both applied and academic anthropology). And class empathy as well, since, after all is said and done, Bourdieu was the prototypical provincial in the lofty academic circles of Paris, a scholar whose intellectual agenda was animated by a deep, Weberian and Goffmanesque suspicion of notions about Western rationality that overlook its historical and sociocultural constructedness.

Our own personal ethnographies of anthropology and academia—our reflexivity—suggest that academic anthropologists often tend to downplay their professional identity as anthropologists in favor of the mantle of academia. Contrarily, personally—and quite likely as a result of our specific histories and social locations—we see ourselves as anthropologists in academia, rather than as academics who are anthropologists—that is to say, not so much Homo Academicus, but Homo [et Muliere] Anthropologicus. In anthropology departments, we suggest, one finds an overlap of these contending—and potentially incommensurate—academic and anthropological fields.[1] Crucially here, the boundaries of a field are policed through the validation of particular practices, discourses, texts, and forms of knowledge over others, which in the case of anthropology has been dominated by academic institutions and those who occupy them.

There is, of course, no intrinsic coherence to these processes. One might expect, since U.S. anthropology developed as committed applied practice—and since the late 1970s over 50 percent of anthropology Ph.D.s have been plying the profession in nonacademic employment (Santiago-Irizarry 2002)—there would be no strong division between academic and applied or practicing anthropology. Yet Vilma had to argue for her ethnographic reports from evaluation work to be considered as part of her professional credentials in her tenure process; she only succeeded by comparing them to archaeological reports, which are conventionally counted. They remained, though, marked and liminal, especially because they were proprietary, as far as actual publication credentials were concerned, tainted by an aura of instrumentality rather than as knowledge production. Fred's work, largely ethnohistorical and archival, equally subsists in a gray zone, for academic anthropologists who like to claim disciplinary distinction and privilege their practice as "ethnographic"—especially now, when many other fields have declared their own allegiance to and dependence on the method. The vaunted mandate to be "ethnographic" is more often than not objectifyingly defined as hanging out and talking to people in faraway places—preferably somewhere best reached by a plane, never a subway—despite many long-standing exceptions who have chosen to work "local" (Darnell 2001, especially Ch. 9; Gleach 2002; Passaro 1997).

As we write this, it has been ten years since Gupta and Ferguson (1997a) published their seminal critique of the fetishization of the field and the epistemological, institutional, and ideological implications that issue from its spatial objectification. But although their critique has been mainstreamed, the exoticization of the field is still being reproduced, making evident how academic anthropology polices the boundaries of its field for the purpose of establishing distinction within the academy. We relate this habitus of the exotic particularly to Chapter 8 here, since Sunderland and Denny organize their discussion of fieldwork around the persistent differentials of ethnoracial identity that prevail in the United States, where one's sociocultural location is inherently marked through the two identity categories of race and ethnicity.

The discussion here of the contradictions that arise in fieldwork when one's focus of inquiry is an objectified identity underscores how we often presume transparency in our interactions with our collaborators. Identity claims are currently both expected and rewarded in U.S. society, as they allow one to locate oneself and to be located in a grid of entitlement. As documented here in nuanced detail, though, the intersubjective encounters of ethnographic fieldwork ambiguate one's own stereotypical expectations. Furthermore, the situation is routinely compounded by widely held unproblematized notions about culture, and a significant potential contribution that this work offers to corporate culture is to disabuse some of those objectified ideas about culture. As Sally Engle Merry has pointed out, in the context of human rights activism and its practitioners' misunderstanding of the anthropological notion of culture:

> Over the last two decades, anthropology has elaborated a concept of culture as un-bounded, contested, and connected to relations of power. It does not consist only of beliefs and values but also practices, habits, and commonsensical ways of doing things. The contemporary anthropological understanding of culture envisions a far more fluid, contested, and changing set of values and practices than that provided by the idea of culture as tradition. Culture is the product of historical influences rather than evolutionary change. Its boundaries are fluid, meanings are contested, and meaning is produced by institutional arrangements and political economy. Culture is marked by hybridity and creolization rather than uniformity or consistency. Local systems are analyzed in terms of national and transnational processes and are understood as the result of particular historical trajectories. This is a more dynamic, agentic, and historicized way of understanding culture . . . moving away from the notion that culture is opposed to capitalism and instead emphasiz[ing] the hybrid, dialectical, historically evanescent character of contemporary culture. (2003:67)

Ultimately, the overarching argument developed here is consonant with Ana Celia Zentella's (1997) notion of anthro*politics*. Working within the field of linguistic anthropology, with its current preoccupation with language ideologies and practices that impinge upon state policies, Zentella coined this as a disciplinary agenda, mandate, and praxis to bridge the gap between researchers and policy makers. She advocates for transcending the ivory towers of academia and for a committed anthropological practice dedicated to the generation of useful knowledge, not just that which can get you tenure, promotion, and academic distinction.

As well as being theoretically strong and politically astute, the research presented here is collaborative on several levels—between multiple researchers, and between researchers and "others" including both those being studied and those commissioning the studies—and these multiple collaborations are highly productive not only for the research itself, but also for our considerations of the process of ethnographic research (cf. Lassiter 2005 on collaborative anthropology). It is notable that the authors do not seek to present themselves as infallible experts at negotiating this minefield, but rather offer examples of projects that have both "succeeded" and "failed"—in different ways and sometimes both simultaneously—and that complicate rather than simplify our understandings of the relationships of identity, representation, and power. Denny and Sunderland's discussion of their research beautifully documents the phenomenological dimensions of fieldwork, with its inherent messiness, contingency, contradictions, intersubjectivity, and relationality—entanglements, indeed, but ones that should not be elided. Sociocultural experience *is* messy, contingent, contradictory, intersubjective, and deeply relational. It is precisely this contextualization that allows the authors to pose their well-articulated arguments concerning visual representations—and the contemporary technologies that produce and reproduce them—as mainstays of the anthropological toolkit.

It is easy to critique many uses of images, still or moving, on grounds of the transparency that is often presumed, the politics of their creation or presentation, and various other issues, but a real contribution of this work is to show that for all the potential pitfalls it is better to work with visual materials, remaining cognizant of the hazards, than to avoid them.

Note

1. We use fields here in the strict sense of Bourdieu: domains of historically constituted and structured activities or practices characterized by a struggle over the power to determine and stratify value through the ranking of divergent sets of practices, as per the operation of a symbolic market.

8

Anthropology and Consumer Segmentation: The Terrain of Race and Ethnicity

In this section of the book our goal is to make explicit some of the entanglements we face as anthropologists working in the consumer research realm. These entanglements have their basis in a knotted network of differing epistemologies, politics of power and professions, institutionalized exigencies and practicalities, and the embedded realities and emergent emotions of differentially positioned social actors. Our goal throughout this section, and particularly in this chapter, is to make these entangled epistemologies, politics, exigencies, and emotions ethnographically explicit. In essence, we want to provide an ethnographic account of what it means to do anthropology in the consumer research arena. We want to provide examples of how things happen and the interventions, thoughts, and feelings that accompany those events.

The examples we use in this chapter are taken from projects in which matters of race and ethnicity have been foregrounded through the process of consumer segmentation. This terrain is an illustrative one because of its highly charged saturation with political, professional, and performative elements as well as the stark epistemological differences and cross purposes we encounter as anthropologists. As anthropologists, it is an analytic given that categories of race and ethnicity, including whiteness, are culturally constituted and, as consumer researchers, it is obvious that many of the practical activities of marketing and consumer research (e.g., the development of products, advertising, or research centered on distinct consumer segments) are constitutive elements of racial and ethnic categorizations.[1] Yet, we have found that this theoretical framework and the constitutive nature of professional activities are too often ignored and overlooked by others in day-to-day practice.[2] The very possibility that race and ethnicity are socially constituted is generally not contemplated, much less considered as due to one's own actions. Rather, race and ethnicity are too often reified as categories, essentialized as identities, and combined with equally reified and essentialized notions of "culture." As we noted in Chapter 2, anthropologists can be called on to research the "culture" of a group, which carries a danger of reinforcing the reification and essentialization, even while trying to illuminate and nuance understandings. In the case of race and ethnicity, our goal as anthropologically oriented consumer researchers is to remain true to an analytic understanding of race and ethnicity as socioculturally constituted and to instantiate that framework in a way that is helpful to our clients. Underlying this goal resides the assumption that the constitution and reconstitution of ethnoracial realities lies in the practices and projects of everyday life, and that inserting the anthropological framework into the projects of business can help decenter reductionistic and problematic social processes. It is an intervention against hierarchical, dehumanizing, and disempowering racism, based on the viewpoint so aptly encapsulated by Rodolfo Stavenhagen's "Race does not beget racism, but rather racism generates races."[3] Without question, inserting and embodying this framework takes effort, one enveloped in a politics of sincerity and hope. And of course, in day-to-day practice, it is not always easy.

We turn now to the ethnographic details, beginning first with the telling of our experiences at a Hispanic marketing conference, in which the frame of the conference and the material we presented help to highlight the terrain and the analytic endeavor. Then we move into the recounting of a specific project, in which the setting up, carrying out, and communicating of research findings evidence the details of the knotted network (entangled epistemologies, politics of power, institutionalized exigencies, and emergent emotions) as instantiated in everyday life. There is a long tradition within anthropology of using stories to convey ethnographic texture. In this chapter, we draw on this narrative form as the means to best convey the ethnographic details of the knotted networks, revealing some of the further embedded knots in endnotes.

Practica = *Práctica?*

In 2005 we were asked to speak at the Strategic Research Institute's (SRI) 11th Annual "Marketing to U.S. Hispanics and Latin America" conference. Speakers and attendees at this conference included advertising and marketing specialists for the Latino/Hispanic market, corporate executives and developers of Latino/ Hispanic media, people responsible for Latino/Hispanic target markets within larger corporate entities (for instance, the multicultural marketing manager for Volkswagen of America), as well as other consumer research professionals. The brochure boasted that conference speakers were a "Who's Who Roster of Trailblazers to Boost Your ROI."[4]

Our featured-speaker status at this conference had been set in motion by the efforts of Rupa Ranganathan, the multicultural conference organizer for SRI. As Rupa told us later, she was often happy to try something or someone new and even accept the risk of possible failure, if the attempt also held the promise of potentially creating more interesting and dynamic conferences. She had been searching the Web for a different kind of speaker and found us. When she called, we assumed that she had found and invited us because of a then recently published article centered on Mexican American identities and the negotiation of ethnicity in the practice of market research.[5] But we told her we did not, by any stretch of the imagination, fancy ourselves specialists in this niche and, moreover, if we did speak we would probably not be saying the kinds of things she or others might expect to be said at a Latino/Hispanic marketing conference. Our talk, we maintained, would center upon notions of ethnicity and race as ideas that often tended to emphasize differences and thus downplay sharing and interchange among people, while in real life people and goods were always in flux—crossing boundaries, diversifying, shifting, blending, and changing.[6] As we promised in the conference brochure and truly hoped we could do, we proposed to show how "appreciating both the permeability of boundaries as well as ethnicity as socially constituted could help marketers see opportunities that might otherwise be dismissed."

Rupa assured us this would be fine. As we later learned, Rupa's Web search discovery of a relevant article had not sparked the telephone call to us. Rather, it was because of our backgrounds in anthropology and because of our company name, Practica. Rupa had just thought that she wanted to do something different and to have an anthropologist speak would be different, and our company name seemed a good fit. In fact, we had no idea how good a fit our name was for a Latino/Hispanic consumer research firm until, as we approached the podium to speak, we heard *Práctica*, clearly announced in Spanish, as our company affiliation. *Práctica* is the Spanish word for practice. As some later told us, based on print, they had never thought that Practica was anything other than the Spanish word. Of course we were *Práctica*.

We had been nervous about this forty-five-minute presentation in any case. We were fearful of being stereotyped as Anglos and thereafter skewered. But, we were also fearful of offending and we feared feeling, sounding, and actually being stupid. This really was not our niche, and how can novices speak to specialists about what matters in their field? Rupa had a good idea, but what were we doing? As part of the fear, in the weeks preceding the presentation, Patti was chatting over dinner with a young journalist friend about the talk. They were ruminating over what kind of opening example might make needed points and draw the audience in—a "lead," in journalistic parlance. The friend suggested that we open by recounting a quotidian experience that all would know. She suggested we discuss the telephone menus encountered almost any time one placed a call to a business, agency, or organization. These initial menus meant that the first thing now encountered when making such a call was the direction to press one (or, in some cases, two) to continue in Spanish. Eh bien voilà (she had a French background), the audience would be drawn in.

This was a potentially good idea, she had grasped the kind of social practices constitutive of a Latino/Hispanic market that we were talking about; yet, it seemed almost too neat, too journalistic for our purposes. Or maybe it just did not seem right because it embodied too much worry. It seemed to us that in all probability those in the audience would be exactly the people who would have been powerful forces in the institutionalization of those kinds of telephone connection options within their organizations.

We decided to proceed instead with the opening example of "LGBTQQ TFAGIPBDSM . . ." or the "endless acronym," as it then circulated on Wesleyan's college campus. The catalyst for this example had been an earlier dinner table conversation in which a young family friend who had recently begun her undergraduate studies at Wesleyan regaled the gathered group with the importance of the endless acronym on Wesleyan's campus. The endless acronym, she had told us, stood for Lesbian, Gay, Bisexual, Transgender, Queer, Questioning, Transsexual, Flexual (a term that reflects the concept of sexuality on a continuum rather than in a binary, i.e., male and female), Asexual, G (which we said at the time we needed to bracket as she could no longer re-member, but now know stands for Genderqueer), Intersex, Polyamourous (which is more a concept of relationship status than gender, as polyamourous indicates more than one sexual partner, regardless of gender); then the BD goes together for bondage/disciple, DS dominance/submission, SM sadism/masochism, and importantly these last four fall under the umbrella of variant—not deviant—sexual practices. Finally, and notably, we pointed out that the three dots were purposefully part of the endless acronym, indicating that the acronym could include other things, and that it was open to and, in fact, likely to change.[7]

The point of starting with this example, based in gender and sexuality rather than race or ethnicity, was simply to set out the tenet of the socially constituted nature of categories with which and within which we live. Thereafter, we invoked notions of European American women of New York City's jazz community who constituted themselves as African American,[8] and finally put an actual toe in the water of Latino issues with the story of Yolanda and the store where she liked to buy meat.

While projecting photographs of rabbits and chickens in what clearly looked more like small farm rather than farming industry cages, as well as an image of a storefront sign and awning that included both *"Pollos"* and "Live and Dressed," we told the story of meeting Yolanda in the course of a study on food and ways of eating in American life. Yolanda had been living in Chicago for seven years. Originally from Ecuador, she had taken us to her favorite meat store where she enjoyed moments of friendship and camaraderie with the owner. She liked to purchase meat there as she found the freshness of the meat as well as the physical and social environment important counterpoints to the large U.S. grocery store experience. The store provided Yolanda with memories of "home." The store did enjoy a Spanish-speaking clientele, as the store sign's inclusion of Spanish would suggest. While cages of live rabbits and chickens, as well as loose chickens that walked about our feet as we chatted, were impressive given the store's location in downtown Chicago (perhaps a mile from the Sears Tower), what was even more impressive was the store's Palestinian owner. He exuded genuine warmth as well as perspicuity in being able to apprehend cultural symbolism and to use it to strategic benefit. Not only was he able to provide Yolanda with memories of Ecuadorian home in downtown Chicago, he deepened the organic "freshness" and prestige value of his chickens by stressing that all of the livestock was raised by the Amish. He was clearly proud of his livestock's Amish roots. While he maintained that there was a taste difference between his freshly slaughtered, Amish livestock and that which was sold in grocery stores, he also told us that he believed that the taste difference was "mostly mental." Able and apt businessman that he was, he had managed to negotiate the selling of his product in a way that touched upon the symbolic memories of "home" of his Latino clientele while simultaneously exploiting the upscale symbolic connections of healthy and organically raised animals in the United States by tapping into the cachet and symbolic associations of the Amish. He also tempted us to buy our next Thanksgiving turkeys there—despite what he had said or maybe because of what he had said—we were also now convinced that the turkeys he sold would taste better.

At around this point in the talk, we let the audience know that what we were trying to be explicit about were the ways in which the categories we live with, be they categories of sex and gender, race, or ethnicity, are social and cultural creations that we—as social and cultural beings—create, recreate, strategically manipulate, resist, contest, work around, embrace, discard, and change. What we were advocating was for us all to keep clearly in our minds, and to appreciate, that ethnicity (as a category, as an entity, as a phenomenon) was socially created. We urged people to think about ethnicity (in general, and of whatever sort) as created by social ideas and by living and acting as if those ideas were true, not because of some sort of differential essence that resides within people or their practices. Our point was that ethnicity, ethnic categories, and ethnic target markets were not based on naturally existing inherent qualities of people, but were ideas and concepts that we as social beings had created. These were then groupings we lived in and with, often as if they were very natural and important because they became meaningful and real, but only because we *made* them meaningful and real through the course of socially constituted thoughts, actions, and institutions in the first place.[9]

To make these somewhat abstract notions come alive, we used examples we thought would have resonance for the audience. We spoke of "Hispanic" as an umbrella category of ethnicity that had gained relevance in the context of the U.S. environment and which created a blending, a sense of comparability, and a kind of sharing between people with origins in Ecuador, Panama, Puerto Rico, Mexico, Venezuela, and *maybe* Cuba (we were trying to joke) that in other contexts would not be viable. We verbalized the obvious: that "Hispanic" was itself a contested term. Should it really be the Latina/Latino, not the Hispanic, marketing conference? And we acknowledged that many Hispanic marketing endeavors had also clearly been successful, citing examples—ranging from banking and mortgage lending through Volkswagen, Hennessey, Clamato, and the National Basketball Association, to the selling of George W. Bush—that we had heard discussed in conference presentations the day before. But, as we told the audience, the questions we all should consider were: What more would be gained? What doors could be opened up by moving beyond these categories? What would fully appreciating the categories' socially constituted nature imply? What would be the expanded and unexpected opportunities? What would be the benefits of thinking about race and ethnicity in terms of semiotics enacted in everyday practice, not naturally occurring traits, charac-teristics, or groupings of people?

As a further concrete example, we then drew upon the study among Mexican American consumers—the one we had assumed, erroneously, had led to our invitation. In this study the client wanted to derive guidelines for developing products that would be of interest to Mexican American consumers. We told how in the process of setting up the research we had gone through difficult negotiations over who would qualify as a respondent. Would it include only people who had immigrated to the United States, or would we also include those whose parents came to the United States or even those whose more distant ancestors were Mexican (because, after all, part of the territorial United States used to be Mexico)? Would we recruit people who spoke only Spanish, mostly Spanish, or both Spanish and English at home? And yet, as it turned out, the splitting of hairs over whom to recruit based on such criteria did not even matter. In the course of the work, it became obvious that these distinctions were not, by any means, key to locating people who considered themselves to be "very Mexican." Nor were these distinctions key to generating ideas for new products. The reality was much more complicated, creative, and inspired.[10]

There was blurring because of consumers' travel between the United States and Mexico: the vacations and summers in Mexico; the people born in the United States but brought up in Mexico; the crossing back and forth for those who lived near the border. There was the interplay of cultural practices: the open enchiladas layered in a pan "like lasagna." There was Isabel, a Mexican American grandmother who wore an apron emblazoned with "Texas," as she cooked scratch tortillas on her *comal,* and told us that *Betty Crocker* was her favorite cookbook. We looked at the Norman Rockwell image of a family praying at a Thanksgiving table hanging on her kitchen wall while tasting the *carne guisada* that sat on her table. If in business minds the goal was to create products that would be of special relevance to Mexican Americans, it was the consumers who pointed out that a clear-cut distinction between what is Mexican and what is American was not easy to make. Wal-Mart and Pizza Hut were places frequented on trips to Mexico; Mexican brands were part of the repertoire in the United States.[11]

We also made explicit how certain respondents, multigenerational inhabitants of the United States, had recreated and reconfigured their identities and consumption practices into "pure Mexican." For instance, Norma, past middle-aged at the time of the interview, told us she had grown up in the United States, barely feeling "Mexican." But then, after marriage to her husband, a professor from Mexico City, that had changed. In essence, she had married the heritage and class status of her husband, which included a search for commodities that were "pure Mexican." In line with "pure Mexican," in her Texas household, there were active efforts to resist "Tex-Mex" mingling. The reach was for the more "pure," "authentic," and "high-level" offerings from the cultural palate, as embodied in a bottle of tequila hand-imported from Mexico. This old, re-cycled Johnnie Walker bottle with a "Tequila Almendrado" label handwritten in marking pen across two pieces of masking tape symbolically embodied the really special, really exclusive, really real, really pure, really Mexican—Johnnie Walker bottle and all (see Figure 8.1).

Figure 8.1 Hand-imported Tequila Almendrado—"authentic" Mexican Tequila in recycled Johnnie Walker bottle

Among the inspirations for the corporation from respondents such as Norma was our suggestion to further mine the "high-end Mexican" realm considered to be "culturally authentic" and "pure" and to market products from this realm to the high-end general as well as Latino market. In so doing, we were suggesting that a U.S. corporation act to further insert high-end Mexican "culturally authentic" and "pure" products into the globalized elite cultural realm of commodities that circulates through our contemporary world. It was unlikely that company clients had this outcome in mind when they began this research (as in the United States, "Mexican" frequently conflates with ideas of low status), but it was an important outcome of the research. And, arguably, it was only in a world of socially constituted ethnicity, international market forces, and deterritorialized national ethnicities that such a thing could happen.

To further illustrate the value of appreciating racial and ethnic categories as social and semiotic constructs—not ones of essentialized difference—we then told the tale of a research project we did for a direct-selling company. In this case our client wanted to expand the success of their in-home selling business among African American and Latina customers, whom they saw as their "ethnic" market and clearly marked as "other." They wondered, Do African American and Latina women like our products? Would they want to attend and host selling parties? Would they be interested in becoming sales consultants?

Per the client's request, we convened separate focus groups of consumers who identified themselves as African American, Latina/Hispanic, and, for comparison, European American. In terms of the results of the study, there was no question that the company's selling process worked for everyone. Many of the African American and Latina respondents talked about experiences they had encountered at home shopping parties of this and other companies. For no one was direct sales perceived as a general mismatch, either as a customer or as a potential seller. The ethnic complexities of work, marriage, and social life also meant that the parties were far from the ethnic enclaves the company had envisioned. This was true not only because of the invitation of coworkers and friends, but also because of the invitation of family members. Realities of marriage often meant that inviting one's family meant inviting those who would be classified as belonging to another ethnic group.

The company's products were assessed as higher-than-average quality among all respondents, and generally liked. Almost everyone owned, or wanted to own, at least some of these products. At the same time, what did become apparent in the groups were the ways the company was missing the mark in the symbolic connotations and presentations of race and ethnicity in their product selection and catalogs. In group after group, there were certain products—one could characterize them as those with Uncle Sam or kitschy, homey-cozy motifs—that would become the brunt of jokes. These products were read as just "too white." And equally importantly, there were jokes about safari motif products as being just "too black," and "candles like the ones you could buy in bodegas" as too stereotypic. Among the egregious semiotic offenses were the ways that the singular "targeted" products in catalogs, akin to a single black baby doll amid a large shelf of otherwise all white dolls, telegraphed both tokenism and "Everything else here is for white people."

The groups expressed the desire to not pigeonhole, presume, or mark consumption preferences with race and ethnicity. Respondents asked for products that did not limit or define or read as being for a certain group of people. There was a desire for a more inclusive product selection, i.e., products that read "could be for anyone" as well as more complicated, nuanced, and diverse evocations of the semiotics of ethnicity.[12] Interestingly in this particular case, the products that at that time were often picked out as desirable and that were currently popular for everyone had motifs explicitly interpreted by respondents as Asian, for instance, those displayed on bamboo mats and on dishes on which sushi was typically served in the United States.

In the end it was garnering a more sophisticated and nuanced understanding of the realities of race and ethnicity in the United States and opening up to greater complexity and diversity, not a focus on static, simplified race/ethnicity seen to reside in the essence of their target customers, that was needed to expand their business. The company needed to examine the semiotics of race and ethnicity as communicated in their product selection and catalogs. They had focused their attention on whether the process of home party shopping would work (or not) for ethnically defined target audiences and on trying to create and offer products that would be of specific interest to these audiences. Yet, their efforts to create products that would be of particular interest for black or Latina consumers were also only marking the rest of their products as "made for whites" and simultaneously positioning the few products offered for black and Latina customers as condescending insults. Meanwhile, the company was totally missing the point that they already had a good thing going—black and Latina consumers were already buying their products.

Thus, the kinds of questions they needed to address to increase their sales were not, "What do African Americans want?" or "Do Latinas like this design?" Instead, they needed to ask questions that would lead to a clear read on the ethnoracial symbolism embedded in their products and product presentations and then act accordingly. They needed to consider whether the embedded semiotics were limiting or diverse, inclusive or exclusive, stereotypic or boundary-breaking. The kinds of questions in need of answering were: "What are communications implicitly saying about what this company thinks about (my/others') ethnicities?" "What do the company's products assume and convey about race/ethnicity?" "Is the unmarked category assumed to be white?"

In the end, we argued to marketers at the SRI conference that—as we felt many of them already knew or believed—for corporations the Latino market is often looked at as a goose that lays the golden egg: If we can just crack that market, we will have another whole source of profits.[13] But, the thing is that there is not one goose (group) out there that is different and that lays golden eggs. Rather, it is all people weaving symbolic matrices, and we are all in these matrices together. Thus, in dealing with ethnicity, we must think of all of us as social actors who actively negotiate, react to, come to terms with, play with, strategically deploy, and also create ethnic symbols and practices. We urged the audience to see the strength in recognizing and capitalizing on arenas of blurring, overlap, and boundary crossing, not only in the stressing of differences. We closed by maintaining that a Palestinian store owner who had managed to make Yolanda feel at home and comfortable, while extolling the upscale virtues of the organic farming practices of the Amish in downtown Chicago, should serve as inspiration.

During our presentation, some audience members had been smiling, some were furiously taking notes, and some were simply intently looking at us. It was hard to know if they were being attentive, attending to other things, or thinking we were nuts. Some of the responses to our talk were also surprising and reminded us—again—that there is no audience that one should simplify or underestimate. One might think of an assembled group of marketers as a highly conservative group, but among the first to approach us was a relatively young woman who came up to say how much she enjoyed hearing our talk. She was herself a recent graduate of a liberal, Wesleyan-like college, and she said it was nice to hear someone talking along the lines of the endless acronym. These were the kinds of things that she was used to hearing and clearly it had been music to her ears to hear it here. Another told us later that he was taking such good notes because he wanted to borrow some of our examples for use in his own internal corporate presentations. Over lunch, he also politely pointed out that while he found it interesting, he was not completely sure what others thought because, really, what we were suggesting was also a questioning of their professional existences. That was true. As Arlene Dávila has pointed out in *Latinos, Inc.*, it is not only that targeted marketing and advertising has helped to create Latino/Hispanic ethnicity as a category, but that these endeavors have simultaneously created the professional existence and credentials of those working within advertising agencies and organizations.[14] Things we had heard in the formal conference presentations made this clear. Conference speakers had hinted that spreading the news within corporations about the increasing numbers of Spanish speakers was a way of retaining and enhancing department budgets.[15] Presentations also made clear the ways in which efforts were undertaken to prove the importance of one's work or department and about carving out expertise within or for a larger entity. Implicit enactments of ethnicity and less formal cocktail party asides hinted at the importance of ethnicity as professional credential. Whispered annoyed gripes on the sidelines over the preponderance of Spaniards among highly valued creatives and creative directors within advertising agencies were cases in point.[16] And, of course, we had been engaged as *Práctica*, not Practica.

Entering the Cells of Authenticity Discourse

We turn now to recounting the constitutive details of a project undertaken in the fall of 2005. The purpose of the study was to conduct a cultural analysis of mothers' desires for kids and family, especially surrounding food. And so, we began organizing this study as we do many, that is, we were trying to assure that our overall sample of families would include families that self-identified as

Latino, African American, and European American, and perhaps also Asian—depending on the city where we did the research. With this understanding we had written the proposal and begun to organize the project. In this case, the various stakeholders' interests and concerns were not made entirely clear to us (or perhaps to anyone else) from the beginning.

Then the e-mail and phone messages started trickling in. As is often the case for large U.S. corporations, this particular corporation worked in partnership with one advertising company for its "general market" advertising, another agency for its Latino/Hispanic advertising, and another for African American advertising. This particular project had potential ramifications in terms of brand positioning and advertising and thus was of great interest and concern to all of the agencies. Before we went too far down any path, the Latino/Hispanic agency wanted a say in terms of the "who" and "how" of the Latino research. They insisted that we only include Spanish-dominant households (i.e., households where people reported speaking more Spanish than English) and that the interviews would be conducted in Spanish. They wanted to assure that the findings would be based on studying the "right" people in the "right" way.

At the same time, corporate definitions provided to us for each ethnic target gave us pause. The European American target included mothers aged 25–44, with household incomes ranging from $20,000 to over $100,000. The African American and Latino/Hispanic targets were mothers aged 18–34, with incomes only up to $50,000. Among the African Americans, it was also required that at least half were single parents. We were asked to recruit respondents for the study according to these target market criteria. One could not help but think that troubling stereotypic and simplistic category-creating assumptions were in play. As Stavenhagen has queried, "Are Indians poor because they are Indians, or are they Indians because they are poor?"[17] In this case, the answer for African American and Latino families would have to be a resounding "yes" to the latter. If incomes were higher, for example, the same people would have become de facto part of the "general market" audience, within which the European American consumers also resided.[18] These ethnicized and racialized demographic constellations defined this company's target audiences. Our concern was in the erasure of the distinction between target audiences and the populations of European Americans, African Americans, and Latinos in the United States. Such an elision could easily occur in the shorthand of later conversation and thinking, and thereby reconstitute assumptions of ethnic differences and hierarchies.

The request for Latino families to be only Spanish-dominant households further signaled a pragmatic of "nonacculturated," "nonassimilated," "authentically Latino" similar to that which had been in the air at the start of the Mexican American study described earlier. It presaged a view of ethnicity as a linear matter which obliterated the view of ethnicity in terms of mixing, ever fluid, everyday practices and semiotics which could be strategically asserted (or resisted). The insistence on Spanish-only interviews simultaneously suggested a notion of difference reduced to differences in language use. We had heard this formulation at its most basic articulated before: English speakers are assimilated to U.S. cultural practices, Spanish speakers are not. Yet, everything we had ever learned as anthropologists regarding the interrelationships of language and cultural practices spoke against anything approaching such a simplistic one-to-one mapping. And it certainly was without question that the situation in the United States was more complicated. It would be entirely possible to identify oneself as Latino and be primarily an English speaker, even if Spanish does seem increasingly important in the United States, undoubtedly for complicated reasons having to do with both Hispanic and Anglo ascendancy.[19]

For us, though, as anthropological consumer researchers, the practical question is about carrying out an analytically rich ethnographic encounter. We trust ourselves (on most days) to be able to do that. Since neither of us are fluent Spanish speakers, we must hand over the reins to another researcher. In doing so, our concern is to assure that the quality of the ethnography and cultural analysis does not suffer. We found ourselves in a bit of a bind in this case as we had already agreed to (and started organizing) the study without securing any Spanish-speaking co-researchers. And when we did make the quick calls to find out the availability of the Spanish-speaking researchers with whom we had worked on past studies, none were available to help due to their academic schedules. We then asked academic colleagues for recommendations for Spanish-speaking Ph.D. anthropologists or advanced graduate students whom they thought might be interested and available.

We hired graduate students Saúl Mercado from U.C. Berkeley and Elise Andaya from NYU. If interviews were going to be in Spanish, this also meant that the telephone screener which local recruiters use to find participants must also be translated in Spanish. In this study we gave respondents homework collages and diary assignments to be completed before the interviews, and these also needed to be translated. The interview guide needed to be translated. This all had to be carried out virtually immediately, and we were grateful that Saúl was able to take on all of these tasks. We felt as if we had needed to scramble, but that we were set. Everything would be okay, it all would work.

◙ ◙ ◙ ◙ ◙

Then the fateful planning meeting occurred. At this meeting were representatives from the corporation as well as from each of the advertising agencies. It had been conceived (in our minds) as a "let's just get to know each other a bit before we all go out to the field" and "just to confirm with everyone what we are doing" kind of meeting. Rita attended in person. Patti and fellow Practica partner and anthropologist Michael Donovan were listening on the speaker phone. After this event, we swore off speaker-phone conferences, at least for start-up meetings.

Before this meeting, we thought we were all set to go as we had already straightened out the issue of Spanish-speaking households and had already engaged Saúl and Elise to carry out these interviews. We had assumed we would carry out the interviews with the European American and African American respondents. Everything was arranged to happen concurrently. Michael would do the European American and African American interviews in Atlanta, Rita would do the European American and African American interviews in Chicago as well as serve as videographer for Elise, and Patti would carry out the fieldwork in Los Angeles, conducting the African American and European American interviews and carrying the camera for Saúl's interviews in the Latino households. While we were geographically dispersed, we only had twenty-five interviews total, all ethnicities included, and it seemed that five interviewing anthropologists were more than enough.

However, at this meeting a senior member of the advertising agency responsible for advertising to the African American target voiced her desires and interests in assuring that an African American would be the interviewer for the African American respondents. She maintained that African American respondents would convey different information to an African American than they would to a European American. At one level this was unquestionably true. On another level it was entirely debatable. Ethnography is always about the interaction. Ethnography is always an encounter co-created by participants. An ethnographic encounter is always, on some level, about attempting to achieve intersubjective understanding and the encounter will always be different between any two people, whoever they are. So just by virtue of having someone else conducting the interview, it would be different. But another truth is that seeming similarities between interlocutors are not an inherent guarantee or necessarily "better" route to understanding. In fact, as John Jackson, an African American anthropologist from New York whose ethnographic work has centered on African Americans in New York, has pointed out, assumed similarities between people can foster assumptions of intersubjective understanding which in fact has not been achieved. One cannot assume and presume that anyone thinks alike, even if we can make our cultural understandings known to one another. As Jackson has poignantly written,

> Being a middle-class African American scholar . . . does not only mean
> deconstructing notions of "race" that would have it operate as some kind of

all-encompassing mechanism for supergluing assumed connections across the material chasm of class differences, and neither is it simply about axiomatically accepting a certain kind of social alienation from non-middle-class black informants. It mandates understanding how both differences and similarities infuse every moment of the intersubjective ethnographic project—even for black anthropologists working in black America.[20]

In the U.S. context, presumed ethnic similarities between researcher and re-searched can also usher intraethnic battles into the encounter. The encounter and the understanding are not necessarily smooth(er) because of perceived or assumed similarities.[21]

Yet, we knew that this was not necessarily how these matters would be per-ceived by our clients-to-be. We had heard this kind of request before; in fact, we had hired an African American moderator in the home party shopping study that we described to the Hispanic marketing conference attendees. The logic draws on essentialist formulations of identity and consumption practices, and it is widespread. The annoying aspect is that it always also seems to be for-gotten that what we are proposing to do is research. Thus, as women, it is often implicitly assumed that we will not be able to understand how or why men drink beer, as white-complexioned persons we are not supposed to understand how or why dark-complexioned persons might use AMBI. But when we provide insight on the lives of men, pickup truck drivers, how people take care of their skin, or those who give their dogs anti-anxiety medications, it is not because we *are* these people, nor because we do these things in our daily lives, but be-cause we are researchers. It is not essential sharing, but rather the ability to decode social life, that is crucial. Clifford Geertz's message that "culture is public because meaning is" was an important one.[22] Anthropology's tradition of studying "the other," despite its colonial and elitist problems, also revealed the revelations that can come from being an outsider. Lessons from Bohannan's "Shakespeare in the Bush" were not all without merit.[23] Difference and initial lack of knowledge can be used to garner knowledge. It can be good when people have to make cultural meanings and practices highly explicit because they feel we do not understand.[24] We often try to explain this to clients, but fre-quently with little success.

For whatever reason, on this occasion we argued strongly that the value of the end results ultimately depended on the ethnographic and analytic skills of the individual and that we felt ourselves capable of conducting the research. Perhaps it was the backdrop of the issues we had already gone through with the organization of the Latino interviews combined with a more generalized fatigue built up from the number of times that we had lived through these discussions and issues before. Perhaps it was because we could not quite imagine how we would manage the insights of eight anthropologists, not to mention the details of scheduling. Recruiting had already begun, dates were set, and interviews in three different cities were to happen *concurrently*, and we would need to find three available anthropologists in very short order. We tried to give examples highlighting that findings were about the value of the interviewer. And we tried to give ourselves credentials by maintaining that we often interviewed African American respondents and we believed that we had success—African American respondents had been among the respondents in the two previous studies we had conducted for this same corporation, in fact. As this argument seemed to be failing, and the agency representatives were insistent on the differences that an African American presence would make, we further pointed out that, in fact, in these and other studies, we often had black videographers with us, and so the research team was not all white. ("Black" was a carefully chosen descriptor here rather than "African American" since these videographers would describe themselves as Ethiopian.) This, they argued, did not matter; in fact, it was potentially distasteful as it meant that the black people on the team were in a lower position than the white interviewers. We stopped short of saying that the videographers were, in fact, often relatives, as Patti was married to a black/Ethiopian man, since we knew that this could (and probably would) also be interpreted as a further instantiation of racism. Once inside the perniciousness of racism and ethnicity defined in terms of issues of essential identity and authenticity, there is no escape and ultimately no winning for anyone.[25] In this particular case, the nadir occurred when Michael, who often expresses himself in lyrical and literary ways, enunciated that he really did not believe that the interview and analysis would be significantly different only because "blackness" entered the room. "Blackness" is a term based in anthropological logic that can also be found in literature. But in this instance, at that pronouncement a senior representative of the African American agency announced that she was offended, and thereafter the argument and the interaction ended. What was really happening in the room was not at all clear to Patti or Michael per telephone, but Rita was assessing the interactions and rapidly announced that we would hire African American interviewers. Case closed. Perhaps none of this would have happened if we all had been there in person and been able to see each other's faces and thus have been better able to judge meanings, intents, and emotions. But in this case the misattributions and misinterpretations were profound.[26]

We hired Vanessa Hayward. She became part of the Atlanta team with Mike. They had worked closely together in the past at the B/R/S Group; it was a good match. For Chicago, we once again leaned on academic colleagues for re-commendations and were led to Paitra Russell, a recent University of Chicago Ph.D. anthropologist then working in the consumer research arena alongside her husband in their marketing agency. For Los Angeles, Patti turned to Saúl to identify fellow students or willing anthropologists who would potentially fit the bill.

Again, there was a scramble involved. We needed to find an African American anthropologist quickly, and one who was able to conduct the interviews on particular days. After some e-mails back and forth, Saúl found a number of potential candidates, not all of whom were interested or available or at least quick enough on the e-mail reply key for the lighting speed with which this needed to be organized. But, as it turned out, Saúl did locate a fellow graduate student who was at the time conducting her dissertation fieldwork in Los Angeles and who was willing, happy, and able to pick up a few days' work. On the phone, Patti explained events and asked her if she would fit the bill as African American anthropologist. Her response was that her mother was African American and her father white. Patti's quick, unconsidered, but heartfelt response was that that was fine and that, in fact, in the current state of affairs, to be both black and white was "the perfect thing to be these days." The younger anthropologist's response was, "Oh really?" in a tone that was truly difficult to decode. Whether she was intending to say, "Do you, senior anthropologist/older person, really believe that and, if so, why?" or "You are a clueless (all) white person who does not understand anything" was completely unclear. In any case, she was hired.[27]

In the meantime, though, on the Latino/Hispanic front, we received from the client a forwarded e-mail request from the Latino/Hispanic agency to see the Spanish translation of the interview protocol, along with pleas such as to be sure to probe on "traditional culture in their lives," e.g., "Do they wish for their kids to speak Spanish, to practice the traditional holidays, to know their cultural history, to eat the traditional foods?" and so on. Moreover, in the e-mail was also a request to "get a brief bio on the Hispanic anthropologist(s). Just basic information like country of origin and time in the U.S. would be great."

Again? More cells of authenticity to assure? Both Saúl and Elise had been personally recommended to us by widely esteemed senior anthropologists with positions in highly recognized departments. We had also asked for curriculum vitas and we had spoken with each of them by telephone. We had no reason to doubt that they had backgrounds which made them suitable candidates for this job. In fact, their vita details were rather humbling: Fulbright-Hays and Wenner-Gren dissertation research grants; undergraduate degrees from Princeton and Cornell, summa and magna cum laude; Mellon fellowships;

minority scholars awards; fieldwork in Cuba centered on issues of the family; fieldwork in Spain on language in media; Latino Anthropological Society membership; many years as a Spanish instructor. How could these not be people worth hiring for this job? How could they not fit the needed bill? While the speed with which anthropological consumer research fieldwork and analysis must be carried out is much faster than typical anthropology endeavors, and thus requires its own art, affinity, and practice, there was no reason not to hire them. And we had never, ever, thought to inquire into countries of origin or time in the United States, what had now been deemed the "basic information."

We generally trade off who takes on the management of a given project, and Patti was the organizer of this one. So she was the lucky one who had to call and ask these questions. Answering was perhaps easiest for Saúl. Even though Saúl was born in the United States, his parents were Dominican-born. Spanish had been his first language, summers had been routinely spent in the Dominican Republic, and even though he had attended private (English-speaking) schools, his parents had also seen to it that he learned to read and write Spanish from an early age. Later, these demographic and language details had converged with his academic interests in linguistic anthropology and language practices in Spain.

For Elise the question was perhaps more difficult as it presaged that she was going to be judged wanting in terms of the vagaries of birth and background—over which one obviously has relatively little control—rather than on linguistic and research qualifications based in experience. When Patti explained the rationale for the question, that it was representatives from the Latino/Hispanic agency who wanted to know, Elise recounted with what seemed a bit of trepidation and concern over the complicated biographical facts. She had come to the United States when she was eighteen, she spoke Spanish because she had learned in school and then through extensive travel through Central America and her fieldwork in Cuba, not because she was a native speaker. She had grown up in New Zealand, with a mother who was Australian and a father whose heritage was from the Philippines, but he had been born in Hawaii. Clearly apologetic, she said she was sure that she had never told us she was of Latina heritage and that she was so sorry if we had been misled. Moreover, she offered that if her background posed a problem, she was more than happy to forego the job. Patti assured her that we had never asked about ethnic background, and that in fact we were sorry to have had to ask. As far as we were concerned, she still had the job. And what an interesting background, Patti could not wait to tell Rita.

Our only problem was that Rita had misspoken in the meeting and said that both Saúl and Elise were native speakers (because she believed they were) and now needed to send a message that this was not true. Patti was sure (hoping?) that it did not matter as the agency would undoubtedly be awed by their vitas. At the same time, however, it was probably at about this time that both of us began talking about resigning. The fantasy contemplated in the wee hours of the morning had become one of escape—if only we could get out of this job. That we never acted on this fantasy was due entirely to our feelings for our primary client liaison who, even when whipsawed by political battles, never lost his keen sense of fairness and integrity, equanimity, and kindness. Resigning would have meant putting him in an untenable position and ultimately making him bear the brunt of the racial and ethnic politics. That was unfair and we liked him too much for that. We tried to find comfort and inspiration for ourselves by framing the situation as being really about the economic battles of business. While it seemed we were caught in the politics of race, really the issue was less about race and ethnicity than it was about three different advertising agencies securing their turf and expertise. Because, at the end of the day, if anything the anthropological consultants (i.e., us) found or suggested contradicted what the agencies had been saying or doing, or if we suggested to the client corporation that the agency should be doing something that the agency did not want to do, then problems could ensue for them. They were guarding their turf and their capital. It could be another arena we were fighting over—it just happened to be race and ethnicity—and we did not need to take it so personally.

Nonetheless, any comfort that the economics-oriented rationale provided did not last long. The plot thickened and the ability of racial and ethnic discourses to imprison us all once again became apparent. This time the intervention was not from one of the agencies, but rather from another of the African American graduate students whom Saúl had suggested. We had exchanged e-mails, but then she had not answered Patti's second e-mail or calls as quickly as needed and so we had gone ahead and moved forward with the other African American anthropologist. When she and Patti did finally talk, Patti had to let her know that while we would love to potentially hire her for a future job, for this one it was too late because we had already promised the job to another student.

The student seemed slightly annoyed. That was okay and even understandable. But then the cells of authenticity were once again brought into view. Patti had fairly openly explained the background and circumstances of the search for an African American anthropologist. What this person wanted Patti to appreciate, however, was that the person we had promised the job to was very light-skinned, in fact, phenotypically white. Did we know this? Of course we did not know this, even if the fact that she had one white parent put the odds on her being lighter rather than darker. Akin to the way we had not asked, or thought to ask, Saúl and Elise for biographies of personal heritage and place of birth, we had not asked the African American candidates about skin tone credentials. This student felt it important to voice her observation that lighter-skinned people seemed to be given these jobs. With imagery of stories of African American social events that allowed entry only if one's skin tone was as light or lighter than a typical brown grocery bag, Patti listened as this student expressed varying degrees of anger and annoyance over the fact of these jobs typically going to people of lighter skin tone.[28] It was something she had seen happening around her, and she wanted that fact to be out there and heard. There was every reason to believe that what she was saying was true, as there is ample evidence that lighter-skinned African Americans have an easier go of things in the racialized world of the United States. But in this particular case the job had gone to the lighter-skinned anthropologist because she had called back first. Nothing more, nothing less, even if, of course, overall the privilege of graduate school education and thus the possibility of being offered this job tended to coincide with the privilege of light skin. Lighter-skinned or darker-skinned, the point was that it was clear that there was no getting out of the imprisoning cells. No exit. Huis Clos.

So, visions of quitting only danced more furiously in our heads because now there was also the worry about what members of the African American advertising agency would say. Would the ethnographer we had hired appear too white? Would she not be "black enough" for this job? "Black enough" is by no means a new issue in the annals of U.S. racial politics, but did it have to rear its head in the midst of this research project, too? The ambiguous "Oh really?" that had answered Patti's exclamation that it was best in today's world to be both black and white echoed. As it turned out, when we went into people's homes in Los Angeles, it was never completely clear if respondents did take both the researcher and the videographer (Patti) as white, or whether the researcher's African Americanness was just not mentioned. It was never brought up as an explicit issue.[29]

And as it turned out, no representatives from the agency responsible for the African American target audience attended any of the Los Angeles interviews, so we did not need to make this particular test case explicit. Clients do often accompany us during fieldwork, and generally this is a positive aspect of the process. As is true for us, going to the field, being in situ, hearing and seeing things first-hand helps clients understand and appreciate the phenomenon under study—whatever or whomever is being studied comes alive. At the same time, this accompaniment introduces additional stresses and intricacies for us. While heightened through the intensifying lenses of race and ethnicity in this instance, there is always the question of whether clients will feel that we are carrying out the study with the "right" people, the "right" questions, and in the "right" way.

Corporations do pay dearly for consumer research, in terms of allocated monetary resources as well as employee time and attention. Clients can thus often be quick to condemn as "a waste" any interactions with respondents who do not fit the target profile. Moreover, in line with a business framework in which "expertise" is valued and is understood as the ability to avoid misunderstandings and gaffes,[30] any of our interaction missteps, instances of social gaffe, or clearly saying the wrong thing can also be quickly judged as failures. Never mind Goffman's ethnomethodological insight that gaffes are precisely the means to illuminate norms of cultural practice.[31] We feel ourselves under the lamp, and at the worst of times believe we can palpably feel the glare of the question: "Why did we hire you?" In this case, the lead-up to the fieldwork simply meant that everything seemed more precarious as we had the specter of being sure we looked like we were asking the "right" questions with the "right" respondents as well as with the ethnically and racially "right" anthropologists.

Thus it was with strong "I just want to quit" thoughts that we had gone into the field. These kinds of political, social, and personal minefields are emotionally exhausting. It is fatiguing terrain to navigate. Sometimes one just wants to live without thinking about the cells of identity and authenticity and appreciate the lived messiness of everyday life, even if being able—and even *wanting*—to live without them is easily perceived as a racially privileged position.[32]

In any case, forgetting was not possible as Patti drove to the first Los Angeles Latino interview. Saúl was in the passenger seat, and an observing representative from the Latino/Hispanic agency was in the backseat. The driving directions supplied by the locally hired recruiter did not seem to be leading to the right place. We were lost and the respondent needed to be called to find out how to get to her home. Saúl was given the job to call. He started in Spanish and then switched to English. As she U-turned the car and began to follow the directions, Patti was quaking and thinking, "Oh, no," and the silent tension emanating from the backseat felt like it was pounding "the wrong people" into the back of her head.

After the phone call, Patti gently asked Saúl what had happened. Did the respondent seem not to speak Spanish, or why had he spoken English? As he explained it, she gave her response in English to his Spanish question and so he switched into English in response. This kind of linguistic accommodation was in line with good anthropological (and general politeness) training, but Saúl did not yet fully appreciate all of the agency-researcher dynamics that also had to be taken into account. He initially did not seem to take it as so important that she had spoken English. As he said, she had simply given the driving directions in English and he answered her in English. Implied in his response was also a "so what?" Again, to assume one-to-one correspondence between language and identity is anathema for someone with training in linguistic anthropology and it likely seemed almost shameful for anthropologists to be having this conversation. Patti tried to explain that people had been recruited to be Spanish speakers. The agency representative reiterated that it was going to be very, very important that we conduct the study with people who were Spanish, not English dominant. Saúl knew then that he had to be apprehensive about accommodating and code-switching to English. Patti quietly indulged in something along the lines of prayer.

Once we got to the house, however, it was possible to take a deep sigh of relief. Almost as if prayers had been magically answered, the decorations in the small home we entered seemed to quickly telegraph a feeling of genuine Latinidad to the agency representative—as we entered she looked around, smiled, and relaxed. At the visual center of the small living room were framed pictures of three wedding couples, each with a bride in a long white wedding dress and groom in tuxedo. These hung above shelves displaying a mixture of framed photographs of babies, children's school photographs, what looked like high school prom photographs, red and violet artificial flowers, religious icons such as a Virgin Mary statuette, candles, fanned-open greeting cards, and various other ceramic pieces and knick-knacks displayed on top of cloth doilies. On the opposite wall hung framed photographs of what looked like extended family groups as well as smaller photographs of sibling groups, taken for special occasions by a professional photographer in a local studio or department store. Near these photographs were other shelves of artificial flowers, ceramics, stuffed animals, more photographs, and a noticeable cache of trophies. We found ourselves for a quick moment alone and the agency representative told us, "This is it. This is the real stuff. This is what I know from my mother's house." As it turned out, the latter observation about her mother was apt. As we found out in the course of the interview, we were not really in the living room of our respondent, a thirty-year-old mother of an eight-year-old. We were in the home of her mother-in-law. The physical dwelling our respondent shared with her husband and son was another, smaller house behind this one. She had decided that we would do the interview in the front home because of the pit bulls that lived in the yard in between.

But while it was not her living room per se, the car club trophies that took up significant space were those of her husband. And this was a home where she and her son lived, in the sense that they spent considerable time there. During our visit, we were also treated to some of the extended family interactions that were part of the everyday food world of her and her son. While we sat in the living room and talked, her husband's younger brother along with a cousin or two arrived with five pounds of fresh meat that he began cooking for us all. Before the brother-in-law was finished preparing it, his mother returned home and took over. She wanted to assure that the *fajitas* were going to taste right. We were treated to first-shift seating at the family's small kitchen table, and we were all happy. The respondent, the agency representative, Saúl, and Patti sat down and ate and talked as a brother-in-law or cousin agreed to hold the research camera and videotape us. And it no longer seemed to matter that sometimes our primary respondent, and definitely her son, spoke in English. The complexity of human life and the humanity of respondents, the people who are willing to let us enter their lives as researchers and fellow human beings, had saved us.

◎ ◎ ◎ ◎ ◎

We had recruited respondents so that the children would always be part of the ethnographic encounter. In the next Latina household we visited, the respondent immediately began with a huge apology that her three young children were not there. The basic situation was that she was divorced and her husband had insisted that the children come with him—it was Saturday and it was his weekend to have the children at his home. She gave us the impression that her insistence on keeping the children with her on that day had been a battle she had lost, but she told us that if it were really, really necessary, she would call him and tell him that he must bring the children. It just was going to cause problems. Putting her in this position did not seem right, so we decided with her that we should just sit with her and talk and then reunite on Sunday evening when her children would be back. We planned that we would then go out to an informal joint dinner with her and her children; in the meantime, we would interview her.

This respondent was a woman whose life efforts and accomplishments could only be admired. As she summed up her basic life philosophy, "It doesn't matter how difficult it is, I can do it!" She also broke us out of the simplistic ethnicity mold. She was from Peru, but one of her grandparents was Chinese. Her ex-husband was half-Japanese and half-Peruvian, thus her children were part Peruvian, part Japanese, and part Chinese. Prior to moving to Los Angeles three years before, she had lived in Japan for eight years. She and her family left Japan as she felt that her children would eventually experience too much educational and employment discrimination there. An acquaintance told them of job opportunities in Los Angeles, catalyzing their move there, and the fact that her brother lived in Los Angeles had also been a reason to choose the city. The employment opportunities she and her husband had been told of did not materialize, nor, as she said, did she actually see her brother very often as in the United States people live their own nuclear, rather than extended, family lives. But, in any case, she was making it, working in a bank and selling vitamin supplements on the side. And in terms of the realities of brands, her children, ages eleven, seven, and five, knew, for example, American fast food from living in Japan, the toys from which were hanging on their bedroom wall. For these Peruvian children, especially the two older ones, American fast food was not just American for them, it was Japanese.

By the end of these two encounters, the agency representative seemed happy with us. The respondents were deemed real and we seemed to have proven ourselves capable of the work. Perhaps we had proven ourselves worthy by our clear interest and willingness in trying to grasp respondents' truths and realities whatever they were. Perhaps it was because she realized that Patti understood some Spanish. Perhaps we had just proven ourselves because we were willing to come back on what would have been our Sunday night off to continue our fieldwork encounter. Or perhaps it was simply because we had started to understand each other's issues.

During this first day together, we had found some time in the car to talk. One problem the agency had was that it had been trying to get the client to provide funds for them to undertake a study such as the one we were now doing. Of course it was a bit of a rub that the client would fund this larger study of which the Latino/Hispanic audience was a part rather than agreeing to provide them the funds to undertake a unique Latino/Hispanic study. Completing this study could also mean that later pleas for research project funding could be rebuffed with the rationale that this study had already been carried out. While the merits of one large, encompassing, tripartite study was understandable from the client side and from our side as contracted consultants, the desire for one unique, fully focused, agency-overseen study was understandable from the agency's side. We had come to a form of mutual understanding, or at least mutual appreciation of some of the realities of the other's point of view and subject position. By the time Sunday evening arrived, we even seemed to have started caring about one another.

Our plan for Sunday evening was to meet in front of the respondent's apartment building. Saúl and Patti were arriving in one car, the agency representative in another. Once en route, we ascertained per cell phone exchange that she was going to arrive slightly ahead of us. Then as we got close to the respondent's home, we came upon a horrific and very fresh car accident. It crossed Patti's mind and lips, "It couldn't involve her, could it?" We had just finished talking on our cell phones when she was probably just arriving at this point. Could it be her in the mangled car? Saúl, applying the logic of chance, reassured that it couldn't be. Patti's visceral response (as if her circulation suddenly slowed and then reversed course) belied logic. She was greatly relieved as she saw the agency representative safely emerging from her car parked in front of the respondent's apartment complex. When everyone regrouped by the cars at the end of the encounter, the agency representative kissed Patti goodbye on the cheek. Back in the car, Saúl repeatedly intoned the import of that kiss. "There's nothing to worry about. It's okay. She kissed you." We had gone with the respondent and her three children for a fun fast food dinner, where amazingly the manager even let us videotape the boisterous activity at our table. It had all been fine.

In the end, the entire fieldwork and analytic experience did turn out to be an exemplary one. We enjoyed being with the respondents, we enjoyed the observing representatives, and we enjoyed being together in research teams. We also managed to incorporate and merge the eight different perspectives of the researchers, and the project was strengthened by the views of the many. It keeps the head lively to have other ideas. And at some level, it had made a difference. We had included people in the study we could not have had without using Spanish. For the African American interviews, Rita sent an e-mail to Patti at one point saying, "By the way, Paitra made a difference. Not that I wouldn't have done as well, just that it would have been different." Everyone had a different perspective that enriched the whole. It ended up being fun. It had been invigorating to work with the graduate students. The new blood of anthropology flowing through their veins enriched our own. Moreover, these pleasures did not end with the fieldwork. Given that we almost always produce a video based on excerpts of the ethnographic encounters, we needed help from a fluent Spanish speaker who could also help us edit and subtitle the video. Ideally the person would also have an ethnographic eye. Once again, colleagues at NYU led us to Ulla Berg, a graduate student in anthropology with a specialty in ethnographic film. From Denmark, her English was impeccable, as seemingly was her Spanish, a skill honed through fieldwork and in daily life with her husband, originally from Puerto Rico. Again, the biographic details of her heritage and life choices burst the boundaries of assumed ethnic realities. We also almost burst our sides laughing together as we worked. Perhaps the laughter was because of the terrible intermittent jerks or inappropriate movements of the anthropologist-held cameras, the antics of children, the way some questions and comments sounded so inane when taken out of context, or the unintended double-entendres created by typographical errors in a subtitle. It is no longer so clear what struck us as funny, but it is clear that it was fun to work together.

◎ ◎ ◎ ◎ ◎

And then we got to the day of the presentation. Most of our consumer research projects are concluded with an in-person presentation to the client. As a rule these presentations are something which we like to do, as they allow us to explain the theoretical points and ethnographic examples embedded along with photographs and video excerpts in the PowerPoint documents which we deliver to clients. Perhaps we also enjoy these presentations as they signal the end of a project. In this case, the still-existing e-mail trail provides a good indication of how difficult it was to organize a time for this presentation when all the important interested parties could attend. As it turned out, finally, near the end of October, we had a date when crucial client representatives as well as representatives from the agencies for the Latino/Hispanic, African American, and general market target audiences could attend. We also luckily (and painstakingly) arranged it so that Saúl and Paitra could attend. We did not want to go it alone. Patti, especially, was not looking forward to her first face-to-face encounter with the woman who had been so inadvertently offended during the fateful pre-fieldwork phone call.

Rita, Patti, and Paitra shared a ride to the client's headquarters on the morning of the presentation. In the free-ranging conversation that moved from kids' school curricula to other projects to reminiscing over favorite moments and occurrences in this fieldwork, we were also still noodling over the issues of the ethnicized and racialized understandings that had so haunted and framed this project. In the course of this conversation, Paitra articulated one of her comments in terms of "blackness." There it was again, the anthropological "b" word, blackness as analytic construct. We were reminded that Michael's use of the word was not out of the realm of our usual discourse and somewhat reassured by the idea that if Paitra had used the term on the phone it might not have been so quickly misread as insulting vernacular. When we got to the presentation, we were also able to feel relatively confident. Rita and Paitra could reconvene with the representatives they knew from the Chicago fieldwork. More kisses were exchanged with the Latino/Hispanic agency representative with whom Saúl and Patti had worked in Los Angeles. The Latino/Hispanic agency headquarters were located in another city and the representatives quickly explained there was some sort of problem at the airport on that day. They wanted to forewarn us before the presentation started to not take it personally, but they would need to leave by a set time, even if we were not finished. Understood. An African American woman sat quietly in a chair in the midsection of the room. Cordial, not cold, introductions held sway. Not bad, Patti thought, comforted by the erroneous thought that this was the woman who had announced her feeling of offense. Only later did Patti find out this was not the woman she had heard on the phone, but at that particular moment, the mix-up helped to smooth all interactions.

Then we were delayed. The most important client representative had been held up at a meeting with the chief marketing officer. That meeting took precedence; the rest of us would wait. There was general consensus that we needed to wait for her arrival to start the presentation because it was her departmental budget that had paid for this project and she ultimately had the decision-making power. She really mattered. There were various notions and ideas about what to do in the meantime—we were, after all, a fairly sizable group, and people had flown in from at least three cities specifically for this presentation. The group did need to be engaged.

In line with notions of video as entertainment, as well as addendum rather than the "real" stuff, we, perhaps not surprisingly, decided to fill the time by showing some of the edited video excerpts.[33] For this project, we had created ten video excerpts. There were three for each of the three identified target audiences. Each excerpt, about ten minutes long, featured a different respondent and each illustrated a particular issue featured in the report. The tenth segment was an amalgam labeled "Kids (Out-takes & Outlooks)" which featured some of the kids' cutest and funniest moments caught on film. This Art Linkletterish move was originally intended to make people laugh at the end. Now we were thinking about using it to fill time. In any case, one of the snippets we did show, one we had intended to leave out of the presentation entirely, was from a European American household in which the four assembled children under age six (two children from the respondent and two from her girlfriend) dominated what looked like a completely chaotic roost. Part of the decisions made in editing this clip was to give a feel of the circumstances of fieldwork—it was purposefully bedlam like. It was also "very white."

We chose to show this segment in this time gap prior to the presentation precisely because we thought that it might give people a feel for the fieldwork circumstances of interviewing pairs of mothers and their children, and because we knew we had not planned to show it in the course of the presentation. But in the end, we regretted having shown this bit of video even to fill the pre-presentation time. As once the presentation got underway, it became apparent that this (very white) video segment had framed and set the stage. It served as a reference point to which other instances became a comparison. Thus, the presentation started to inadvertently take on, and feed into—much to our chagrin and dismay—a very European American defined framework. We had all noticed and discussed during the fieldwork that the African American target mothers tended to expect a level of children's politeness and polish vis-à-vis others which was not necessarily insisted on by the European American target mothers. When asked during the presentation, we had been able to answer the question about the African American mothers' expectations for children's behavior and obedience in a way that foregrounded and acknowledged mothers' recognition that because of American racism, their children's out-of-home behavior was likely to be refracted differently than would be the behavior of European American children. But what was also important about this, in the first place, was that the comparison had been set-up by the "out of control" kids seen in the white video.

The view from the front of the room, with the spatial setting of our client liaison sitting with the senior representative from the general market agency in the front row, also brought into stark relief the degree to which it seemed largely the representative from the general market agency who had such a strong voice in the report revisions that the client had asked for in the weeks leading up to the presentation. It is fairly common for us to deliver clients a draft report prior to our presentations. As a rule clients change little—but it gives the client liaison, the one who has gone out on a limb to hire us, the chance to see first what we are planning to deliver to the organization. It also gives clients a chance to let us know the parts of the report which seem unclear or need more explanation or empirical support to be accepted by their internal audiences. In this way, the delivery of a draft report, with the understanding that some changes might be requested before acceptance of a final report, is structurally similar to the academic processes of peer-review for journal publications. The process is also similar in that one is allowed to argue the case for certain aspects and, at times, even to succeed in leaving parts as they were in the original. In this case, the requests for revisions had been both substantial and picky. We had been treated to the return of our manuscript with marks or requests for further material or refinements on virtually every page. Hours had been spent on the phone in explanation and negotiation. In the end, as is also often the case after meeting peer review requests, we thought that the overall report was actually stronger and better. We were confident that we had produced an acceptable final product.

Yet, what the spatial arrangement had brought into stark relief was who had most likely really had a voice in these revisions and who had not. Our client contact had been the one who discussed the revisions with us, on one occasion also with the general market agency representative taking part, but now it was becoming crystal clear to us that in all likelihood the general market agency had been the one with the most, if not the only, input on suggested changes. We were too overwhelmed by the sheer volume of revisions requested (on top of demand from other projects) to do much more than react. We did what we needed to do to get it done, and now, on reflection during the presentation, it was clear to us who had been shortchanged. We felt for the African American and Latino/Hispanic target market agencies. No wonder the annoyance. No wonder the turf battles. There are only small pleasures in step-child and second-class citizenship status. The cells of authenticity in which the Latino/ Hispanic and African American agencies resided clearly were those of less over-all voice and influence. Yet, this reality of less influence also spoke to the fact, as many have argued, that the cells serve to allow a voice at all. And that would be a reason why they should *not* be dismantled. Was there not power located in being able to affect the definitions of the cells? But was not the paradox exactly that imprisoning cells of disempowering difference were what created the need for empowering cells in the first place? In essence, cells producing cells producing cells. And so we found ourselves feeling the need and value of cells organized around ethnoracial identity. Yet these same cells are what we would also consider part of the dynamic of the problem.[34]

Thus, while in this presentation we had managed successfully to answer crucial questions and to dodge external accusations of European American cluelessness, we nonetheless left feeling disappointed in ourselves. Yes, we had been able to answer questions in ways that acknowledged racism, for instance the question about target mothers' expectation for children's out-of-home behavior. African American mothers depicted on the video also seemed to have been accepted as saying the kinds of things that would be said to other African Americans, the need the agency representatives had expressed during the initial telephone meeting. The audience had borne witness to the video snippets in which African American mothers were speaking openly about their focus on fulfilling their children's educational needs and dreams, almost at any cost, because and in spite of racism. Yet, none of this general acceptance from the African American agency representatives helped us overcome the feeling that the general market agency was the one sharing mutual embrace with the client and we had supplied additional adhesive to that relationship. The African American agency was clearly on the periphery. And we had played into it by not thinking about how the "very white" video snippet might frame the presentation and by not paying attention to whether all voices had a say in report revisions. In this situation, in which power relations were simultaneously racialized, we felt that we had unwittingly become contributors to the white hegemony.

Adding to the sentiment, we also felt that we did not give due justice to the findings surrounding the Latino/Hispanic target audience. Because of the initial video shown, because of our attention to not further alienating the African American agency, and because of the succession of particular pages and points we had brushed by rather too quickly, it seemed to us by the end that we had in fact also given the Latino/Hispanic respondents short shrift. In the report we had taken great care to call out the issues for which the Latino/Hispanic target audience mothers had different ideas about family, brands, food, and so on. On a number of issues, the Latino/Hispanic target had expressed differences where the African American and European American mothers expressed similarities. On other issues, all were similar and it was the similarities which ended up stressed in the presentation. Moreover, by the time the representatives of that agency needed to leave for the airport, we had not finished and thus the Latino/Hispanic agency representations had not seen the Latino/Hispanic video that we had inserted in the final section of the report and which we considered one of the best.

In our own personal Practica postmortem lunch, Saúl repeatedly expressed that he had not seen it as so bleak. It was not that bad; he thought we were being harsh on ourselves. We had presented, persuasively, a finely grained analytic report, and one which showed, importantly, that similarities among groups, e.g., the significance of education in their children's lives, could be meaningful and the differences insignificant. Also, hadn't it been well-received and hadn't kisses once again been exchanged? This was, nonetheless, not really comforting. Thus, a few days later, Patti decided to send an e-mail to the client expressing the parts of the Latino story that had been overlooked. She also crafted an e-mail to the agency representative, copying to the client, that included the message that it had been a shame about the flight problems because she had missed the best Latino/Hispanic target market video and that another video which had been skipped had also set up nicely some of the differences in understandings of family among the Latino/Hispanic audience. Finally, there was acknowledgment that without the video and some of the nuanced slides (which unfortunately in the time crunch were glossed over too quickly), we feared that the Latino/Hispanic component got lost in the telling. We reiterated that the good news was that it all *was* in the report, and the CD with the presentation and embedded videos would be arriving in her office shortly.

We received an appropriate and friendly message in response about looking forward to seeing all of the videos and reading the full report, and even more importantly, an eventual invitation to present at the agency headquarters. As it turned out, this presentation was postponed until the following February, but it felt like a chance for exoneration. Saúl was once again able to join us and we spent a considerable amount of time between the three of us, discussing which videos to show, how to best present the Latino/Hispanic aspects, and how to contextualize this story with the European American and African American stories. Patti felt like she had the chance to make things right. And for a brief moment the world was right.

It was also a pleasure to leave New York and Chicago for a warm weather climate in February. The night before the presentation included a relaxing dinner at an outdoor restaurant. Preparation for the next day's presentation could not have been better. Patti would begin the presentation; Saúl would contextualize, elucidate, and answer any questions about the videos; Rita would do the second part. We were prepared, or so it seemed.

Patti began the presentation and had barely gotten through reviewing the objectives of the project and the demographic specifics of the target audience when the unexpected challenge came. A young woman, perhaps in her late twenties or early thirties and seemingly important in the agency but whom we had not met before, challenged the fact that only families of Mexican and Peruvian descent were represented in the sample. Why these people? Did we really believe that our findings applied to everyone? You know there would be differences between Mexican and Cuban families (don't you)? Why were Caribbean families excluded? Of course we knew there would be differences. Of course we were sensitive to diverse backgrounds. The countries of origin of the respondents also had been a topic of discussion during the recruiting and we, the agency representatives, and the client were all well aware of the choices, limitations, and possibilities given our small sample. We had all done our best given these limitations.

Moreover, trafficking in specifics had always been our point and the deeply troubling aspect for us all along in this study had been the fact that the client and agencies had insisted that we follow their pre-established demographic criteria in recruiting target group respondents for the study, target groupings that were troubling in their underlying assumptions. Thus from the very start of the report, in the information and language we used, we specifically made clear that what we were finding should in no way be construed as ethnic group distinctions in the United States as a whole, but referred to these ethnicized and racialized categories as defined in terms of the brand's target audience. That the target group categories were never anything more than imposed and artificial ethnoracial group distinctions was our very point. We had only accepted—and had to accept—that these were our clients' (and the associated agencies') target audience definitions. And once again, in practice, the unreality of it all had been illustrated in the wondrous boundary-blurring and fluidity of respondents' actual practices. There were the Peruvian-Chinese-Japanese permutations already noted; the European American single mother and son household in which her male, gay African American roommate provided the household with a sense of family and family meals; the single mother who spoke Spanish in the home she shared with her parents, but who was recruited as a general market respondent because her income was too high and she identified herself as white on the phone with recruiters. For this respondent, Rita had actually come back from the interview confused as to how to count her. The woman clearly identified herself in the interview as Puerto Rican, but per the recruiting specifications she was a member of the "general target market" audience.[35]

At the moment of challenge regarding the countries of origin of our respondents, we were also purposefully making it clear that among the Latino families, we only had those of Mexican and Peruvian national origin represented in this sample. The question of generalizability of our findings to Latino families as a whole was a shared one. One could thusly argue that it was a challenge with which we were in agreement. Was not this the essence of the problem we had been having the whole time? But in this case, it was difficult to retain equanimity, as it did not feel that the risk of potential elisions was at the heart of the challenge. Rather, it seemed a "demonstrate that you're a clueless Anglo" challenge, a ritual of imprisonment in preparation for the skewering. It was perhaps difficult to retain equanimity as the invitation had been so warm and our preparation so thorough. The challenge was unexpected, and the woman voicing it acted as if she was not about to let up. In fact, the moment was not smoothed over until another member of the assembled audience stepped in to tell her, more or less, to back down, that they had known the situation all along, and that we should continue. Her challenge did then stop, at least until dinner when Saúl was challenged with the assertion that he did not sound "Dominican" and that he probably did not go to "the Island" much.

For Patti, however, this minor challenge had been simply too much. It hit and wounded where there had been so much care and concern. While she continued to present, she also largely closed down to caring, thereby limiting her vulnerability. Thus, she also really stopped trying to assure an intersubjective, anthropological understanding that was based on caring, vulnerability, and the willingness to risk a broken heart. In her book, *The Vulnerable Observer,* anthropologist Ruth Behar maintained that "anthropology that doesn't break your heart just isn't worth doing anymore."[36] While up until this point in our endeavors we might have also lived up to this anthropological challenge, we now had to stop as a heart needed to first mend in order to continue.

Segmentation and Sincerity

While we have illustrated this chapter with projects that have foregrounded racial and ethnic categorizations, in practice, implicit or explicit customer segmentation is operative in virtually all of the work we do. For many clients, we recruit respondents based on the clients' pre-existing attitude and behavior segmentation schemas (e.g., "beginners" versus "experts," "admirers" versus "disdainers"). A financial service company requests that we examine small owners of construction, IT, or retail businesses, as well as requests information on the special issues and "needs" of female business owners. For a cleaning products study we are instructed to interview only homeowners, not renters. Segmentation is a fundamental marketing tool that started with demographics and later added lifestyle, psychographic, and, more recently, value mindsets as variables to identify and target potentially profitable segments of the population. As in other realms, segmentation schemas are deployed by marketers pragmatically to achieve actionable goals. Carving up the world is done to make a messy world manageable—in the same way that the management of brands is generally carried out by separate fiefdoms within organizations (not infrequently in implicit or explicit competition).

Yet, as we have argued, catering to consumer segments in fact gives credence to and creates the categories themselves, in ways that invariably invoke a sense of homogeneity, and often assume that the created differences are based on essential qualities of individuals in the group. Segmentation schemas can also be based on—and serve to reconstitute—deeply problematic social hierarchies. In today's world in which the market is increasingly a key metaphor of, and prism for, all experience, corporations (and other agencies) hold the power to define and segment markets on their own terms, regardless of the realities or nuanced similarities or differences of individuals within a targeted segment.[37] Segmentation schemas too often lead to presumptions of homogeneity and the static existence and privileged nature of "traits," even when consumers demonstrate that the countercurrents of heterogeneity, situational and strategic deployments of ethnoracial identities, and hybridity are normative practices. Schemas hide the inherent processual nature of identity construction and belie the power of consumption practices to contextualize—to presuppose, recreate, or forge anew. If our current world is witnessing the globalization of fragmentation, then it is precisely these processes and acts of consumption in which race and ethnicity (and identity in general) is productively created that deserve the attention of not only marketers, but government agencies, policy groups, nongovernmental organizations, and foundations.[38]

As this chapter shows, if at times we cannot help but almost give up hope of undoing the knots and constraints that current consumer segmentation practices in business foster, it is also the complexity of real life and the humanity of respondents that tends to keep us going. On an analytic and theoretical level, we have also found recent inspiration in anthropologist John Jackson's 2005 ethnography, *Real Black: Adventures in Racial Sincerity*. In his careful, nuanced portrayal of race and ethnicity and the process of ethnographic research, Jackson tries to help us move beyond the all-imprisoning cells of authenticity discourse by bringing forward notions of racial sincerity. A crucial element of sincerity is that it is defined from within. It is a subject-defined state, not an objectified property. And as an internal, subjective experience, it is never thoroughly knowable or definable from the outside. It can also change over time. Thoughts and feelings and allegiances and situations and contexts and selves change. And importantly, Jackson's notion and his analysis give one hope. Hope helps to provide a strong heart, and hope means one can imagine a way out of essentialism and authenticity discourse, and thus one can care.

About the time we were setting about writing the first draft of this chapter, Patti went to dinner with the journalist who had suggested that we use the "press one (or two) for Spanish" telephone menu example in our conference talk. The dinner was celebrating the fact that the journalist would be leaving New York shortly because she had landed a position with the then newly forming French international news network, FRANCE 24. Her dual French and American cultural and linguistic background was going to pay off. She was completely and ideally suited to the job. At dinner we were talking about world and other affairs. A recurring motif, a topic on many Americans' minds at the time, was the economic power and cultural ascendancy of China. One of the most personally comforting and laughter-inducing stories for Patti was about how in France, rather than finding busloads of American tourists offensive, it had now become busloads of Chinese tourists who so offended French sensibilities. Equivalent to conceptions of American tourists, the Chinese were seen to speak loudly and wear terrible clothing combinations. But, in addition to this, the Chinese tourists had added spitting. "They spit all the time." The busloads of spitting Chinese tourists were making the busloads of American tourists look good. Funny. There is comfort on the moral high ground, and perhaps along with the loss of economic power there are also some symbolic rewards. But one cannot rely on the moral high ground or economic palliatives; we must also remember that in every instance we are co-creators. The audience also creates the categories: We are all in these matrices together.

Notes

1. For anthropologists, notions of the cultural constitution of race and ethnicity draw upon and build from the early 20th-century analyses of Boas (1940), the work of Barth (1959, 1969), and others in the 1950s and 1960s, investigations and interventions during the 1970s, 1980s, and 1990s such as those from Baker (1998), Blu (1979, 1980), Domínguez (1986), Harrison (1995), Shanklin (1994), Sollors (1989), Waters (1990), Williams (1989), and the authors included in Gregory and Sanjek's (1994) volume, *Race*. This outlook continues to animate and inform analyses published in the 2000s, for instance, John Jackson's (2005) *Real Black: Adventures in Racial Sincerity* and John Hartigan's (2005) *Odd Tribes: Toward a Cultural Analysis of White People*. See also Darder and Torres (2004) and Mullings (2005) in terms of appreciating the need to interrogate racism, not only race.
2. Dávila (2001) has clearly argued that the practices of marketing worlds have had an important role in the social constitution of Latino/Hispanic identity in the United States. Whether through familiarity with this or other scholarship (Appadurai 1996; Bourdieu 1984; Brodkin 2000; Costa and Bamossy 1995; Firat 1995; García Canclini 1995, 2001; Miller 1997; Tharp 2001; Thompson and Tambyah 1999; Vélez-Ibáñez and Sampaio 2002) or by virtue of being a citizen of the contemporary world, few can doubt that the organization of consumption in relation to international market forces has had a significant impact on the production and reproduction of contemporary notions, expectations, and lived realities of ethnoracial identities. The current keen interest within business in segmenting customers in terms of Latino/Hispanic ethnicity is no doubt creative and inseparable from other societal dynamics: the huge growth of Spanish language media in the last decade, projected population figures for individuals of Caribbean, Mexican, Central and South American descent in the United States, the importance of Latino identity in politics.
3. Stavenhagen (1999:8). With thanks to Leith Mullings (2005) for calling our attention to this quotation.
4. Conferences that include the sharing of experiences through papers, presentations, and workshops among various corporate executives, marketers, consumer research professionals, and "gurus" (a label we have actually seen applied) are not uncommon. From an academic standpoint these conferences can themselves be tangled affairs. For instance, one of the major organizations that sponsors conferences of this type requests sizable fees from consumer researchers for the right to present

at the conference. Part of the "package" the consumer researcher receives in return for the fee is the promise of brokered and targeted introductions to those identified as potential clients. We have turned down offers to pay for such a privilege—such offers grate against academic norms and assumptions, however chimerical, regarding appropriate rationales and values surrounding the exchange of information among peers. We also became incensed on one occasion when a client wanted to include us in the presentation slot she had been offered (corporate parties do not pay for the right to speak, in fact they are often sought after) but were excluded because another party had already received the exclusive right to be the only ethnographic research supplier featured at the conference. Thus we learned that for an even larger fee (one can presume), the right to be the sole ethnographic supplier featured at a marketing conference could be garnered. At the conference we describe in this chapter, no fees were paid by either side for this speech, and we paid our own plane and accommodations, thus it fit well with our academic conference expectations.

5. See Sunderland, Taylor, and Denny (2004).

6. In essence, this also meant recognizing the inherent hybridity of ethnicity, not only, per Rosaldo, because the symbols and practices surrounding ethnicity are inherently blurred, mixed, in flux, and changing, but also that we were all part of its constitution. See Renato Rosaldo's comments on hybridity in his foreword in García Canclini (1995:xv). Note that today, if we were asked to give this talk, we may have foregrounded processes of racism rather than socially constituted ethnicity, but we have tried to remain true in this recounting to what we actually said at that time.

7. In preparation for the talk we further explored the meaning of the acronym in a follow-up call as well as through Wesleyan's Web site. At the time of this writing, a listing and brief discussion of the endless acronym could be found at www.wesleyan.edu/queer/whyqueer.htt. Last accessed June 16, 2007.

8. Sunderland (1997).

9. Many scholars have pointed out that what is important about ethnoracial identities—for the individual or as a category—is not a question of their authenticity (historical or otherwise) but of the ways in which these are invoked and used. In whose interest are these invoked? For what ends? To serve what goals? Many scholars have indicated that important questions are the ways in which intertwined networks of power organize the deployment of these socially constructed identities; see, for instance, García Canclini (2001), Lipsitz (2006), Santiago-Irizarry (2001), and also Vila (2000). As Lipsitz (2006:2) succinctly sums up the issues, "Race is a cultural construct, but one with deadly social causes and consequences."

10. See also Keefe and Padilla (1987), Limón (1998), Peñaloza (1994), and Vila (2000).

11. Note Dávila's (1998) analysis of *El Kiosko Budweiser*, a local and locally perceived television show in Puerto Rico, developed in and through the marketing efforts of Budweiser.

12. Note Mahon's (2004) *Right to Rock*, a detailed ethnographic analysis of the Black Rock Coalition and participants' activities and efforts to assert and affirm African American identity with and within rock music. See also Jackson (2005) for an exploration in the deconstruction of African American authenticity discourse.

13. With thanks to John Prevost for this formulation.

14. Dávila (2001, 2002).
15. See also Santiago-Irizarry's (2001) discussion of "the numbers argument" in the establishment of Latino-focused psychiatric programs.
16. Cf. Dávila (2002).
17. Stavenhagen (1999:12).
18. As Dávila has noted, the "general market" can be a gloss for "white" consumers, but at the same time this category in actual practice in corporations does often encompass and include diversity, in terms of both category definition and research.
19. See De Genova and Ramos-Zayas (2003), Flores and Yúdice (1990), Mendoza-Denton (1999), Santiago-Irizarry (2001:88–115), and Urciuoli (1996). See also Darder and Torres (1998) and Woolard (1998), and Waterston's (2006) article on social processes, including those of marketing, on Latino ascendancy and "whitening" thus perpetuating the racial binary in the United States.
20. Jackson (2005:163–164). See also May and Pattillo-McCoy (2000) for a thoughtful explication of the divergent experiences and analyses of two African American ethnographers carrying out research in an African American community in Chicago. The elision in the quotation from Jackson refers to May and Pattillo and himself as middle-class African American scholars. Jackson provides a thoughtful discussion of these issues in terms of a rigorous reflexivity incorporating Ginsburg's (1995) parallax effect and Behar's (1996) notions of vulnerability. See also Narayan's (1993) important "How Native is a 'Native' Anthropologist?" and Domínguez (2000), "For a Politics of Love and Rescue," in which she discusses some of the social problematics in the study of minoritized groups by minoritized scholars, including a reproduction of the institutionalized discrimination it is meant to challenge.
21. See Sunderland, Taylor, and Denny (2004).
22. Geertz (1973:12).
23. See Bohannan (1966).
24. See Chapters 2 and 3.
25. Notably, in terms of the Latino context, Patti's father had been born and raised in Cuba. She had grown up with *arroz con pollo, café con leche*, and hearing Spanish at gatherings with relatives, even though per his parents, he was of Anglo heritage. The world is complicated.
26. Notably, while Patti and Michael had assumed all speakers representing the agency for the African American target audience were black, the first woman from that agency to bring up this issue was white. The reality of this telephone meeting was that it was a very complex and multilayered racialized encounter, complete with mis-, under-, and overinterpretations. As Paitra Russell later pointed out, the explanation of the race/ethnicity of interviewers as *not* integral to the research could have also been taken by the agency representative who expressed her offense as a personal affront. It may have been interpreted as an assertion that nonwhite people don't "matter," which could easily be extrapolated to be a suggestion that "white people think they know everything" and do not need input from anyone—not interviewers and not niche market advertising agencies.
27. As she explained in response to a draft of this chapter, in fact, she had no idea what Patti meant by the statement, but since it was about thirty seconds into a conversation in which she was in the process of being hired, she felt it was not the

best time to explore it. Moreover, she has actually retold the story of that first conversation many times, always with a chuckle.

28. For discussion of "the paper bag principle," see Kerr (2005). For a broader and more detailed analysis of the social importance of this and other complexion lore in African American communities, see Kerr (2006).

29. As this anthropologist later disclosed, she had herself been concerned whether she would appear to us as "black enough" for the project, but that she was not worried about what interviewees would think as African Americans, accustomed to seeing various mixtures and skin tones, almost always knew that she was part black. As she also pointed out, "It's always interesting to me that so much attention is focused on how people self-identify, when what has always mattered most in my life is how other people are identifying me." Without question, racial assignment has been, and continues to be, a powerful social force.

30. We thank Paitra Russell for pointing to this explicit understanding of expertise within business realms.

31. See Goffman (1961, 1963, 1978).

32. See McLarin (2006) for a contemporary example. See also comments by Mullings (2005) on "color-blindness."

33. Implicit notions of entertainment usher in their own set of entanglements and conundrums, as discussed in Chapter 9.

34. We are grateful to Paitra Russell for aspects of this formulation and for her reminder of the argument that "now that nonwhites are making strides, [white] people want to eradicate race." As she also pointed out, those who are deeply, *personally* committed to what we would consider to be essentialist understandings of race and ethnicity may not view essentialism as a problem at all and may, in fact, feel empowered by it. Thus, destabilizing the categories themselves can often be interpreted as assisting in the devaluation of identities people hold dear, and is why anthropologists can come to be seen as the enemy in racial/ethnic identity politics debates. At the same time, anthropologists, often in agreement, continue to point to the dangers of the hierarchical oppositions and the need to emphasize interstitial and intragroup diversity, as well as to keep in mind the structural inequalities and destructiveness of racism while embracing that race is socially constituted; see, for instance, Mendoza-Denton (1999), Mullings (2005), and Shanklin (1998).

35. See note 18.

36. Behar (1996:177). Note also Domínguez' (2000:365) argument for the virtues of study based in "real love and real respect for real people" rather than one built in and upon identity politics.

37. See Firat (1995).

38. See, as examples from consumer research, Costa and Bamossy (1995), Crockett and Wallendorf (2004), Fennell and Saegert (2004), Firat (1995), Mehta and Belk (1991), and Oswald (1999).

9

Ethnographic Video in Consumer Research: Fulfilling the Promise?

Above all, the visual media allow us to construct knowledge not by "description" (to borrow Bertrand Russell's terms) but by a form of "acquaintance."[1]
—David MacDougall, theorist in visual anthropology

Let's go to the videotape.
—Iconic refrain of Warner Wolf, former New York television sportscaster

In the preceding chapter we described entanglements that ensue when instantiating an anthropological approach in the midst of marketing's practice of segmenting consumers. Here we address entanglements that have arisen with the increased use of moving imagery as a medium of ethnographic research and representation. Again the entanglements are formed in a network of differing epistemological assumptions, practical and strategic goals. In this instance the discrepancies among assumptions and goals for video as a methodological and representational tool are knotted together with broader sociocultural assumptions and practices surrounding moving imagery. The fact that video and digital technologies are rapidly changing adds complexity: The terrain is a swiftly changing one, not only in terms of video production, but also in the social practices of video consumption.

Videographic recording of ethnography is currently exceedingly commonplace within applied consumer research. Our primary concern arising from this practice is that moving imagery's apprehension, use, and viewing are often not carried out in ways that ensure the generative promise of enhanced ethnographic understanding. The use of video in ethnographic consumer research is *not* problematic per se—video can be a tool for enhancing ethnographic understanding and representation—but our uneasiness surrounds the problematic ways video is apprehended and utilized. In the first section of what follows, we describe some of the principal epistemological tangles we encounter in the use of video as a methodological tool. We then turn to matters of reception and representation in the second section. Both build to the ultimate question of how ethnographic consumer researchers can fulfill the generative promise of video in practice.

Bringing Video into Ethnographic Consumer Research

When we first began conducting ethnographic consumer research for corporate clients in the 1980s, video was only occasionally a requested component. We used stationary video to record kitchen activities such as refrigerator and microwave use or the washing of dishes, and for the rare project we created video reports. Yet even in the mid-1990s, we, not clients, were usually the catalysts for video's inclusion in research projects.[2] We embraced the virtues and creative possibilities of moving imagery; clients were not always convinced of the benefit of the added expense. However, by the end of the 1990s, this had radically changed. By the late 1990s video was a frequent request and an expectation of clients. Since 2000, videographic recording and representation of ethnographic work have been virtually assumed requirements within the industry as a whole.

Thus, in the early 2000s many consumer research firms began to feature "video ethnography" (labeled in those or similar terms) as a research modality they could provide and highlighted the filmmaking credentials of their team. "Professional videographers" became a selling point for consumer research firms and corporate research departments. In the mid-2000s, video examples appeared on research company Web sites.[3] At present, it often seems as if, for many, it is no longer imaginable that ethnographic work could be carried out without the presence of a recording camera.[4]

Videotaping = "Doing Ethnography"

A troubling aspect in the initial embrace of video in applied ethnographic consumer research was the way in which the recording of video was often represented as not only co-terminus, but somehow synonymous with "doing ethnography." At times, video seemed to even be replacing ethnography as the fantasy du jour.[5] For instance, a May 2001 column in the trade publication *Adweek* was headlined, not with ethnography as the newcomer, but video: "Candid Camera: Will video replace focus groups as the core of research?" As the column concluded, "The ability to see into lives as they are lived, rather than as they are reported, could prompt advertising's next evolution."[6] A month later, *Adweek* chose Emma Gilding, then head of Ogilvy & Mather's Discovery Group, as among five who had the "coolest jobs in advertising" and the subtitle here was: "The ex-theatre director moves in, then films consumers in their own homes." The accompanying article included the quotation, "With a video camera you can see the difference between what people say they do and what they actually do."[7]

In 2000, a *Wall Street Journal* article had also reported: "Videotape, P&G hopes, will help get at the whole truth." As that article detailed, "[T]he maker of Tide laundry detergent, Pampers diapers and Crest toothpaste plans to send video crews and cameras into about 80 households around the world, hoping to capture, on tape, life's daily routine and procedures in all their boring glory.... In a recent test of the program, P&G marketers huddled around a computer in a Cincinnati conference room to watch a mother make breakfast in a tidy kitchen in Thailand."[8] In the concluding paragraph, the author wrote of P&G's eventual goal of amassing a large, searchable video database "organized by key words." Thus, the eventual possibility that you could "search for 'eating snacks' and find clips from all over the world on that topic."[9] An enormous undertaking, laudable for the effort, but the problem P&G researchers would face would be how to globally apply socioculturally constituted and specific conceptual terms such as "snack" or "meal." How would one get beyond the constricting filter and imposition of U.S.-relevant categories when viewing the clips in the United States? What would be the interpretative frame?

In our own practice, we also experienced ways in which clients began to think of the video recording as "the ethnography." For instance, in a project done in 2003 we were asked to send the day's video by overnight FedEx so that the client team could review it the next morning. As they told us, their goal was to assess the ethnographic content, to make sure they were getting what was needed: "an opportunity to make adjustments." Wanting to make adjustments or be assured of getting at the issues deemed relevant are understandable—and often helpful—client goals. What was problematic in this request for videotapes, as it is in the overall embrace of video-as-ethnography, was the evident reprise of the epistemological problem of rendering and reducing ethnography to observation that we described in Chapter 2. In turn, this rendering was re-ushering in the epistemological assumption of a transparency of meaning (as if every observer attends to, sees, hears, and thinks the same thing *and* that ethnographic understanding does not necessarily need to include appreciation of observers' internal thoughts and analysis).

If, in general, the notion of observable, transparent meaning has been generated in consumer research circles by the ongoing aura of positivistic science, the promise of an observable truth is supported in video's case by socioculturally constituted understandings of video's "monitoring" lens. The ongoing recording, the sense of video's continuousness, the surveillance we have come to know from mounted cameras, has carried the promise of a total record. In our experience, within consumer research, the fact that filming and editing means choosing, excluding, and potentially reordering is easily over-looked. Credibility anxiety is often only provoked when a badly placed dissolve (a convention that signals an exclusion or time lapse) violates the sense of viewing a seemingly continuous, i.e., uncut, reality or "truth." Even if the sociocultural assumptive terrain surrounding cameras' recording is shifting as digital retouching of photographs and video editing become the province of the everyday user (and thus hands-on realizations of the fictions that can easily be made to look "true"), videotaping (monitoring) cameras within consumer research have continued to evoke traditional cultural notions of the objectivity, reliability, and neutrality of the recording lens. However ironic, then, the wide-scale embrace of monitoring video in ethnographic consumer research practice seems to have helped refuel a scientist dream that one unadulterated, unfiltered, uninterested truth can exist.

But, of course, even monitoring camera lenses necessarily take in very small slices of life, and some things will be out of the frame. The narrow camera lens is also always placed and directed by a human eye, which, in turn, is always informed by sociocultural context, history, and situation. Even when a camera moves from spot to spot, some things will be missed, and of course cameras are sometimes turned off. Moreover, as ethnographic filmmaker and theorist David MacDougall has contended, what often distinguishes good filmmakers is not "seeing," but their ability to look and to look carefully. As he has also pointed out, citing Dai Vaughan, ongoing life and film are not the same thing because film is always "about something" and "reality is not."[10] Video representations are always about a slice of life and always involve some editing (at the least, in designated start and stop points). That is reality. The video record is never "total" and the "reading" of the record will always depend on the viewer.

For anthropologists, the assumptions about observation and univocal meaning surrounding video are also problematic because the potential power of cultural analysis is simultaneously left unutilized. As Donna Romeo has noted about her work in the retail environment, videography as an end unto itself reduces the role of the anthropologist to "the collector of 'cool customer clips.'"[11] The interpretive contribution can be lost. A nuanced cultural reading and analysis of consumer behavior can go by the wayside. The risk in this rendering, as Christina Wasson has discussed in relation to the use of video in the field of design, is the danger of producing analytically anemic accounts that in turn can pose a danger to the perceived value of ethnography.[12] When ethnography is judged by the videotaped encounter rather than the analysis, it is not really a fair assessment of the method's potential. As has been queried before, can we imagine the potential ramifications if quantitative research were rendered synonymous with raw data files?

As Suchman and Trigg's work in video-based interaction analysis demonstrated in the early 1990s, videotaping during fieldwork and later careful examination of the record can be exceedingly useful for observing small, telling details and interactions that otherwise could go unseen or unnoticed.[13] Their design-oriented research on technology and work practices implicitly and explicitly brought the theory of ethnomethodology and conversation analysis into the observational lens. But "cool customer clips," or ethnography reduced to videographic observational research, undermines the medium's potential for enhanced ethnographic understanding. To record moving imagery is not to *do* ethnography, even if ethnographic work can include and benefit from the use of video cameras.[14]

Performance Anxiety

Beyond the use of video to record ethnographic encounters, one of the important ways in which we often use video as an ethnographic tool is to have respondents create their own video documentaries. We were originally inspired to try out this method in 2000 at the request of clients at an advertising agency.[15] Their desire was to better understand the worlds of pickup truck owners and the advertising agency came to us with the request to include video diaries in the research process. This experiment with video was enormously successful and we became enamored with the possibilities of video diaries as ethnographic methodology. The video diary method was ideally suited to documenting pickup truck owners' active lives which centered on activities involving their trucks. We were treated to scenes of home and yard reconstruction, fishing, hunting, off-road hill climbing, and families at drive-in movies, as well as the more mundane matters of going to work, completing errands, or shopping. The owners could also talk freely and easily about what it meant to have a truck versus a car and about the meanings of different truck brands. They were proud of their trucks and how they could live with and through their trucks.

Since then we have used video diaries successfully in projects ranging from young people's everyday and social lives, home cleaning, the use of air fresheners, the routines and rituals of going to bed, the purchase of consumer electronics, what it means to cook dinner, and the documentation of both pleasant and unpleasant experiences in the use of new products. Part of what makes these video diaries successful is the degree to which respondents become involved and engaged in the process of documentation. Their reflections about themselves, their thoughts, and their actions are often the key to our understanding. As we have written elsewhere, in making these diaries, respondents become our partners in the ethnographic research endeavor and, as we have also noted, they are performers.[16]

One of the knotty conversations we have oft had to repeat with clients involves this performance element of diarists. Sometimes clients become concerned in anticipation of what and how respondents will produce their diaries; sometimes they become concerned on seeing their result. Will we influence consumers if we interview them before they do their diaries? Would they have done that if there was not a camera around? Of course, the respondents are influenced by any questions we ask and by our implicit presence, just as they would be influenced in a different way if they had not encountered us and if they did not have any images in their minds of who would be seeing the tape as they created their diaries. And of course, they are performing. It is an improvised performance, not a scripted one, and they—not we—are the directors, but there are performative elements.

Embedded in our clients' questions is the epistemological concern that if performance is any part of the data, then it is not reality, it is not real information, it is fiction.[17] Yet, similar to what we argued for focus group performances in Chapter 7, we would suggest that respondent performance does not make video diaries any less real or ethnographically telling. Yes, just as entering the space of a focus group room, grocery store, classroom, or gym are cues for performative routines, so is the presence of a camera. And, without question, the presence of a shooting camera is a highly salient sociocultural cue for specified routines. One can note, for example, the way frequently photographed children know the social conventions of being photographed and most can perform the appropriate behaviors before they can talk. In 2002 Kodak reported equipping its dual-mode digital cameras, which could record video or stills, with a dual indicator light when (ethnographic) research showed that people needed to know whether a still or video was being shot so they could act appropriately, i.e., move or stay still.[18]

There is also, without question, the special cultural and performative space of "movie" productions, ethnographic and otherwise. The culturally special ciné-unique performative context—for those filmed and for filmmakers—has been discussed as the participatory cinema space per David MacDougall and with notions such as ciné-attitude, ciné-vois, ciné-entends, ciné-bouge, ciné-pense, and ciné-regarde by Jean Rouch, muse and mentor of many an ethnographic filmmaker.[19] As Weinberger has also bluntly put it, people depicted in the first ethnographic film, the 1895 *L'Arivèe d'un Train en Gare*, were "with a few exceptions, the last filmed people who were not actors, self-conscious participants in the filmmaking."[20] We are all involved when we know that a camera is rolling.[21]

But from our point of view, the performance of routines—including those associated with the act of movie-making—do not in any way impede the possibilities of cultural analysis. To consider that because something is performed it does not convey "real" information is to force oneself into a needlessly confining box. For one, as ethnomethodology and ethnography of communication research made abundantly clear many years ago, culturally specified, learned, rehearsed, performative routines (in physical and verbal actions) are part of what make life both predictable and intelligible.[22] We know to say "excuse me" after bumping into someone on the street. Embedded, implicated, reflective, and productive of the convoluted sociocultural matrix in which we live, such routines are part of the grammar we draw on (whether in conformity or in protest) to know what to do and how to act. Performances *are* culturally telling and revealing.

Thus, as Pini has pointed out in her own discussion of video diary performance in a study for which she used the method to explore social class among British teenage girls, while the girls performed things from secret confessionals to the mocking of middle-class norms, nonetheless:

> Social class thoroughly saturates each and every one of these diaries. It speaks through bodies, in accent, in composure, in dress, in a diarist's level of ease and so forth. It speaks through objects, through a room's decoration, through what hangs on a girl's wall, through what shows through her window (a large green garden or a crowded street or block of other flats for example). It speaks through the *mise en scene* of the diary. In short, it speaks itself through the whole feel, style and theme of the diary.[23]

As Pini further argued, genres of reality and confessional television served as cultural context and model for the girls as individuals, performers, and research participants. We witness this influence of the popular sphere in our research practice as well. We have seen shifts in respondent performance along with shifts in popular genres. Younger respondents once talked about (and mimicked) MTV's *The Real World*, then shifted to other reality shows, and at the time of this writing, seemingly the conventions and assumptions of their own prior experience in video productions and/or YouTube. For older respondents, television cooking shows often seemed the implicit model for diarists in the 1990s and early 2000s, whereas home makeover shows seemed the more relevant frame by 2006.

What is perhaps particularly interesting and telling in the expressed concern over video diarists' performances is that we rarely hear this concern expressed in relation to the recording of in situ ethnographic encounters where we are present. In these encounters, there is also performance—again one which does not negate the possibilities for cultural analysis—but it is rarely questioned. One has to ponder, then, the extent to which the concern over performance in video diaries implicitly revolves around concerns over who has authorial and directorial control. In in situ encounters, researchers, professional videographers, and clients implicitly engage in these roles (even if respondents sometimes implicitly and explicitly contest that situation by how they respond to queries, what they are willing to show, and whom they include in the conversation). Is the disquiet about performance in consumer video diaries, then, in actuality about giving consumers' directorial control of the research process? And, then, what does this have to say about the implicit assumptions surrounding the research process, and, importantly, what constitutes ethnographic knowledge?

Our own anthropological goal of gaining participants' points of view is perhaps the core reason we are enamored with participant-created video diaries as an ethnographic methodology. But these self-produced video documentaries provide us additional benefits. They stretch the traditional boundaries of consumer research in terms of space and time—we cannot always be there. Diaries tend also to retain in their making the social worlds and relations of respondents. The help (and hindrances) from friends and family in the creation of diaries, as well other life events and context, infuse the diaries. We gain insight into the social context that frames respondents' lives. One notes how exasperated a mother becomes with her toddler right before she turns off the camera. A boy videotaping his mother's commentary turns the camera on himself to playfully contradict what his mother just said. A videotaping teenager pleads to her (charmingly clueless) father to please not unplug her iPod at the moment he pulls it out of its charger to show us. The conventions the diarists use to create their videotapes provide further insight into sociocultural worlds and how consumers locate themselves within those worlds. Setting the diary to self-produced music, creating titles, inserting credits at the end, and making us sign a form that protected her copyright over potential public reuse—as a diarist in her early twenties did in March 2007—is telling about herself, her world, and her perception of research endeavors. We ask respondents to reflect at the end of their tapes on their own realizations during the research process as well as on a few of the key issues that we know need answering. From an anthropological point of view, what is there *not* to like?

For us, then, the problem of performance is not that it exists, but that it must be decoded. Worry over the performance of video diarists is unneeded. What is needed, however, is to consider video productions as cultural documents requiring interpretation. With video diaries (and video and film more generally), one must take into account the semiotic and social conventions drawn upon for their production, the assumptions brought to their interpretation, and the practices that surround their social use. This taking into account of the assumptions, conventions, and social practices is the real challenge we see in bringing video into the quotidian ethnographic toolkit. We begin a consideration of these matters with the discussion of some of the entanglements that ensue in the reception of video during presentations.

Bringing Video into the "Deliverables"

In the vocabulary of the applied market research world, "deliverables" refer to what research consultants agree to materially provide ("deliver") to commissioning clients. Ours generally include PowerPoint reports, original recordings of ethnographic encounters or focus groups (and occasionally transcripts), original video diary tapes (increasingly DVDs), and, for ethnography, some form of edited video product. As a rule, as described in Chapter 8, an in-person presentation is also part of the deliverables.

For the most part, these presentations consist of us explaining the import of written bullet points, as well as the implications we see in a multitude of accompanying digital photographs, scanned drawings, collages, and other images inserted into projected PowerPoint slides. And at strategic points, we show edited video clips. A few years ago this meant switching from projected PowerPoint slides to a DVD player; more recently this has meant simply clicking on the compressed "movie" file linked to the PowerPoint document.

When we first began using and producing videotapes for clients, the modality was VHS tapes (and the masters were Beta). Interestingly, in those first years, we tended *not* to show the video interspersed at points within the presentation, but rather as one piece at the beginning or end of the presentation. While we began to intersperse video into the main body of the presentation when they were still in VHS format—doing so by starting and stopping a tape—these tapes were generally created as "whole stories," thirty to sixty minutes in length, broken into "sections," largely to facilitate our starting and stopping.

We call out these aspects of early practices with videotape because they so clearly mirrored more general sociocultural assumptions and practices surrounding moving imagery. Specifically, the lengths of the edited products corresponded to the standard 30-, 60-, and 120-minute lengths of VHS video-tapes, lengths which in turn corresponded to the typical lengths of television shows and movies. The practice of interspersing was clearly influenced by the start-stop capabilities learned and made possible with the use of VCRs. The original practice of showing without interspersing also seems a product of the special cultural space traditionally afforded in the United States (and many other places) to moving imagery—the space of entertainment, the telling of stories, and inspiration set apart from ordinary life, and, particularly, the mundane activities of work.[24] This is the cultural space we know from the traditional place of moving imagery in our lives: television shows, movies, and ads. We were similarly marking and setting apart this space during our presentations by screening our videos in this way.

The Entertainment Space

The existence of the entertainment space cued by moving imagery is easily observed in the posture of those assembled to hear our "findings."[25] When covering the material presented in PowerPoint slides, the posture of the audience reflects "business meeting" or "serious lecture." That is, there is attention (at least feigned) to what is said; if handouts have been made from the PowerPoint slides or original collages put out on the table, these are perused; participants' pens are in hand, notes jotted. When the switch is made to video (or even in anticipation of video), pens are put down, notebooks pushed away, people sit back ever so slightly in their chairs and often smile. The palpable sense in the room is that the good stuff is coming. Turning off lights in the room, frequently a necessity for viewing, only adds to the allure. If video starts the presentation, this is not usually taken as part of the presentation, but rather—as we had intended it to be in the example in Chapter 8—as the inspirational set-up.

If in a classroom setting it would be possible to insist that students take notes while watching a video to disrupt these viewing conventions, we never have felt that we had this option in corporate conference rooms.[26] To say that we have never seen a client take notes during the screening of video involves only a tiny bit of exaggeration. Moreover, if not engaged by it, people also freely "turn off" from video. Rather than make attempts to sharpen their focus on the content (often done on a "text" thought to be "work"), most people will shift their attention. We might hope that people would appreciate the socio-cultural complexity of the consumption context or the way in which the social environment influences the meaning of a brand, even if the drama drags. But generally this appreciation does not occur; more likely the video will not even be watched if it does not tell an entertaining story. If it was, until quite recently, a widespread cultural articulation in the United States that documentaries were "always boring," most filmmakers accepted—and continue to accept—that if they want their work to be watched, they had better make it interesting. With video and film, the entertainment expectation and posture is a predominant frame.

Thus, entertainment value has always been a conscious consideration in our choice of material to present in video. While we always try to accurately illustrate analytic findings within their sociocultural context, we do so by trying to find the bits that do this in the most compelling and engaging fashion. The video *must* have the power to capture and hold viewer attention. Does it tell a good story, either directly by the respondents' telling of a story or in the unfolding of drama akin to what we expect from cinema and television? Is there "action" in addition to "talking heads"? We also take some pains to leave in humorous bits that will make people laugh. We try to be careful to make this entertainment value not that of "laughing at" but rather "laughing with" respondents in response to moments of shared humorous recognition, purposeful jokes, and the like (including moments of laughing at ourselves). Ideally, these are moments when laughing would have occurred had we all been there, for instance, when a video diarist who has been showing what life is like in her car—and it almost always entails being behind schedule—deadpans ironically to the camera that now, once again late, they are "speeding to the bus stop" so her daughter can get to school on time. She wants us to shake our heads and chuckle; she was being funny. As this example also shows, our video diary respondents clearly share the convention that they should be entertaining and tell good stories in their video productions.

This fact of moving imagery's association with entertainment, not work, does have entangling repercussions. It can mean that the ethnographic video production is taken as not serious, not as the "real" or "important" informational resource, but simply as the "fun" stuff. And so when we switch to video, assembled audiences may not only smile and sit back in their chairs, but also seize upon those moments as the time when they can stop paying attention to the presentation and instead check—and respond to—messages on their PDAs. Or, it can be seen as the time to make a run out of the conference room for a bathroom break. It is the time when audience members will lean toward those sitting near them and engage in side conversations.

To not oversimplify, as a cultural event, there are undoubtedly many things going on here. In part, the context also shifts because we move from center stage, and thus, there may be less felt pressure to be attentively polite to a speaker. Individuals working in corporate worlds frequently live with multiple commitments and extraordinary time pressures. Any kind of a break in an event can be seen as time to check up on things, to answer a message, to get something else done. With the advent of mobile, individual, digital technologies, the cultural conventions for group face-to-face meetings are also in flux; attending to calls, messages, or interacting with information stored on a personal device is, in fact, generally becoming more commonplace.[27] We do see evidence of this in the corporate conference rooms before the video goes on as well. But what is important is the relative relationship. The sense that there is less need to give "serious" attention while the video is playing (what are all the reasons we call it "playing"?) as when we are lecturing or just talking is often palpable. More messages are checked. Talk is instituted. People relax. People leave. This common reaction to video segments provided the space in 2005 for one of our partners who is slightly less enamored with video (and probably also tired of admonitions to pay attention to lighting, audio, and editing needs) to exact joking revenge. During a presentation he and Patti did together, when the videotape started to roll, and the assembled crowd started checking messages and talking, and a few got up to leave, he leaned over and quipped, "Yes, Patti, we'll pay more attention to lighting, audio, and labeling the tapes, and maybe one day they'll watch it."

If moving imagery as a signal of a space apart from work and seriousness is currently being attenuated by its use as a medium for communicating information (witness the popularity of twenty-four-hour television news and documentaries, video clips on Web sites framed as serious information sources), the ability of the medium to signify "less important than text" clearly still exists.[28] In our most recent instance, occurring in the spring of 2007, when we screened video excerpts during a presentation those in research and brand positions paid very close attention. However, the most senior person in the room, the person to whom, in many ways, we were *really* presenting, consistently stopped paying attention whenever we switched to video. During those moments, he examined the PowerPoint handout and wrote notes on it. But clearly his notes were based on what was written in the document or perhaps on something we had said. His notes were not sparked by the video's content. He did not watch the video; he was "working." Even if expository prose and educational lecture are not the dominant communication modalities of our time, culturally these genres are still constituted as the forms through which serious learning takes place. Moving imagery is not the medium we believe we learn from, even if we do; and so, the switch to video remains a contextual key that frames the event as one of "entertainment."

For us, in trying to accurately and adequately represent and convey ethnographic consumer research findings, this reality has always perplexed.[29] We invest our analytic heads and hearts in the videos. We see these as productions that illustrate the issues we deem most important for the client. We rely on the edited videos to show cultural and behavioral complexity in ways we feel we never could with PowerPoint documents filled with bullet points and photographs and accompanied by speech, or even interpretive dance (as one favorite client has quipped should be our next move). By virtue of video's multimodal presentation of auditory, visual, expository, foreground, background, multi-person and multi-place information, we expect them to inform. We use them to communicate ethnographic, sociocultural texture. Our objective, for us the raison d'être of the video, is the transmittal of truly exciting cultural analytic findings. Our own "Let's go to the videotape" (like that of sportscaster Warner Wolf) is not supposed to be about spice, it is not just about illustration, it is supposed to be a substantial part of the main course.

Moreover, we note a shift over the years toward the growing importance we have ourselves placed on video as a medium of communication. The first videos we produced tended to illustrate one or several parts of the analysis. In the edited excerpts we now produce, we often attempt to cover *all* crucial nodes of the analysis—there is rarely an important concept in the written report that is not also communicated with video. And also hence the importance we see for people to pay attention to them. In the interest of time in a presentation, in fact, we often now skip the provision of verbal commentary on some of the written bullet points or still images in order to communicate the information with the video. Again, we do so because we feel that video is a superior medium for providing sociocultural texture and our respondents' points of view than is our own in vivo show-and-tell of static text and imagery.

And so, the fact that moving imagery signals entertainment rather than crucial informational resource is often a conundrum for us. Without question, however, there is also a clear upside to the bracketed entertainment space of moving imagery—for corporations and for us—and that is when moving imagery serves to take people out of the mundane, out of the ordinary world of work. Captivating and compelling videos can become vehicles of inspiration.

Vehicles of Inspiration

In 1998 we created a composite video focused on fabric refreshers. Febreze was new to the market and our client wanted to understand how and why consumers were using this product. What was the "consumer magic" that was allowing fabric refresher to seemingly take the world by storm? The tape we produced included a smoker—who wanted to keep the actualities and volume of her smoking unknown to her husband—demonstrating the lengths she would go to when having a cigarette. She first donned a thick robe that covered her other attire, and then tucked her hair into a full coverage plastic shower cap. After slipping a cigarette pack taken from her (not his) bathroom into her pocket, she headed down the hallway, past the kitty litter box (for others, the ostensible reason she used Febreze), and went outside to the patio where ashtray and a bag for wrapping finished cigarette ends were stored in a cabinet. She then showed the routine she went through once she finished the cigarette. For this, she took off her robe and hung it up on the inside of the bathroom door and proceeded to spray Febreze (profusely and steadily) on the robe. As she noted, she paid special attention to the cuffs and collar where the smoke would tend to accumulate. After spraying the robe, she would wash her face, brush her teeth and tongue, floss her teeth, and so on. She followed up by talking about how on the occasional times when she would have a cigarette in the bathroom (contradicting what she had told us earlier about never smoking in the house) she then would spray the towels, the toilet seat cover, and any other fabric in the bathroom. If, as sometimes happened, her husband surprised her before she was finished with her routine and was knocking on the door, she would quickly shut her eyes, spray Febreze onto her face and open up the door with a big smile and "hi." As we were later told, this tape went around the world. It was passed to far-flung planners and creatives of globally affiliated agencies. People talked to us about it years after its making. This poorly lit, grainy, client-shot video was "famous."

In 2005, an issuer of credit cards requested that we conduct a study that would involve interviewing small business owners we had interviewed in 2000. Most importantly, the desire, the enthusiasm, and the impetus to reinterview was driven by the video of small business owners we had produced five years before. As our client contacts told us, these business owners lived within the organization. They were individual customers felt to be known by "everyone," including the CEO, and "everyone" wanted to know what had happened to them during that five-year interval. During the telephone conversation in which we discussed the project with our clients, there was excitement in their voices. The bar owner, the guy who owned the gym, the leather restorer, the antique dealer who had told the story of the furry massage mitts (inspired by a James Bond film) he had tried to sell in college, the musician, the man in Chicago who owned the toy store—"We can't wait to hear what happened to them." Perhaps it goes without stating, but the desired deliverables included a comparative edited video that would juxtapose footage from the first video we had produced with the newly garnered stories. If the reason for requesting this follow-up study was truly to gain greater insight into the longitudinal outcomes of small business endeavors (a question with considerable implications for a credit card issuer), the impetus here was also the desire for a stimulating sequel to refresh the inspiration achieved by the original stories.

Another Practica production that served as inspiration was created for a national retailer in December of 2006 based on research carried out by partner Michael Donovan. The DVD created as accompaniment to the PowerPoint report was something the commissioning client began showing at meetings of field teams, regional offices, and licensees. Screenings seemed to consistently catalyze requests from viewers for copies so that they could show it to their own colleagues and constituents. Michael began receiving requests for extra copies: first a request for ten, then ten more, then in May of 2007, for twenty-five more. In the May e-mail request, sent five months after the research had been completed and presented, the client used the language of "hits." As he wrote, "The ethnography DVD continues to be a smash hit . . . I need to get 25 more DVDs . . . at this rate, the DVD will go platinum soon." The client also ended his message with, "I am hopeful that the approach has proven itself and we will come back in the future on another project."

In each of these examples, people clearly derived pleasure from watching the videos, and they liked to share them with others. They found it worthwhile to pass them around. In doing so, they were acting no differently with moving image media than many now do in their social lives. Rita has a friend (and former client) who routinely e-mails humorous video bits (sometimes hysterical ads from other countries, sometimes political spoofs) to her. Rita looks at them and forwards the ones she believes will strike a chord with colleagues. Rita's friend is a dependable source, we almost always take a moment out to watch them and laugh. They keep us going. They can also inspire. Recently, a friend sent Patti, and a score of others, a Web link to watch a videotaped presentation (spoken from a podium and assisted with projected computer presentation) on global trends in life expectancy, child mortality, and the like. Importantly, she wrote in the e-mail: "All, don't miss this presentation—especially those of you who care about poverty, data, communications, policy, teaching, and/or statistics. You won't regret it." The link was to Ted.com and the blurb there included: "You've never seen data presented like this. With the drama and urgency of a sportscaster, Hans Gosling debunks myths about the so-called 'developing world' . . . global trends become clear, intuitive and even playful."[30] As the friend wrote in a follow-up to Patti, "Do watch this presentation. It will inspire you for the rest of the day."

In the past few years, we certainly have felt the pressure to up the ante on the technical and artistic qualities of our productions even if, per Jean Rouch, one should be less worried about technical aspects and more concerned with content.[31] In today's climate, especially in corporate circles, not worrying about technical quality does not seem an option. In our own ethnographic research practice, we have always liked to put the camera in the hands of the client during fieldwork. We have done so, in part, to cut down on the number of participants on the ethnographic team (clients often like to attend ethnographic encounters) and also because it increases client participation in the research process as well as the final product, and thus helps fuel the enthusiasm necessary to see the implications carried through the organization. To facilitate this practice of clients-as-videographers, we have used relatively easy-to-operate cameras and largely depended on the cameras' internal microphones for audio.

But, more recently, we have also often had to shift to the use of professional videographers and external microphones in our ethnographic encounters when clients have made it clear that the technical quality of the final product must truly be first-rate. These requests for high-quality footage are often accompanied with the explicit rationale of wanting to ensure that the deliverable will be in its most attention-grabbing form. They, with a rationale similar to our own for wanting them to videotape, want to be sure the research results will "live" within the corporation. PowerPoint research reports can now end up gathering dust or lost on the hard drive, rarely re-read, their implications forgotten. Clients need something that will capture the imaginations of their colleagues and their own internal or external clients. Video that involves others, that captures imaginations, can make this work. If just a little over a decade ago reports were largely text, occasionally illustrated (and that was fine), now, without "great video," reports are "uninteresting."

In a recent issue of *Cultural Anthropology*, Teri Silvio drew on new media theorists' Bolter and Grusin's concept of remediation to discuss a digital video serial popular in Taiwan, "digital video knights-errant hand-puppetry." As Silvio explained, knights-errant hand-puppetry, a combination of knight-errant, fantasy, and science fiction genres, is a pop culture phenomenon that knits traditional Taiwanese themes, media, and cultural forms with contemporary technologies and concerns into "a utopian vision of what globalization might look like if Taiwan were at the center." If business arenas (except perhaps those in related industries) seem conceptually distant from knights-errant hand-puppetry and matters of new media, parallels can be drawn between ways new media have been formed and fit into social concerns and the ways video has been inserted into the concerns of business realms. The concept of remediation is helpful. As Silvio explains, quoting Bolter and Grusin, "A medium is that which remediates. It is that which appropriates the techniques, forms, and social significance of other media and attempts to rival or refashion them in the name of the real." Importantly, as she points out, the real here refers not only to an aesthetic sense of "real," but an institutional, sociological, and phenomenological one as well.[32]

In essence, then, in the three client examples discussed, what clients were doing with the ethnographic videos was remediating older means of inspiring others with videographic ones. They used the ethnographic video to inspire those they hoped to influence—colleagues in associated companies, internal clients, and so on. In the last example—in which, in fact, a media metaphor of a hit song (it "will go platinum soon") was invoked to frame the video's popularity—the ethnographic video remediated older tools (e.g., in-person presentations) to sell the ethnographic method and the research "supplier" to the organization. This could be noted in the client's comments at the end of the e-mail that he hoped the approach had proven itself and that ethnography would again be used in the future. In this way, the use of video was fundamentally akin to what consumer researchers were doing when they posted ethnographic videos onto their Web sites, instead of only written explanations and perhaps a few photos.

If these purposes of refitting the ethnographic videos into traditional business needs are not inherently problematic for us, the ways in which our videos-as-analytic-representations become reinserted, repurposed, remediated into traditional frameworks often are.

Complicities and Complexities of Representation

A cultural analytic perspective has always been embedded in our productions, though largely implicitly (e.g., via content and editing decisions and from a few strategically worded section titles) *because* we consciously decided not to use explanatory voiceover or excessive text among the moving images. We forewent documentary's traditional voice of authority in favor of the more cinema-verité and observational cinema approaches, allowing the voices of those filmed and the ongoing action to structure and communicate. We did not want the power of words to override the multidimensional, felt experience of visual and auditory imagery of multiple people and multiple places, some in the foreground, some in the background. If we also made these decisions to create videos without explanatory text or voiceover precisely out of a desire to make them (somewhat) open to multiple points of view and interpretations, in our presentations we also have always brought in cultural analysis and the implications we draw via written text and verbally delivered messages. We have interspersed the showing of the video with the explaining of the PowerPoint text to enhance the appreciation of both. We have always wanted the cultural theoretical perspective to be brought to bear on the questions at hand because we know that otherwise things can be interpreted in other fashions.

For instance, as wonderful and gratifying as it has been that virtually every watcher of our fabric refresher video remembers and continues to mention it to us years after the fact, tempering that elation is the reality that virtually everyone also interprets the actions of the woman described earlier as those of an obsessive, even slightly mad, individual. We had purposefully tried to circumvent such readings by immediately following her demonstration in the video with the demonstration of another woman, approximately twenty years her senior and personally quite different, yet conceptually doing the same things. We ordered both of these described clips in a section of the video that dealt with smoking. The analytic issues that this video imagery illustrated—issues covered in the written report—included the way that odor was an issue of the moral and social order.[33] Odors considered negative were ones associated with the socially devalued (e.g., cigarettes, deep fried food, inexpensive perfume, disliked houseguests). Also discussed in the report was how Febreze use fit into the moral order of the day, as said at the time, one more in line with Oscar Wilde than Dostoevsky. The instances illustrated in the video were not those of idiosyncratic personalities, but of widespread cultural phenomena. Closet smoking, a culturally produced and defined phenomenon, is not idiosyncratic in a social environment that devalues smokers. The woman featured was not anomalous, nor was she nuts. And even if she were, there would be cultural phenomena to discern.[34]

One of the truisms of film and video—like all texts—is the uncertainty and instability of the interpretive meanings that the viewer brings to the viewing. Even in the context of a presentation, it can be difficult to assure that the cultural analytic read is what occurs. The ethnocentric and oppositional readings of anthropological films that occur among anthropology undergraduates in classroom settings, brought to life by Wilton Martínez, are cautionary tales.[35] In our context, in many cases, well-practiced psychological frameworks reinscribe our analyses when the video is viewed. This has been the case for the viewing of the fabric refresher video, and has often happened with the excerpt from the gold video discussed in Chapter 2. Furthermore, room for prevailing analytic frameworks (whatever they are) to be invoked is compounded when the ethnographic videos are taken out of their original context—analytically, spatially, performatively—as they so frequently and it would seem, inevitably, now are.

Given the contemporary possibilities, expectations, and practices surrounding media, there is a strong pull toward the creation, use, and consumption of movable, extractable video clips. Thus, we have in our own work witnessed the shift toward producing ever shorter, separate segments of edited video, created with explicit attention to their serviceability in being used by clients as files that they can link to their own PowerPoint documents. If we started with long VHS tapes and then DVDs telling "whole stories" in sections, we now clearly think of the edited video segments we produce foremost as separate and linkable digital files. They are also clearly becoming shorter and shorter—now generally three to ten minutes, not ten to twenty minutes as they were not so long ago. We still create DVDs, but now as a collection of edited videos, ordered in a sequence on the DVD that mirrors the flow of our report (and which we also know, and expect, will not necessarily be viewed in that way, as viewers will go anywhere on the menu they want). In essence then, what we are now creating are extractable EthnoBites, as are many others in the applied consumer research arena.[36]

We once bristled over short lengths because they conflicted with the assumption in anthropological research that understanding requires considerable time, a time frame that has been incorporated into the typical modes of representation for anthropologists: the book-length ethnographic account, the tendency toward the monographic in Sherry's terms.[37] Yet, we bristle less now, perhaps out of an acceptance of the unreality (even surreality) of this epistemological assumption within the contemporary socio-cultural milieu, combined with a realization and appreciation that sometimes length does not matter. Consider the dense, meaning-packed, evocative pro-perties of a good Haiku. Anthropologists' own epistemological assumptions can get in the way.

What remains a concern, however, is whether short videos represent ethnographic research findings. Do they serve as vehicles for appreciating the sociocultural worlds of consumers, the sociocultural context in which consumption takes place? Do they fulfill the generative promise of providing ethnographic insight? Or, are the representations simply re-inserted into psychological, entertainment, or other frameworks? As we noted above, to videotape is not to *do* ethnography. An edited representation produced from ethnographic research footage is not inherently ethnographic or anthropological, either. For instance, as Lucy Suchman included in a juxtaposed "yes, but" list between desires for representation and counter-concerns in her 1995 "Making Work Visible" article, do video records "make evidence for claims open to contest" or do they "persuade, close down debate"? Does video "maintain the animation, dynamics of lived experience" or "freeze activity, while affording a (mis)illusion of experience"?[38]

And what happens if or when few-minute, talking-head, quotation-come-alive video clips become a kind of ethnographic consumer research standard? The longstanding practice of the "telling" consumer quotations that dominate written focus group reports allows for this form of remediation in video to easily occur. Another catalyst for the creation of such clips is the frequent assumption that the less ambiguous the video message, the greater impact it will have for the intended audience. Will talking-head, one-unambiguous-point video clips be considered the normative standard, ones that tend to "persuade, close down debate" rather than ones that "maintain the animation, dynamics of lived experience"? And once a standard is in operation, its conventions can be reproduced, perhaps especially easily in today's digital world.

We have been witnesses—and participants—of some of the mechanisms by which such standards are reproduced within corporations and among consumer researchers, not only by word of mouth, but in instantiated practice. For instance, there have been occasions when clients have provided us with the videos produced by other research firms and insisted that we comply with that style in the video we produced for them. (We have also noticed Request for Proposals [RFPs] coming from former clients that seem to have embedded our conventions into their general expectations.) Thus, consumer researchers do influence one another's practices and thereby create the genre. Expectations and exigencies of those in corporations also play a role.

Late in 2006, when in the final stages of one of the largest projects of the year, we were also thoroughly complicit in (re)creating corporate expectations of ethnographic video. Our task was to bring to life four distinct customer segments.[39] The company was interested in reorganizing its business strategy to differentially target these four different customer groups. The assignment was to deliver, for each group, a thorough and fundamental understanding that the company could rely and build upon in developing this differentiated strategy. The research did yield the material for a thorough, ethnographic understanding of each of the four segments. We were fortunate, actually, that a priori demographic differences (e.g., income, age, marital status, ages of children, type of primary residence, and *not* ethnoracial categories) made it fairly easy for us to provide very different ethnographic portrayals.

Our ingoing agreement had been to produce thirty minutes of edited footage, in separate files corresponding to important themes for each customer segment. In the thirty-plus hours of footage we had obtained from each segment, we found many gems. We decided, therefore, to submit to the client an approximately forty-minute version per segment, each organized into four ten-minute "stand alone" portions that spoke to the relevant business issues in specific sections of our PowerPoint report. When we sent it to them as a preview, we argued that we thought that it could stay as it was—that the video could tell most of the story.

We also felt that these extra ten minutes for each customer group could be useful to the company. Why excise them solely for the purpose of achieving an arbitrary (no doubt, outdated, television-influenced) minute limit that we had suggested in the first place? We also suggested that the longer-than-promised video provided them the opportunity to excise parts they deemed less important for their audience and their business goals. During the course of the research, we had already many times been jokingly forewarned by the client who had been with us in the field that even if he seemed an easy-going research partner—and he was—he could be tough to please when it came to video editing because of his own considerable experience editing consumer research footage.

In the course of this project, there were complicated, mitigating circumstances. The original thirty minutes of video per segment had been conceived as part of two-hour presentations. In the end, the time the corporation allotted to the presentation was cut in half. So, now we had produced forty minutes of video for sixty-minute presentation frames. We still wanted to leave the forty minutes of video on the presentation discs even if we only screened twenty to thirty minutes in the presentation, because then the longer version of the video would continue to live with the version of the presentation most people would see. We liked that idea.

However, our clients felt that it had to be, without question, shorter. They felt strongly that their constituents would have neither the time in their schedules nor the patience to view that much video. We had to shorten it. Perhaps it was the despondency surrounding a shortened presentation time—as well as the need to shorten a video that we liked so much—which led us to suggest that, as a first step in the shortening process, our client (who had promised his attention to the editing) should be the first to go through and choose the clips he thought should be cut. Whatever the motivation was, that is what we did.

He returned an extremely detailed, clip-by-clip suggestion list, laid out in an Excel spreadsheet. Who could ask for more? What he had done represented hours of viewing and undoubtedly considerable contemplation. He clearly did have abundant experience in editing. Cutting the video according to his suggestions (with only minor instances of resistance, reordering, and further cutting on our part) led to twenty-minute versions for each segment, segmented in four approximately five-minute videos. In so doing, with some chagrin, we also realized that frequently the indirect, multifaceted, lived sensual examples of the ethnographic themes hit the cutting room floor while the talking-head, "you can sum it up like this" type of statements remained and reigned. The ethnographic moment of a father soothing his infant daughter by playing a tune on his cell phone was cut, as was a video diary excerpt showing the drama of ceding the favorite TV to an eighteen-month-old. Parents' lively explanations and demonstrations of the way Webkinz had taken their kids' (and their own) imaginations by storm were cut, as was a video diarist's evident thrill as he ordered online something he had wanted for two years and could finally now do because of the extra money earned from doing the diary. Those in the video with nonstandard U.S. accents (from South Africa to South Asia) were almost all cut.

So, the edited videos became shorter. But we worried whether they were as memorable and ethnographically communicative. Findings were told, but were they communicated?[40] Would it really help company representatives have a feeling of "lived knowledge" of their customers? Without evoking this lived knowledge and this feeling, would the video really be as effective as a tool to assist them in devising and implementing business strategies for each customer segment? We had voiced these types of concerns to our clients; and they had voiced theirs. Their concern was that their audience wanted implications and that if the video did not seem to provide clear implications, their colleagues would feel that the research was a waste.

Without question, their argument was grounded. Companies expect consultants to provide the implications that can be drawn from their research. We always put statements of implications in the PowerPoint reports, as we did in this case. But for the videos, we were also convinced that the enormous and far-reaching implications for changes in business strategy and the means to target each customer segment virtually "screamed" upon watching them. As we told our client and now also co-editor, we were convinced that the most generative method for communicating the implications was to establish that foundational base of understanding by letting people really feel the sociocultural texture of the lives of these customers. Once they had that feeling, they would devise relevant business strategies because they would know what to do. In essence we were pleading for the construction of knowledge by acquaintance, not description, that visual media can afford, as formulated by David MacDougall in the quotation at the start of this chapter. We wanted that ethnographic feeling, that knowledge by acquaintance to be accomplished by the video. Our client agreed, but corporate expectations for clips that communicated a clear idea as unambiguously as possible were stronger. We all complied.

Importantly, this was—by no means—the first time we had been asked to conform to corporate conventions for less ambiguous, straightforward, talking-head clips rather than inherently ambiguous ethnographic moments of real-life events. While we had never before gotten an Excel spreadsheet with exact time codes, other clients have asked that we make clips shorter or "more to the point." But when we are asked to cut in the name of clarity (or attention spans of internal clients), we wonder if there is a structural similarity with what is said to cause the re-creation of formulaic Hollywood productions, i.e., do assumptions about what audiences want and expect (and desires to stick with "safe" choices) fuel the creation of the formulaic, even if many creators and audiences would welcome other forms?

The entangled epistemological and emotional knots we feel as anthropologists at these junctures are unquestionably similar to those that have been expressed by visual anthropologists trained in observational cinema who then have gone to work in traditional television documentary contexts. Julie Moggan, for instance, has evocatively voiced the dilemmas that arose in a broadcast documentary situation that "denigrated almost every tenet of the observational [cinema] approach."[41] Rather than giving time to develop relationships and letting events emerge, and to thereby create the documentary around this unfolding, she was instructed to quickly find out what was important based on videotaped interviews, then create a script and shot list, and thereafter carry out subsequent videotaped encounters to get the planned-for answers and actions. In the end, to her, the finished product, which included explanatory voiceover and dubbed translation instead of subtitles, was an "othering," exoticising film which only added to the original ethical dilemmas she experienced arising from the truncated conversations and artificial staging.[42]

Questions concerning the (re)presentation of ethnographic data have never been separate from questions of epistemology and ethics.[43] As communicators of ethnographic research, a strength and opportunity we now have lies in the access to the production and dissemination of visual imagery. There is little question that moving imagery is a powerful means to transmit and represent ethnographic data. And if we are going to achieve phenomenological and sensory understandings, which many now see as an important goal of ethnographic research, we need to find ways that let us feel cultural issues, ways that allow cultural issues to resonate.[44] It is not easy to do so in the abbreviated forms sought by corporate audiences and, it would seem, the larger popular sphere. Anthropologists are not by training masters of any sort of Haiku. But in our own three- to ten-minute EthnoBites, we do try to retain as much ethnographic, sociocultural texture as possible.[45] We aim to convey the look and feel of consumption within everyday life, including the visual surroundings, sounds, actions, interactions, and inherent symbolic and practical messiness of it all.

As Maureen Mahon wrote of "cultural producers" (e.g., musicians, film-makers, and other artists) who begin as critics but whose work becomes part of the mainstream terrain, "cultural producers must manage the complicit and contestatory dimensions of their work as they balance their desire for acceptance and cultural legitimacy"[46] If, as anthropologists, we are the critics of positivist outlooks, understandings that essentialize and reify culture, simplistic notions of language use, and all the other matters we have been railing about in this book, we must also manage the complicit and contradictory ways in which we produce representations of ethnographic research.

Video offers tremendous opportunities. The entanglement of consumer segmentation discussed in the previous chapter involved a hard-to-escape, firmly established scaffold in business. In the case of ethnographic video, the terrain is very much a shifting one, and the productive control is more firmly in our hands, even if negotiation and the pull to recreate and fulfill normative expectations play a strong part. Yet, if each new technological or media innovation has the potential not only to reproduce but also to transform quotidian practices, interactions, and assumptions, there are enormous possibilities.[47] Perhaps the generative promise of ethnographic video can be fulfilled.

To achieve this promise, as researchers, (re)presenters, and consumers of ethnographic research, it is incumbent on us to really think about what we produce and thereby reproduce. We need to gain a deeper appreciation of the epistemological, cultural, and practical intricacies involved in moving imagery.[48] As the move is made toward more frequent representation of ethnographic analysis in forms beyond (increasingly outmoded) text-only forms, we need to interrogate the ways cultural and epistemological assumptions reside amid our (re)presentational choices as well as consider the ways these operate in the reception of ethnographic knowledge. For instance, do close-up head shots, conventions that we have all learned from cinema and television as indicative of personal intimacy and emotion, reawaken and foster psychological interpretations? Do unambiguous, decontextualized quotations, or even longer "descriptive" excerpts, taken from ethnographic encounters serve us well?

This plea to become masters of the genre of moving imagery, including its socially constituted semiotic conventions as well as the practices surrounding its reception and use, is not new. As Jay Ruby has pointed out, an important goal of Russian filmmaker Dziga Vertov's work in the 1920s was to create a better understanding for the audience, one that demystified and demonstrated how film worked, "in a mechanical, technical, methodological, as well as conceptual way."[49] Anthropology as a discipline also has a long history of dealing with moving imagery, even if, until quite recently, video's use and surrounding epistemological debates have been bracketed from the mundane, ordinary work of scholarship.[50] Within the academic field of consumer research, Russell Belk and Robert Kozinets have been active and persuasive agents in trying to move toward a greater embrace and integration of moving imagery.[51] As Belk and Kozinets have pointed out, this entails the epistemological and institutional migration of visual media into the mainstream of the field.

Complicating matters, while there is much that we can and should learn from existing works dedicated to understanding the making and reception of moving imagery, there is also the jarringly uncomfortable feeling that as the intertwined technological, cultural, and theoretical terrain shifts, how we should (re)present our data will also shift. It is always shifting. A question we have as we write this (and tomorrow it might be different) about videographic representation of ethnography in consumer research is the impact of professionalization and democratization. What does the polish of professional shooting and editing do to the reading of these as "research" documents? Does it help or hinder clients in meeting their research objectives or inspiring a business strategy? Either way, how so? And what of the impact of the democratization of video-making, in which six-year-olds are making and directing video diaries for their households and teenagers can show us their YouTube creations? If ethnographic video in consumer research, as a genre, is in process, it is a process in which corporate sensibilities, research participant creativities, and epistemologies of the shooters (and editors) all interweave in its definition. What conventions, what sources of semiosis are being introduced? What will prevail? How will we know?

We also cannot stop worrying about how to make cultural analysis stick. To assure that the EthnoBites we create are seen in context and kept "to-gether" with the analysis, we compress and embed them on disks with the PowerPoint report. We deliver multiples of these disks to clients. Even so, the video EthnoBites on the disks can be copied and put into other reports. And importantly, clients want the videos to be separable and usable for their purposes. To this end, we create stand-alone, full-resolution DVDs which can stand up to large-screen projection on disks that do not include the report. And most recently, we include versions of the video clips that are small enough to make them easy to pass around (internationally) by e-mail. Clips from ethno-graphic consumer research now travel, inbox to inbox, clearly without their reports (at least without the necessities of seeing/reading the report as well).

At times clients have videotaped our in-person presentations, maintaining that they "get so much more" out of our explanations and commentaries than when the text report and/or video "stands alone." We have always found it hard to believe that anyone would have the time or inclination to actually watch these two- to three-hour affairs, except perhaps those in explicitly research positions (or those in new or junior positions). But perhaps we need to take both heart and cues from Ted.com and Al Gore's *An Inconvenient Truth* and realize that moving imagery of someone giving a multi-mediated PowerPoint presentation, including embedded video, is a doable, not to mention inspirational, way to go. Perhaps then, there would be more literal stickiness of the analysis, and therefore our ethnographic videos would have more of the impact that we desire, and not simply the indeterminate meanings of decontextualized EthnoBites, which was what we read in an enthusiastic, "received and enjoyed by many" e-mail response we recently got when we inquired about the status of small-byte video clips we had placed on our FTP site for our client to download. In business arenas today, the sending or responding to e-mail is often calibrated by the degree of urgency. The timing of our own query, in fact, was motivated because our FTP site was out of space (because of videos) and another partner needed space to send images to a client. If e-mails had gone unwritten and unsent, the videos had already been watched.

Notes

1. MacDougall (2006:220).
2. Rita had used video as a data source in projects from the mid-1980s and worked in partnership with professional videographers to create video reports for selected projects in the late 1980s and early 1990s. Patti also had a longstanding interest in ethnographic film, sparked by the influence and importance of it to members of the anthropology department at NYU. She gained further experience in the merits of videography in consumer research while working as a freelance researcher for PortiCo Research, a firm which incorporated videographers and video reporting into its research process from its inception in 1992.
3. See, for example, http://www.innovare-inc.com/srv_ethno_techniques.htm, http://www.edlglobal.net/clips.html. Note also http://www.snippies.com.
4. As Belk and Kozinets noted in 2005, what happened was a revolution in demand, as well as expectations, for videographic consumer research. As they reasoned, these increased demands were based on an appreciation of the power of video-based re-search as well as a social environment in which not only was video production more feasible, but consumers and clients were also more accustomed to interacting with visual imagery as a result of television, film, computers, and the Internet (Belk and Kozinets 2005b). See also Kozinets and Belk (2006).
5. We borrow here from Thomas Frank (1999:78). Reporting on his experiences at an advertising account planning conference, Frank wrote: "These days, with the media world grown as fragmented as the American demographic map, the sales fantasy du jour is anthropology."

6. Mitchell (2001:16).
7. O'Leary (2001:27). Also see and compare Maddox (2006). Maddox also featured Emma Gilding, at this time managing director of Omnicom DAS' in:site. In this article, it did seem that the video aspect was framed in more of a supporting role to the anthropology—Emma Gilding was referred to as a cultural anthropologist and as working with "her team of sociologists and anthropologists."
8. Nelson (2001:B1).
9. Ibid., p. B4. There is nothing novel in the dream of an ethnographic database. The general idea was evident in the early comparative culture work of explorers, naturalists, and theoreticians and continued in the form of the research process and prose publications of Boas and Malinowski. The Human Relations Area Files is a classic example of the attempt to create an ethnographic database. These files, conceived as a resource for scholars, were developed at Yale in the late 1930s by anthropologist Murdoch and are still in existence today (http://www.yale.edu/hraf/collections.htm). The impulse to collect and catalog ethnographic films *and* film footage, and to have them serve as a database for future researchers, has also been evident from the time the first footage was developed (see Ruby 2000, Chapter 1). Databases of ethnographic materials are replete with problems, interpretive as well as the context and intent of the original research. Nonetheless, there are good reasons for clients to attempt to create a database of their own consumer ethnographic video footage. The sheer number of hours of produced video in any given consumer research project is daunting (25–150 hours typically). In our experience it is rare that the client stakeholders in a project have the time (even if the inclination is there) to view the material. Corporations rarely have the internal resources to integrate the viewing of raw material into daily business life. As a result, ethnographic video footage goes unviewed and unused. The idea of a complete database, indexed for any search request, is an alluring concept, one which promises that the valuable resource can be mined. Nonetheless, a useful database requires longitudinal commitment in time and resources, and awareness that the information must be filtered and interpreted. And it will never be complete—neither social life, nor social ideas, stand still.
10. MacDougall (2006:3).
11. Quoted from a preliminary abstract of a paper for the 2006 annual meeting of the American Anthropological Association.
12. Wasson (2000:384–385).
13. Suchman and Trigg (1991).
14. It may be that most recently, the inclination to equate ethnography with video recording is lessening, e.g., see Note 7 above. While a positive development, at the time of this writing, the potential for the simplistic reduction of ethnography to videotaping remains.
15. The video diary method also has been used with tremendous success by Michael Rich and Richard Chalfen in efforts to better understand and improve treatment for patients with asthma, cystic fibrosis, diabetes, and other health concerns. See Chalfen and Rich (2004) and the Video Intervention/Prevention Assessment Web site at http://www.viaproject.org/home/. See also Holliday (2000) and Pini (2001) for other examples and discussion of the use of video diaries in research and representation. Also note BBC's *Video Nation* series, begun in 1993 with the

sending of Hi-8 cameras for participants to create diaries and still continuing. Interestingly, *Video Nation* links its history and impulse with the "anthropology of ourselves" of the U.K. social organization Mass-Observation. See http://www.bbc.co.uk/videonation/history/index.shtml. Last accessed June 20, 2007.

16. See Sunderland and Denny (2002). Note also that participatory and collaborative filmmaking projects with research participants are not novel. Such projects have been repeated and reinvented numerous times by anthropologists and ethnographic filmmakers. *Nanook of the North*, a classic of ethnographic film, was realized by the partnership of Robert Flaherty and the Inuit in the 1920s. Starting in the 1950s, Jean Rouch was also a strong advocate of collaborative filmmaking.

17. See Pini's (2001) remarks on performance signaling fiction and her counterarguments in her work with video diaries. See also Okely's (2005) compelling account of her performative anthropological explorations of the British boarding school of her youth. As Okely (2005:122) noted regarding the filming of her school re-visit, "It was self-conscious. It was a performance, but in no way scripted."

18. Kodak Research and Development (2002).

19. See Rouch (2003:98-99) and Chapters 3 and 6 in MacDougall (1998). See articles included as part of a tribute and commemoration to Jean Rouch (1917–2004) published in the *American Anthropologist* in March 2005.

20. Weinberger (1994:4). Note, even if this was not "the first" ethnographic film, it does classify as a very early example.

21. Anxieties over performance underlie consumer research practices that include "spy" or hidden cameras. These kinds of practices create anxiety for us; they are too great of a violation of the ethical and moral obligation we feel toward research respondents and research processes. See Chapter 10.

22. See, for instance, Goffman (1959, 1963), Gumperz and Hymes (1972), Schegloff (1986).

23. Pini (2001:8).

24. As Drotner (1996:30) observed in a 1996 study of Danish teenagers' video productions, while the teens clearly learned extensively in the process of video-making, they would not speak of it in terms of learning. In fact, rather, as she wrote, "the attraction of video to young people . . . lies in its being regarded as non-schooling. It is self-defined, fun, and rarely planned ahead. Watching videos as well as making them are processes lodged outside the realm of regularity. Hence they are deemed insignificant and that is precisely their attraction." Note Belk and Kozinets' (2005a, 2005b) comments regarding the association of video and entertainment and the symbolic disconnect of entertainment with knowledge production. Also see Dávila (1998). The frequent practice at academic conferences of organizing videographic presentations apart from the papers is also telling.

25. In general, this space is keyed by the pragmatics of the communicative frame of moving imagery. On the pragmatics of the communicative frame, see Goffman (1974), Hymes (1964), and Silverstein (2004). Of course, conventions of editing play a role in how video is interpreted. Conventions (and expectations of conventions) which telegraph "educational video" could produce different forms of viewing. This assumption may also be interrupted by the extent to which one explicitly foregrounds the videographic presentation as "the analysis." See Martin, Schouten, and McAlexander (2006).

26. It is a standard practice in courses in visual anthropology, film, and video to have students take notes while watching. Sarah Teitler, an ethnographic filmmaker who has edited many of our productions, instructs students in her classes to watch twice—first with no notes and the second time with "total notes."

27. Brigitte Jordan presented a fascinating paper that discussed her observations of some of these changes in attention during face-to-face group meetings based on the use of mobile technologies at the annual meeting of the Society for Applied Anthropology in 2005.

28. As noted, as we write this, with changes in the presence and use of digital video ✔ (on informational Web sites and DVDs), the increasing popularity of documentaries, and growing corporate use of video for information (e.g., for trainings and presentations), some of these associations of moving imagery as primarily entertainment may be in the process of change. Yet, paying serious attention to moving imagery as if it were work is not what is usually done; close attention is largely given to the extraordinarily compelling, and the frame is still often one of entertainment. Note the way Hans Rosling's presentation is described in the text. A social environment laced with infotainment and edutainment also produces blurring, bringing the frame of entertainment into information and vice versa.

29. See also Martin, Schouten, and McAlexander's (2006) essay on presenting ethnographic research to corporate audiences, stressing the role and importance of guiding metaphors. Note also their use of a "making movies" metaphor to describe the research process.

30. See "Talks Hans Rosling: Debunking third-world myths with the best stats you've ever seen." http://www.ted.com/index.php/talks/view/id/92. Last accessed June 22, 2007.

31. See articles by Colleyn and Ruby regarding Rouch's emphasis on the importance of content vs. technical perfection included as part of a tribute and commemoration published in the *American Anthropologist* in March 2005.

32. Silvio (2007:286, 308).

33. Corbin's (1986) *The Foul and the Fragrant* is a classic work on the ways in which the assessments of odor are matters of the moral and social order. See also Mary Douglas's (1966) classic sociocultural analysis of pollution, *Purity and Danger.*

34. See Comaroff and Comaroff (1987).

35. See Martínez (1992, 1995, 1996). Note also the arguments by those who have discussed the "preferred" readings of films constrained by the context and text or discursive space of film even in the case of "active" viewers (see Crawford and Hafsteinsson 1996).

36. We are using the term EthnoBite here as a narrative shorthand for ethnographic video clips. It is not a term we use in our practice.

37. Sherry (2006:273)

38. Suchman (1995:60).

39. Cf. Schouten and McAlexander (2006).

40. Inspiration for this question comes from notions of differences in ethnographic film versus documentary. Specifically, it is inspired by Julie Moggan's (2005) recounting of her own experiences melding her training in visual anthropology with work in British television documentary. As she sums up the observational cinema tradition in which she had been trained (Moggan 2005:32): "This approach

is cinematic—words are not necessarily privileged over images and informal conversation between filmmaker and subject takes the place of interviews. In this way the audience is given a great deal of space to form their own conclusions on what they are viewing. They are shown something rather than told something and the evocation of experience takes precedence over the communication of information."

41. Ibid., p. 34.

42. See also Robertson (2005) in the same volume edited by Anna Grimshaw and Amanda Ravetz.

43. Note Arnould and Thompson (2005), Behar (1996), Belk (1998), Clifford and Marcus (1986), Geertz (1988), Lassiter (2005), Ruby (1991), and Sherry and Schouten (2002).

44. Within academic anthropology, debates on these issues have considered the use of visual imagery as well as written forms. Gifted and highly evocative writers can create very sensual and moving imagery in a reader's mind—and this can happen in the writing of academic prose, novels, or poetry. Even if, as Ruth Behar (1999) has so eloquently pointed out, this has not generally been the rule in the books anthropologists write, the "ethnographies" by which they acquire tenure as well as professional identity. Instead, as Behar writes, these accounts "explain rather than show, tell rather than narrate, cite rather than imagine, justify rather than dream, and most tragically, turn vigorous flesh-and-blood people into ponderous slugs of theory" (1999:482–483). The poetically told—and shown—is important.

45. Posted on www.practicagroup.com are two versions of a few-minute video of a woman eating and driving. Notably, the shorter version is one the client asked us to create because the other (few-minute) version was too long.

46. Mahon (2000:477).

47. See Chapter 4 and Bolter and Grusin (1999). See the 2005 review by Bishop regarding the new possibilities that DVDs have brought to the viewing and apprehension of Robert Gardner's ethnographic film classic *Dead Birds* as well as Cooper's (2005) review of Gardner and Östör's 2002 Making *Forest of Bliss* book-DVD combination. See also Ginsburg, Abu-Lughod, and Larkin (2002).

48. Foundational works and good places to begin include Askew and Wilk (2002), Barbash and Taylor (1997), Belk (1998), Ginsburg (1995), Ginsburg, Abu-Lughod, and Larkin (2002), Kozinets and Belk (2006), MacDougall (2006), Pink (2006a), Pink, Kürti, and Afonso (2004), Ruby (2000), Taylor (1994), Worth (1977).

49. Ruby (1980:168).

50. See Chapter 3 in Askew and Wilk (2002), "On the Use of the Camera in Anthropology," a dialogue between Mead and Bateson. Strong proponents and vocal advocates and analysts for contemporary ethnographic filmmaking include, among others, Faye Ginsburg, Anna Grimshaw, David MacDougall, Jay Ruby, Lucien Taylor, and, for the applied as well as academic realm, Sarah Pink. This list prioritizes the most visible to us, widely published, or frequently cited. Our apologies to many important others.

51. See Belk (1998, 2006), Belk and Kozinets (2005a, 2005b), Kozinets (2002), and Kozinets and Belk (2006). Our apologies, again, to others who are active agents for the visual in consumer research.

10

Photographs, Ethics, and Exoticization in/of Practice

Figure 10.1   Morón

The taking of photographs currently holds, as does video, a central position in our ethnographic work. We use photographs as data, as a means to illustrate, and as a medium to think with and through. As we move through spaces or places, or even while sitting and talking, we generally have a digital still camera in hand, taking photographs of telling details, significant actions, what catches our eye as potentially meaningful, configurations of people and objects we imagine as valuable illustrations for an eventual report, as well as, at times, simply someone or something that holds the promise of producing an aesthetically pleasing photograph. In Figure 10.1, the photograph that opens this chapter, it is easy to imagine that all of these motivations were at work in its taking and it is difficult to discern which of these might have been in the forefront.

In this final chapter on entanglements, we have chosen photographs because they provide both a muse and illustrative case in point of entanglements in the representation of analytic frameworks as well as the representation of ourselves and of those with whom we conduct research.[1] In doing so, we build on issues brought forward in the last chapter and we return to issues of the refractive filters brought to analysis as well as the importance of iterative reexaminations of ethnographic details initially discussed in Chapters 2 and 3. In closing this circle with photographs, in which the relationship between the researcher and researched is so much a part, we also use ethical questions which must be asked of photo-taking as a jumping-off point for a discussion of ethics in anthropology and consumer research more generally.

Like video, the current use of photographs in consumer research has been made possible by the availability and affordability of technologies. The centrality of photographs in our own work started in the late 1990s, at about the time disposable cameras began to fill drugstore shelves and scanners became consumer goods. We initially incorporated significant numbers of photographs in reports for studies in which we had respondents complete homework assignments with photographs—diaries of activities, collections of photographs which depicted the meaning of a brand to them, and so on. Availability of disposable cameras and one-hour processing made it easy to request photographs from respondents; scanners made it easy to include the photographs in the reports. Again, available technologies do influence methodologies.

The advent of inexpensive digital cameras, obviating the need for developing and scanning, allowed photographs to attain their important position in our work (and no doubt consumer research more generally). We started with clunky Sony Mavikas and 3.5-inch floppy disks—boxes of disks filled with project photographs can still be found in our offices. We have since moved to slimmer and lighter cameras in which large memory capacity and fast downloading via a USB port have made it even easier to take and include many more photographs in reports. Now when we take our cameras out of our bags, respondents also often begin comparing and contrasting their own cameras with ours. For homework assignments involving photographs we no longer send along disposable cameras. We ask people to use their own digital cameras (or to go buy a disposable one) and to create a digital file of photos for us along with the prints. Sometimes they send us pictures taken by their phones.

As available technology changed the terrain in visual representation (for both researchers and those researched), photographic representation has simultaneously, like video, been embraced as a compelling narrative of "what is real." Whether advertising planners and creatives or brand managers and researchers, illustrative photographs are frequently used to bring a sense of visual verisimilitude with the goal of fostering both understanding and inspiration. That photographs have been implicitly edited along the way, from the initial framing in the viewfinder to their insertion into PowerPoint, or, indeed, are edited in their viewing, often goes unconsidered. Thus, photos can be taken quite literally at face value rather than being seen as produced, as are our notes, as contingent records, dependent both on the context of their production and the interpretations that are brought to bear.

It is because of their inherent contingency that photos can become part of the process of ethnographic understanding, both at the moment of taking them and later during the poring over of them. We often find new and further meanings in photographs we took, those which we took with the explicit intention of creating a record for later perusal as well as those taken for other telling details, significant moments, representational or aesthetic purposes. During steps in the representational process, in the moving, juxtaposing, and cropping of photographs we also find and create new meanings.[2] In this chapter we explore that contingency of meaning—we want to call attention to the constitutive nature of unexamined assumptions in the taking and viewing of photographs. We then use our analysis as a means for bringing the relationship between researcher and researched into reflective focus.

Documenting Cuba

We took the photographs that appear in this chapter in the course of a round-trip journey between Havana and Pina, a small town located in the central Cuban province of Ciego de Ávila.[3] Many of the photographs were taken in Morón, a mid-sized municipality not far from Pina, although others were taken in Havana and Pina as well as other towns, rest stops, and halting places along the highway. Morón had the most because it was there that we gave ourselves the task of documenting both transportation and commerce. We walked up and down the street, stopping to look at and take pictures of market and consumption activities and modes of transportation, meanwhile asking questions of a Cuban traveling companion, who, de facto, took on a kind of primary informant role.

The first time we prepared these photographs was for a photo essay in which we wanted to tell a story of Cuba as a place of connections between people as well as between people and things. In doing this preparation, we selected, cropped, and framed the photographs we thought could best tell the story of these connections. We selected photographs that highlighted people's gaze and hands upon objects. We included photographs that represented the relationships among people, as seen in the closeness and touch between their bodies as well as in their gaze at us. Note, for instance, the ways hands and eyes touch bikes, utensils, food, and people in Figures 10.2 through 10.8.

Figure 10.2 Morón

Figure 10.3   Morón

Figure 10.4   Morón

Figure 10.5 Gas station rest stop by the highway, Pina-Havana

Figure 10.6 Pina

Figure 10.7 Morón

Ultimately we wanted our photographs to illustrate our experience of Cuba as a place where connections between people constituted an infrastructure, were a currency seemingly more salient than money, and were among the most important elements of exchange.[4] We cropped out backgrounds to bring the viewer's focus in on the hands, connection, and gaze—we thought that at times the effects were gripping. We were not intending to participate in touristy fantasies of Cuba. Nor were we interested in replicating and reinforcing

Figure 10.8 Morón

simplistic myths of consumption. As Daniel Miller has outlined, these myths include notions that consumption is opposed to sociality or authenticity as well as the simultaneously contradictory ideas that mass consumption necessarily drives either global homogenization or global heterogeneity.[5] Rather we hoped, as anthropologists and consumer researchers, to bring theoretical traditions and research experience to bear in a way that could provide a richer, more informative portrait of Cuba as a contemporary site of intriguing instances of consumption and exchange.

However, as we began to prepare a photo essay and supporting text for publication,[6] we were both confronted and inspired by Ana María Dopico's insightful 2002 essay, *Picturing Havana*.[7] Focused primarily on documentary works of still and moving imagery internationally distributed during the late 1990s, Dopico aptly delineated the way visual tropes and cultural fantasies coincided in the production of images of Cuba, images which in turn were put into service as strategic commodities of global tourism as well as the cultural and political projects of varied nations. She pointed to the way imagery of suspended and slowed time had appeal for "consumers overrun by speedup"[8] and noted how imagery of Cuba served "as a contrasting and broken-down background for first-world travelers and their luxuries," useful for purposes of both politics and nostalgia.[9] She called attention to the recurrent signification of contradictory temporalities in representations of Cuba. Cuba was depicted as a place of movement where time had stopped through images of vintage American cars, bicycles, and manually powered taxis on otherwise emptied streets, and decaying colonial structures. Cultural and consumption practices that seemed to belong to (an idealized) time past were shown to live currently and vibrantly. There was often a juxtaposed focus on the very young and the very old, or on the voluptuous among the ruins. As Dopico wrote, "The gaze of the lens in Havana has accompanied the eye of the market, reflecting the fashionable status and historical exceptionalism of the city as living ruin, and the allure of a scarcity still set apart from the flawed and normative narratives of development, democratization, or global economic integration."[10] And as she put it in a sentence that summed up much, "The allure of Cuba lies precisely in both its suffering and its surviving collapse."[11]

As we thereafter looked carefully at the body of images we had shot as well as selected, we realized—with chagrin—the degree to which our images reflected, appealed to, and continued many of the same problematic sentiments, tropes, and myths. Elements of these sentiments and tropes are discernable in the opening photograph, the photographs we had intended about connection, as well as in other of our photographs shown in Figures 10.9–10.13.

The process we then went through was to go back and look at the corpus of the photographs we had taken to examine the constitutive nature of these assumptions in the taking as well as viewing of the photographs. We asked ourselves how much our analytic framework, our assumption about the connections between people as a currency potentially more salient than money, was also part of the mythic opposition of consumption with sociability. Also, were we seeing authenticity because it was in comparison to what we knew as normative based on consumption-infused life in the United States? We then set out to deconstruct in the photo essay some of the tropes and ideas—however problematic—that had seemed in play in our visual choices.

Figure 10.9　Güines

Figure 10.10　Havana

Figure 10.11 Havana

Figure 10.12 Morón

Figure 10.13   Güines

Documenting the Allure of Scarcity

As the photographs in Figures 10.14–10.18 indicate, the fascination of relative scarcity, modes of nonmotorized transportation, and practices that could be interpreted easily as instances of improvisation and making-do (from the vantage point of those accustomed to an abundance of specialized consumer goods) had clearly proved a visual temptation difficult to resist. Farming with oxen and using old phone books for toilet paper in bathrooms also made implicit analytic comparisons to both the past and other "less affluent world" countries, to use the terminology of Ger and Belk,[12] all too ready and easy, even if these comparisons were quickly followed by a satisfied smile of a simplistic interpretation overcome. Without doubt, notions of outhouses and the paper of Sears Roebuck catalogs from a former era in the United States were difficult to keep from entering the mind. But to imagine that countries can follow each other in historical time or that one social milieu can exist in a state of some prior historical time of another is an ontogeny-recapitulating-phylogeny form of conceptual slippage which anthropologists take pride in not making.[13] Thus, even while looking down at the toilet and the overflowing can of used newspaper toilet paper, there was a certain intellectual fascination in observing that the tiles seemed relatively new and in line with contemporary European bathroom tile fashion. It was also easy to appreciate that farming with oxen was not an instance of premechanized practices, but rather that oxen had replaced many tractors in Cuba in the 1990s due to scarcities of fuel, tires, and machinery that followed the withdrawal of Soviet Union support.[14]

Nonetheless, the use of oxen for farming, phone books for toilet paper, and the general improvisational reuse of things had still been deemed interesting to-be-documented phenomena; and this interest was constituted in romanticized

Figure 10.14 Güines

Figure 10.15 Morón

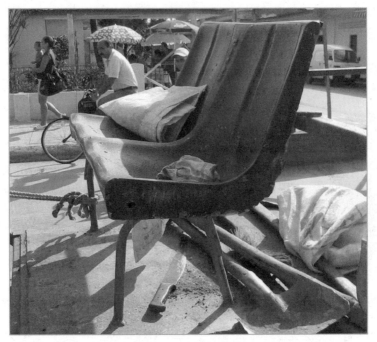

Figure 10.16 Morón

Figure 10.17 On the side of the highway, Pina–Havana

Figure 10.18 On the side of the highway, Pina-Havana

notions of the past as well as based in the privileged position of seeing the poverty of others as interesting.[15] That we also saw the general improvisation and reuse of things as so emblematic of scarcity also clearly implied that an assumed absence (of something we knew, expected, considered important) was supplying the definitional terms. In many ways, the perceived realities clearly told at least as much about us, our interests, and our implicitly assumed audience as it did about what was observed.

As residents of the "more affluent world," we are not accustomed to a general state of scarcity in consumable goods, but of living in a world filled with consumables, even if these are not all within one's own personal reach. As professionals who spend much of their time talking with people about the symbolic meanings of goods and brands as they permeate life, the social fact that many goods were not wrapped in branded packaging or infused with an aura of aspirational luxury was also striking. Relative scarcity and making do were without question themes in our minds as we documented the commerce surrounding food in Morón, as seen in Figures 10.19–10.25.

Many people do live amid relative scarcity in Cuba. We had been prepared to find that desired (and basic) items were scarce because of the recommendations from those who had spent time in Cuba of what to take along for people there: Band-Aids, pencils, aspirin, ibuprofen, vitamins, notebooks, soap, shampoo, and so on. We had stocked up at a Miami drugstore before leaving. We also

Figure 10.19 Morón

Figure 10.20 Morón

Figure 10.21   Morón

Figure 10.22   Morón

Figure 10.23 Morón

Figure 10.24 Morón

Figure 10.25   Morón

brought coffee, as an earlier trip in 1987 had made it clear that this was a beverage not always readily available. In 2003, for those with dollars to spend,
coffee was no longer in scarce supply. Yet in one private home, the home of a
physician in Pina, we were given apologies for the fact that they did not have
any coffee to offer.

To what extent, though, in our documentation of Morón commerce was
it our own picture-taking that further created the view of food and money as
scarce resources? Why the many images of people gazing onto food or money
as if it were highly precious, akin to the way a U.S. resident might stare at
the offerings in a Cartier window? Likewise, we initially thought to include
a set of photographs taken in Güines (Figures 10.26 and 10.27) that evoked
a feeling of people's desire for goods as well as a sense of scarcity, rather than
Figure 10.28, a photograph of a smiling vendor in a Havana market. Is it
because the photograph of the vendor in the Havana market evoked a sense
of plenty as well as indifference to the displayed meat? He requested a copy of
the photograph and handed over an e-mail address. Surely there was a story
about commerce and connection there as well.

Brand (E)Scapes

News that Cuba had faced serious economic problems and significant shortages
after the demise of the Soviet Union's considerable support was widely reported in the international media. Less well reported, or perhaps less noted,

Figure 10.26 Güines

Figure 10.27 Güines

Figure 10.28   Havana

were the economic measures and agreements put in place during the "Special Period" and other provisions of the 1990s and early 2000s.[16] In October 1990 Fidel Castro declared "a special period in time of peace," which was intended to address increased hardships encountered after Soviet assistance stopped. In the mid-1990s the U.S. dollar was legalized, foreign investment and joint business ventures were instituted (Canada and countries of Western Europe became important partners), and even agricultural agreements with the United States were undertaken.[17]

Although, as Dopico mentions, the Special Period also ushered in tremendous growth (and an aura of chic) in the global circulation of Cuban imagery by and for scholars, journalists, and tourists, the most common aspects of knowledge about Cuba in the United States remained a sense of U.S.-Cuban political differences and trade and travel embargos. Timing of our own trip, in fact, was hastened as new laws put in place by the Bush administration were to go into effect at the start of 2004. These new regulations would make it even more difficult for U.S. citizens to travel legally to Cuba. Though, the word "sense" regarding knowledge of U.S.-Cuban trade and travel is carefully chosen. Little about the specifics, including agricultural agreements, was widely disseminated or known. "Embargo" is what was known. Thus we were truly shocked when we realized that the chartered flight we took from Miami to Cuba was handing out Continental branded boarding passes and using Continental branded planes. One of us is a gold elite member on Continental. It really was only half in jest that we asked if frequent flyer miles were available. The agent laughed.

To anthropologists and consumer researchers, the impact and dissemination of brands across national and cultural boundaries are important and intriguing questions.[18] As Americans accustomed to hearing a fairly steady refrain of "no trade with (communist) Cuba," things like the Continental charter or the Coca-Cola and Sprite we saw on sale at a highway rest stop (see Figure 10.29) were their own humorist tropes of the power, reach, and interests of global commerce as well as human ingenuity and endurance. We reasoned that Coke and Sprite must arrive from countries such as Canada, Mexico, or Jamaica the same way that many illegally traveling Americans do.

As attuned and interested as we may have been in brands and the cultural interplay of brands, and as much as we were in tune with globalscapes and global cultural processes, the romance of times past, the allure of scarcity, and the ingenuity of improvisation still had the ability to cloud vision. Thus, for instance, what does one focus on in the scenes and artifacts depicted in the photographs in Figures 10.30 and 10.31? In observation of the actualities as well as observation of the next two photos, does one focus on the age of materials, the improvisation in tools, the ingenuity in keeping things (from cars to the economy) moving, or the cargo pants? Does one revel in the age of the car or wonder about just how long Chevrolet has used the brand logo affixed to the rear window and how it got onto that particular car window in any case? Does one question the presence of the Volkswagen? Or, was what appears to be a "piss on" joke sticker in the back window of the car in Figure 10.10 noticed?

Notions of scarcity (and having experienced the need for reflectors on slow-moving vehicles traveling amid fast-moving cars on unlit streets) might have initially made it seem to us that the Mercedes hubcap on the vehicle depicted in Figure 10.32 was serving as not much more than a functional reflector and that its irony was solely that. But could this really be possible?[19] In an age of mass and electronic media, and in the visibility of this icon on diplomatic vehicles in Cuba, could the affixer not know of the symbolic meanings attached to this global brand? And was he—or she—not thus also making a contribution to that conversation? Likewise, as we gaze upon the photograph in Figure 10.33, is it the scarcity and improvisation in the accoutrements for a (long since internationally disseminated) chess game that summons our attention? Or, is it the more contemporary fashion statements that also popped

Figure 10.29 On the counter at the highway rest stop, Havana-Pina

Figure 10.30 Morón

Figure 10.31   On the side of the highway, Pina-Havana

up in varied global locations: the backwards baseball cap or the half-shaved, half-saved Low and Tight haircut that can itself be seen as a modification of the once popular (and politically incorrectly named) Mohawk? Were the backwards baseball cap, shoes, and overall matching outfit of the little boy in front of the Güines store in Figure 10.26 noticed?

Alternative Conversations, Alternative Frameworks

Dopico, quoting Rafael Hernández, invoked the fable of an elephant described by four blind monkeys. Each able to touch and "see" only one part of the elephant, they derived highly diverse conclusions about the overall make-up of an elephant, despite being true to their own individual experience and observation. There are many stories that can be told about Cuba through photographs or other means. For those accustomed to the cultural notion of access regulated by money, other means of regulating access can readily appear as human rights violations. Our Cuban traveling companion was not allowed to stay in the same hotels as we were, not because of money but because of nationality. Cubans assured us that there were ways around the restrictions; for

Figure 10.32   Havana

Figure 10.33   Havana

instance, one must only know the tricks to get to Caya Coco, the upscale barrier island tourist resort officially off-limits to Cuban nationals. Yet in the tired dark of the night in Morón, after it proved so difficult to find an open bed in one of the private homes officially licensed to lodge overnight Cuban travelers (while the large tourist hotel had empty rooms), was it an overwhelming sentiment of the "senseless" restriction of movement and inequality that produced the iconicity of apartheid in the composition of the photograph (see Figure 10.34) taken when a room was finally located?

Would a photograph in New York, taken with a backdrop of frustration over lack of funds to stay in a hotel, have led instead to a juxtaposition of an expensive hotel and a homeless person? Likewise, how do the cultural conceptions and expectations we all bring to the photographs affect what is seen and read in them? Are the lines for foodstuffs in the Morón photographs (Figures 10.19 and 10.25) assumed akin to the past bread lines of Moscow, so easy for older residents of the traditionally capitalist countries to imagine? Or, are they akin

Figure 10.34 Morón

to those that began to form in the early 2000s for the famed cupcakes at New York City's Magnolia bakery, where no one person was allowed to buy more than a dozen?

The point, again, is that what we see and what we report—as observers, as researchers, as photographers, as theorists—always depends on the experience as well as prior experience, with the theoretical conversation one has in the head as well as with each other, with larger symbolic associations and meanings, with history, with comparisons, with context. And as with the coproduction of goods on the part of consumers, meaning is always reciprocally produced by sender and receiver, creator and user, research producer and research consumer. We are all always in a multiperson, multifaceted conversation whether in Cuba, daily consumer research practice, a classroom, or even a two-person encounter.

Traditionally, anthropologists have had a generally dismissive relationship with the accounts and activities of tourists and casual travelers.[20] Ironically, however, among our own photographs, those that in the end often told the richest and fullest tale of Cuba as a place of people and things and of connections between people are those that fall most fully into the "tourist snapshot" genre. It is the photographs of friends caught off guard as well as the kinds of stereotypic tourist photos in which people are together in "here we are in this place" type of shots that tell the stories of connection and consumption. For instance, it is the photograph in Figure 10.35 that documents the connection between our companion and the two young men who late at night guided him through the maze of Morón streets and private homes, and thereby forged a bond of friendship among us all. The photograph also displays a kind of inattention to the pressed shirts, baseball caps, notebook, and even centrally visible watch. These items appear normative in this photograph. While not necessarily the usual case, in the context of a morning meeting with two visiting Americans, these items were normative, as they were for the viewer via the composition of the photograph.

It was also the photographs in Figures 10.36 and 10.37 as our traveling companion interacted with us, kidding, explaining, guiding us through the process of what we needed to do to navigate situations and environments about which we had so little knowledge (as he was doing in the background of the photograph in Figure 10.6) that retained the Transtur rent-a-car location, the interaction, the images that do not flatter ourselves, our own image, or our preconceptions. It is these images that seem to tell as much—or more—about what is happening in Cuba in terms of contemporary consumption, rather

Figure 10.35   Morón

Figure 10.36   Havana

Figure 10.37 Havana

than the idealized images that may have romanticized Cuban practices, but also ultimately served to make the U.S. economic situation look "better."[21]

Why was it that all along the way, we had not taken, nor subsequently prioritized, a different set of images, for instance, the one in Figure 10.38 which includes bicycles and a manually powered taxi, but also shows fairly contemporary automobiles in the background? Or, note the stylish and relatively well-equipped manual taxi depicted in Figure 10.39. In this case the yellow highlights on the driver's shirt and socks coordinated with the yellow painted metal further highlighted with a red stencil design.

An Ethical Excursion?

As Dopico has maintained regarding global visual imagery of Cuba, "While exploiting Cuba's exceptionalism (its transgressive status and revolutionary reputation), the image machine reproducing Cuba for a global market in fact relies on tourism's capacity to camouflage revolutionary Havana into consumable mirages, visual clichés that disguise or iconize the city's economic and potential crises."[22] In this chapter, through the interrogation of our

Figure 10.38 Morón

Figure 10.39 Morón

practices and the illumination of dynamics surrounding the taking, cropping, and presentation of photographs, we have attempted to avoid being unwitting coproducers in this process as well as to interrupt (however meagerly) others' future production of visual imagery of Cuba or other places without consideration of such dynamics. We wanted to call attention to the constitutive nature of unexamined assumptions in the taking as well as the viewing of all photographs. We simultaneously wanted to demonstrate that the consideration of representations is part of seeing as well as part of the process of understanding cultural dynamics that are in play in any situation. We have also implied that understanding the dynamics of power, in whatever context, helps one understand the kind of knowledge produced.

Yet, there are issues of ethics that still remain clouded in the background. Among anthropologists, taking seriously the ethical ramifications of one's endeavors has long been valued. Concerns for those with less social power and for the ignored or deplored have been virtual hallmarks of the field. In this vein, as we have done here, anthropologists have interrogated the ways their own as well as anthropological work as a whole has fit hand in hand with colonial, capitalist, gendered, racialized, nationalized, or other hegemonic powers.[23] Anthropologists have also worried over the ethics of interpersonal interactions in the field and the ways interlocutors are represented. Considerable ink and emotion have been spilled over issues of whether consent for participation is truly informed and the power and profit dynamics among anthropologists and research participants interrogated.[24] These ethical concerns are not to be scoffed or jeered—attention to these issues is one of the positive aspects of the field.[25]

Through these photographs and the accompanying exposition, we have taken pains to tackle how these representations might contribute to simplistic thinking and social self-aggrandizement. Yet we must also question the degree to which these photographs could still be considered emblematic of anthropological reductionism and exploitation. By contemporary standards, a valid question to pose is how it can seem analytically, socially, or morally correct to use nameless people to synecdochically stand for "Cubans" as a social type? We must also contemplate whether through the use of aesthetically appealing photographs in this essay, we—no matter what we say—remain productive participants in the process of the commodification of Cuban imagery akin to the ways those who show pornographic images in the interest of combating pornography also perpetuate pornography. One must also ask in what ways permission and informed consent were granted? Who profits from the use of these photographs? Has potential harm been considered?

The answer to the last three questions is that, at some level, of course we are culpable and contributors to the aged problem (with reach well beyond anthropology or consumer research) of using another, relatively uninformed and uncompensated, for one's own research purposes. In the taking of many of the photographs, we clearly implicitly relied on the presumption of legality and social acceptance of taking and using photographs of those in public, given the general legality and acceptance of this practice in the United States.[26] Throughout the preparation of this chapter, we have tried to quiet our own and imagined accusatory voices by taking pains to largely use photographs where the closeness of the photograph or the person's gaze upon us clearly telegraphed knowledge of our picture taking. We did ask permission, in one form or another, of many of the people we photographed. For instance, Figures 10.5, 10.7, 10.8, 10.28, 10.31, and 10.33 were explicit poses for the camera, and Figures 10.2, 10.17, and 10.20–10.25 were ones taken of activities that participants explicitly allowed us to watch and record. Many others were of objects and things or snapshots of friends, e.g., Figures 10.14–10.16, 10.29, 10.32, and 10.34–10.37. The truly problematic remain just a few, with perhaps the ones depicting children (given our cultural ideas, assumptions, and laws) seeming the most troublesome. Yet overall, we believe we have remained within the parameters of professional codes of ethics as well as a combinatory framework of the formal, do-no-harm model, along with the more informal, less lofty, but as Daniel Bradburd has pointed out, often quietly instituted "no harm, no foul" sentiment.[27] We have omitted images, real names, and details if we thought they could be problematic or harmful. Moreover, we have tried to pay homage to and show respect for the people we photographed, with feelings perhaps akin to what Stoller has maintained was the embodied bond he felt with Hauka in Niger that demanded he write "with remembrance and respect."[28] We are hoping that homage will prevail as moral force.

In our own consumer research work, we take ethical and moral issues seriously and we strive to maintain moral and ethical standards from multiple vantage points: that of the project, the clients, and the respondents.[29] We make moral choices about which projects we will take and how we will carry them out (e.g., the choice of video diaries over concealed cameras). Once we agree to a project, we also take our ethical contract with our clients very seriously. As we enter into contractual relationships with clients, we enter into personal, human, and professional (anthropological) relationships with them. We want to do a good job, a job that helps them in their efforts, not simply because it is a professional obligation, but because it becomes a moral and personal obligation. We are also highly conscious about showing and giving respect to our research respondents during the research encounter and thereafter. We are acutely aware of how we represent respondents to our commissioning clients' constituencies. We do not want research respondents to be laughed at, disparaged, othered, or exoticized. We are careful about how we portray people in video and photographs. We want them to be accorded the same human complexity and dignity that those trying to understand accord themselves. Our anthropological hackles are quickly raised when someone complains that a non-American accent is difficult to understand or when an accent or aesthetic of one less powerful is found comical.

But, of course, we can neither completely control nor contain these responses as we see them happening and definitely not once we have left the scene. We do our best to engender for others the understanding and appreciation of our research respondents as we see them, but this cannot always be assured given the contingencies of corporate and professional discourses. Moreover, we have little to no control over uses to which the materials will be put once we leave, although clients also are generally bound by their own (often strict) legal, ethical, and moral frameworks. Thus, we have had clients contact us for help in obtaining permission from consumers to use poems, written in the course of a research project, on a corporate Web site. But, we all know that in professional situations, or any time "they read what we write," anthropological and cultural research can be put to all kinds of uses and misuses.[30] And corporate representatives, like the rest of us, are not uninterested parties.

We chose the photographs from Cuba to illustrate our points in this chapter in part because these are photographs that we particularly like. Taken in a time of relative leisure, and without the constraints of an externally driven research goal, we could give more attention to aesthetics in the taking of the images. Yet part of the reason we chose to highlight the Cuba photos in this chapter rather than photographs from one of our contracted projects was also precisely because our access to reuse materials produced in a client-sponsored project is more limited. Client companies—not us—own the materials. We sometimes negotiate special permission for the use, presentation, or discussion of research results after projects have been completed, or we make special arrangements in advance as we did with the advertising agencies that were our research partners in the projects described in Chapters 5 and 6. Most respondents who participate in a project with us sign permission forms which grant the use of their first names and images for internal presentation and business development purposes, but guarantees to them that their images and names will not appear in any advertising medium, on television, or the Internet without further permission (thus the request to us from our client to help acquire permission to use respondents' materials on the corporate Web site). So, for us too, how could we use project respondents' photographs here, without first asking? In this way, it was easier to use the photographs from Cuba. They were ours to use, even if not to abuse. We do not always have that luxury.

We also bring up these issues of ethics because, as indicated in Chapter 1, in interrogations of ethics, too often practice is imagined as necessarily more problematic. Rather than acting in concert with shared ethical and moral concerns, those of us working outside the academy are seen as ethically more compromised by the exigencies of the practical research world (which is also why we used the Cuba photos, an independent research project, to interrogate ethical dilemmas). We wonder the extent to which the notion that work outside the academy is necessarily ethically lesser is generated in the longstanding dichotomy of theory versus practice, one that elevates theoretical issues pondered at some distance above the messiness of everyday life. Metaphorically higher (note: "elevated" and "above"), this puts academic work on a plane of higher value, higher status, and "purer" (not part of "the messiness of everyday life"). As also noted in Chapter 1, consumer researchers are often presumed (explicitly or implicitly) particularly polluted given our part not only in the analysis, but also in the actualities of consumption and commerce (yes, including trafficking in the development or marketing of products and in earning money for carrying out research).[31] In part this harkens to a critique of capitalism. In part this notion appears to be yet another instantiation of the assumption that sociability and authenticity live in opposition to consumption.

Figure 10.40 is a photograph of Havana's Malecón, the famed seawall. We want to use this photograph as a lens to examine the pollution assumptions of consumption and practice, and as our final example of the value of photographs as a medium to think with and through. The visual scape depicted, despite the seawall, seems unscathed by consumable goods. The perturbations appear only to be the strange dark shadows, the traces of the researcher's hair pushed and pulled by the wind to the front of the lens—as if the only disrupting influence on the "purity" was on the part of the researcher's view. But, have not consumable goods and consumption also played a role in the production of this photograph? Where did the concrete originate? What of the dye in the photographer's hair or its distinctive cut? The camera and computers implicated in the production of the photograph? What of the composite look of the Malecón, the sea, and the hitting of the wave which currently has the power

Figure 10.40   Havana

to symbolize numerous treacherous journeys to Miami? What of Cuban soil itself and its saturation with meaning? In the United States, as singer Celia Cruz was mourned, a crystal bowl of Cuban soil was placed under her coffin.[32] What if one magnified the image, and in doing so noticed that on the upper left, cars actually become visible? People also become visible, and undoubtedly, at least some are dressed in clothes esteemed for their statements of fashion and value. We need to remember that we are all connected; we are part of one, interconnected world that is permeated by sociability, consumption, one another, and our conversations.

   We must also, just as examples in the photographs provided here demonstrate, not be afraid of closeness and interconnection. It was in the closeness of relationships evident in the "tourist" photographs that led to imagery which depicted a more complicated, less flattering to ourselves rendition of Cuban consumption and connection. We cannot be afraid of close, personal relationships—they are the stuff of ethnographic knowledge and the stuff of in-depth, empirical details of social life that are the strength of that knowledge.[33] We cannot exoticize others, even each other. We must all remember that wittingly or not, we are all part of the same social world, the same research community, the same theoretical milieu, and that no one is really separable from contemporary consumption practices.

Notes

1. There are some affinities of the approach we take in the utilization and deconstruction of photographs in this essay with that of Morris Holbrook, e.g., Holbrook (1998, 2006a, 2006b). See also Heisley, McGrath, and Sherry (1991), Lovejoy and Steele (2004), Peñaloza and Cayla (2006), Pulman-Jones (2005), and Schroeder (1998) on the use of photographs in consumer research. For discussions and examples of photography and anthropology see Collier and Collier (1986), Domínguez (2000), Edwards (1992, 2001, 2005), Edwards and Hart (2004), MacDougall (1992), Pink (2001) and chapters by Edwards and MacDougall in Banks and Morphy (1997). Classic works detailing socio-philosophical issues surrounding photography include Sontag's (1973) *On Photography* and Roland Barthes' (1981) *Camera Lucida*. See also Sontag's (2003) *Regarding the Pain of Others* and Tagg's (1993) *The Burden of Representation*.
2. See and compare Berger (1973).
3. The trip to Pina, where Patti's father grew up, was one of homage.
4. For examples of exchange as classically discussed by anthropologists, see Appadurai (1986), Mauss (1990), Sykes (2005), and Weiner (1992).
5. See Miller (1995b and 1995c) for an outline of these and other myths of consumption. See also Mazzarella's (2004) points about the typical analytic slippage in discussions of culture, mediation, and globalization, e.g., the notion of authentic cultural life tarnished by global media rather than co-constituted by media.
6. See Sunderland and Denny (2005) and the DVD which accompanied that special issue of *Consumption, Markets and Culture*.
7. Dopico (2002). Note also Quiroga's (2005) fascinating *Cuban Palimpsests*.
8. Dopico (2002:452).
9. Ibid., 453-454.
10. Ibid., 451.
11. Ibid., 463.
12. Ger and Belk (1996).
13. See Chapter 5.
14. See Rosset (1998) and Warwick (1999).
15. Note Szörény's (2006) deconstruction of refugee "coffee-table" books as ones which create and reinforce the privileged viewing of a refugee as objectified, reified category of (subordinate, nameless, timeless) person.
16. See Dopico (2002), News Bites (2002), Warwick (1999).
17. Leake (2002). In 2004, the dollar was pronounced still legal for Cubans to possess, but not for circulation; dollars had to be changed by Cubans into convertible pesos for use as legal tender.
18. Note Appadurai (1996), Belk (1997), Burke (1996), Ger and Belk (1996), Hannerz (1996), Johansson (2004), Mazzarella (2003b), Miller (1995b, 1997), Ritzer (2004), Solomon (2003), and Wilk (2006).

19. As a friend who had spent many years in Cuba said to us after reading a draft with this question, "It's not possible."
20. See Clifford (1988, 1997). See also Dopico (2002).
21. As Kleinman and Kleinman (1997:8) wrote in the context of a discussion of Kevin Carter's Pulitzer Prize–winning photograph taken in the Sudan of a hungry young girl on the ground and a vulture perched in the background: "One message that comes across from viewing suffering from a distance is that for all the havoc in Western society, we are somehow better than this African society. We gain in moral status and some of our organizations gain financially and politically, while those whom we represent, or appropriate, remain where they are, moribund, surrounded by vultures. This 'consumption' of suffering in an era of so-called 'disordered capitalism' is not so very different from the late nineteenth-century view that the savage barbarism in pagan lands justified the valuing of our own civilization at a higher level of development—a view that authorized colonial exploitation."
22. Dopico (2002:464).
23. See, for instance, Argyrou (2000), Behar and Gordon (1995), Caplan (2003), Farmer (1992, 2003), Fluehr-Lobban (2003a), Hymes (1999), Marcus and Fischer (1986), Pels (2000), and the 1995 articles by D'Andrade and Scheper-Hughes and commentaries in *Current Anthropology.*
24. See Battaglia (1999), Behar (1993, 1996), Fluehr-Lobban (2003b), Jackson (2004), Lassiter (2005), Marvin (2006), Ruby (1991), Stoller (1997), Sunderland (1999), and Sykes (2005, Chapter 12).
25. Anthropologists' concerns surrounding ethics and their own interrogation of the ethics of anthropology as a field makes some of the criticisms and disparagements from those outside the field regarding anthropology as an unwitting handmaiden of power feel unjust (Santiago-Irizarry, pers. comm.). In recent years, issues of ethics more generally have also been a notable substantive and analytic concern for anthropologists; see, for instance, Ong and Collier (2005) and Strathern (2000). See also the informative and thoughtful essays and commentaries surrounding Institutional Review Board (IRB) practices and the ethics of ethnographic research in the November 2006 *American Ethnologist* Forum, "IRBs, Bureaucratic Regulation, and Academic Freedom." See also the U.K.'s Association of Social Anthropologists 2006 Ethics Blog at http://anthropologists.blogspot.com.
26. Note Hammond's (2004:137) point, even if somewhat overstated, that "[c]oming from societies in which laws protect people who wish to photograph others in public contexts, many anthropologists have not considered the ethics of creating images of others in different cultural contexts."
27. Bradburd (2006:495) presents an enlightening essay regarding the typical informal practices of ethnographic research undertaken in times, like this one, of vacation, personal, informal interaction, and so on. In the context of university IRB review, he points to the way that use of IRB review and codes of ethics, even with the best of intentions, are at heart about interested, protective practices on the part of researchers and institutions and not about "protection of subjects." In other words, when its sensitive or controversial nature might cause problems for researchers or institutions, IRB review is instituted. See also comments by

Fassin (2006) on the need for ethnographers to invent a model that can seriously address the applicable moral and political questions and to move beyond the biomedical model of ethics, and by Lederman (2006) on the competing epistemic cultures of research confronted via IRB review, the twists and turns of researching IRB processes, and the implications for ethnographic researchers. At the time of this writing, the most recent Code of Ethics approved by the American Anthropological Association was from June 1998. See http://www.aaanet.org/committees/ethics/ethcode.htm. The Society for Applied Anthropology also had a Statement of Ethical and Professional Responsibilities for its members to follow, http://www.sfaa.net/sfaaethic.html, as did the National Association for the Practice of Anthropology, titled "Ethical Guidelines for Practitioners," http://www.practicinganthropology org/inside/?section=resources_ethical_guidelines. See also the U.K.'s Association of Social Anthropologists (ASA) Ethical Guidelines for Good Research Practice approved in 1999, http://www.theasa.org/ethics/ethics_guidelines.htm, as well as the ASA's June 2005 statement from the chair on the new ethics initiative.

28. Stoller (1997:73). Also as the AAA Code of Ethics states, in Section III, part A, numbers 1 and 2: "Anthropological researchers have primary ethical obligations to the people, species, and materials they study and to the people with whom they work. . . . Anthropological researchers must do everything in their power to ensure that their research does not harm the safety, dignity, or privacy of the people with whom they work, conduct research, or perform other professional activities."

29. Professional guidelines of organizations listed in note 27 recognize these multiple levels of obligations. As Don Brenneis, AAA past-president, has also noted (2006:538), research projects have "life histories" and that each stage in a research project's life "presents a different set of ethical concerns and opportunities." As Brenneis further noted (2006:540), the explicitly situated social practice and social relationship orientation of the ethical guidelines of the British ASA is a particularly helpful approach. We would agree.

30. See Brettell (1993) and Terrio (1998).

31. For instance, note the clause (italics ours) embedded in the Association of Social Anthropologists (1999) Ethical Guidelines for Good Research Practice, "Under some research conditions, *particularly those involving contract research*, it may not be possible to fully guarantee research participants' interests. In such cases anthropologists would be well-advised to consider in advance whether they should pursue that particular piece of research." Note also Levy's (2003:103–104) comments about the offense to commercial applications of qualitative research taken within academic consumer research, including Morris Holbrook's view of consultants as "obsequious dogs." Even if Holbrook's comments must be contextualized to be fully appreciated, including the backdrop of the debate over managerial relevance of research and the acknowledgment and importance of consumer research per se, note the comparison to freethinking cats (such as those named Morris) who are "ready to starve—or at least to dwell in dignified academic penury—before succumbing to the pressures implicit in the dictates of managerial relevance" (Holbrook 1995:303).

32. See the final chapter in Quiroga (2005).

33. With homage to Mazzarella (2004) for his eloquence in reminding us of the power and place of empiricism in distinguishing ethnography, and to Domínguez (2000) for her reminder of the importance of foregrounding love in ethnographic work and photographs. See also Strathern's and others' points in the 2006 *American Ethnologist* Forum about the importance of relationships in ethnographic knowledge and ethics.

Part IV
Engaging One Another

Engaging One Another

In the introductory chapter of her 1999 book, *Goodthinking*, U.K. practitioner Wendy Gordon recounted her surprise, with some amount of exasperation, that a then current handbook in qualitative methods made no mention of the work of applied qualitative market research. Despite a trail of published work, and the huge industry that marketing research constitutes globally, applied market research protocols and thinking remained invisible in academic treatises sharing a common subject.[1] Academic anthropology, at least in the United States, United Kingdom, and parts of Europe, has construed and constituted theory and application in oppositional terms for decades. Consumer culture theory (CCT) in academic marketing, developed explicitly in the last two decades in response to prevailing models of consumption and marketing in business schools, has also rested on a perhaps unavoidable, but equally unfortunate, bifurcation between managerial practice and consumption theory.[2]

In 2006, one could observe the impact of the separateness and insularity of discussions for the practice of ethnography in business. The ten articles devoted to ethnography in the September issue of *Journal of Advertising Research* ("Can ethnography uncover richer consumer insights?") veered kaleidoscopically between observational analysis, cultural analysis, application of archetypes to segmentation analysis, multivariate analysis of universal (read cross-cultural) values, and experimental treatments assessing the impact of "culture" on readings of advertising.[3] As an exemplar of industry's notion of ethnography, one had to conclude that "ethnography" referenced an observational method, and/or "in-depth" interviews, and/or the topic of culture, often with attendant assumptions (observation as truth, culture as a separable singularity, words as transparent) that we have problematized throughout the chapters of this book.

One must also observe that if the discourse of marketing is often problematized in academic discourses, the discourses of academia are often problematic for practice. Though linked by the quest for, indeed love of, knowledge-making through ethnography, those of us in the worlds of practice, academic marketing, and anthropology are often all talking past each other, that is, if we even acknowledge one another.

But there is great reason to talk to each other, if for no other reason than a convergence in the subject of scrutiny. If anthropology's concerns and theoretical developments have been, per Geertz, grounded by surrounding contemporaneous history and are, per Fischer, by emergent sciences, then one should also add the foci of consumers and consumption.[4] Issues of *American Anthropologist* over the last decade attest to the discipline's expansion into consumption as object of study.[5] Even more importantly, anthropology's contemporary concern for the "us" and "here" (versus "them" and "there") has rendered ethnographers and anthropology explicitly part of the show, which includes practice.[6] In applied consumer research, practice often retains a rhetoric and rationale of instrumentality, in which a heuristic of reflexivity is not a standard element of the analytic process.[7] Here, the tropes of marketing and prevailing models of brands can too often stymie a more reflexive, cultural understanding of both subject matter and the process of analysis. In academic consumer research, in which consumption is the focal interest, anthropology's voice is present, but highly niched.[8] Moreover, the voices of anthropology within academic consumer research that do exist appear largely ignored by academic anthropology. If we are convergent in our topical interests, which we would argue we are, it is a moment (an opportunity in marketing vernacular) to merge and coalesce, not retain the historical separations of interest and understanding.[9] We all—whether as practitioners or academics—are meaning makers, producers of cultural practices.

In these chapters we have tried to be an interlocutor of practice, academic consumer research, and anthropology, and to bring together disparate trajectories to illuminate the value of cultural analysis in the practice of consumer research. We have also tried to bring disparate sources of understanding together in our references. It was not easy. Whether our muse in analysis was language, conversation, advertising, or other visual media, our goal was to nuance standard consumer research methods (focus groups, ethnography, segmentation, photo taking, video reports) and contemporary topics of consumer research attention (emotion, ethnicity, culture) as culturally produced or constituted. We hope we have shown that these methods or topics are what they are because the constituent interlocutors (consumers, corporations, media, academics) continually define them in ongoing life (whether reflexively or not, scholarly or not). Each chapter is grounded by ethnographic analysis in a here-and-now that consumer research practice readily affords. If projects collide, juxtapose, conflict, fragment, and interweave by dint of corporate timelines and contingencies, we are the beneficiaries, by being able to constantly participate and observe and reflect on the quotidian of everyday living. We would hope that this vantage point is inspiring to others.

A more pragmatic, but no less theoretically important, reason to speak to each other and gain mutual intelligibility is that, in many ways, technology in the current marketplace presents a challenge to academic representational infrastructure. Practice routinely incorporates visual images, blogs, videography, written or auditory consumer texts (and us), not only in the research process but in reporting. While in itself such reporting becomes an ethnographic text of doing ethnography in the commercial world, these inclusions also, arguably, routinely bring interlocutors' voices into texts in ways academic journals have not (though one can be encouraged by poetry, photographs, and video that is increasingly making an appearance in journals).[10] In the production of cultural practices, such reporting is significant.

Today's technological infrastructure makes it easy for consumers' voices, visual and auditory details of their lives or experiences to be brought into corporate meeting rooms, e-mail inboxes, and laptops in ways that go far beyond usual boundaries of scholarly representation, if not transgressing them. With or without a mediating voice of cultural analysis, these practices will continue, fueled, as they are, by ever-changing technological capability. In the world of commerce and consumption (which includes selling, marketing, branding, and advertising), where do we, as anthropologists and/or consumer culture theorists, want to play? Do we want to write about ethnography in business or do we also want to contribute to the writing (representation) of it? Do we want to have a voice in—or care enough about—the edits in video and how ethnographic video is looked at and upon (Chapter 9)? Would we wish that photographs, a ubiquitous form of illustration, are scrutinized for their attendant assumptions in the photograph-taking and viewing (Chapter 10)? Do we demand that attention be paid to the language of interlocutors to make evident that language (clients', consumers', and ours) is not only a constitutive element of consumption practice but of marketing practice (Chapter 7)? How do we effectively take on the representational practices that reconstitute hierarchical ethnoracial difference (Chapter 8)?

Playing in the interstitial spaces between anthropology, academic marketing, consumer research practice, and real-life consumption has great merit, as, for example, McCracken's blog (www.cultureby.com) which continually engages diverse audiences in his relentless quest to make cultural matters visible, or

Pettigrew's online journal which targets both academics and lay audiences (www.jrconsumers.com). The ongoing bifurcation between applied (i.e., commercial) and academic treatments of consumption that is evidenced in the trade press, in articles on ethnography or anthropology, for example, is not only unfortunate but counterproductive to achieving mutual intelligibility. Commercial representation of ethnography cannot neglect the needed tension between the practical and the theoretical, and the ensuing reflexivity of our actions in the world at large—as brand managers, as consultants, or as academics.

This book in many ways is an ethnographic account of doing anthropology in practice. It is a volume that, at its heart, takes on the implications of "here" and "us" when cultural analysis is conducted in business (vs. more acceptable realms of the environment, science, medicine). It reflects a continued interest, fascination, and heart for understanding, challenging, and (hopefully) mediating prevailing commercial and market worldviews by what we do in the field and produce as texts. Project by project, success is achieving mutual intelligibility between the discourse of marketing and the goals of cultural analysis. The process requires a constant switch of perspective. Doing a good job is meeting expectations of our clients (getting the "right" recruits, successfully coordinating all those involved, accommodating timeline needs, helping to solve a problem) and meeting our own (foregrounding cultural analysis, not worrying too much about the "rightness" of respondents or nuancing ideas quite consciously through representational practices). It is a process in which collaboration and liking among respondents and research team are often palpable emergent phenomena (see Chapter 8). "Doing research," as is doing ethnography, is grounded fundamentally by the contingencies and desires of its interlocutors.

In taking on the "here" and "us" in consumer research we would cite the benefit of a parallax effect, in which perspectives from divergent locations lead—via their collaborative convergence—to a fuller view of an object of scrutiny.[11] Applied to consumer research practice, the vantage points are consumer-produced texts, us as (anthropological) researchers, and our client team members (whether they are in R&D, brand management, advertising, or research). Each brings a perspective to bear on the subject of study that, in the process, illuminates not only what is studied (e.g., what is a cell phone, what is cleaning), but also illuminates the primary means by which understanding occurs in the realm of commercial market research. The parallax in this case is grounded by constituent parties of the research project simultaneously with our own reflexivity of doing cultural analysis—of being anthropologists—in business. Such a convergence also needs to happen for academic anthropology, academic consumer research, and applied consumer research. Let us put to rest the tired dichotomies of data vs. analysis, applied vs. pure, native vs. nonnative, instrumental vs. intellectual, practicing vs. critiquing, and commercial vs. academic. We are all productive components in the world of consumption and we have interrelated questions. We would benefit by acknowledging and consciously incorporating each other's conversations.

The chapters in this book represent working knowledge, not perfect knowledge.[12] What often seems to be forgotten, however, is that working knowledge, not perfect knowledge, is what we operate with almost all the time—in research and in life. One of the refreshing things about working in the corporate world is that working knowledge is prioritized and appreciated. The partiality of information is an accepted heuristic in corporate worlds—there is little masquerading of having told the whole story. There is a need to produce ideas and products quickly; there is a realization that if one waits another six months, the world and its demands will be different.

By accepting the partiality of knowledge, we do not mean superficial or lesser. We would disagree with apologetic tones of anthropologists in corporations who view what they do in practice as a "weird bastardization" or compromise.[13] As practicing consumer research anthropologists, we are engaged in fairly continuous fieldwork—in the field, writing reports, or editing video, full time, year after year. And in doing so, the anthropological theory with which we were equipped as students is brought to the work and, moreover, we are constantly—in good anthropological fashion—inductively and iteratively, based on our fieldwork and the questions at hand—developing new analytic tools. It does not need to be looked at as bastardization; it melds every ounce of brain matter and practical skills. When we need, for instance, to work out a way to do ethnographic multiperson, multisited research of multimediated social worlds, we accept the challenge. And we accept the challenge to influence, as influence begets a source of understanding not possible otherwise.

In their ethnographic account of dilemmas facing toxicology scientists in a 2005 article in *American Anthropologist*, Fortun and Fortun suggested that usual forms of critique had become perhaps less valuable: "Scientists are, inevitably, coded—by the technologies with which they work, by hegemonic cultural formations, and by forceful political-economic currents. This is inevitable and pointing it out does not suffice as critique."[14] We would suggest the parallel to brand managers, even though brand managers bring an inflection to their work that is quite different from scientists. Fortun and Fortun propose, as we would, that a focus on the imaginaries important in a social terrain (scientific in their case, marketing in our case) is a contribution to the ethnographic record and that friendship as an ethnographic methodology is part and parcel of a more collaborative ethnographic process. Being the accepted outsider, "the nudge" in collegial terms, to aid in the framing of clients' tasks and dilemmas, is what we do. Entanglements such as those addressed in Chapters 8, 9 and 10 can only come from engagement.

In 1995, in *Contemporary Marketing and Consumer Behavior*, John Sherry observed that if it was a propitious time for anthropologists given the interest in ethnography in marketing domains, it was also a crucial time in the marketing of anthropology. Sherry's concern was that if ethnography were to be viewed as only a method (i.e., anything behavioral that occurred outside of a focus group room), then anthropology's impact on marketing practice would indeed be attenuated. Twelve years later, we would observe that ethnography is still seen as a method and, somewhat ironically, notions of culture that have been problematized in academic discourse have become co-opted by a business discourse.

Thus, if anthropology and academic consumer research are to have a voice in the practice of consumer research, we still need to reattach cultural analysis to ethnographic as well as other research in marketing practice. The theoretical foundations of cultural analysis must be continually made explicit in practice, and both the theory and the voices must be pushed through into reporting (and representation more generally). Academic anthropologists and academic consumer researchers will also need to speak with one another and with consumer researchers engaged in applied practice, recognizing, refracting, and reflecting the strengths of each. Otherwise, the shared social terrain of the knowledge production process will go unacknowledged and the parallax possibilities for a fuller vision will go unrealized, undone, and unachieved. We, collectively, will have to find delight in working in the interstitial spaces between and among consumers, marketing, academic consumer research, and anthropology. Otherwise, culture as a theoretical construct will remain invisible, caricatured (read essentialized), or be seen as important only when doing multinational or ethnic studies. Ethnography and related research practices will continue on as misused terms and co-opted techniques. The practice of business or consumer research will remain undervalued by academic audiences and thus untapped as a means of elucidating substantive issues or driving forces in contemporary methodological-theoretical developments. Anthropology will be rendered by the market in ways that trivialize, marginalize, and exoticize it.[15] The campus divide between anthropology departments and business schools will remain a large, and largely untraveled, territory.

Notes

1. See Gordon (1999:19). The handbook she referred to was Denzin and Lincoln (1994), *Handbook of Qualitative Research*, whose contributors spanned multiple continents and disciplines. ESOMAR and Britain's Market Research Society have a long history in publishing and making visible the work of market research practice. Gordon herself published a volume on qualitative methods in 1988.

2. For a bit of history and perspective, see Arnould and Thompson (2005) as well as their chapter in Belk and Sherry (2007), Holbrook (1995), and Pettigrew's (2001b) introduction to the *Journal of Research for Consumers*. Pettigrew framed the journal as a needed corrective in bridging the gap between academic and lay audience understandings of consumption. The journal's mission in part is to educate consumers about consumption, enabling a more savvy and, no doubt, reflective consumer, at the same time that it speaks to fellow academics.

3. See the *Journal of Advertising Research* 46(3). The difficulty is not the many uses for which ethnography can be enlisted (e.g., Internet texts, family life, interaction with technologies). The problem is that ethnography can come to mean anything vaguely cultural, vaguely observational, or vaguely interpersonal in its method, e.g., questionnaire results from 2,000 individuals plus seven "in-depth interviews."

4. See Fischer (2007) and Geertz (2002).

5. See also Mazzarella (2003b) and Miller (1995a, 1995b, 1997). See also Baba and Hill (2006) who argue that convergence of applied and pure will gain momentum by dint of globalizing forces in the market.

6. See Fischer (2007) and Ginsburg (2006).

7. Applbaum (2000) provides ethnographic examples of marketing managers' constructions of consumers and of their own work. While his paper addresses the construction of globalization through (self-fulfilling) globalizing practices, the tenor and rationales for marketing practice could be applied to the domestic realm as well. New products, for example, are imagined by marketers (or R&D) as really being better, and thus provide a moral foundation for practices.

8. Sid Levy has long argued for an anthropological presence in marketing (see a number of relevant essays in Levy and Rook 1999).

9. See Catterall and Clarke's (2000) plea to make market research curricula more relevant to marketing practices. They also suggest that marketing academics in the United Kingdom take on a broader intellectual perspective of their purview.

10. Poetry has appeared in the *Journal of Consumer Research*, e.g., Sherry and Schouten (2002). Also *Consumption, Markets and Culture* issued a special DVD issue in 2005 for the first time and has continued this annually. We hope such examples are trends. See also the online *Journal of Research for Consumers* (www.jrconsumers.com), whose mission is to speak directly to lay audiences on consumption topics of academic concern. Fischer (1999) has argued that an important challenge for anthropologists in postmodernity is "juxtaposing, complementing, or sup-plementing other genres of writing" (1999:459), such as journalists, media critics, or filmmakers. We would suggest that brand managers and other marketing pro-fessionals are crucial additions to the list.

11. See Ginsburg (1995) who used this concept to reference the benefit of convergent perspective offered by indigenous and anthropological lenses in ethnographic film-making. Jackson (2004) also uses the concept of the parallax effect in teasing apart assumptions about native anthropologists and, more generally, the particularity of subjectivities brought to bear in doing ethnography.
12. See Fortun and Fortun (2005:49).
13. See Wellner (2002).
14. Fortun and Fortun (2005:50).
15. The trade press, as illustrated in Chapter 2, has, in the last decade, been a significant force that defines and obscures what anthropologists do and can contribute. In the absence of anthropological attention to, or voice in, markets and marketing, anthropology will continue to be defined by others. See also Mills (2006) who, in *Anthropology Today*, takes on this issue explicitly in the U.K. context.

References

Aaker, Jennifer, and Susan Fournier. 1995. A brand as character, a partner and a person: Three perspectives on the question of brand personality. *Advances in Consumer Research* 22:391–395.

Aaker, Jennifer, and Patti Williams. 1998. Empathy versus pride: The influence of emotional appeals across cultures. *Journal of Consumer Research* 25 (3):241–261.

Abel, Sue. 2004. Mrs Lee's knowing wink: Reading race in New Zealand advertising. In *Television in New Zealand: Programming the nation*, edited by R. Horrocks and N. Perry, 116-134. South Melbourne, Vic.: Oxford University Press.

Abrams, Bill. 2000. *The observational research handbook: Understanding how consumers live with your product*. Lincolnwood, Ill.: NTC Business Books.

Abu-Lughod, Lila. 1991. Writing against culture. In Fox, *Recapturing anthropology*.

———. 1999. The interpretation of culture(s) after television. In *The fate of "culture": Geertz and beyond*, edited by S. B. Ortner, 110-135. Berkeley: University of California Press.

Adams, Paul C. 1997. Cyberspace and virtual places. *Geographical Review* 87 (2): 155–171.

Ahuvia, Aaron. 2005. Beyond the extended self: Loved objects and consumers' identity narratives. *Journal of Consumer Research* 32:171–184.

Albers, Patricia, and William James. 1988. Travel photography: A methodological approach. *Annals of Tourism Research* 14:134–158.

Alverson, Hoyt. 1991. Metaphor and experience: Looking over the notion of image schema. In Fernandez, *Beyond metaphor*, 94–117.

American Anthropological Association. 1998. *Code of ethics of the American Anthropological Association*. http://www.aaanet.org/committees/ethics/ethcode.htm. Last accessed December 26, 2006.

———. 2006. IRBs, bureaucratic regulation, and academic freedom. *American Ethnologist* 33 (4):477–548.

Anderson, Benedict R. 1983. *Imagined communities: Reflections on the origin and spread of nationalism*. London: Verso Editions/NLB.

Appadurai, Arjun, ed. 1986. *The social life of things: Commodities in cultural perspective*. Cambridge: Cambridge University Press.

———. 1996. *Modernity at large: Cultural dimensions of globalization*. Minneapolis: University of Minnesota Press.

Applbaum, Kalman. 2000. Crossing borders: Globalization as myth and charter in American transnational consumer marketing. *American Ethnologist* 27 (2):257–282.

Argyrou, Vassos. 2000. Self-accountability, ethics and the problem of meaning. In Strathern, *Audit cultures*, 196–211.

Arnould, Eric, and Linda Price. 1993. River magic: Extraordinary experience and the extended service encounter. *Journal of Consumer Research* 20:24–45.

———. 2006. Market-oriented ethnography revisited. *Journal of Advertising Research* 46 (3):251–262.

Arnould, Eric, and Craig Thompson. 2005. Consumer Culture Theory (CCT): Twenty years of research. *Journal of Consumer Research* 31 (4):868–882.

Arnould, Eric, and Melanie Wallendorf. 1994. Market-oriented ethnography: Interpretation building and marketing strategy formulation. *Journal of Marketing Research* November:484–504.

Askew, Kelly, and Richard R. Wilk, eds. 2002. *The anthropology of media: A reader*. Malden, Mass.: Blackwell.

Association of Social Anthropologists (ASA). 1999. *Ethical guidelines for good research*. http://www.theasa.org/ethics/ethics_guidelines.htm. Last accessed December 27, 2006.

———. 2005. *Our new initiative on ethics: A statement from the chair. Developing anthropological ethics in the ASA*. http://www.theasa.org/ethics/ethics_position.htm. Last accessed December 27, 2006.

———. 2006. *ASA ethics blog*. http://anthropologists.blogspot.com. Last accessed December 27, 2006.

Austin, J. L. 1962. *How to do things with words*. Cambridge, Mass.: Harvard University Press.

Baba, Marietta. 2005a. Anthropological practice in business and industry. In *Applied anthropology: Domains of application*, edited by S. Kedia and J. van Willigen, 221–261. Westport, Conn.: Praeger.

———. 2005b. To the end of theory-practice apartheid: Encountering the world. *EPIC* 2005:205–217.

Baba, Marietta, and Carole Hill. 2006. What's in the name "Applied Anthropology"? An encounter with global practice. *National Association for the Practice of Anthropology Bulletin* 25 (1):176–207.

Baker, Lee D. 1998. *From savage to Negro: Anthropology and the construction of race, 1896–1954*. Berkeley: University of California Press.

Banks, Marcus, and Howard Morphy, eds. 1997. *Rethinking visual anthropology*. New Haven: Yale University Press.

Barbash, Ilisa, and Lucien Taylor. 1997. *Cross-cultural filmmaking: A handbook for making documentary and ethnographic films and videos*. Berkeley: University of California Press.

Barnett, Steve. 2003. Understand and apply sociology and anthropology: Build brands and leadership through anthropology and scenario planning. In *The change champions fieldguide*, edited by D. Ulrich, M. Goldsmith, L. Carter, J. Bolt, and N. Smallwood, 121–132. New York: Best Practice Publications.

Barnett, Steve, and JoAnn Magdoff. 1986. Beyond narcissism in American culture of the 1980s. *Cultural Anthropology* 1 (4):413–424.

Barrand, Drew. 2004. Closer encounters. *Marketing* (July 14):48.

Barrett, Stanley R. 1996. *Anthropology: A student's guide to theory and method*. Toronto: University of Toronto Press.

Barth, Fredrik. 1959. *Political leadership among Swat Pathans*. London: University of London Athlone Press.

———. ed. 1969. *Ethnic groups and boundaries: The social organization of culture difference*. Boston: Little Brown.

Barthes, Roland. 1972. *Mythologies*. New York, N.Y.: Hill and Wang.

———. 1981. *Camera lucida: Reflections on photography*. Translated by R. Howard. New York: Hill and Wang.

Battaglia, Deborah. 1999. Toward an ethics of the open subject: Writing culture in good conscience. In *Anthropological theory today*, edited by H. L. Moore, 114–150. Cambridge, U.K.: Polity Press.

Bauman, Richard, and Charles L. Briggs. 1990. Poetics and performance as critical perspectives on language and social life. *Annual Review of Anthropology* 19:59–88.

———. 2003. *Voices of modernity: Language ideologies and the politics of inequality*. Cambridge: Cambridge University Press.

Bauman, Richard, and Joel Sherzer, eds. 1974. *Explorations in the ethnography of speaking*. Cambridge: Cambridge University Press.

Behar, Ruth. 1993. *Translated woman: Crossing the border with Esperanza's story*. Boston: Beacon Press.

———. 1996. *The vulnerable observer: Anthropology that breaks your heart*. Boston: Beacon Press.

———. 1999. Ethnography: Cherishing our second-fiddle genre. *Journal of Contemporary Ethnography* 28 (5):472–484.

Behar, Ruth, and Deborah A. Gordon, eds. 1995. *Women writing culture*. Berkeley: University of California Press.

Belich, James. 1996. *Making peoples: A history of the New Zealanders, from Polynesian settlement to the end of the nineteenth century*. Honolulu: University of Hawai'i Press.

———. 2001. *Paradise reforged: A history of the New Zealanders from the 1880s to the year 2000*. Honolulu: University of Hawai'i Press.

Belk, Russell. 1988. Possessions and the extended self. *Journal of Consumer Research* 15 (2):139–168.

———. 1990. Me and thee versus mine and thine: How perceptions of the body influence organ donation and transplantation. In *Organ donation and transplantation: Psychological and behavioral factors*, edited by J. Shanteau and R. J. Harris, 139–149. Washington, D.C.: American Psychological Association.

———, ed. 1991. *Highways and buyways: Naturalistic research from the Consumer Behavior Odyssey*. Provo, Utah: Association for Consumer Research.

———. 1996. Metaphoric relationships with pets. *Society and Animals* 4 (2): 121–146.

———. 1997. Been there, done that, bought the souvenirs: Of journeys and boundary crossing. In *Consumer research: Postcards from the edge*, edited by S. Brown and D. Turley, 22–45. London: Routledge.

———. 1998. Multimedia approaches to qualitative data and representations. In Stern, *Representing consumers*, 308–338. London: Routledge.

———. 2006. You ought to be in pictures: Envisioning marketing research. In *Review of marketing research*, edited by N. Malhotra, 193–205. Armonk, N.Y.: M.E. Sharpe.

Belk, Russell, Güliz Ger, and Søren Askegaard. 2003. The fire of desire: A multisited inquiry into consumer passion. *Journal of Consumer Research* 30:326–351.

Belk, Russell, and Robert Kozinets. 2005a. Introduction to the resonant representations issue of consumption, markets and culture. *Consumption, Markets and Culture* 8:195–203.

———. 2005b. Videography in marketing and consumer research. *Qualitative Market Research: An International Journal* 8:128–141.

Belk, Russell, and John F. Sherry Jr., eds. 2007. *Consumer culture theory.* Oxford: Elsevier.

Belk, Russell, John F. Sherry Jr., and Melanie Wallendorf. 1988. A naturalistic inquiry in buyer and seller behavior at a swap meet. *Journal of Consumer Behavior* 14 (4): 449–470.

Belk, Russell, Melanie Wallendorf, and John F. Sherry Jr. 1989. The sacred and the profane: Theodicy on the Odyssey. *Journal of Consumer Behavior* 16 (1):1–38.

Belk, Russell, and Joel Watson. 1998. Material culture and the extended and unextended self in our university offices. *Advances in Consumer Research* 25:305–310.

Bell, Avril. 2004. "Half-castes" and "white natives": The politics of Māori-Pākehā hybrid identities. In Bell and Matthewman, *Cultural studies in Aotearoa New Zealand,* 121-138.

Bell, Claudia. 2004. Kiwiana revisited. In Bell and Matthewman, *Cultural studies in Aotearoa New Zealand,* 175-187.

Bell, Claudia, and Steve Matthewman, eds. 2004. *Cultural studies in Aotearoa New Zealand: identity, space and place.* South Melbourne, Vic.: Oxford University Press.

Bendelow, Gillian, and Simon J. Williams, eds. 1998. *Emotions in social life: Critical themes and contemporary issues.* London: Routledge.

Berger, John. 1973. *Ways of seeing.* New York: Viking Press.

Bergin, Paul. 2002. Māori sport and cultural identity in Australia. *The Australian Journal of Anthropology* 13 (3):257–269.

Berland, Jody. 2000. Cultural technologies and the "evolution" of technological cultures. In *The World Wide Web and contemporary cultural theory,* edited by A. Herman and T. Swiss, 235–258. New York: Routledge.

Beyer, Hugh, and Karen Holtzblatt. 1998. *Contextual design: Defining customer-centered systems.* San Francisco: Morgan Kaufmann.

Biella, Peter. 1993. Beyond ethnographic film: Hypermedia and scholarship. In *Anthropological film and video in the 1990s,* edited by J. R. Rollwagen, 131–176. Brockport, N.Y.: The Institute Press.

———. 1994. Codifications of ethnography: Linear and nonlinear. http://www.usc.edu/dept/elab/welcome/codifications.html. Last accessed January 27, 2007.

Biener, Lois, Ming Ji, Elizabeth Gilpin, and Alison Albers. 2004. The impact of emotional tone, message, and broadcast parameters in youth anti-smoking advertisements. *Journal of Health Communications* 9:259–274.

Biener, Lois, and T. M. Taylor. 2002. The continuing importance of emotion in tobacco control media campaigns: A response to Hastings and MacFayden. *Tobacco Control* 11:75–77.

Bignell, Jonathan. 1997. *Media semiotics: An introduction.* Manchester, England: Manchester University Press.

Bishop, John. 2005. *Dead Birds* migrating: DVD reinvigorates classic ethnographic film. *American Anthropologist* 107 (3):475–484.

Black, Stephanie. 2001. *Life and Debt*. 80-minute film. New York: New Yorker Films.

Blackston, Max. 1992. Beyond brand personality: Building brand relationships. Paper presented to the Advertising Research Foundation, New York, February.

Bloor, Michael, Jane Frankland, Michelle Thomas, and Kate Robson. 2001. *Focus groups in social research: Introducing qualitative methods*. London: Sage.

Blot, Richard K., ed. 2003. *Language and social identity*. Westport, Conn.: Praeger.

Blu, Karen I. 1979. Race and ethnicity: Changing symbols of dominance and hierarchy in the United States. *Anthropological Quarterly* 52 (2):77–85.

———. 1980. *The Lumbee problem: The making of an American Indian people*. Cambridge: Cambridge University Press.

Boas, Franz. 1896. Limitations of the comparative method in anthropology. *Science N.S.* 4:901–908.

———. 1940. *Race, language and culture*. New York: The Macmillan Company.

Bohannan, Laura. 1966. Shakespeare in the bush. *Natural History Magazine* (August/September):28–33.

Bohannan, Paul. 1980. You can't do nothing: Presidential address for 1979. *American Anthropologist* 82:508–524.

Bolter, J. David, and Richard A. Grusin. 1999. *Remediation: Understanding new media*. Cambridge, Mass.: MIT Press.

Bourdieu, Pierre. 1984. *Distinction: A social critique of the judgement of taste*. Translated by R. Nice. Cambridge, Mass.: Harvard University Press.

Bradburd, Daniel. 2006. Fuzzy boundaries and hard rules: Unfunded research and the IRB. *American Ethnologist* 33 (4):492–498.

Brenneis, Don. 2006. Partial measures. *American Ethnologist* 33 (4):538–540.

Brettell, Caroline, ed. 1993. *When they read what we write: The politics of ethnography*. Westport, Conn.: Bergin & Garvey.

Brodeur, Paul. 1989. *Currents of death: Power lines, computer terminals, and the attempt to cover up their threat to your health*. New York: Simon and Schuster.

———. 1990. Danger in the schoolyard. *Family Circle* (September 25):61–66.

Brodkin, Karen. 2000. Global capitalism: What's race got to do with it? *American Ethnologist* 27 (2):237–256.

Brown, Stephen. 1995. *Postmodern marketing*. London: Routledge.

———. 2006. *The marketing code*. London: Cyan Communications and Marshall Cavendish Business.

Brown, Stephen, Anne Marie Doherty, and Bill Clarke, eds. 1998. *Romancing the market*. London: Routledge.

Brown, Stephen, Lorna Stevens, and Pauline Maclaren. 1999. I can't believe it's not Bakhtin! Literary theory, postmodern advertising, and the gender agenda. *Journal of Advertising* 28 (1):11–24.

Burke, Timothy. 1996. *Lifebuoy men, Lux women: Commodification, consumption, and cleanliness in modern Zimbabwe*. Durham, N.C.: Duke University Press.

Butz, Andreas, and Antonio Krüger. 2006. Applying the peephole metaphor in a mixed-reality room. *IEEE Computer Graphics and Applications* 26 (1):56–63.

CAANZ. 2006. Saatchi & Saatchi "Back To Glory Days." *Caanz (Communication Agencies Association New Zealand)* www.caanz.co.nz/v2/news_view.asp?id=245, 15 March. Last accessed March 29, 2007.

Caillat, Zahna, and Barbara Mueller. 1996. Observations: The influence of culture on American and British advertising. *Journal of Advertising Research* 36 (3):79–88.

Caplan, Patricia, ed. 2003. *The ethics of anthropology: Debates and dilemmas.* London: Routledge.

Carù, Antonella, and Bernard Cova, eds. 2007. *Consuming experience.* London: Routledge.

Catterall, Miriam, and William Clarke. 2000. Improving the interface between the profession and the university. *International Journal of Market Research* 42 (1):3–15.

Catterall, Miriam, and Pauline Maclaran. 2006. Focus groups in marketing research. In *Handbook of qualitative research methods in marketing,* edited by R. W. Belk, 255–267. Cheltenham, U.K.: Edward Elgar.

Chalfen, Richard, and Michael Rich. 2004. Applying visual research: Patients teaching physicians about asthma through visual illness narratives. *Visual Anthropology Review* 20 (1):17–30.

Chernela, Janet M. 2003. Language ideology and women's speech: Talking community in the Northwest Amazon. *American Anthropologist* 105 (4):794–806.

Chun, Elaine. 2001. The construction of white, black and Korean American identities through African American vernacular English. *Journal of Linguistic Anthropology* 11 (1):53–64.

Clark, Nigel. 2004. Cultural studies for Shaky Islands. In Bell and Matthewman, *Cultural studies in Aotearoa New Zealand,* 3–18.

Clayton, Antony. 2003. *London's coffee houses: A stimulating story.* London: Historical Publications.

Clifford, James. 1986. On ethnographic allegory. In Clifford and Marcus, *Writing culture,* 98–121.

———. 1988. *The predicament of culture: Twentieth-century ethnography, literature and art.* Cambridge, Mass.: Harvard University Press.

———. 1997. *Routes: Travel and translation in the late twentieth century.* Cambridge, Mass.: Harvard University Press.

Clifford, James, and George E. Marcus, eds. 1986. *Writing culture: The poetics and politics of ethnography.* Berkeley: University of California Press.

Cohen, Lizabeth. 2003. *A consumers' republic: The politics of mass consumption in postwar America.* New York: Knopf.

Cohn, Carol. 1987. Sex and death in the rational world of defense intellectuals. *Signs* 12 (4):687–718.

Colleyn, Jean-Paul. 2005. Jean Rouch: An anthropologist ahead of his time. *American Anthropologist* 107 (1):113–116.

Collier, John, and Malcolm Collier. 1986. *Visual anthropology: Photography as a research method.* Rev. and expanded ed. Albuquerque: University of New Mexico Press.

Comaroff, Jean, and John L. Comaroff. 1987. The madman and the migrant: Work and labor in the historical consciousness of a South African people. *American Ethnologist* 14 (2):191–209.

Cook, Guy. 1992. *The discourse of advertising.* London: Routledge.

Cooper, Tom. 2005. Making *Forest of Bliss*: The film, the book, the DVD, and the breakthrough. *American Anthropologist* 107 (3):484–488.

Coover, Roderick. 2004. Working with images, images of work: Using digital interface, photography and hypertext in ethnography. In Pink, Kürti, and Afonso, *Working images*, 185–203.

Corbin, Alain. 1986. *The foul and the fragrant: Odor and the French social imagination*. Translated by Miriam L. Kochan. Cambridge, Mass.: Harvard University Press.

Costa, Janeen Arnold, and Gary J. Bamossy, eds. 1995. *Marketing in a multicultural world: Ethnicity, nationalism, and cultural identity*. Thousand Oaks, Calif.: Sage.

Coulter, Robin, and Gerald Zaltman. 2000. The power of metaphor. In *The why of consumption: Contemporary perspectives on consumer motives, goals, and desires*, edited by S. Ratneshwar, D. G. Mick and C. Huffman, 259–281. London: Routledge.

Cova, Bernard. 1996. The postmodern explained to managers: Implications for marketing. *Business Horizons* 39 (6):9.

Crawford, Peter Ian, and Sigurjón Hafsteinsson, eds. 1996. *The construction of the viewer: Media ethnography and the anthropology of audiences*. Hojbjerg, Denmark: Intervention Press.

Crockett, David, and Melanie Wallendorf. 2004. The role of normative political ideology in consumer behavior. *Journal of Consumer Research* 31:511–528.

Curasi, Carolyn, Linda Price, and Eric Arnould. 2004. How individuals' cherished possessions become families' inalienable wealth. *Journal of Consumer Research* 31:609–622.

Dahl, Darren, Kristina Frankenberger, and Rajesh Manchanda. 2003. Does it pay to shock? Reactions to shocking and nonshocking advertising content among university students. *Journal of Advertising Research* September:268–280.

D'Andrade, Roy. 1995. Moral models in anthropology. *Current Anthropology* 36 (3):399–408.

Darder, Antonia, and Rodolfo D. Torres, eds. 1998. *The Latino studies reader: Culture, economy, and society*. Malden, Mass.: Blackwell.

———. 2004. *After race: Racism after multiculturalism*. New York: New York University Press.

Darnell, Regna. 2001. *Invisible genealogies: A history of Americanist anthropology*. Lincoln: University of Nebraska Press.

Dávila, Arlene M. 1998. El Kiosko Budweiser: The making of a "national" television show in Puerto Rico. *American Ethnologist* 25 (3):452–470.

———. 2001. *Latinos, Inc.: The marketing and making of a people*. Berkeley: University of California Press.

———. 2002. Culture in the ad world: Producing the Latin look. In Ginsburg, Abu-Lughod, and Larkin, *Media worlds*, 264–280.

De Genova, Nicholas, and Ana Y. Ramos-Zayas. 2003. *Latino crossings: Mexicans, Puerto Ricans, and the politics of race and citizenship*. New York: Routledge.

Denny, Rita. 1999. Consuming values: The culture of clients, researchers and consumers. In *The race for innovation*, 375–384. Amsterdam: ESOMAR.

———. 2006. Pushing the boundaries of ethnography in the practice of market research. In *Handbook of qualitative research methods in marketing*, edited by R. W. Belk, 430–439. Cheltenham, U.K.: Edward Elgar.

Denny, Rita, and Victor Russell. 1994. Fighting bias through public relations. *Fortnightly* August 1:14–17.

Denzin, Norman K., and Yvonna S. Lincoln, eds. 1994. *Handbook of qualitative research*. Thousand Oaks, Calif.: Sage.

Desjeux, Dominique. 2001. La méthode des itinéraires comme méthode comparative appliquée à la comparaison interculturelle. www.argonautes.fr/sections.php?op= viewarticle&artid=103. Last accessed January 19, 2007.

———. 2004. *Les sciences sociales*. Paris: Presses Universitaires de France.

———. 2006. *La consommation*. Paris: Presses Universitaires de France.

———. 2007. NAPA news. *Anthropology News*. Forthcoming.

Diamond, Nina, Mary Ann McGrath, Albert M. Muniz Jr., John F. Sherry Jr., Robert Kozinets, and Stefania Borghini. n.d. Creation and propagation of brand complexity: The case of American Girl. Manuscript under review.

Dodd, Sarah D. 2002. Metaphors and meaning—A grounded cultural model of US entrepreneurship. *Journal of Business Venturing* 17:519–535.

Domínguez, Virginia R. 1986. *White by definition: Social classification in creole Louisiana*. New Brunswick, N.J.: Rutgers University Press.

———. 2000. For a politics of love and rescue. *Cultural Anthropology* 15 (3):361–393.

Doostdar, Alireza. 2004. "The vulgar spirit of blogging": On language, culture, and power in Persian Weblogestan. *American Anthropologist* 106 (4):651–662.

Dopico, Ana María. 2002. *Picturing Havana: History, vision, and the scramble for Cuba*. *Nepantla: Views from the South* 3 (3):451–493.

Douglas, Mary. 1966. *Purity and danger: An analysis of concepts of pollution and taboo*. London: Routledge & K. Paul.

Downey, Gary Lee. 1998. *The machine in me: An anthropologist sits among computer engineers*. New York: Routledge.

Drotner, Kirsten. 1996. Less is more: Media ethnography and its limits. In Crawford and Hafsteinsson, *The construction of the viewer*, 28–46.

Dufrenoy, Mary-Louise, and Jean Dufrenoy. 1950. Coffee, the "exotick drug." *The Scientific Monthly* 70 (3):185–188.

Dumit, Joseph. 2004. *Picturing personhood: Brain scans and biomedical identity*. Princeton, N.J.: Princeton University Press.

Duncker, Elke. 2002. Cross-cultural usability of the library metaphor. *Joint Conference on Digital Libraries* (July):223–230.

Edwards, Elizabeth, ed. 1992. *Anthropology and photography, 1860–1920*. New Haven: Yale University Press in association with The Royal Anthropological Institute, London.

———. 2001. *Raw histories: Photographs, anthropology and museums*. Oxford: Berg.

———. 2005. Photographs and the sound of history. *Visual Anthropology Review* 21 (1–2):27–46.

Edwards, Elizabeth, and Janice Hart, eds. 2004. *Photographs objects histories: On the materiality of images*. London: Routledge.

Elliot, Luther. 2004. Goa trance and the practice of community in the age of the Internet. *Television and New Media* 5 (3):272–288.

Emanatian, Michele. 1999. Congruence by degree: On the relation between metaphor and cultural models. In *Metaphor in cognitive linguistics*, edited by R. W. Gibbs and G. Steen, 205–218. Amsterdam: J. Benjamins.

Erickson, Kenneth, and Martin Høyem. 2006. Research blogs for team ethnography: What kind of notes are these? Poster presented at EPIC2006 Poster Session, Portland, Oregon, September 24–26.

———. 2007. Using blogs for ethnography in China. Paper read at International Seminar on Qualitative Research Techniques Applied to Understanding Consumers, Sorbonne-Université de Paris 5, January 9–11.

Erickson, Ken C., and Donald D. Stull. 1998. *Doing team ethnography: Warnings and advice.* Thousand Oaks, Calif.: Sage.

Eriksen, Thomas Hylland. 2006. *Engaging anthropology: The case for a public presence.* Oxford: Berg.

Ernst, Thomas. 1990. Mates, wives and children. In *Writing Australian culture: Text, society, and national identity,* edited by J. Marcus, 110–118. Adelaide: University of Adelaide.

Eubanks, Philip. 1999. The story of conceptual metaphor: What motivates metaphoric mappings? *Poetics Today* 20 (3):419–442.

Fabian, Johannes. 1983. *Time and the other: How anthropology makes its object.* New York: Columbia University Press.

Farmer, Paul. 1992. *AIDS and accusation: Haiti and the geography of blame.* Berkeley: University of California Press.

———. 2003. *Pathologies of power: Health, human rights, and the new war on the poor.* Berkeley: University of California Press.

Fassin, Didier. 2006. The end of ethnography as collateral damage of ethical regulation? *American Ethnologist* 33 (4):522–524.

Fennell, Geraldine, and Joel Saegert. 2004. Diversity: Population vs. market. In *Diversity in advertising: Broadening the scope of research directions,* edited by J. D. Williams, W.-N. Lee, and C. P. Haugtvedt, 301–318. Mahwah, N.J.: Lawrence Erlbaum.

Fernandez, James W., ed. 1991. *Beyond metaphor: The theory of tropes in anthropology.* Stanford, Calif.: Stanford University Press.

Firat, A. Fuat. 1995. Consumer culture or culture consumed. In *Marketing in a multicultural world: Ethnicity, nationalism, and cultural identity,* edited by J. A. Costa and G. J. Bamossy, 105–126. Thousand Oaks, Calif.: Sage.

Firat, A. Fuat, and Alladi Venkatesh. 1995. Liberatory postmodernism and the reenchantment of consumption. *Journal of Consumer Research* 22:239–267.

Fischer, Michael M. J. 1999. Emergent forms of life: Anthropologies of late or postmodernities. *Annual Review of Anthropology* 28:455–478.

———. 2007. Culture and cultural analysis as experimental systems. *Cultural Anthropology* 22 (1):1–65.

Flores, Juan, and George Yúdice. 1990. Living borders/Buscando America: Languages of Latino self-formation. *Social Text* (24):57–84.

Fluehr-Lobban, Carolyn, ed. 2003a. *Ethics and the profession of anthropology: Dialogue for ethically conscious practice.* 2nd ed. Walnut Creek, Calif.: AltaMira Press.

———. 2003b. Informed consent in anthropological research: We are not exempt. In Fluehr-Lobban, *Ethics and the profession of anthropology,* 159–177.

Fortun, Kim, and Mike Fortun. 2005. Scientific imaginaries and ethical plateaus in contemporary U.S. toxicology. *American Anthropologist* 107 (1):43–54.

Foster, George. 1965. Peasant society and the image of limited good. *American Anthropologist* 67 (2):293–315.

Fournier, Susan. 1998. Consumers and their brands: Developing relationship theory in consumer research. *Journal of Consumer Research* 4:343–373.

Fox, Richard Gabriel, ed. 1991. *Recapturing anthropology: Working in the present*. Santa Fe, N.M.: School of American Research Press.

Frank, Thomas. 1999. Brand you: Better selling through anthropology. *Harper's Magazine* July (1790):74–79.

Friedrich, Paul. 1966. Structural implications of Russian pronominal usage. In *Sociolinguistics*, edited by W. Bright, 214–259. The Hague: Mouton.

García Canclini, Néstor. 1995. *Hybrid cultures: Strategies for entering and leaving modernity*. Translated by C. Chiappari and S. Lopez. Minneapolis: University of Minnesota Press.

———. 2001. *Consumers and citizens: Globalization and multicultural conflicts*. Translated by G. Yúdice. Minneapolis: University of Minnesota Press.

Gardner, Burleigh, and Sidney Levy. 1955. The product and the brand. *Harvard Business Review* 33 (2):33–39.

Geertz, Clifford. 1973. *The interpretation of cultures*. New York: Basic Books.

———. 1983. *Local knowledge: Further essays in interpretive anthropology*. New York: Basic Books.

———. 1988. *Works and lives: The anthropologist as author*. Stanford, Calif.: Stanford University Press.

———. 2002. An inconstant profession: The anthropological life in interesting times. *Annual Review of Anthropology* 31:1–19.

Ger, Güliz, and Russell Belk. 1996. I'd like to buy the world a Coke: Consumptionscapes of the "less affluent world." *Journal of Consumer Policy* 19 (3):271–304.

Gibbs, Raymond W. 1994. *The poetics of mind: Figurative thought, language, and understanding*. Cambridge: Cambridge University Press.

———. 1999. Taking metaphor out of our heads and putting it into the cultural world. In Gibbs and Steen, *Metaphor in cognitive linguistics*, 145–166.

Gibbs, Raymond W., and Gerard Steen, eds. 1999. *Metaphor in cognitive linguistics*. Amsterdam: J. Benjamins.

Gibson, Ross. 1993. Camera natura: Landscape in Australian feature films. In *Australian cultural studies: A reader*, edited by J. Frow and M. Morris, 209–221. Urbana: University of Illinois Press.

Ginsburg, Faye. 1989. *Contested lives: The abortion debate in an American community*. Berkeley: University of California Press.

———. 1995. The parallax effect: The impact of Aboriginal media on ethnographic film. *Visual Anthropology Review* 11 (2):64–76.

———. 2006. Ethnography and American studies. *Cultural Anthropology* 21 (3): 487–495.

Ginsburg, Faye D., Lila Abu-Lughod, and Brian Larkin, eds. 2002. *Media worlds: Anthropology on new terrain*. Berkeley: University of California Press.

Gladwell, Malcolm. 2001. Java man: How caffeine created the modern world. *The New Yorker* July 30:76–80.

———. 2005. *Blink: The power of thinking without thinking*. New York: Little Brown.

Glaser, Barney G., and Anselm L. Strauss. 1967. *The discovery of grounded theory: Strategies for qualitative research*. Chicago: Aldine.

Gleach, Frederic W. 2002. Anthropological professionalization and the Virginia Indians at the turn of the century. *American Anthropologist* 104 (2):499–507.

Gleick, James. 1999. *Faster: The acceleration of just about everything*. New York: Pantheon Books.

Goff, Phil. 2001. The Trans-Tasman relationship: A New Zealand perspective. *The Drawing Board: An Australian Review of Public Affairs* 2 (1):1–9.

Goffman, Erving. 1959. *The presentation of self in everyday life*. Garden City, N.Y.: Doubleday.

———. 1961. *Asylums: Essays on the social situation of mental patients and other inmates*. Garden City, N.Y.: Doubleday.

———. 1963. *Stigma: Notes on the management of spoiled identity*. Englewood Cliffs, N.J.: Prentice-Hall.

———. 1974. *Frame analysis: An essay on the organization of experience*. New York: Harper & Row.

———. 1978. Response cries. *Language* 54 (4):787–815.

———. 1979. *Gender advertisements*. New York: Harper & Row.

———. 1981. *Forms of talk*. Philadelphia: University of Pennsylvania Press.

Goldman, Robert. 1992. *Reading ads socially*. London: Routledge.

Goldman, Robert, and Stephen Papson. 1998. *Nike culture: The sign of the swoosh*. Thousand Oaks, Calif.: Sage.

Gomes, Lee. 2006. Talking tech: Companies hire anthropologists to better understand customers. *The Wall Street Journal*, October 3:A20.

Goode, Luke. 2004. Keeping in (and out of) touch: Telecommunications and mobile technocultures. In Bell and Matthewman, *Cultural studies in Aotearoa New Zealand*, 268–284.

Gordon, Wendy. 1999. *Goodthinking: A guide to qualitative research*. Oxfordshire, U.K.: Admap Publications.

Gordon, Wendy, and Roy Langmaid. 1988. *Qualitative market research: A practitioner's and buyer's guide*. Aldershot, England: Gower.

Goto, Kelly, and Subha Subramanian. 2004. Culture matters: An interview with Genevieve Bell. *Gotomedia Publication,* http://www.gotomedia.com/gotoreport/november2004/news_1104_bell.html. Last accessed January 31, 2007.

Gould, Stephen Jay. 1981. *The mismeasure of man*. New York: Norton.

Green, Penelope. 1999. The anthropologist of dressing rooms. *The New York Times*, May 2 (9):4.

Gregory, Steven, and Roger Sanjek, eds. 1994. *Race*. New Brunswick, N.J.: Rutgers University Press.

Grimshaw, Anna, and Amanda Ravetz, eds. 2005. *Visualizing anthropology*. Bristol, U.K.: Intellect Books.

Gross, Jane. 2004. A dream life Freud would have envied. *The New York Times*, November 7 (9):1–2.

Gumperz, John Joseph, and Dell H. Hymes, eds. 1972. *Directions in sociolinguistics: The ethnography of communication*. New York: Holt Rinehart and Winston.

Gupta, Akhil, and James Ferguson, eds. 1997a. *Anthropological locations: Boundaries and grounds of a field science*. Berkeley: University of California Press.

———, eds. 1997b. *Culture, power, place: Explorations in critical anthropology*. Durham, N.C.: Duke University Press.

Hackenberg, Robert. 1993. Reflections on the death of Tonto and the new ethnographic enterprise. *High Plains Applied Anthropologist* 13:12–27.

Hackenberg, Robert, and Beverly H. Hackenberg. 2004. Notes toward a new future: Applied anthropology in century XXI. *Human Organization* 63 (4):385–399.

Hakken, David. 1999. *Cyborgs@cyberspace? An ethnographer looks to the future*. New York: Routledge.

Hamilton, Annette. 1990. Beer and being. In *Writing Australian culture: Text, society, and national identity*, edited by J. Marcus, 17–29. Adelaide: University of Adelaide.

Hammond, Joyce. 2004. Photography and ambivalence. *Visual Studies* 19:135–144.

Hanby, Terry. 1999. Brands—dead or alive? *Journal of Market Research Society* 41 (1): 7–18.

Hanks, William F. 1996. *Language and communicative practices*. Boulder, Colo.: Westview Press.

———. 2005. Pierre Bourdieu and the practices of language. *Annual Review of Anthropology* 34:67–83.

Hannerz, Ulf. 1996. *Transnational connections*. London: Routledge.

Harrison, Faye V. 1995. The persistent power of "race" in the cultural and political economy of racism. *Annual Review of Anthropology* 24:47–74.

Hartigan, John. 2005. *Odd tribes: Toward a cultural analysis of White people*. Durham N.C.: Duke University Press.

Harvey, David. 1990. *The condition of postmodernity: An enquiry into the origins of cultural change*. Cambridge, Mass.: Blackwell.

Hastings, Gerard, and L. MacFadyen. 2002. The limitations of fear messages. *Tobacco Control* 11:73–75.

Hattox, Ralph S. 1985. *Coffee and coffeehouses: The origins of a social beverage in the Medieval Near East*. Seattle: University of Washington Press.

Havránek, Bohuslav. 1964. The functional differentiation of the standard language. In *A Prague school reader on esthetics, literary structure, and style*, edited by P. L. Garvin. Washington, D.C.: Georgetown University Press.

Heisley, Deborah A., Mary Ann McGrath, and John F. Sherry Jr. 1991. "To everything there is a season": A photoessay of a farmers' market. In Belk, *Highways and Buyways*, 141–166.

Helms, Mary W. 1988. *Ulysses' sail: An ethnographic odyssey of power, knowledge, and geographical distance*. Princeton: Princeton University Press.

Henley, Margaret. 2004. Going mainstream: Women's televised sport through a case study of the 1999 Netball World Championships. In Horrocks and Perry, *Television in New Zealand*, 167–183.

Hill, Carole, and Marietta Baba. 1997. The international practice of anthropology: A critical overview. In *The global practice of anthropology*, edited by M. Baba and C. Hill, 1–24. Williamsburg, Va.: Dept. of Anthropology College of William and Mary.

———, eds. 2000. *The unity of theory and practice in anthropology: Rebuilding a fractured synthesis, NAPA Bulletin 18*. Alexandria, Va.: American Anthropological Association.

Hinton, Alexander. 1993. Prolegomenon to a processual approach to the emotions. *Ethos* 21 (4):417–451.

Hirschman, Elizabeth C. 2002. Dogs as metaphors: Meaning transfer in a complex product set. *Semiotica* 139 (1–4):125–159.

Hobsbawm, Eric, and Terrance Ranger, eds. 1983. *The invention of tradition*. Cambridge: Cambridge University Press.

Hochschild, Arlie Russell. 1983. *The managed heart: Commercialization of human feeling*. Berkeley: University of California Press.

Hockings, Paul, ed. 2003. *Principles of visual anthropology*. 3rd ed. Berlin: Mouton de Gruyter.

Holbrook, Morris B. 1995. *Consumer research: Introspective essays on the study of consumption*. Thousand Oaks, Calif.: Sage.

———. 1998. Journey to Kroywen: An ethnoscopic auto-auto-auto-driven stereographic photo essay. In Stern, *Representing consumers*, 231–263.

———. 2006a. Consumption experience, customer value, and subjective personal introspection: An illustrative photographic essay. *Journal of Business Research* 59 (6): 714–725.

———. 2006b. Photo essays and the mining of minutiae in consumer research: 'Bout the time I got to Phoenix. In *Handbook of qualitative research methods in marketing*, edited by R. W. Belk, 476–493. Cheltenham, U.K.: Edward Elgar.

Holliday, Ruth. 2000. We've been framed: Visualising methodology. *The Sociological Review* 48:503–521.

Holt, Douglas B. 1995. How consumers consume: A typology of consumption practices. *The Journal of Consumer Research* 22 (1):1–16.

———. 2004. *How brands become icons: The principles of cultural branding*. Boston: Harvard Business School Press.

hooks, bell. 2004. *We real cool: Black men and masculinity*. New York: Routledge.

Horrocks, Roger, and Nick Perry, eds. 2004. *Television in New Zealand: Programming the nation*. South Melbourne, Vic.: Oxford University Press.

Howard, Alan. 1988. Hypermedia and the future of ethnography. *Cultural Anthropology* 3 (3):304–315.

Hudson, Wayne. 1997. Cultural undergrounds and civic identity. In *Creating Australia: Changing Australian history*, edited by W. Hudson and G. C. Bolton, 165–177. St. Leonards, N.S.W., Australia: Allen & Unwin.

Hymes, Dell H. 1962. The ethnography of speaking. In *Anthropology and human behavior*, edited by T. Gladwin and W. C. Sturtevant, 15–53. Washington, D.C.: Anthropology So-ciety of Washington.

———. 1964. Introduction: Toward ethnographies of communication. *American Anthropologist* 66 (6):1–34.

———, ed. 1972. *Reinventing anthropology*. New York: Pantheon Books.

———. 1974a. *Foundations in sociolinguistics: An ethnographic approach*. Philadelphia: University of Pennsylvania Press.

———. 1974b. Ways of speaking. In *Explorations in the ethnography of speaking*, edited by R. Bauman and J. Sherzer, 433–452. Cambridge: Cambridge University Press.

———, ed. 1999. *Reinventing anthropology*. Ann Arbor: University of Michigan Press.

Imms, Michael. 1999. A reassessment of the roots and theoretical basis of qualitative market research in the UK. Paper read at Market Research Society, Annual Conference, London, March 18–19.

Ishida, Toru. 1998. Towards computation over communities. *Lecture Notes in Computer Science* (1519):1–10.

Jackson, John L. 2004. An ethnographic *film*flam: Giving gifts, doing research, and videotaping the native subject/object. *American Anthropologist* 106 (1):32–42.

———. 2005. *Real Black: Adventures in racial sincerity*. Chicago: University of Chicago Press.

Jackson, Steven, and Brendan Hokowhitu. 2002. Sport, tribes and technology. *Journal of Sport & Social Issues* 26 (2):125–139.

Jakobson, Roman. 1960. Linguistics and poetics. In *Style in language*, edited by T. A. Sebeok, 350–377. Cambridge: Technology Press of Massachusetts Institute of Technology.

———. 1980. *The framework of language*. Ann Arbor: University of Michigan Press.

Jardine, Andrew. 2004. A discursive analysis of a television advertisement: The I'd Like advertisement for Xenical. *Proceedings of the Association for Consumer Research*. http://www.acrwebsite.org/volumes/display.asp?id=12076. Last accessed June 2007.

Johansson, Johny K. 2004. *In your face: How American marketing excess fuels anti-Americanism*. Upper Saddle River, N.J.: Financial Times Prentice Hall.

Johnson, Gerald. 1994. Of metaphor and the difficulty of computer discourse. *Communications of the ACM* 37 (12):97–102.

Jones, Del. 1999. Hot asset in corporate: Anthropology degrees. *USA Today*, February 18:B1.

Jones, Rachel, and Martin Ortlieb. 2006. Online place and person-making: Matters of the heart and self-expression. *EPIC* 2006:214–228.

Joos, Martin. 1962. *The five clocks*. New York: Harcourt, Brace & World.

Jordan, Ann. 2003. *Business anthropology*. Prospect Heights, Ill.: Waveland.

Jordan, Brigitte. 2005. Managing global teams: Bookkeeping or herding cats? Paper read at *The Society for Applied Anthropology 65th Annual Meeting*, Santa Fe, New Mexico, April 5–10.

Joy, Annamma, and John F. Sherry Jr. 2003. Speaking of art as embodied imagination: A multisensory approach to understanding aesthetic experience. *Journal of Consumer Research* 30 (2):259–282.

Jutel, Thierry. 2004. *Lord of the Rings: Landscape, transformation, and the geography of the virtual*. In Bell and Matthewman, *Cultural studies in Aotearoa New Zealand*, 54–65.

Kaarst-Brown, Michelle, and Dan Robey. 1999. More on myth, magic and metaphor. *Information Technology and People* 12 (2):192–218.

Kapferer, Judith. 1996. *Being all equal: Identity, difference and Australian cultural practice*. Oxford: Berg.

Katz, Jack. 1999. *How emotions work*. Chicago: University of Chicago Press.

Keefe, Susan E., and Amado M. Padilla. 1987. *Chicano ethnicity*. Albuquerque: University of New Mexico Press.

Kerr, Audrey Elisa. 2005. The paper bag principle: Of the myth and the motion of colorism. *Journal of American Folklore* 118 (469):271–289.

———. 2006. *The paper bag principle: Class, colorism, and rumor and the case of Black Washington, D.C.* Knoxville: University of Tennessee Press.

King, Larry. 1993. Electromagnetic health scare. *Larry King Live*, Broadcast January 28. USA: CNN.

Kleine, Susan, Robert Kleine, and Chris Allen. 1995. How is a possession "me" or "not me"? Characterizing types and an antecedent of material possession attachment. *Journal of Consumer Research* 22:327–343.

Kleinman, Arthur, and Joan Kleinman. 1997. The appeal of experience, the dismay of images: Cultural appropriations of suffering in our times. In *Social suffering*, edited by A. Kleinman, V. Das, and M. M. Lock, 1–23. Berkeley: University of California Press.

Kodak Research and Development. 2002. Kodak researchers take anthropology from the jungle to the living room. http://www.kodak.com/USen/corp/researchdevelopment/productFeatures/anthropology.shtml. Last accessed October 2002.

Koerner, Brendan. 1998. Into the wild unknown of workplace culture: Anthropologists revitalize their discipline. *U.S. News & World Report* (August 10):56.

Koppel, Ted. 1990. *Nightline*, Broadcast March 9. USA: ABC.

Kövecses, Zoltán. 1999. Metaphor: Does it constitute or reflect cultural models? In Gibbs and Steen, *Metaphor in cognitive linguistics*, 167–188.

———. 2002. *Metaphor: A practical introduction*. Oxford: Oxford University Press.

Kozinets, Robert. 2002. Can consumers escape the market? Emancipatory illuminations from burning man. *Journal of Consumer Research* 29 (1):20–38.

Kozinets, Robert, and Russell Belk. 2006. Camcorder society: Quality videography in consumer and marketing research. In *Handbook of qualitative research methods in marketing*, edited by R. W. Belk, 335–344. Cheltenham, U.K.: Edward Elgar.

Labov, William. 1972. *Sociolinguistic patterns*. Philadelphia: University of Pennsylvania Press.

Lakoff, George. 1987. *Women, fire, and dangerous things: What categories reveal about the mind*. Chicago: University of Chicago Press.

Lakoff, George, and Mark Johnson. 1980. *Metaphors we live by*. Chicago: University of Chicago Press.

Lamphere, Louise. 2004. The convergence of applied, practicing, and public anthropology in the 21st century. *Human Organization* 63 (4):431–443.

Lane, E. 1993. SDG&E prepares for March court date in key EMF case. *Energy Daily* (February 22):4.

Larson, E. 1993. Attention shoppers: Don't look now but you are being tailed. *The Smithsonian* 23 (10):70.

Lassiter, Luke E. 2005. *The Chicago guide to collaborative ethnography*. Chicago: University of Chicago Press.

Leake, Linda. 2002. Cashing in on Cuba. *Agri Marketing* 40 (9):54, 56–58.

Leavitt, John. 1996. Meaning and feeling in the anthropology of emotions. *American Ethnologist* 23 (3):514–539.

Lederman, Rena. 2006. Introduction: Anxious borders between work and life in a time of bureaucratic ethics regulation. *American Ethnologist* 33 (4):477–481.

Lee, Nick, and Amanda Broderick. 2007. The past, present and future of observational research in marketing. *Qualitative Market Research: An International Journal* 10 (2):121–129.

Lefkowitz, Daniel. 2003. Investing in emotion: Love and anger in financial advertising. *Journal of Linguistic Anthropology* 13 (1):71–97.

Leiss, William, Stephen Kline, and Sut Jhally. 1986. *Social communication in advertising: Persons, products, & images of well-being*. Toronto: Methuen.

Leonard, Dorothy, and Jeffrey F. Rayport. 1997. Spark innovation through empathic design. *Harvard Business Review* (November):102–113.

Lessig, Lawrence. 1999. *Code and other laws of cyberspace*. New York: Basic Books.

———. 2001. *The future of ideas: The fate of the commons in a connected world*. New York: Random House.

Levy, Sidney J. 1978. Hunger and work in a civilized tribe. *American Behavioral Scientist* (21):557–570.

———. 2003. Roots of marketing and consumer research at the University of Chicago. *Consumption, Markets and Culture* 6:99–110.

———. 2006a. History of qualitative research methods in marketing. In *Handbook of qualitative research methods in marketing*, edited by R. W. Belk, 3–16. Cheltenham, U.K.: Edward Elgar.

———. 2006b. The consumption of stories. In *Handbook of qualitative research methods in marketing*, edited by R. W. Belk, 453–464. Cheltenham, U.K.: Edward Elgar.

Levy, Sidney J., and Dennis W. Rook. 1999. *Brands, consumers, symbols, & research: Sidney J. Levy on marketing*. Thousand Oaks, Calif.: Sage.

Limón, José Eduardo. 1998. *American encounters: Greater Mexico, the United States, and the erotics of culture*. Boston: Beacon Press.

Lindquist, Julie. 2002. *A place to stand: Politics and persuasion in a working-class bar*. Oxford: Oxford University Press.

Lindstrom, Lamont. 1993. *Cargo cult: Strange stories of desire from Melanesia and beyond*. Honolulu: University of Hawai'i Press.

Linnett, Richard. 2000. BellSouth Yellow Pages recast as virtual store. *Advertising Age* (June 5):1, 62.

Lipsitz, George. 2006. *The possessive investment in whiteness: How white people profit from identity politics*. Philadelphia: Temple University Press.

Lovejoy, Tracey, and Nelle Steele. 2004. Engaging our audience through photo stories. *Visual Anthropology Review* 20 (1):70–81.

Low, Graham, and Lynne Cameron, eds. 1999. *Researching and applying metaphor*. Cambridge: Cambridge University Press.

Lupton, Deborah. 1998. *The emotional self: A sociocultural exploration*. Thousand Oaks, Calif.: Sage.

Lutz, Catherine. 1986. Emotion, thought and estrangement: Emotions as a cultural category. *Current Anthropology* 1 (3):287–309.

Lutz, Catherine, and Lila Abu-Lughod, eds. 1990. *Language and the politics of emotion*. New York: Cambridge University Press.

Lutz, Catherine, and Jane L. Collins. 1993. *Reading National Geographic*. Chicago: University of Chicago Press.

Lyotard, Jean François. 1984. *The postmodern condition: A report on knowledge*. Translated by G. Bennington and B. Massumi. Minneapolis: University of Minnesota Press.

MacClancy, Jeremy, and Chris McDonaugh. 1996. *Popularizing anthropology*. London: Routledge.

MacDougall, David. 1992. "Photo wallahs": An encounter with photography. *Visual Anthropology Review* 8 (2):96–100.

———. 1998. *Transcultural cinema*. Princeton, N.J.: Princeton University Press.

———. 2006. *The corporeal image: Film, ethnography, and the senses*. Princeton, N.J.: Princeton University Press.

Maddox, Kate. 2006. Researchers learn more from what people do than say. *BtoB Online*, April 3, http://www.btobonline.com/article.cms?articleId=27580. Last accessed January 15, 2007.

Maglio, Paul, and Teenie Matlock. 1998. Metaphors we surf the web by. Paper read at Workshop on Personalized and Social Navigation in Information Space, Stockholm, Sweden, March 16–17.

Mahon, Maureen. 2000. The visible evidence of cultural producers. *Annual Review of Anthropology* 29:467–492.

———. 2004. *Right to rock: The Black Rock Coalition and the cultural politics of race*. Durham: Duke University Press.

Malefyt, Timothy D. 2003. Models, metaphors and client relations: The negotiated meanings of advertising. In *Advertising cultures*, edited by T. D. Malefyt and B. Moeran, 139–164. Oxford: Berg.

Malinowski, Bronislaw. 1984. *Argonauts of the Western Pacific*. Prospect Heights, Ill.: Waveland. Originally published in 1922.

———. 1989. *A diary in the strict sense of the term*. Stanford: Stanford University Press. Originally published in 1967.

Mandelbaum, David G., ed. 1949. *Selected writings of Edward Sapir in language, culture and personality*. Berkeley: University of California Press.

Marcus, George E. 1998. *Ethnography through thick and thin*. Princeton, N.J.: Princeton University Press.

Marcus, George E., and Michael M. J. Fischer. 1986. *Anthropology as cultural critique: An experimental moment in the human sciences*. Chicago: University of Chicago Press.

Mariampolski, Hy. 2006. *Ethnography for marketers: A guide to consumer immersion*. Thousand Oaks, Calif.: Sage.

Marketing Week. 2004. It's time to get personal. *Marketing Week* (June 24):43.

Mars, Gerald. 2004. Refocusing with applied anthropology. *Anthropology Today* 20 (1):1–2.

Martin, Diane, John Schouten, and James McAlexander. 2006. Reporting ethnographic research: Bringing segments to life through movie making and metaphor. In *Hand-book of qualitative research methods in marketing*, edited by R. W. Belk, 361–370. Cheltenham, U.K.: Edward Elgar.

Martin, Emily. 1987. *The woman in the body: A cultural analysis of reproduction*. Boston: Beacon Press.

———. 1994. *Flexible bodies: Tracking immunity in American culture from the days of polio to the age of AIDS*. Boston: Beacon Press.

Martínez, Wilton. 1992. Who constructs anthropological knowledge? Toward a theory of ethnographic film spectatorship. In *Film as ethnography*, edited by P. I. Crawford and D. Turton, 130–161. Manchester: Manchester University Press.

———. 1995. The challenges of a pioneer: Tim Asch, otherness, and film reception. *Visual Anthropology Review* 11 (1):53–82.

———. 1996. Deconstructing the "viewer": From ethnography of the visual to critique of the occult. In Crawford and Hafsteinsson, *The construction of the viewer*, 69–100.

Marvin, Garry. 2006. Research, representations and responsibilities: An anthropologist in the contested world of foxhunting. In Pink, *Applications of anthropology*, 191–208.

Matthewman, Steve. 2004. More than sand: Theorizing the beach. In Bell and Matthewman, *Cultural studies in Aotearoa New Zealand*, 36–53.

Mauss, Marcel. 1990. *The gift: The form and reason for exchange in archaic societies*. Translated by W. D. Halls. New York: W.W. Norton. Original work published in 1950.

May, Reuben A. Buford, and Mary Pattillo-McCoy. 2000. Do you see what I see? Examining a collaborative ethnography. *Qualitative Inquiry* 6 (1):65–87.

Mazzarella, William. 2003a. Critical publicity/public criticism: Reflections on field-work in the Bombay ad world. In *Advertising cultures*, edited by T. D. Malefyt and B. Moeran, 55–74. New York: Berg.

———. 2003b. *Shoveling smoke: Advertising and globalization in contemporary India*. Durham, N.C.: Duke University Press.

———. 2004. Culture, globalization, mediation. *Annual Review of Anthropology* 33: 345–367.

McClain, Dylan. 1999. Toronto TV station adopts Web-page format. *New York Times*, December 27.

McClintock, Anne. 1995. *Imperial leather: Race, gender, and sexuality in the colonial contest*. New York: Routledge.

McCracken, Grant. 1988a. *Culture and consumption: New approaches to the symbolic character of consumer goods and activities*. Bloomington: Indiana University Press.

———. 1988b. *The long interview*. Beverly Hills: Sage.

———. 1990. Culture and consumer behavior: An anthropological perspective. *Journal of the Market Research Society* 32 (1):3–11.

———. 1996. *Big hair: A journey into the transformation of self*. Woodstock, N.Y.: Overlook Press.

———. 2005. *Culture and consumption II: Markets, meaning, and brand management*. Bloomington: Indiana University Press.

———. 2006a. *Flock and flow: Predicting and managing change in a dynamic marketplace*. Bloomington: Indiana University Press.

———. 2006b. *Lovemark*. www.cultureby.com February 24, 2006. Last accessed March 29, 2007.

McFarland, Jennifer. 2001. Margaret Mead meets consumer fieldwork. *Harvard Management Update* (August):5–6.

McGrath, Ann. 1997. Sexuality and Australian identities. In *Creating Australia: Changing Australian history*, edited by W. Hudson and G. C. Bolton, 39–51. St. Leonards, N.S.W., Australia: Allen & Unwin.

McLarin, Kim. 2006. Modern love: Race wasn't an isssue for him, and that was an issue to me. *New York Times*, September 8: http://www.naplesnews.com/news/2006/sep/08/modern_love_race_wasnt_issue_him_and_was_issue_me. Last accessed June 16, 2007.

McQuarrie, Edward F., and David Glen Mick. 1992. On resonance: A critical pluralistic inquiry into advertising rhetoric. *Journal of Consumer Research* 19 (2):180–197.

———. 1996. Figures of rhetoric in advertising language. *Journal of Consumer Research* 22 (4):424–438.

———. 1999. Visual rhetoric in advertising: Text-interpretive, experimental, and reader-response analyses. *Journal of Consumer Research* 26 (1):37–54.

Meerwarth, Tracy, Elizabeth Briody, and Devadatta Kulkarni. 2005. Discovering the rules: Folk knowledge for improving GM partnerships. *Human Organization* 64 (3):286–301.

Mehta, Raj, and Russell W. Belk. 1991. Artifacts, identity, and transition: Favorite possessions of Indians and Indian immigrants to the United States. *Journal of Consumer Research* 17 (4):398–411.

Mendoza-Denton, Norma. 1995. Pregnant pauses: Silence and authority in the Anita Hill–Clarence Thomas Hearings. In *Gender articulated: Language and the socially constructed self*, edited by K. Hall and M. Bucholtz, 51–66. New York: Routledge.

———. 1999. Sociologists and linguistic anthropology of US Latinos. *Annual Review of Anthropology* 28:375–395.

Merry, Sally Engle. 2003. Human rights law and the demonization of culture (and anthropology along the way). *PoLAR* 26 (1):55–76.

Mewett, Peter. 1999. Fragments of a composite identity: Aspects of Australian nationalism in a sports setting. *Australian Journal of Anthropology* 10 (3):357–375.

Mick, David G. 1986. Consumer research and semiotics: Exploring the morphology of signs, symbols, and significance. *Journal of Consumer Research* 13 (2):196–213.

———. 1997. Semiotics in marketing and consumer research: Balderdash, verity, pleas. In *Consumer research: Postcards from the edge*, edited by S. Brown and D. Turley, 249–262. London: Routledge.

Mick, David G., and Claus Buhl. 1992. A meaning-based model of advertising experiences. *Journal of Consumer Research* 19 (3):317–338.

Mick, David G., James Burroughs, Patrick Hetzel, and Mary Yoko Brannen. 2004. Pursuing the meaning of meaning in the commercial world: An international review of marketing and consumer research founded on semiotics. *Semiotica* 152 (1):1–74.

Mick, David G., and Susan Fournier. 1998. Paradoxes of technology: Consumer cognizance, emotions, and coping strategies. *Journal of Consumer Research* 25 (2): 123–143.

Miller, Daniel, ed. 1995a. *Acknowledging consumption: A review of new studies*. London: Routledge.

———. 1995b. Introduction: Anthropology, modernity and consumption. In *Worlds apart: Modernity through the prism of the local*, edited by D. Miller, 1–22. London: Routledge.

———. 1995c. Consumption as the vanguard of history: A polemic by way of an introduction. In Miller, *Acknowledging consumption*, 1–57.

———, ed. 1997. *Capitalism: An ethnographic approach*. Oxford: Berg.

Miller, Daniel, and Don Slater. 2000. *The Internet: An ethnographic approach*. Oxford: Berg.

Mills, David. 2006. Trust me, I'm an anthropologist. *Anthropology Today* 22:1–2.

Miner, Horace. 1956. Body ritual among the Nacirema. *American Anthropologist* 58 (3): 503–507.

Mitchell, Colin. 2001. Candid camera: Will video replace focus groups as the core of research? *Adweek* 42 (May 28):16.

Moeran, Brian. 1996. *A Japanese advertising agency: An anthropology of media and markets*. Honolulu: University of Hawai'i Press.

Moeran, Brian. 2003. Imagining and imaging the other: Japanese advertising international. In *Advertising cultures*, edited by T. D. Malefyt and B. Moeran, 91–113. Oxford: Berg.

Moggan, Julie. 2005. Reflections of a Neophyte: A university versus a broadcast context. In Grimshaw and Ravetz, *Visualizing anthropology*, 31–41.

Moisander, Johannna, and Anu Valtonen. 2006. *Qualitative marketing research: A cultural approach*. London: Sage.

Mosca, Vincent. 2000. Webs of myth and power. In *The World Wide Web and contemporary cultural theory*, edited by A. Herman and T. Swiss, 37–60. New York: Routledge.

Mukařovský, Jan. 1977. Dialogue and monologue. In *The word and verbal art: Selected essays by Jan Mukařovský*, edited by J. Burbantz and P. Steiner, 81–112. New Haven: Yale University Press. Original work published in 1940.

Mullings, Leith. 2005. Interrogating racism: Toward an antiracist anthropology. *Annual Review of Anthropology* 43:667–693.

Muniz, Albert M., Jr., and Thomas O'Guinn. 2001. Brand community. *Journal of Consumer Research* 27 (4):412–432.

Murphy, Richard. 2005. Getting to know you. *Fortune Small Business* (June):41–46.

Musharbash, Yasmine. 2007. Boredom, time, and modernity: An example from Aboriginal Australia. *American Anthropologist* 109 (2):307–317.

Myerhoff, Barbara G. 1978. *Number our days*. New York: Dutton.

Nader, Laura. 1972. Up the anthropologist—perspectives gained from studying up. In Hymes, *Reinventing anthropology*, 284–312.

Nafus, Dawn, and Ken Anderson. 2006. The real problem: Rhetorics of knowing in corporate ethnographic research. *EPIC* 2006:227–241.

Narayan, Kirin. 1993. How native is a "native" anthropologist? *American Anthropologist* 95 (3):671–686.

Nelson, Emily. 2001. P&G checks out real life. *The Wall Street Journal*, May 17:B1.

News Bites. 2002. Courting Cuba: U.S. food concerns open trade with Castro and company. *Food Processing* 63 (11):12.

Nguyen, Doan, and Russell Belk. forthcoming. This we remember: Consuming representation in remembering. In *Consumption, Markets and Culture*.

Nippert-Eng, Christena E. 1996. *Home and work: Negotiating boundaries through everyday life*. Chicago, Ill.: University of Chicago Press.

O'Leary, Noreen. 2001. "Ogilvy's Emma Gilding" in "The 5 Coolest Jobs in Advertising." *Adweek* 42 (June 4):27.

Ochs, Elinor, and Lisa Capps. 2001. *Living narrative: Creating lives in everyday storytelling*. Cambridge, Mass.: Harvard University Press.

O'Hanlon, Michael. 1993. *Paradise: Portraying the New Guinea Highlands*. London: British Museum Press.

Ohnuki-Tierney, Emiko. 1991. Embedding and transforming polytrope: The monkey as self in Japanese culture. In Fernandez, *Beyond metaphor*, 159–189.

Okely, Judith. 2005. The filmed return of the natives—to a colonizing territory of terror. In Grimshaw and Ravetz, *Visualizing anthropology*, 121–132.

Oliker, Stacey J. 1989. *Best friends and marriage: Exchange among women*. Berkeley: University of California Press.

Olwig, Karen Fog, and Kirsten Hastrup, eds. 1997. *Siting culture: The shifting anthropological object*. London: Routledge.

Ong, Aihwa, and Stephen J. Collier, eds. 2005. *Global assemblages: Technology, politics, and ethics as anthropological problems*. Malden, Mass.: Blackwell Publishing.

O'Reilly, Karen. 2005. *Ethnographic methods*. London: Routledge.

Ortony, Andrew, ed. 1993. *Metaphor and thought*. 2nd ed. Cambridge: Cambridge University Press.

Oswald, Laura R. 1999. Culture swapping: Consumption and the ethnogenesis of middle-class Haitian immigrants. *Journal of Consumer Research* 25 (4):303–318.

Palmer, Catherine. 2002. "Shit happens": The selling of risk in extreme sport. *Australian Journal of Anthropology* 13 (3):323–336.

Palmquist, Ruth. 1996. The search for an Internet metaphor: A comparison of literatures. *American Society for Information Science Conference Proceedings*, October.

Pantzar, Mika. 2000. Consumption as work, play, and art: Representation of the consumer in future scenarios. *Design Issues* 16 (3):3–18.

Partridge, William L. 1985. Toward a theory of practice. *American Behavioral Scientist* 29:139–163.

Passaro, Joanne. 1997. "You can't take the subway to the field!" Village epistemologies in the global village. In Gupta and Ferguson, *Anthropological locations*, 147–162.

Peacock, James. 1997. The future of anthropology. *American Anthropologist* 99:9–17.

Pels, Peter. 2000. The trickster's dilemma: Ethics and the technologies of the anthropological self. In Strathern, *Audit cultures*, 135–172.

Peñaloza, Lisa. 1994. Atravesando fronteras/border crossings: A critical ethnographic exploration of the consumer acculturation of Mexican immigrants. *Journal of Consumer Research* 21 (1):32–54.

Peñaloza, Lisa, and Julien Cayla. 2006. Writing pictures/taking fieldnotes: Towards a more visual and material ethnographic consumer research. In *Handbook of qualitative research methods in marketing*, edited by R. W. Belk, 279–290. Cheltenham, U.K.: Edward Elgar.

Perry, Nick. 2004. Boots, boats, and bytes: Novel technologies of representation, changing media organization, and the globalisation of New Zealand sport. In Horrocks and Perry, *Television in New Zealand*, 74–89.

Pettigrew, Simone. 1999. An analysis of Australian beer advertisements. Paper read at Australian and New Zealand Marketing Academy Conference, University of New South Wales, Sydney, November 30–December 2.

———. 2001a. King or pawn? The role of the Australian beer drinker. *Journal of Research for Consumers* 2, www.jrconsumers.com. Last accessed January 15, 2007.

———. 2001b. Why a journal of research for consumers? *Journal of Research for Consumers* 1, www.jrconsumers.com. Last accessed January 15, 2007.

———. 2001c. The beer drinking female: An Australian anomaly. *Asia Pacific Advances in Consumer Research*, 4.

Piller, Ingrid. 1999. Extended metaphor in automobile fan discourse. *Poetics Today* 20 (3):483–498.

Pinch, Trevor, and Colin Clark. 1986. The hard sell: "Patter merchandising" and the strategic (re)production and local management of economic reasoning in the sales routines of market pitchers. *Sociology* 20:169–191.

Pine, B. Joseph, and James H. Gilmore. 1999. *The experience economy: Work is theatre & every business a stage*. Boston: Harvard Business School Press.

Pini, Maria. 2001. Video diaries: Questions of authenticity and fabrication. *Screening the Past* 13: http://www.latrobe.edu.au/screeningthepast/current/cc1201.html. Last accessed January 15, 2007.

Pink, Sarah, ed. 2001. *Doing visual ethnography: Images, media and representation in research.* Thousand Oaks, Calif.: Sage.

————. 2004a. Conversing anthropologically: Hypermedia as anthropological text. In Pink, Kürti, and Afonso, *Working images*, 166–184.

————. 2004b. *Home truths: Gender, domestic objects and everyday life.* Oxford: Berg.

————. 2006a. *The future of visual anthropology: Engaging the senses.* London: Routledge.

————. 2006b. The practice of anthropology in Great Britain. *NAPA Bulletin* 25: 123–133.

————. 2006c. *Applications of anthropology: Professional anthropology in the twenty-first century.* New York: Berghahn Books.

Pink, Sarah, László Kürti, and Ana Isabel Afonso, eds. 2004. *Working images: Visual research and representation in ethnography.* New York: Routledge.

Plummer, Joseph. 2006. Up close and personal: The value of ethnography. *Journal of Advertising Research* 46 (3):245.

Pulman-Jones, Simon. 2005. Using photographic data to build a large-scale global comparative visual ethnography of domestic spaces: Can a limited data set capture the complexities of "sociality"? *EPIC* 2005:128–139.

Quinn, Naomi. 1991. The cultural basis of metaphor. In Fernandez, *Beyond metaphor*, 56–93.

————, ed. 2005. *Finding culture in talk: A collection of methods.* New York: Palgrave Macmillan.

Quiroga, Jose. 2005. *Cuban palimpsests.* Minneapolis: University of Minnesota Press.

Rappaport, Roy A. 1993. The anthropology of trouble. *American Anthropologist* 95: 295–303.

Reddy, William M. 2001. *The navigation of feeling: A framework for the history of emotions.* Cambridge: Cambridge University Press.

Reed-Danahay, Deborah. 2005. *Locating Bourdieu: New anthropologies of Europe.* Bloomington: Indiana University Press.

Richards, B. 1993. Electric utilities brace for cancer lawsuits though risk is unclear. *The Wall Street Journal*, February 5:A1.

Ritson, Mark, and Richard Elliott. 1999. The social uses of advertising: An ethnographic study of adolescent advertising audiences. *Journal of Consumer Research* 26 (3):260–277.

Ritzer, George. 2004. *The McDonaldization of society.* Thousand Oaks, Calif.: Pine Forge Press.

Roberts, Kevin. 2004. *Lovemarks: The future beyond brands.* New York: PowerHouse Books.

Roberts, Simon. 2006. The pure and the impure? Reflections on applying anthropology and doing ethnography. In Pink, *Applications of anthropology*, 72–89.

Robertson, Rachael. 2005. Seeing is believing: An ethnographer's encounter with television documentary production. In Grimshaw and Ravetz, *Visualizing anthropology*, 42–54.

Robinson, Rick. 2005. Let's have a conversation: Theory session introductory remarks. *EPIC* 2005:1–8.

Rosaldo, Michelle. 1980. *Knowledge and passion: Ilongot notions of self and social life.* Cambridge: Cambridge University Press.

———. 1983. The shame of headhunters and the autonomy of self. *Ethos* 11:135–151.

———. 1984. Toward an anthropology of self and feeling. In Shweder and LeVine, *Culture Theory*, 137–157.

Rosaldo, Renato. 1980. *Ilongot headhunting: 1883–1974.* Stanford: Stanford University Press.

———. 1984. Grief and a headhunter's rage: On the cultural force of emotions. In *Text, play, and story: The construction and reconstruction of self and society*, edited by E. Bruner, 178–195. Washington, D.C.: American Ethnological Society.

Roseberry, William. 1996. The rise of Yuppie coffees and the reimagination of class in the United States. *American Anthropologist* 98 (4):762–775.

Rosenzweig, Linda W. 1999. *Another self: Middle-class American women and their friends in the twentieth century.* New York: New York University Press.

Rosset, Peter. 1998. Alternative agricultural works: The case of Cuba. *Monthly Review* 50 (3):137–46.

Rouch, Jean. 2003. *Ciné-ethnography.* Translated by S. Feld. Minneapolis: University of Minnesota Press.

Ruby, Jay. 1971. Towards an anthropological cinema. *Film Comment* 7 (1):35–40.

———. 1975. Is an ethnographic film a filmic ethnography? *Studies in the Anthropology of Visual Communication* 2 (2):104–111.

———. 1976. In a pic's eye: Interpretive strategies for deriving significance and meaning from photographs. *AfterImage* 3 (9):5–7.

———. 1980. Exposing yourself: Reflexivity, anthropology, and film. *Semiotica* 30 (1/2): 153–179.

———. 1991. Speaking for, speaking about, speaking with, or speaking alongside: An anthropological and documentary dilemma. *Visual Anthropology Review* 7 (2):50–67.

———. 1996. The viewer viewed: The reception of ethnographic films. In Crawford and Hafsteinsson, *The construction of the viewer*, 193–206.

———. 2000. *Picturing culture: Explorations of film & anthropology.* Chicago: University of Chicago Press.

———. 2005. Jean Rouch: Hidden and revealed. *American Anthropologist* 107 (1): 111–112.

Rylko-Bauer, Barbara, Merrill Singer, and John van Willigen. 2006. Reclaiming applied anthropology: Its past, present, and future. *American Anthropologist* 108 (1):178–190.

Sachs, Patricia. 2006. Bushwacking a career. *NAPA Bulletin* 26:152–162.

Sacks, Harvey, Emanuel A. Schegloff, and Gail Jefferson. 1974. A simplest systematics for the organization of turn-taking for conversation. *Language* 50 (4):696–735.

Sanders, Elizabeth. 2004. Ethnography and the empowerment of everyday people. www.maketools.com/pdfs/EthnographyandEmpowerment_Sanders_04.pdf. Last accessed June 2007.

Sando, Ruth, and Donna Sweeney. 2005. Shedding new light on an old flame. *Quirk's Marketing Research Review* 19 (5):30–35.

Santiago-Irizarry, Vilma. 2001. *Medicalizing ethnicity: The construction of Latino identity in a psychiatric setting.* Ithaca, N.Y.: Cornell University Press.

Santiago-Irizarry, Vilma. 2002. Head counting and accounting: Minority anthropologists in departments of anthropology. Paper read at 100th American Anthropological Association Annual Meeting, New Orleans, Louisiana, November 20–24.

Saussure, Ferdinand de. 1966. *Course in general linguistics*. Translated by W. Baskin. New York: McGraw-Hill.

Schegloff, Emmanuel. 1986. The routine as achievement. *Human Studies* 9 (2–3): 111–151.

Schensul, Jean J., and Gwen Stern, eds. 1985. Collaborative research and social policy. *American Behavioral Scientist* 29:133–264.

Scheper-Hughes, Nancy. 1992. *Death without weeping: The violence of everyday life in Brazil*. Berkeley: University of California Press.

———. 1995. The primacy of the ethical: Propositions for a militant anthropology. *Current Anthropology* 36 (3):409–440.

Schieffelin, Bambi B. 1990. *The give and take of everyday life: Language socialization of Kaluli children*. Cambridge; New York: Cambridge University Press.

Schieffelin, Bambi B., Kathryn Ann Woolard, and Paul V. Kroskrity, eds. 1998. *Language ideologies: Practice and theory*. New York: Oxford University Press.

Schouten, John, and James McAlexander. 1995. Subcultures of consumption: An ethnography of the new bikers. *Journal of Consumer Research* 22:43–61.

Schrage, Michael. 2000. An interview with Jaron Lanier. *Adweek* 41 (40):IQ44.

Schroeder, Jonathan. 1998. Consuming representation: A visual approach to consumer research. In Stern, *Representing consumers*, 193–230.

———. 2006. Critical visual analysis. In *Handbook of qualitative research methods in marketing*, edited by R. W. Belk, 303–321. Cheltenham, U.K.: Edward Elgar.

Schroeder, Jonathan, and Miriam Salzer-Mörling, eds. 2006. *Brand culture*. London: Routledge.

Schroeder, Jonathan, and D. Zwick. 2004. Mirrors of masculinity: Representation and identity in advertising images. *Consumption, Markets and Culture* 7:21–52.

Scott, Linda M. 1994. The bridge from text to mind: Adapting reader-response theory to consumer research. *Journal of Consumer Research* 21 (3):461–480.

Scott, Linda M., Edward McQuarrie, John Sherry, and Melanie Wallendorf. 2005. Roundtable on advertising as a cultural form. *Advertising and Society Review* 6 (4):1–23.

Shanklin, Eugenia. 1994. *Anthropology and race*. Belmont, Calif.: Wadsworth.

———. 1998. The profession of the color blind: Sociocultural anthropology and racism in the 21st century. *American Anthropologist* 100 (3):669–679.

Sherry, John F., Jr. 1983. Gift giving in anthropological perspective. *Journal of Consumer Research* 10 (2):157–168.

———, ed. 1984. Some implications of consumer oral tradition for reactive marketing. *Advances in Consumer Research* 2:741–747.

———. 1987. Advertising as a cultural system. In *Marketing and semiotics: New directions in the study of signs for sale*, edited by J. Umiker-Sebeok, 441–461. Berlin: De Gruyter.

———. 1988. Market pitching and the ethnography of speaking. *Advances in Consumer Research* 15:543–547.

———. 1991. Postmodern alternatives: The interpretive turn in consumer research. In *Handbook of consumer behavior*, edited by T. S. Robertson and H. H. Kassarjian. Englewood Cliffs, N.J.: Prentice-Hall.

Sherry, John F., Jr., ed. 1995a. *Contemporary marketing and consumer behavior: An anthropological source-book.* Thousand Oaks, Calif.: Sage.

———. 1995b. Bottomless cup, plug-in drug: A telethnography of coffee. *Visual Anthropology* 7 (4):355–374.

———. 1998. *Servicescapes: The concept of place in contemporary markets.* Lincolnwood, Ill.: NTC Business Books.

———. 2000. Place, technology and representation. *Journal of Consumer Research* 27:273–278.

———. 2006. Fielding ethnographic teams. In *Handbook of qualitative research methods in marketing*, edited by R. W. Belk, 268–276. Cheltenham, U.K.: Edward Elgar.

Sherry, John F., Jr., and Eduardo G. Camargo. 1987. "May your life be marvelous": English language labeling and the semiotics of Japanese promotion. *The Journal of Consumer Research* 14 (2):174–188.

Sherry, John F., Jr., Robert Kozinets, Diana Storm, Adam Duhachek, Krittinee Nuttavuthisit, and Benét DeBerry-Spence. 2001. Being in the zone: Staging retail theater at ESPN Zone Chicago. *Journal of Contemporary Ethnography* 30 (4): 465–501.

Sherry, John F., Jr., and John Schouten. 2002. A role for poetry in consumer research. *Journal of Consumer Research* 29:218–234.

Shore, Cris, and Susan Wright. 1997. Colonial gaze to critique of policy: British anthropology in policy and practice. In *The global practice of anthropology*, edited by M. L. Baba and C. E. Hill, 139–154. Williamsburg, Va.: Dept. of Anthropology College of William and Mary.

Shweder, Richard A., and Robert Alan LeVine, eds. 1984. *Culture theory: Essays on mind, self, and emotion.* Cambridge: Cambridge University Press.

Silverstein, Michael. 1976. Shifters, linguistic categories and cultural description. In *Meaning in anthropology*, edited by K. H. Basso and H. A. Selby, 11–55. Albuquerque: University of New Mexico Press.

———. 2004. "Cultural" concepts and the language-culture nexus. *Current Anthropology* 45 (5):621–652.

Silvio, Teri. 2007. Remediation and local globalizations: How Taiwan's "digital video knights-errant puppetry" writes the history of the new media in Chinese. *Cultural Anthropology* 22 (2):285–313.

Smallbridge, Justin. 2003. The human zoo. *Canadian Business* 76 (10):155.

Smith, D. V. L. 2007. Walk before you run. *Research World* (January):35.

Smith, Philippa Mein, and Peter Hempenstall. 2003. Australian and New Zealand: Turning shared pasts into a shared history. *History Compass* 1:1–8.

Snyder, Gerald S. 1972. *The computer: How it's changing our lives.* Washington, D.C.: U.S. News & World Report.

Sollors, Werner, ed. 1989. *The Invention of ethnicity.* New York: Oxford University Press.

Solomon, Michael R. 2003. *Conquering consumerspace: Marketing strategies for a branded world.* New York: Amacom.

Sontag, Susan. 1973. *On photography.* New York: Farrar Straus and Giroux.

———. 2003. *Regarding the pain of others.* New York: Farrar Straus and Giroux.

Squires, Sue. 2006. Solving puzzles. *NAPA Bulletin* 26:191–208.

Squires, Susan E., and Bryan Byrne, eds. 2002. *Creating breakthrough ideas: The collaboration of anthropologists and designers in the product development industry*. Westport, Conn.: Bergin & Garvey.

Stanley, Liz. 2001. Mass-observation's fieldwork methods. In *Handbook of ethnography*, edited by P. Atkinson, A. Coffey, S. Delamont, J. Lofland and L. Lofland, 92–108. Thousand Oaks, Calif.: Sage.

Stavenhagen, Rodolfo. 1999. Structural racism and trends in the global economy. Paper read at International Council on Human Rights Policy, Consultation on Racism and Human Rights, Geneva, December 3–4.

Stern, Barbara B. 1988. How does an ad mean? Language in services advertising. *Journal of Advertising* 17 (2):3–14.

———. 1989. Literary criticism and consumer research: Overview and illustrative analysis. *Journal of Consumer Research* 16 (3):322–334.

———. 1996. Textual analysis in advertising research: Construction and deconstruction of meanings. *Journal of Advertising* 25 (3):61–73.

———, ed. 1998. *Representing consumers: Voices, views, and visions*. London: Routledge.

Stoller, Paul. 1997. *Sensuous scholarship, contemporary ethnography*. Philadelphia, PA: University of Pennsylvania Press.

Strathern, Marilyn, ed. 2000. *Audit cultures: Anthropological studies in accountability, ethics, and the academy*. London: Routledge.

———. 2006. Don't eat unwashed lettuce. *American Ethnologist* 33 (4):532–534.

Strauss, Anselm L. 1987. *Qualitative analysis for social scientists*. Cambridge: Cambridge University Press.

Streeter, Thomas. 2005. Hypertext essay and tutorial on using semiotic techniques to analyze advertising, media and contemporary culture. www.uvm.edu/~tstreete/ semiotics_and_ads/. Last accessed January 15, 2007.

Suchman, Lucy. 1995. Making work visible. *Communications of the ACM* 38 (9):56–64.

———. 2000. Anthropology as a "brand": Reflections on corporate anthropology. http://www.lancs.ac.uk/fss/sociology/papers/suchman-anthropology-as-brand.pdf. Last accessed January 15, 2007.

Suchman, Lucy, and Randall Trigg. 1991. Understanding practice: Video as a medium for reflection and design. In *Design at work: Cooperative design of computer systems*, edited by J. M. Greenbaum and M. Kyng, 65–89. Hillsdale, N.J.: L. Erlbaum Associates.

Sunderland, Patricia. 1997. "You may not know it, but I'm Black": White women's self-identification as black. *Ethnos* 62 (1–2):32–58.

———. 1999. Fieldwork and the phone. *Anthropological Quarterly* 72 (3):105–117.

Sunderland, Patricia, and Rita Denny. 2002. Performers and partners: Consumer video documentaries in ethnographic research. In *Qualitative ascending: Harnessing its true value*, 285–303. Amsterdam: ESOMAR.

———. 2003. Psychology vs. anthropology: Where is culture in marketplace ethnography? In *Advertising cultures*, edited by T. D. Malefyt and B. Moeran, 187–202. New York: Berg.

———. 2005. Connections among people, things, images, and ideas: La Habana to Pina and back. *Consumption, Markets and Culture* 8:291–312.

Sunderland, Patricia, Elizabeth Gigi Taylor, and Rita Denny. 2004. Being Mexican *and* American: Negotiating ethnicity in the practice of market research. *Human Organization* 63 (3):373–380.

Suri, Jane Fulton, and Suzanne Gibbs Howard. 2006. Going deeper, seeing further: Enhancing ethnographic interpretations to reveal more meaningful opportunities for design. *Journal of Advertising Research* 46 (3):246–250.

Swain, Tony. 1993. *A place for strangers: Towards a history of Australian Aboriginal being.* Cambridge: Cambridge University Press.

Sykes, Karen Margaret. 2005. *Arguing with anthropology: An introduction to critical theories of the gift.* London: Routledge.

Szörény, Anna. 2006. The images speak for themselves? Reading refugee coffee-table books. *Visual Studies* 21 (1):24–41.

Tagg, John. 1993. *The burden of representation: Essays on photographies and histories.* Minneapolis: University of Minnesota Press.

Taylor, Lucien, ed. 1994. *Visualizing theory: Selected essays from V.A.R., 1990–1994.* New York: Routledge.

———. 1996. Iconophobia. *Transition* (69):64–88.

Terrio, Susan J. 1998. Deconstructing fieldwork in contemporary urban France. *Anthropological Quarterly* 71 (1):18–31.

Tett, Gillian. 2005. Lost tribes of Acme Accounting. *Financial Times* (May 21):W1.

Tharp, Marye C. 2001. *Marketing and consumer identity in multicultural America.* Thousand Oaks, Calif.: Sage.

Thomas, Suzanne, and Tony Salvador. 2006. Skillful strategy, artful navigation and necessary wrangling. *EPIC* 2006:104–119.

Thompson, Craig. 1997. Interpreting consumers: A hermeneutical framework for deriving marketing insights from the texts of consumers' consumption stories. *Journal of Marketing Research* 34 (November):438–455.

Thompson, Craig, Eric Arnould, and Barbara Stern. 1997. Exploring the difference: A postmodern approach to paradigmatic pluralism in consumer research. In *Consumer research: Postcards from the edge*, edited by S. Brown and D. Turley, 150–189. New York: Routledge.

Thompson, Craig, and Zeynep Arsel. 2004. The Starbucks brandscape and consumers' (anticorporate) experiences of globalization. *Journal of Consumer Research* 31 (3): 631–642.

Thompson, Craig J., and Siok Kuan Tambyah. 1999. Trying to be cosmopolitan. *Journal of Consumer Research* 26 (3):214–241.

Thorpe, Mark. 2003. Virtual connections: Representation and commercial qualitative research. *Qualitative Market Research: An International Journal* 6:184–193.

Tischler, Linda. 2004. Every move you make. *Fast Company* (April):73.

Tsing, Anna Lowenhaupt. 2005. *Friction: An ethnography of global connection.* Princeton: Princeton University Press.

Turkle, Sherry. 1984. *The second self: Computers and the human spirit.* New York: Simon and Schuster.

———. 1995. *Life on the screen: Identity in the age of the Internet.* New York: Simon and Schuster.

———. 1997. Computational technologies and images of the self. *Social Research* 64 (3): 1093–1111.

———. 1999. Cyberspace and identity. *Contemporary Sociology* 28 (6):643–648.

Turner, Stephen. 2004. Representing the country: Adidas Aotearoa. In Horrocks and Perry, *Television in New Zealand*, 90–104.

Urciuoli, Bonnie. 1996. *Exposing prejudice: Puerto Rican experiences of language, race, and class*. Boulder, Colo.: Westview Press.

Valentine, Virginia. 1995. Opening up the black box: Switching the paradigm of qualitative research. In *Looking through the kaleidoscope: What is the qualitative mission?*, 25–47. Amsterdam: ESOMAR.

———. 2001. Repositioning research: A new *market research* language model. Paper presented to the Market Research Society, Annual Conference, London.

Valentine, Virginia, and Malcolm Evans. 1993. The dark side of the onion: Rethinking the meanings of "rational" and "emotional" responses. *Journal of Market Research Society* 35 (2):125–144.

Valentine, Virginia, and Wendy Gordon. 2000. The 21st century consumer: A new model of thinking. *International Journal of Market Research* 42 (2):185–206.

van Maanen, John. 1988. *Tales of the field: On writing ethnography*. Chicago: University of Chicago Press.

———, ed. 1995. *Representation in ethnography*. Thousand Oaks, Calif.: Sage.

van Veggel, Rob J. F. M. 2005. Where the two sides of ethnography collide. *Design Issues* 21 (3):3–16.

———. 2006. An anthropologist at a bed manufacturer. *Medische Antropologie* 18 (1): 117–132.

van Willigen, John, and Timothy L. Finan, eds. 1991. *Soundings: Rapid and reliable research methods for practicing anthropologists*, *NAPA Bulletin 10*. Alexandria, Va.: American Anthropological Association.

Varman, Rohit, Russell Belk, and Janeen Arnold Costa. 2006. Recapturing humanity: Embeddedness in market communities. *Academy of Marketing Science Review* 4: www.amsreview.org/articles.htm.

Vélez-Ibáñez, Carlos G., and Anna Sampaio, eds. 2002. *Transnational Latina/o communities: Politics, processes, and cultures*. Lanham, Md.: Rowman & Littlefield.

Venkatesh, Alladi. 1998. Cyberculture: Consumers and cybermarketscapes. In *Servicescapes: The concept of place in contemporary markets*, edited by J. F. Sherry Jr., 343–376. Lincolnwood, Ill.: NTC Business Books.

Venkatesh, Alladi, Norman Stolzoff, Eric Shih, and Sanjoy Mazumdar. 2001. The home of the future: An ethnographic study of new information technologies in the home. *Advances in Consumer Research* 28:99–97.

Vestergaard, Torben, and Kim Schrøder. 1985. *The language of advertising*. Oxford: B. Blackwell.

Vila, Pablo. 2000. *Crossing borders, reinforcing borders: Social categories, metaphors, and narrative identities on the U.S.-Mexico frontier*. Austin: University of Texas Press.

Wallendorf, Melanie, and Eric Arnould. 1988. "Some of my favorite things": A cross-cultural inquiry into object attachment, possessiveness, and social linkage. *Journal of Consumer Research* 14:531–547.

Warwick, Hugh. 1999. Cuba's organic revolution. *The Ecologist* 29 (8):457–460.

Wasson, Christina. 2000. Ethnography in the field of design. *Human Organization* 59 (4):377–388.

———. 2002. Collaborative work: Integrating the roles of ethnographers and designers. In *Creating breakthrough ideas: The collaboration of anthropologists and designers in the product development industry*, edited by S. E. Squires and B. Byrne, 71–90. Westport, Conn.: Bergin & Garvey.

Waters, Mary C. 1990. *Ethnic options: Choosing identities in America*. Berkeley: University of California Press.

Waterston, Alisse. 2006. Are Latinos becoming "white" folk? And what that still says about race in America. *Transforming Anthropology* 14 (2):133–150.

Weinberger, Eliot. 1994. The camera people. In *Visualizing theory: Selected essays from V.A.R., 1990–1994*, edited by L. Taylor, 3–26. New York: Routledge.

Weiner, Annette B. 1976. *Women of value, men of renown: New perspectives in Trobriand exchange*. Austin: University of Texas Press.

———. 1992. *Inalienable possessions: The paradox of keeping-while-giving*. Berkeley: University of California Press.

Wellner, Alison. 2002. Watch me now. *American Demographics* 24 (9):S1.

White, Richard. 1981. *Inventing Australia: Images and identity, 1688–1980*. Sydney: Allen & Unwin.

Whorf, Benjamin Lee. 1956. The relation of habitual thought and behavior to language. In *Language, thought, and reality: Selected writings of Benjamin Lee Whorf*, edited by J. B. Carroll, 134–159. Cambridge: Technology Press of Massachusetts Institute of Technology.

Wilk, Richard R. 2006. *Home cooking in the global village: Caribbean food from buccaneers to ecotourists*. Oxford: Berg.

Williams, Brackette F. 1989. A class act: Anthropology and the race to nation across ethnic terrain. *Annual Review of Anthropology* 18:401–444.

Williams, Patti, and Jennifer Aaker. 2002. Can mixed emotions peacefully coexist? *Journal of Consumer Research* 28 (4):636–649.

Williamson, Judith. 1978. *Decoding advertisements: Ideology and meaning in advertising*. London: Boyars.

Wilson, Samuel M., and Leighton Peterson. 2002. The anthropology of online communities. *Annual Review of Anthropology* 31:449–467.

Wolf, Michael J. 1999. *The entertainment economy: How mega-media forces are transforming our lives*. New York: Times Books.

Woolard, Kathryn A. 1998. Introduction: Language ideology as a field of inquiry. In *Language ideologies: Practice and theory*, edited by B. B. Schieffelin, K. A. Woolard, and P. V. Kroskrity, 3–47. New York: Oxford University Press.

Wooten, David. 2006. From labeling possessions to possessing labels: Ridicule and socialization among adolescents. *Journal of Consumer Research* 33 (2):188–198.

Worth, Sol. 1977. Toward an ethnographic semiotic. In *Utilization de l'ethnologie par le cinéma/Utilization du cinéma par l'ethnologie*. Paris: UNESCO.

Yin, Sandra. 2001. The power of images. *American Demographics* 23 (11):32–33.

Zaltman, Gerald. 1997. Re-thinking market research: Putting people back in. *Journal of Marketing Research* 34:424–437.

Zaltman, Gerald, and Robin H. Coulter. 1995. Seeing the voice of the customer: Metaphor-based advertising research. *Journal of Advertising Research* 35 (4):35–51.

Zentella, Ana Celia. 1997. *Growing up bilingual: Puerto Rican children in New York*. Malden, Mass.: Blackwell.

Index

About the Authors

Patricia L. Sunderland, Ph.D., and Rita M. Denny, Ph.D., are anthropologists and founding partners of Practica Group, LLC, along with Ed Bovich, George Hunt, and Michael Donovan. Patti has been melding cultural analysis with ethnographic video and photographs to bring consumer environments to life for clients for more than a decade. Rita has been listening to what is presupposed in consumer and client talk for even longer. Their research, like this book, is a collaborative effort to examine sociocultural meanings of products and services in everyday life. Contrary to what it may sometimes seem, they are not the same person. Patti is the one who speaks German and French; Rita is the Lake Michigan swimmer.

Contributing Authors

Russell Belk (Kraft Foods Canada Chair of Marketing at York University) is a Fellow and past president of the Association for Consumer Research as well as cofounder of the association's annual film festival. His research involves the meanings of possessions, collecting, gift-giving, materialism, and emerging consumer cultures.

Frederic W. Gleach (Senior Lecturer and Curator of Anthropology at Cornell University) is a historical anthropologist with focuses on material and visual culture, author of *Powhatan's World and Colonial Virginia: A Conflict of Cultures*, and founding coeditor of *Histories of Anthropology Annual*.

Vilma Santiago-Irizarry, author of *Medicalizing Ethnicity: The Construction of Latino Identity in a Psychiatric Setting*, addresses identity construction in U.S. institutional cultures—particularly legal and medical contexts—and is currently studying ethnohistorical constructions of the Spanish-speaking Caribbean. She is Associate Professor of Anthropology and Latino Studies at Cornell University.

John F. Sherry Jr. (Herrick Professor and Chair of Marketing, University of Notre Dame) is a past president of the Association for Consumer Research, a former associate editor of the *Journal of Consumer Research*, a Fellow of AAA and of SfAA, and a diligent inquirer into the evolving character of spectacle.

Donald D. Stull, Ph.D., M.P.H., is Professor of Anthropology at the University of Kansas, as well as a former editor of the journal *Human Organization* and past president of the Society for Applied Anthropology.